ESSAYS IN MODERN ENGLISH HISTORY

LONDON : HUMPHREY MILFORD
OXFORD UNIVERSITY PRESS

ESSAYS IN MODERN ENGLISH HISTORY

IN HONOR OF

WILBUR CORTEZ ABBOTT

CAMBRIDGE · MASSACHUSETTS
HARVARD UNIVERSITY PRESS
1941

PRINTED AT THE HARVARD UNIVERSITY PRESS
CAMBRIDGE, MASS., U. S. A.

THESE ESSAYS ARE DEDICATED BY THE AUTHORS, HIS FORMER PUPILS AT YALE, HARVARD, AND RADCLIFFE

TO

WILBUR CORTEZ ABBOTT

CONTENTS

FOREWORD

It is a high privilege to be given this opportunity to participate in a tribute to Wilbur Cortez Abbott. I accept it with a certain sense of unworthiness, as one who has turned his feet aside for the moment from the path of historical scholarship and has thereby forfeited, or nearly, the right even to bring homage to the scholar. There still lingers in my memory the caustic phrase of a French historian on learning that a professor had become a president: "Est-ce bien vrai qu'il est descendu dans les fonctions administratives?" Tribute from a pupil to his master finds its proper expression not in mere words but rather in faithful fulfilment of the master's ideals, in undeviating emulation of his scholarship, and in unremitting pursuit of the tasks and the opportunities which he has indicated. Such tribute, of a worthy kind, is found in the essays that follow. It is with humility that I dare to speak a prefatory word.

The titles of the essays reveal the field of the master's main interest, even were it not known by his own writings. They reveal also a principle that has characterized both his writing and his teaching, a preoccupation with the human aspect of history. For him it is vital that in studying the men of the past, in their various activities and relationships, we should appreciate them as men and not merely as pieces on a chess-board whose moves we record. In his seminary, if we studied an institution, it was constantly borne in on us that we were dealing with something more than an abstraction; that we must understand it as an instrument created, operated, maintained or destroyed by human beings; and that unless we came to know those human beings through every scrap of available evidence, we could not understand the institution. For him a battle was a conflict of human individuals and not merely a colored diagram; troops were more than mere block squares, they had legs to get tired and stomachs to be fed, and emotions that could be aroused; headquarters was not merely a dot on the map, but a gathering of personalities who must be understood as men if the generals' orders were to be explained. An English borough was not merely a geographical expression that sent two members to the House of Commons; it was a group of living individuals, working in field or factory, guided by their economic interests, or by blind tradition, voting independently or with a bribe; but always human beings who must be so regarded if a parliamentary election were to be understood. The influence of Professor Abbott on historical teaching and scholarship in this regard was broad and beneficent. With the introduction of the "new history," the emphasis upon "institutional history," "social history," "the economic interpretation of history," there was danger of forgetting that as historians we are always concerned with men and the interests of men. "It was men who made history," he said, "and the greatest of historians have been the most human." Against the danger of writing historical abstractions he warned us by precept and example.

On the relationships of men among each other and to things, he laid great stress. The isolated study of an individual or of an event apart from the circumstances that surrounded them seemed to him of little value. His primary interest in the teaching and writing of history lay in the pulling together of the significant facts so that they provided an explanation of why things happened as they did. In his seminary his pupils were expected not merely to analyze the problem before them, to discover and expose the materials necessary to its investigation, but also to bring together the findings in a co-ordinated whole. He insisted upon synthesis because without it the historical process was incomplete; whether the problem was small or large, it must be viewed in its entirety. In his own writing, whether in his general history of Europe or in a short biographical essay, this quality is outstanding. With equal emphasis he insisted that to create an adequate synthesis, the highest sort of mental effort was necessary. The pieces would not fall into their places automatically. "History is no mere accumulation of facts;" he wrote, "it is not masses of notes and information; it is not the product of a 'lifetime of horrid industry' alone. It requires more than the ability to read endless volumes and manuscripts and make endless references. It requires thought. It needs the mind as well as the eye and hand. Without thought it is but sounding brass and tinkling cymbal, out of tune and harsh. Without informing ideas it becomes a chaos without form and void."

Professor Abbott's seminary assumed a willingness on the part of the student to devote painful labor to the investigation of a problem. It also assumed a capacity for rigorous analysis. Inexactitude in facts or slovenliness in critical apparatus were not tolerated. It was, in the language of the time, a "scientific approach" to history. But it was much more than that, for as teacher and as exemplar he did not fail to drive home to us that there is no history until it is written, and that in true historical literature manner may not be sacrificed to matter, nor form to substance. He warned us that in "the eternal triangle of history, science, and literature" the historic muse must divide her attentions discreetly. "While one may admit that in its method history should and must be scientific, this need not and ought not to prevent its being literary on the side of presentation. Unless it is, it will not be read. If it is not read, it will lose much or most of its value as a guide to thought and action."

Thus his seminary became an exercise in, as his own writings served as an example of, the art of presentation. The construction of reports and theses provided a means of training in literary form, whereby the method of the budding scholar and the substance of his newly acquired learning might be capitalized at their highest value. In sum, his recipe for the production of historical students who would and could write was simple: broad reading and constant writing. He used to quote the remark of the Oxford don: "If we can only teach men to read and write we are satisfied." Conscious of the myriad of professional activities in academic life, into which most historians of our day must enter, activities that offer constant distraction from the literary life, Professor Abbott sought to instill in his students an unbreakable habit of reading the historical classics; he led them to write and rewrite their papers with the example of the great historians always before them. His courses in historiography showed us the way; but he never failed to make plain that the persistence of the essential habits of reading and writing must depend upon ourselves. There was in his teaching not merely a spirit of intellectual guidance and artistic criticism, but also an inspiration to the personal pride of the student, a challenge to his moral fibre.

For this we who were his pupils are above all grateful. Just as the characters of whom he wrote emerged on the pages of his historical writings as human beings alive with human interest, so the students in his seminary not merely learned lessons in the craft of historical scholarship, but found themselves in a confraternity which, because of the personality of the instructor, taught us something of the essentials of human life.

CHARLES SEYMOUR

ESSAYS IN
MODERN ENGLISH HISTORY

A RESTORATION GOLDSMITH-BANKING HOUSE: THE VINE ON LOMBARD STREET

Two generations were amply sufficient in seventeenth-century London to bridge the transition from the shop of a working goldsmith to a bank with widespread transactions in private and public finance—witness the history of the Vine on Lombard Street and its owners, Sir Thomas Vyner and his nephew, Sir Robert Vyner. In the development of the Vine, in fact, appear in miniature and in rapid succession some of the stages through which the financial structure of English life had been moving ponderously in preceding centuries. Thomas Vyner, in the first decades of the seventeenth century, began his career by accepting the well-worn pattern laid through hundreds of years by London goldsmiths: he sold the gold and silver plate fashioned in his shop to the country gentry who regarded it as the best of investments because it was easily hoarded and as tangible as land; and, in turn, he relieved the necessities of these gentlemen by loaning money on their plate as pawn. By the time he was forty-five, Vyner had taken on the rôle of London merchant and City magistrate and was following the lead of those merchants who had begun in Tudor times to find in joint-stock companies the opportunities they sought to increase their surplus by investments in active enterprises. As a member of the East India Company, Vyner found eager market not only for his traffic in bullion, traditionally allied with the practice of the goldsmith's craft, but also for investment in various ventures. Indeed, such was Vyner's reputation in the City that he was in demand as treasurer of funds for the East India Company, and for the Commonwealth of England as well. And herein, no doubt, lay the seeds of the bank at the Vine, which Vyner, in his old age, had developed to the full stature of deposit, loan, and issue. It was in this final phase of his career that Sir Thomas, emerging from traditions and tried practices, appeared as a particularly notable example of a phenomenon peculiar to his own country and time — the goldsmith-banker.

Bankers and banks, to be sure, had long been familiar enough to Vyner and his contemporaries. The memory of Italian financiers who had controlled the fortunes of thirteenth- and fourteenth-century London was kept green by the name of their street — Lombard Street — where English goldsmith-bankers now lived; the agents of the great German houses of the Welsers and the Fuggers had made themselves known to fifteenth-century Europe wherever money was in demand; Sir Thomas Gresham, mercer, Elizabethan financier and builder of the Royal Exchange, was but recently dead when Thomas Vyner came to London; and familiar to all English merchants who dealt in foreign bills of exchange were the public banks of the cities of Genoa, Venice, and Amsterdam, particularly this last — financial bulwark of England's most formidable commercial competitors, the Dutch.

But none of these banks manifested all the phases which characterize banking in the modern sense, and which characterized the Vine — deposits and loans at interest, and the issue of negotiable paper. Some of these earlier financiers, it is true, had been money-lenders on a large scale, but the money which they lent was their own, not that of depositors. Others had loaned funds deposited with them, but, content with verbal contracts or the entries in their journals, had not yet developed negotiable notes as receipts for deposits. And the great public banks received deposits and exchanged foreign money, but discounted no bills and, for many years after their founding, lent no money. There were, to be sure, in seventeenth-century London, contemporaneous with the Vine, scriveners who appear to have operated banks as a logical development of their duties as notaries and negotiators of loans, and a surviving ledger, probably of Robert Abbott,[1] and the multitudinous references to the firm of John Morris and Robert Clayton are evidence that these bankers exercised all the primary functions of a modern bank; but the majority of scriveners, even such financiers as Hugh Audley[2] and Sir Martin Noel,[3] appear not to have advanced beyond lending from their own resources. It was the goldsmiths, not the scriveners, who were destined to dominate the money market of the Restoration years.

By the second half of the seventeenth century, the proprietors of the Vine, and four or five great rival goldsmith-bankers and a hundred lesser goldsmiths who "kept running cashes" had, in fact, developed into full-fledged banks which discounted domestic and foreign bills of exchange, solicited interest-bearing deposits to form a fund from which to loan at higher rates, and issued "goldsmiths' notes" which were reassignable and circulated freely. All this had come about as a natural extension of their traditional trade in gold and silver, their pawnshops, their bullion traffic of a century's growth,[4] and their foreign-money-changing. In addition, the outstanding few possessed an ability and daring which made

[1] *Guildhall MS.* 2931 (London).

[2] Cf. *The Way to be Rich, According to the Practice of the Great Audley who began with 200 l. in 1605 and dyed worth 400,000 l. Nov. 1662* (London, 1662).

[3] Cf. page 16.

[4] The bullion traffic was legalized in the reign of Elizabeth.

them capable of fishing in troubled political waters with notable though not always lasting success.

It remained for Sir Thomas Vyner's nephew, Robert, to carry his uncle's policies to their natural conclusion. For Sir Thomas, not content with a clientele of gentry and merchants for his bank and investment in private enterprises, had joined his fortunes with the Restoration of Charles II. Through more than a decade Sir Thomas, as also his nephew after him, was a chief underwriter of the government of England, concerned in tax-farms, loans to various departmental treasurers on all branches of hereditary revenue, extraordinary funds, and Parliamentary grants, until the Vine had become so inextricably bound up with the inadequate and mismanaged governmental income that the repudiation of paper orders at the Stop of the Exchequer in January, 1672, inevitably crippled the bank, and doomed it to a decade of slow decline, which ended, despite Sir Robert's best efforts, in bankruptcy. Thus it is evident that the story of the Vine forms a paragraph not only in the history of private banking but also in the sad tale of the financial difficulties of Charles II.

In the first year of the seventeenth century Thomas Vyner came to London and at the tender age of eleven began work as an apprentice in the shop of his brother-in-law, Samuel Moore, a working goldsmith.[5] By 1623, Thomas had married Anne, daughter of Richard Parsons, a London merchant,[6] and had graduated to a goldsmith's shop of his own,[7] where, as goldsmiths had done for hun-

5 *Dictionary of National Biography*, article on Sir Thomas Viner.

6 *Ibid.*

7 Sir Ambrose Heal, *The London Goldsmiths, 1200–1800* (Cambridge, Eng., 1935), p. 88.

dreds of years, he also conducted a pawnshop.[8] Seven years later the craftsmanship of his shop had become of sufficient note that the City of London bought from him a gold cup and cover as a baptismal gift to the young Prince Charles.[9] It was forty-six years, however, from the beginning of Vyner's apprenticeship before he began through his election as alderman from Billingsgate Ward to emerge from the obscurity of the hundreds of his fellow-craftsmen whose shops lined Cheapside and Lombard Street in the heart of the City. Two years later he was chosen sheriff of London; and the Goldsmiths' Company of which he was a member not only lent him their plate for the year but gave him £50 to help him support this expensive honor.[10] It was a fateful year in which to be sheriff of London, for in January, 1649, Charles I was tried and condemned to death in Westminster Hall. Thomas Vyner's fellow-sheriff was arrested for his refusal to be present at the execution of his king, but Vyner, it is said, lacking either courage or scruples, carried out all the duties of his office; and that he rode bareheaded in the rain carrying the sword of state before Oliver Cromwell and "proclaimed No Kingship" was remembered against him in later years by royalists who had counted principle above purse.[11]

It is evident that in the obscure earlier years Vyner's business had been growing steadily, for now the master of the Vine in St. Clement's Lane off Lombard Street[12] emerged as a merchant of influence and consequence. He

[8] In 1631 he lent money on plate at 4 per cent for five months — *Cal. St. Papers*, 1629–31, p. 498; 1631–33, p. 133.

[9] Sir Walter S. Prideaux, *Memorials of the Goldsmiths' Company, 1335–1815* (London, 1897), I, 149. Prince Charles was later Charles II.

[10] *Ibid.*, I, 251, 253.

[11] *The Mystery of the Good Old Cause Briefly unfolded* (London, 1660), p. 46.

[12] A little alley running south opposite the church of St. Edmund the King and Martyr. *Notes and Queries*, 9th series, V, 127.

had built up an account with a scrivener-banker, probably Robert Abbott, one of the few accounts at that shop which showed annual deposits of more than £5000.[13] He had been admitted to the freedom of the East India Company in March, 1648,[14] and the next year was essaying ventures in benzoin and calicoes in the Second General Voyage of the Company ships.[15] His foreign connections, probably made through his trade in bullion, were such that, in 1650, in a general scarcity of money from Spain, he was able to furnish 7000 ryals of eight (c. £1700) for the fleet which the Admiralty Commissioners were sending on a voyage south.[16] In 1648 he was one of the trustees appointed to advance £50,000 for the relief of Ireland to be collected from the estates of certain notorious royalists;[17] and he invested, too, in "adventures" in Irish lands which had been seized from royalist owners.[18]

Because of the ejection of all royalists from the ranks of the aldermen of London, Thomas Vyner's advance to seniority was rapid, and in 1653 he was elected Lord Mayor. Again the Goldsmiths' Company lent him their plate, with a doubled contribution for his expenses;[19] and Cromwell, taking upon himself the prerogative of conferring knighthood, made Vyner his first knight.[20] But Vyner's new interests and duties did not hinder the work of his goldsmith shop. In 1649 he had served on a jury of the most prominent goldsmiths in London to plan and

[13] Scrivener's ledger, Feb. 1645–May, 1652, *Guildhall MS.* 2931 (London).

[14] Ethel E. Sainsbury, *A Calendar of the Court Minutes, etc. of the East India Company, 1644–49* (Oxford, 1912), p. 261.

[15] *Ibid.*, p. 352.

[16] *Cal. St. Papers*, 1649–50, p. 450.

[17] *Ibid.*, 1649, p. 98.

[18] *Cal. St. Papers, Ireland*, 1647–60, pp. 443, 548; *Adventurers*, 1642–59, p. 380.

[19] Prideaux, *Memorials of Goldsmiths' Company*, II, 44, 51.

[20] *The Mystery of the Good Old Cause*, p. 46.

supervise the coining of the new Commonwealth money;[21] and during his mayoralty he was commissioned to make two services of plate for Cromwell and his lady, at a cost of £3183/14/1.[22]

It was a tribute to Vyner's reputation and resources that he, with Sir Andrew Riccards, was appointed by the East India Company to act as receiver and treasurer for the £85,000 which the Dutch in 1654 agreed to pay for the damage done by vessels of their East India Company to the English East India trade in the war which had just been ended by the Treaty of Westminster.[23] Such a large sum of money, however, was not permitted to remain in the hands of the treasurers; the Council of State of the Commonwealth at once demanded a loan of the whole sum, and, although they were forced to be content with £50,000,[24] the East India Company would have been both wiser and wealthier had they been able to resist the demand altogether, for the loan seems never to have been repaid.[25]

Vyner also served as treasurer, with Sir Christopher Packe, of funds collected to relieve the poor and distressed Protestants in the territory of the Duke of Savoy, and, subsequently, those driven out of Poland and Bohemia.[26] To the Nonconformists who controlled the government of England, every oppressed Protestant of Independent tendencies seemed an obligation. They accordingly appointed a Sunday in June, 1655, for a house-to-house canvass by ministers and church wardens for

[21] William Chaffers, *Gilda Aurifabrorum* (London, 1899), p. 57.

[22] *Cal. St. Papers*, 1653–54, p. 402; 1654, p. 454.

[23] Sainsbury, *East India Company, 1655–59* (Oxford, 1916), p. v; *Cal. St. Papers*, 1655, p. 240.

[24] They received only £46,000 when all charges had been deducted.

[25] *Cal. St. Papers*, 1655, pp. 256, 275; Sainsbury, *East India Co., 1655–59*, p. 53.

[26] *Ibid.*, pp. 182, 248.

these unfortunates;[27] and, although a part of the contributions proved to be "counterfeit, or light and clipped money not current,"[28] the surprising sum of £38,232 was collected.[29] Before all the money had been distributed, however, Cromwell's régime came to an end, and the interim Council of State, drawing on all possible sources for money, demanded the remaining £7978/8/9 from the treasurers.[30] Parliament after the Restoration piously resolved "detestation of any diversion of the money from the distressed foreign Protestants,"[31] but there is no evidence that the sum was ever repaid, and, at all events, it was not until October, 1668, that an account of the fund passed the Exchequer and the business was declared closed.[32]

Another measure of Sir Thomas Vyner's financial resources and enterprise appears in his arrangement to purchase, in partnership with another goldsmith, Alderman Edward Backwell, the treasure which, in September, 1656, a squadron under Blake had captured from the Spanish Plate Fleet, a prize estimated to be worth over £300,000.[33] Thirty-eight wagons laden with chests full of pieces of eight which came rumbling up from Portsmouth to London under military escort did not suffice to convey the entire amount for which the partners had agreed to pay £10,000 or £15,000 weekly and to advance £50,000 at once[34] — ready cash without which Cromwell's government would have been in a sorry case to

[27] *Cal. St. Papers*, p. 197.
[28] *Ibid.*, 1659–60, p. 161.
[29] Samuel R. Gardiner, *History of the Commonwealth and Protectorate* (London, 1901), III, 417.
[30] *Cal. St. Papers*, 1659–60, p. 589.
[31] *Ibid.*, 1660–61, p. 321 (11 May, 1660).
[32] *Cal. Treas. Books*, 1667–68, pp. 285, 291, 457.
[33] Henry W. Henfrey, *Numismata Cromwelliana* (London, 1877), pp. 98–101.
[34] *Cal. St. Papers*, 1656–57, pp. 143, 147.

maintain the Navy and the troops. Under the terms of the contract, all this treasure was coined at the Tower Mint at the expense of the partners, and they exported a substantial amount as bullion for the East India Company, which traded gold and silver for calicoes and spices in the East Indies and India.[35]

Already in 1658, as the serious nature of Cromwell's illness became apparent, the fate of the Commonwealth was a matter of general concern, productive of all stages of reaction from idle speculation to practical plotting; and after Cromwell's death in August, a few months of the inefficient Richard made the return of Charles II seem the logical solution to a majority of Englishmen. It is evident that in the case of Sir Thomas Vyner his attachment to the Cromwell régime had no deeper foundation than his pocketbook. When General Monk occupied London, late in March, 1660, and the Restoration was rapidly becoming a reality under his skilful leadership, Sir Thomas joined ardently in planning a feast which was tendered the General, his staff, and the Council of State, at a cost of £462/3/9 by the Goldsmiths' Company; and Vyner's newly-wed third wife, Alice, widow of the goldsmith John Perryn,[36] was a specially invited guest.[37] That the brother of Vyner's second wife, Sir William Humble, of no known fortune, was credited with a present of £20,000 to Charles during his exile,[38] and that Vyner's confidential servant, James Temple, was sent to Holland in September, 1659,[39] are facts suggestive that Vyner thus quietly despatched gifts to the King which did much to blot out inconvenient

[35] Henfrey, *op. cit.*, p. 116; Sainsbury, *op. cit.*, 1655–59, p. 250.

[36] Charles J. and Henry W. Vyner, *Vyner Family History* (1885), p. 28. His second wife died, 25 June, 1656, Richard Smyth, *Obituary* (1849), p. 42.

[37] Prideaux, *op. cit.*, II, 131 (26 Mar., 1660).

[38] *Vyner Family History*, p. 27.

[39] *Cal. St. Papers*, 1659–60, p. 567.

memories of his past. At all events, in common with others of known liberality to Charles in his exile, Vyner was granted a baronetcy immediately on the King's arrival in London,[40] while another Cromwellian Lord Mayor and Vyner's erstwhile associate, Sir Christopher Packe, escaped execution only by vote of a lenient House of Lords under promise never again to engage in public business.[41]

In the fashioning of gold plate in the intricate and fanciful style which was the current mode, the owner and apprentices of the Vine were master-craftsmen.[42] Charles II had already seen pieces from the shop in the plate which the East India Company had presented him on his arrival in London;[43] and it was not a purely politic appointment with an eye to future loans which made Robert Vyner, thirty-year-old nephew of Sir Thomas, the King's goldsmith.[44] His first undertaking was to prepare the regalia for the coronation — a herculean task since most of the traditional articles had been melted down to supply the urgent needs of royalists and roundheads in the years just past; but by Coronation Day, April 23, 1661, Robert Vyner had delivered two crowns and two sceptres, a jewelled orb and St. Edward's staff; the armilla and ampulla for the ceremony; a crown and mace for the Garter-King-at-Arms; twenty-seven collars, Georges and garters for the order of St. George; seventy-five badges for the order of the Bath; plate for New Year's and christening gifts — and his bill for £31,978/1/11.[45] There-

[40] *Cal. St. Papers*, 1660–61, p. 598.

[41] James T. Granger, *Biographical History of England* (London, 1824), V, 28.

[42] Some of their work may be seen in the plate owned by the Goldsmiths' Company and other livery companies of London; some of the coronation regalia still in use was made by Vyner.

[43] Sainsbury, *op. cit.*, 1660–63, p. 36.

[44] *Cal. St. Papers*, 1661–62, p. 60; he had already occupied the position *de facto* for months. *Cal. St. Papers*, 1661–62, pp. 25, 35, 41.

[45] *Archeologia*, XXIX, 265; *Cal. St. Papers*, 1660–61, p. 35.

after, the Vyner shop turned out plate for the Jewel House which in the reign of Charles II averaged perhaps £8000 a year, and in the more frugal régime of James II came to rather less than £1000 annually — articles for the King's personal use and for his gifts, for his ambassadors and for his mistresses.[46]

But after the Restoration the Vyners were by no means chiefly known as working goldsmiths; nor was Sir Thomas' reputation in the City based altogether on his career as an East India merchant and bullion trader; he was, in fact, in 1660, already doing a sizable banking business at the Vine, now situated on Lombard Street next the church of St. Mary Woolnoth. Since, regrettably, none of the actual records of this bank have come down to us, details must necessarily remain meager and uncertain, but it is possible, nevertheless, to reconstruct from the surviving ledgers of Vyner's contemporary and rival, Edward Backwell of the Unicorn,[47] and from Treasury and Exchequer documents, notably the books recording assignments to creditors of the Vine,[48] a partial history of the bank and its depositors.

To discover when Sir Thomas Vyner began to keep "running cashes," as the seventeenth century termed the practice of loaning out deposits, or to set a date for the issue of assignable receipts from the Vine, is impossible; but the earliest surviving Backwell ledger (1663) gives evidence of such large and intricate transactions carried on by Vyner, with merchants, other bankers, and government treasurers, that there can be no doubt that the Vyner bank had already been in operation for several years.

[46] *Cal. Treas. Books, passim.*

[47] Ledgers I–T (1663–71), preserved at Child's Bank (Glyn, Mills and Company), 1 Fleet Street, London, where I was kindly permitted to examine them.

[48] E 406/16–19 (Goldsmiths'); E 406/27–32 (Pells').

In 1662, Sir Thomas Vyner, now seventy-three years old, took up his residence in Hackney, northeast of London, where he had rebuilt an ancient mansion known as "the Black-and-White House";[49] and thereafter he left the conduct of the Vine more and more to his nephew Robert, although he continued to have a hand in some of the transactions of the bank until his death in 1665. Under the guidance of Robert Vyner, the banking end of the Vine apparently developed rapidly, and the bank's clientele grew to include most of the prominent men of the day. The large and multifarious dealings with government officials are, of course, herein reflected in accounts which often included personal as well as public business: Sir Denis Gauden, Surveyor of Navy Victualling; Samuel Pepys, Secretary to the Navy Board and Treasurer for Tangiers; Thomas Povey, Navy Commissioner for Tangiers; William Chiffinch, Keeper of the Privy Closet; Stephen Fox, Paymaster of the Guards, and his cashier, Richard Kent; Richard Mounteney, Cashier for the Customs Commissioners; Lord Robartes, Privy Seal; Exchequer officials — the brothers Squibb and Sir George Downing, Exchequer tellers, and John Spicer, Oliver Gregory, and Nicholas Dering, clerks to Exchequer tellers; and tax receivers from half the counties of England. The Earl of Anglesey, successively Vice-Treasurer of Ireland, Treasurer of the Navy, and Lord Privy Seal, regarded Vyner as his London agent and kept his personal accounts and a large part of his official accounts at the Vine; so too the Earl of Ormonde, Lord Lieutenant of Ireland, however he might deplore the exorbitant rates of interest charged by Vyner.[50] Indeed, for public and private purposes together, the Vyners ad-

[49] *Vyner Family History*, p. 28.
[50] Cf. page 26.

vanced to Ormonde in the first years of his Lord Lieutenancy £1,004,000; [51] and even in 1680 Ormonde was struggling to pay off to Vyner a debt of £13,000.[52]

The company of large private depositors was no less distinguished. Joseph Williamson, newspaper proprietor, clerk of the Privy Council, Secretary of State 1675–1679, not only maintained a personal account with Vyner but was on such terms of intimacy that Sir Robert kept his cellar stocked with Canary, Claret, and "Hocomer," [53] and Vyner's niece, Elizabeth,[54] entertained him in what she termed "accomodations . . . so disproportional to his merit," [55] and drew him as her valentine.[56]

Of the Irish gentry, Viscount Conway and Sir George Rawdon continued to bank at the Vine [57] where their fathers had raised money on the family plate in the early 1630's; [58] and Sir James Shaen, whose business was to serve inconspicuously as agent for greater men,[59] paid bribes in the guise of presents through Vyner's hands for the Irish lord of Munster, the Earl of Orrery.[60]

The great landlords, the Earls of Exeter and Bath; Sir John Bennett, brother of Secretary of State Arlington; Sir John Wynn of Denbighshire, Wales; Sir Thomas Player, father and son, both Chamberlains of the City of London; Sir John Robinson, Lieutenant of the Tower; Sir John Maynard, distinguished lawyer; Sir Thomas

[51] Report from an examination of actual accounts. *Hist. MSS. Comm. Reports, Ormonde*, N. S. III, 340.

[52] Cf. page 46; *Hist. MSS. Comm. Reports, Ormonde*, N. S. IV, 320.

[53] *Cal. St. Papers*, 1671, p. 327.

[54] Probably the daughter of Sir Robert's brother, Sir Thomas; she afterward married the goldsmith-banker, John Snell.

[55] *Cal. St. Papers*, 1671, p. 456.

[56] *Ibid.*, 1671–72, p. 380.

[57] *Cal. St. Papers, Ireland*, 1663–65, p. 587.

[58] *Cal. St. Papers*, 1629–31, p. 498; 1631–33, p. 133.

[59] Agent for the Duke of York; a farmer of the Irish revenue.

[60] Rev. Thos. Morrice, *A Collection of the State Papers of the First Earl of Orrery* (Dublin, 1743), I, 90.

Allen, hero of many a sea-battle, and later Comptroller of the Navy; Sir Thomas Meres, eloquent Opposition M.P.; the Bishop of Sarum, the Dean of St. Paul's, and the Archdeacon of Canterbury — all these and many more of equal distinction stepped from their coaches into the spacious reception room of the Vine.

Here, too, came the great merchants of London — Sir Martin Noel, scrivener and East India merchant, who, under the Commonwealth, had farmed the Post Office, the excise on salt, wines, tobacco, silk, linen, and sea-coals,[61] and at his death in 1665 was farming the Irish Customs;[62] Sir John Moore, Lord Mayor in 1683; Thomas Winter, East India merchant; Anthony Power, dealer in tobacco and Cashier for the Commissioners of Wine Licenses; Duarte Da Silva and Gomes Rodrigues, Portuguese Jews and representatives of great houses which dealt in bullion, jewels, wines, and sugar all over the world.

And here, too, came Vyner's neighbors — other Lombard Street goldsmith-bankers: George Snell of the Acorn who had married Mary Vyner;[63] his son John, of the Fox, who continued the alliance by marrying Sir Robert's niece Elizabeth;[64] Alderman Edward Backwell of the Unicorn, Vyner's sometime rival, sometime partner; John Colvile, and John Lindsey who, in 1676, married Colvile's widow and his fortune; Thomas Rowe, Backwell's erstwhile apprentice who prospered at the Three Tuns; Peter Fontaine of the Golden Cup in Soho; the Meynells, and Gilbert Whitehall who inherited their shop after the

[61] Edward Hughes, *Studies in Administration and Finance*, 1558–1825 (Manchester, Eng., 1934), p. 134; Thos. Burton, *Diary* (London, 1828), IV, 415–421.

[62] *Stowe MSS.*, 489, f. 61.

[63] In 1631 — Brooke and Hallen, *op. cit.*, p. 146.

[64] *Vyner Family History*, p. 53.

death of Isaac in November, 1675;[65] Alderman John Morris and Sir Robert Clayton, scrivener-bankers.[66]

Customers with smaller accounts came from all walks of life. There were lesser London tradesmen — butchers, chandlers, dyers, apothecaries, coach-makers, milliners, vintners, mercers; there were clerks and scholars from Oxford; agents for great estates from Yorkshire to Devon; widows and spinsters who invested their small inheritances at the Vine; country gentlemen and London lawyers — a cross-section not only of middle-class London but of the whole of England.

Best measure of the extent and prosperity of the private banking phase of the Vine is found, however, in the very large and very frequent loans which the Vyners, and particularly Sir Robert, were thereby enabled to make to the department treasurers who administered the revenues of the Crown; for, in fact, the Vyners' resources of cash and credit were as much needed to keep their King on his throne as they had been to put him there. The King of England was still expected in the 1660's to "live of his own," and since a blundering Parliament granted revenue to support the King and the governmental machinery of England which was barely adequate even at their estimate of £1,200,000 a year but which at the actual average yield of £800,000 posed a problem in finance that not even a mathematical wizard could have solved satisfactorily,[67] anticipations on revenue were the obvious result; and the Vyners, the Meynells, Edward Backwell, and lesser goldsmith-bankers stood ready with

[65] Brooke and Hallen, *op. cit.*, p. 242.

[66] They had large accounts also with Backwell, and with Blanchard and Child.

[67] W. A. Shaw, *Introduction to Cal. Treas. Books,* 1676–79, I, ix.

loans — at a price, to be sure, which averaged 10 per cent per annum but sometimes ran to 15 or 20 per cent.[68]

In fact, on the triumvirate of Vyner, Meynell, and Backwell, in the first years of the Restoration, much of the credit of the government seems to have rested. Together or separately they advanced large sums on nearly all the sources of revenue available to the Crown, and, indeed, it is very probable that an abortive proposal which was being considered in 1663 to farm the whole revenue may have emanated from this consortium.[69]

Francis Meynell had begun his career as a goldsmith's apprentice fresh from Derbyshire,[70] but by 1660 the Goldsmiths' Company were so eager to persuade him to become a member of their Court that they reduced his fine to a nominal sum, and when he was elected sheriff in 1661 they voted him £50 for "tryming" his house.[71] In the same year Meynell was made Receiver-General of the Eighteen-Months' Assessment granted by Parliament.[72] Pepys, who was continually in a state of shock at the deplorable condition of the country's finances, denominated Meynell "the great money-man," [73] and hoped that the Earl of Southampton, Lord Treasurer, would no longer suffer him "to go away with 10,000 £ per annm, as he do now get, by making people pay after this manner (15–20 per cent) for their money . . . which is," he opined, "a most horrid shame." [74]

Alderman Edward Backwell of the Unicorn in Ex-

[68] The legal limit was 6 per cent but it was evaded by disguising the additional percentage as a "reward."

[69] *Hist. MSS. Comm. Reports*, *Ormonde*, N. S. III, 69.

[70] He was the third son of Godfrey Meynell of Willington, Derbyshire. *Pepys' Diary* (Braybrooke ed.), (London, 1865–67), I, 326–327 note.

[71] Prideaux, *op. cit.*, II, 137, 142.

[72] E 401/1934, pt. I. Receipt Books (Pells').

[73] *Diary* (Braybrooke), I, 326–327.

[74] *Ibid.*, p. 374.

change Alley and Lombard Street — working goldsmith, dealer in bullion, East India merchant, and banker — bears for us a special interest because his ledgers alone, of the records of the great goldsmith-bankers of his day, have come down to us.[75] In the first years of the 1660's he seems to have been the least wealthy of the three, but such was his reputation for dependability that Charles II appointed him to receive in person the £325,000 which the French paid for the Flanders port of Dunkirk bought from England in the autumn of 1662.

On the security of these chests of silver, the three advanced £36,000 to the Household and £30,000 to Sir George Carteret for the Navy, and gradually they were repaid in Charles II's new currency now being made at the Mint out of the French specie.[76] The making of the new coins was, in fact, another joint enterprise, begun by these three in 1661 when the coins current in the country still bore the imprint of the "usurper" although Charles II now sat securely on the throne of England. The royalists, to be sure, had long maintained that the legends, "God with us," on one face of these coins, and "The Commonwealth of England" on the other, made it patent to all that God and the Commonwealth were on different sides, but this reasoning could hardly reconcile Charles II to the continued circulation of these reminders of "the late troubles." [77] Accordingly, in the autumn of 1661, he ordered the "Harp and Crown" money into the Mint to be recoined in his own likeness.[78] Since, however, the country was already suffering from a scarcity of gold and silver currency, and the Tower Mint could handle

[75] Cf. page 13 note 47.
[76] *Cal. Treas. Books,* 1660–67, pp. 459–460.
[77] J. W. Ebsworth, *Bagford Ballads* (Hertford, 1878), II, 756 note.
[78] British Museum Collection of Proclamations, 7 Sept., 1661.

no more than £10,000 a week, he contracted with Sir Thomas Vyner, Meynell, and Backwell to undertake the recoining and to make an immediate advance of £100,000 to the Exchequer.[79] They found this a most profitable undertaking, for not only was their loan repaid in new money as it came from the Mint, but the expense of recoining was borne by the Crown, while they were allowed 5s 10d on each £100 in old money which they turned in to the Mint.[80] Vyner's share in the profit alone was £19,456/1/2.[81]

In June, 1662, Charles II's new Queen, Catherine of Braganza, came to England. Her arrival was eagerly awaited, not only because of the curiosity as to her person but because her marriage contract specified a dowry of two million crusadoes (£350,000 [82]), half of which she was supposed to bring with her, the other half to be paid within the year following her arrival. To the impecunious King, actual cash was always of tremendous concern, but government treasurers, and the bankers as well, awaited the coming of the lady with impatience.

The prevailing disappointment was correspondingly bitter. The Queen herself was well enough, but her promised million crusadoes materialized as a few chests of specie, a few jewels, some sugar, and the rest in more or less dubious bills of exchange.[83] The Vyners, however, armed with tallies for £22,000 issued on the security of the dowry as early as the preceding February,[84] had first claim on what funds there were,[85] and that debt was dis-

[79] *Pepys' Diary* (Braybrooke), II, 306.
[80] *Cal. Treas. Books*, 1660–67, p. 417.
[81] *Ibid.*, p. 508.
[82] *Ibid.*, p. 435, gives the rate of exchange as 3/7 per crusado.
[83] *Ibid.*, p. 360.
[84] *Hist. MSS. Comm. Reports*, *Heathcote MS.*, p. 30.
[85] *Ibid.*; *Cal. Treas. Books*, 1660–67, p. 398.

charged at once; but repayment of the £24,000 they had advanced for the Royal Household in company with Meynell and Backwell [86] was delayed until well into the winter, when the Queen's agent, Edward DaSilva, under the surveillance of a King's messenger, managed to make good the bills of exchange sent in his name.[87]

There was soon need for the triumvirate's services again. In November, 1662, an ambassador from Russia arrived in town for a six months' stay at the King's expense,[88] with "attendants in their habits and fur caps" who impressed Pepys as "very handsome, comely men"; but his townsfellows, Pepys observed, after "the absurd nature of Englishmen," could "not forbear laughing and jeering." [89] The purpose of this visit shortly appeared. The cavalcade had come to collect the loan which the Emperor of Russia had made to Charles II in the years of his exile, and the price of their departure was, obviously, the payment of the debt. The triumvirate accordingly advanced a total of £33,169/11/8 in Lübeck dollars to speed the parting guest.[90]

With the death of Sir Thomas Vyner in 1665 and of Francis Meynell the following year, these joint operations ceased. The reason for this may lie partly in the increasing capital at the command of each of these flourishing banking houses which made large independent transactions possible, but, since Vyner and Backwell occasionally undertook ventures in partnership thereafter, the probability is that Isaac Meynell, who succeeded his

[86] *Cal. Treas. Books*, 1660–67, p. 398.

[87] He was a member of the great family of Portuguese Jews. *Stowe MSS.* 489, ff. 41, 55.

[88] *Calendar of Wynn of Gwydir Papers*, 1515–1690 (London, 1926), p. 373.

[89] *Pepys' Diary* (Braybrooke), I, 353.

[90] Backwell Ledger I (1663), "King's Most Excellent Majtie" account; *Cal. Treas. Books*, 1660–67, p. 564.

brother, preferred to carry on his own prosperous business [91] without interference or obligation.

It was in May, 1665, that Sir Thomas Vyner died, at the age of seventy-six, the "two hares feete" which he wore "at the wast band of his breeches on each syde within next his shirt" [92] having at length failed to protect him. The funeral was held from Goldsmiths' Hall and an overflow at Haberdashers' Hall, both so crowded that Pepys preferred to view the funeral procession to St. Mary Woolnoth Church from a balcony on Cornhill — a procession "which was with the blue-coat boys and old men, all the Aldermen, and Lord Mayor, &c., and the number of the company very great." [93] Sir Thomas evidently had died from old age, and not from the plague, but the plague was terrifyingly prevalent in London that spring; already merchants and gentry had begun to realize that "the sickness is not far from Lombard St.," [94] and it is very probable that the great gathering at Sir Thomas' funeral hastened the spread of the epidemic among the goldsmiths. The proprietors themselves, either because they were made of stern stuff, or more probably because they fled from London, for the most part seem to have escaped infection, but their servants left behind were not so fortunate. By the middle of June "the affairs of the Bankers were in such Disorder by the Death of Servants, and the Plague having been in some of their Houses, that the usual Course of advancing Money by Assignations could not be depended upon." [95] More-

[91] After the death of Francis, the total of deposits in the Meynell account at Backwell's continued to reach or exceed £35,000 a year.

[92] *Notes and Queries*, 2nd series, X, 322, from a herald's work book.

[93] *Diary* (Braybrooke), II, 174.

[94] Margaret M. Verney, *Memoirs of the Verney Family* (London, 1899), IV, 117.

[95] Edward Hyde, Earl of Clarendon, Continuation of *Life* (London, 1759), p. 305.

over, it was generally realized that if the sickness "should visitt the Goldsmiths twill be hazardous to have too great a stock there,"[96] and "the feare of the Plague," observed Sir Ralph Verney, "makes many willing to take their Estates out of the Goldsmiths' hands, & the King's greate want of money makes many very unwilling to lend any money to these that advance greate summs for him. I know some friends," he added, "that have 1000 l. & 1500 l. a peece that they cannot dispose of."[97]

War with the Dutch, brought on by the perennial disputes between English and Dutch merchants, had been declared in February of that year, and although Parliament had provided the Royal Aid, estimated at £2,477,500, for the expenses of war, this was to be collected over a period of three years and was by no means adequate. Pepys in June complained that the tallies assigned the Navy to be offered the bankers as security would "not be money in less than sixteen months, which," he added, "is a sad thing for the King to pay all that interest for every penny he spends"; nor would the goldsmiths, with deposits from their regular customers drastically cut, "be moved to part with money," even "upon the increase of their consideration of ten per cent. which they have."[98]

Robert Vyner, however, fared much better in this disastrous year of 1665 than his colleagues Backwell and Meynell. Backwell's "right hand,"[99] his cashier Robert Shaw, died of the plague,[100] and his bank suffered a run,[101] while, in Meynell's family, his sister-in-law Elizabeth and his nephew and apprentice John Meynell died in the epi-

[96] Verney, *Memoirs of the Verney Family*, IV, 117.
[97] *Ibid.*, p. 116.
[98] *Diary* (Braybrooke), II, 184.
[99] *Ibid.*, p. 201.
[100] Brooke and Hallen, *op. cit.*, p. 235. 25 July, 1665.
[101] *Pepys' Diary* (Braybrooke), II, 192.

demic.[102] Vyner, however, by his uncle's death, came into full proprietorship of the shop and house at the Vine.[103] He was able to loan, "in the heat of the plague," £330,000 for Navy, household, and guards;[104] he was knighted by Charles II; and ten days after his uncle's funeral he married Mary Whitchurch Hyde, widow of a month, who brought him not only exceptional beauty of form and face — though now a little faded — but £100,000 as a marriage portion.[105] Sir Robert at once bought as a country house Swakeleys, in Ickenham, south of London[106] and away from the infection of the city — a great house, pleasant despite its exuberant architecture, set in a formal garden.[107] The ubiquitous Pepys dined there in September, 1665, and was rapturous over the marble window cases, door cases, and mantels, and the splendid furniture, and fascinated by Vyner's little black boy who, having died of consumption, had been "dried in an oven, and lies there entire in a box."[108]

The full impact of the nation's losses from the plague came in the following year, 1666, in the decrease in trade from the death of so many merchants and the drop in revenue from all kinds of taxes; while at the same time the Dutch War called for expenditures even beyond the Additional Aid, estimated at £1,250,000, which Parliament had granted in November, 1665. Sir Robert Vyner, with his great resources of cash and credit, in large degree controlled the financial fate of the government.

[102] Brooke and Hallen, *op. cit.*, pp. 234–235.

[103] *Vyner Family History*, p. 29. Sir Thomas' son George inherited the baronetcy and lived at Hackney, died Aug., 1673; his son Thomas was Clerk of Chancery, died Feb., 1667.

[104] *Cal. St. Papers*, 1666–67, p. 433.

[105] *Vyner Family History*, p. 54.

[106] Near Uxbridge Common.

[107] London Survey Committee, Monograph No. 13, *Swakeleys, Ickenham* (London, 1933), gives a very detailed study of this house, built in 1638.

[108] *Diary* (Braybrooke), II, 226.

From the earliest days of the Restoration he had accepted as his special province the supplying of funds for the troops in Ireland. In May, 1660, he had furnished £30,000; [109] a year later he bought a like sum in foreign gold and silver for transportation to Ireland, advancing the specie on the security of Customs.[110] Payment was slow, and in November, 1661, although he "ought to have been repaid . . . long since," he had received but £500; [111] nevertheless, the following March he was agreeing to furnish the Irish service with £100,000 — this time, however, on the security of an Eighteen-Months' Assessment which Parliament had granted,[112] his loan made doubly sure by the provisos that all the proceeds of this tax from seven counties be paid directly to him and that, although the estimated total from these sources exceeded his loan by more than £30,000, he was to receive the whole and deduct his expenses before he paid any surplus into the Exchequer.[113]

When £60,000 was assigned to Ireland out of the four subsidies which Parliament had voted [114] in 1663, the Vice-Treasurer of Ireland, the Earl of Anglesey and the Lord Lieutenant, the Earl of Ormonde made every effort to secure the whole amount from Sir Thomas Vyner, who had already advanced £15,000 in English money and promised to send the remainder in English coin to Chester, where Robert Vyner was to put it safely aboard a "yaght" — all at their personal expense.[115] Alderman Edward Backwell, however, not only "circumvented the

[109] *Cal. St. Papers*, 1660–61, p. 597.
[110] *Ibid.*, 1661–62, p. 8.
[111] *Cal. Treas. Books*, 1660–67, p. 300.
[112] Estimated at £1,260,000. 13 Car. II st. 2, c. 3.
[113] *Cal. St. Papers, Ireland*, 1660–62, p. 520 (24 Mar., 1662).
[114] 15 Car. II, c. 9.
[115] *Cal. St. Papers, Ireland*, 1663–65, p. 164; *Hist. MSS. Comm. Reports, Ormonde*, N. S. III, 76.

Council" into contracting with him for half the total grant but secured their consent that it be sent in foreign specie and shipped to Ireland at the expense of the Crown.[116]

Now in 1666, when £15,000 was needed imperatively in Ireland to pay mutinying troops and to preserve the very government from dissolution,[117] Vyner was less obliging. Ormonde objected strenuously to his greedy insistence on "Irish interest, which is 10 per cent., and 6 per cent. for the exchange," [118] but Lord Treasurer Southampton was forced to admit himself to be "under some kind of necessity for transacting by Sir Robert Viner's hand," although he was frank in "acknowledging . . . Vyner's conditions to be exorbitant ones." [119] In the end, with Vyner's expenses, allowances, and discounts all subtracted, the disgusted Lord Lieutenant received £11,700 out of the promised £15,000.[120] The Exchequer was, moreover, still paying interest to the tune of £8632 a year on the £100,000, as yet only partially repaid, which Vyner had advanced for Ireland in 1661.[121]

Vyner was actuated by no motives of altruism in his financial dealings with the government, and, in these war years particularly, he was very careful to protect his own interests. On the Royal Aid he had pledged a large advance for the Navy, £49,480 of which was to be repaid him directly by the receivers for London and Oxfordshire. The disasters of these years, however, affected the returns from this revenue immediately and severely; local tax-receivers died, went bankrupt, or defaulted; but it was the Excheq-

[116] *Hist. MSS. Comm. Reports, Ormonde,* N. S. III, 76.

[117] *Cal. St. Papers, Ireland,* 1666–69, p. 120.

[118] *Ibid.*, p. 259.

[119] T[homas] Brown, *Miscellania Aulica* (London,1702), p. 400.

[120] *Cal. St. Papers, Ireland,* pp. 164, 180, 206.

[121] *Ibid.*, pp. 258, 259 — 5 per cent for exchange, 3 per cent for interest, and £632 for Exchequer fees.

uer that suffered, and not Vyner. He paid to the Navy Treasurer scarcely more than a third of his pledge, and was finally allowed to close the account by paying only an additional £6000 into the Exchequer.[122]

In May of 1666 Sir Robert was granted a baronetcy, and in June he was elected sheriff of London. The Goldsmiths' Company honored his shrievalty by lending him the Company plate, but the more expansive days of his uncle's incumbency were past, and no money for the expenses of his office was forthcoming.[123] He was destined to hold this office in a time quite as memorable in its way as had been that of his uncle's tenure, for in September occurred the Great Fire which consumed almost the entire City of London. Sir Robert's part in coping with the disaster does not appear, so that it is probable that if he showed no outstanding heroism, neither did he reach the abysmal depths of panic which caused the unfortunate Lord Mayor to stand about in everyone's way, wringing his hands. What is certain is that Vyner showed immediate solicitude for the fate of his own business, so that "almost twenty four hours before the furious Fire entred Lumbardstreet" his bonds, papers, and money had been removed from the Vine[124] and carted off for safe-keeping at his brother's quarters in Windsor Castle "under a convenient guard."[125] This was a very temporary move, however, for almost at once he was advertising to do business at the headquarters in Broad Street of the Royal African Company,[126] of which he was a member,[127] and shortly after he had moved to Winchester Street near by.[128]

[122] *Cal. Treas. Books*, 1672–75, p. 406. [123] Prideaux, *op. cit.*, II, 159.
[124] *London Gazette*, No. 85, 3–10 Sept., 1666.
[125] *Vyner Family History*, p. 57. His brother, Thomas, was prebendary of Windsor.
[126] *London Gazette*, No. 85, 3–10 Sept., 1666.
[127] Blome, *Britannia*, p. 161. [128] *Cal. St. Papers*, 1666–67, p. 322.

If government treasurers had thought money tight before the Fire, they found it almost impossible to borrow thereafter. Panic was again imminent, and Charles II found it necessary to deny by proclamation rumors of an intended devaluation of coinage,[129] and to beg from Vyner his promise to hold in readiness £145,000 for immediate use in case a general panic or a revolt should actually break out in the excitement following the disaster.[130] In the middle of October, both Vyner and Backwell, at a meeting of the King and cabinet, flatly refused to advance further funds,[131] but several days later the threat of any immediate emergency had passed and Vyner was prevailed upon to loan the £145,000 reserve in gradual installments to the Treasurer of the Navy.[132]

Parliament that autumn, feeling the pinch from plague and fire, voted only a poll tax estimated at no more than £480,000, and although the text remains of a proposal made by Vyner and Backwell to farm this tax for £800,000 on the ground that the difference would be saved by paying the money directly into their shops instead of the Exchequer,[133] there is no indication that this proposal was accepted, and the receipts from this tax seem to have been actually less than £265,000.[134]

The damage which the Dutch War inevitably brought to English shipping, augmented by the death of so many merchants in the epidemic, made renewal of the Customs

129 *London Gazette*, No. 93, 4–8 Oct., 1666.

130 *Cal. Treas. Books*, 1669–72, II, 1169; he was paid £2000 for this service in Jan., 1672.

131 *Pepys' Diary* (Braybrooke), II, 425.

132 *Cal. Treas. Books*, 1669–72, II, 1169.

133 *Cal. St. Papers*, 1666–67, p. 541 (? Feb., 1667). The disparity in estimates is so great, however, that the possibility of an error in the text as printed in the Calendar must be considered.

134 W. A. Shaw, "Beginnings of the National Debt," *Historical Essays* (London, 1902), p. 395.

Farm at the same rental a doubtful matter even before the additional disaster of the Fire. The Farm was not, to be sure, actually due to end until Michaelmas, 1665, but in August, 1666, a tentative lease for four years had been arranged with a combination which included Sir Robert Vyner and his prospective nephew, Francis Millington,[135] as new investors; two of the former signatories — Sir John Wolstenholme and Sir John Shaw; and Edward Backwell and Sir Edmond Turner, who had increased their stakes sufficiently to entitle them to sign the contract. The partners had advanced only £15,000,[136] however, when the Great Fire, by destroying much of the property of London merchants and even the Customs-house itself, reduced still further the probable revenue from the Farm. King and Council, however, urged the undertakers to tender new proposals,[137] and their necessities forced them to accept the niggardly terms offered — £200,000 in advance, £350,000 annual rent for the first three years, and £370,000 for the last,[138] instead of the £390,000 a year pledged in 1662.[139]

The Hearth Farm fell into even more desperate case, and it was Sir Robert Vyner alone who saved it from complete failure. The tax on chimneys, from the time of its granting in 1662, had been collected by local receivers on a fixed salary from the Crown, but this method had proved unproductive and the King had resolved instead to farm out the Chimney tax, beginning at Michaelmas, 1665.[140] Preliminary terms for the Farm had been signed by Perient

[135] He subsequently married Martha, daughter of Vyner's brother Samuel.

[136] *Hist. MSS. Comm. Reports*, VIII, *House of Lords MSS.*, 131.

[137] *Cal. Treas. Books*, 1669–72, II, 961.

[138] T 64/37 — 26 March, 1667 — the terms of the final indenture. After peace was declared the following July, the rent was raised to £400,000 per annum. *Stowe MSS.* 489, f. 168 — 6 Sept., 1667.

[139] *Cal. St. Papers*, 1661–62, p. 503.

[140] British Museum Collection of Royal Proclamations, 19 Dec., 1666.

Trott, Humphrey Beane, and Sir Richard Piggott, Vyner's cousin, just before the plague reached frightening proportions — terms which called for an advance of £250,000 and an annual rental of £145,000; [141] but one by one, these signatories and their several partners found it impossible to meet the payments on the advance, and, in the end, Trott supplied £20,000, James Hoare, goldsmith-banker, £10,000, Captain John Ryves £10,000 which he had borrowed from Backwell,[142] and Vyner the remaining £210,000 [143] on a promise of 6 per cent interest from his nominal partners in addition to the 6 per cent pledged by the Crown.[144] For the first half year, ending Lady Day, 1666, Vyner was able to pay no more than £48,000 rent; [145] and the Great Fire still further reduced the income, so that the Hearth tax was as much in arrears under the farmers as when directly under the Crown. By October, 1667, however, Vyner's partners had sufficiently recovered actually to invest in the Farm, and Sir Allen Broderick, Alderman John Bence, George Cock, goldsmith-banker, and James Temple, Vyner's "chief man," took shares, although Vyner continued to control the Farm with an investment of two-fifths; [146] and eventually a reduction of £7000 in the annual rent was allowed for the losses from the burning of London.[147]

The rebuilding of London went on very slowly, and it was not until the middle of 1670 that Vyner and other temporary residents of the Broad Street region advertised

[141] *Cal. St. Papers*, 1665–66, p. 290. The indenture provided for an increased rental for the sixth and seventh years — £150,000, £170,000.

[142] In partnership with Thomas Leigh who married Vyner's niece Honor, daughter of his brother Thomas, the Dean of Gloucester and Prebendary of Windsor.

[143] Backwell, Dunkirk Ledger. Indenture of 17 Oct., 1667.

[144] *Cal. St. Papers*, 1666–67, p. 433.

[145] *Cal. Treas. Books*, 1667–68, p. 134.

[146] Backwell, Dunkirk Ledger, Indenture.

[147] *Cal. Treas. Books*, 1669–72, I, 22.

in the *London Gazette* their return to Lombard Street.[148] Vyner's new house occupied not only the site of the old Vine but the site of a large tavern as well, and was a wandering expanse of buildings and courtyard covering a quarter of an acre. A large gate and broad entry led from Lombard Street into a "handsome Court neatly paved with freestone" behind which was "a yard for stabling and coaches with a back gate to Sherborn Lane."[149] The house itself was "a very curious Building with good Rooms," and gave ample space for goldsmiths' work-rooms and melting-kitchen, a reception room for banking business, and living quarters for household, apprentices, and servants.

St. Mary Woolnoth Church adjoining was desolated like the rest of Lombard Street after the Fire, but, largely due to Sir Robert's efforts, it was "suddenly" rebuilt, equipped with an organ,[150] and decorated with vines all over the front façade in tribute to the principal donor.[151]

Sir Robert was instrumental, too, in advancing, in partnership with Backwell, funds for rebuilding the Customs-house;[152] and he was generous in contributing toward the hall of the Goldsmiths' Company. Not only did he give £300 for repairing and beautifying their Great Parlour,[153] but he donated the silver bell and ivory hammer which are still used at business meetings of the Company.[154] And it is only fitting that portraits of Sir Robert and Sir Thomas even now look down from the walls of the Great Parlour,[155] with proprietary gaze on the splendid plate, some of which is their own handiwork.

148 No. 479, 16–20 June, 1670.

149 John Stow, *A Survey of the Cities of London and Westminster, Enlarged by John Strype* (London, 1720), I, 163.

150 *Stowe MSS.* 186, f. 26.

151 Stow, *Survey*, I, 160.

152 *Cal. Treas. Books*, 1667–68, p. 149.

153 Prideaux, *op. cit.*, II, 165.

154 *Ibid*, p. 161.

155 James Temple presented the portrait of Sir Thomas in his robes of Lord Mayor, in October, 1671. Both portraits are reproduced in Prideaux, *op. cit.*, II, 164, 248.

Sir Robert had not been left at his uncle's death to carry on the business unaided. Sir Thomas in his will had bequeathed to James Temple, "cousin and servant," £500, five times the sum he had designated for his nephew;[156] and Temple, "the fat blade" of Pepys' *Diary*, continued as Vyner's "chief man"[157] until his death, probably early in the 1670's.

Henry Lewis, "servant," also remembered in Sir Thomas' will,[158] was taken into partnership with Sir Robert, and, with the other partner, Richard Stratford, shared in the fortunes of the Vine as long as Sir Robert lived. By 1668 both Lewis and Stratford had attained the dignity of accounts in their own name at Backwell's;[159] in 1671 Stratford was advancing money on Customs;[159a] and Sir Robert seems to have tried to evade some of his obligations to the Crown by transacting business under cover of Stratford's name.[160] It is probable that Sir Robert's nephew, Robert Vyner,[161] usually distinguished as "Junior," learned the goldsmith's trade in his uncle's shop. He did not remain at the Vine, however, but set up in business for himself in 1678[162] on the north side of Lombard Street near Cardinal's Cap Alley, in partnership with Bernard Eales.[163]

If the years 1665 and 1666 were disastrous for England,

[156] *Vyner Family History*, p. 29.

[157] *Pepys' Diary* (Braybrooke), II, 306, erroneously identifies Vyner's servant as *John* Temple who was a goldsmith-banker at the Three Tuns, Lombard St., 1670–83 (Heal, *op. cit.*, p. 87), in partnership with John Seale in 1677 (*Little London Directory*); in which Chaffers (*op. cit.*), p. 69, and Price (*Handbook of London Bankers*), p. 130, followed him.

[158] *Vyner Family History*, p. 29.

[159] Ledger Q.

[159a] E 401/1948 (3 Nov., 1671).

[160] *Cal. Treas. Books*, 1681–85, I, 298.

[161] Son of Sir Robert's brother, Samuel.

[162] First mention of the two partners occurs in 1678; they do not appear in the list of goldsmith-bankers in the *Little London Directory* of 1677.

[163] E 401/1961. Robert, Jr., died in 1690; Eales in 1694.

1667 proved a proportionate culmination. The condition of all connected with the Navy, which was bearing the brunt of the war with the Dutch, was indeed lamentable. As early as October, 1665, Pepys had reported that "merchantmen, victuallers, water- and hospital-ships lie uselessly unpaid. The victualler, the slopseller, the smith, the workmen in the yard, in fine, all people, are out of humour because out of purse, so that nothing can be found fault with or enquired after but you are straightly answered, 'We want money.'"[164] Fifteen months later, the seamen had grown openly mutinous, and when "a young fellow sounded a horne at Tower hill . . . and cryed — for Whitehall,"[165] the sailors "went tumultuously," breaking open Newgate-prison on their way.[166] In this emergency, Vyner came to the rescue by lending at least £60,000 on Hearth tax and Customs on what he called good terms, for the purchase of stores and goods for the fleet, refitting ships, and paying sailors' wages.

But although this crisis was tided over, the course of the war went more and more definitely against the English, until the climax came in June, 1667, with the raid by the Dutch up the Thames as far as Chatham, where they destroyed English ships, lying idle for want of stores and men. This bordered on actual invasion of the island, and it added terror to the state of nerves into which the City had been plunged by the death of the old and trusted Lord Treasurer Southampton in the middle of May and by the appointment of Commissioners to succeed him who were rumored to be unfriendly to the bankers who had tied up the Crown revenues by their large advances at exorbitant

164 J. R. Tanner, *Further Correspondence of Samuel Pepys, 1662–1679* (London, 1929), p. 70.

165 *Stowe MSS.* 489, f. 151.

166 *Cal. St. Papers*, 1667–68, p. 148.

rates of interest.[167] These bankers now found themselves besieged by their creditors, who were convinced by the Dutch raid that the government was foundering and that the bankers must be dragged down with it.

Vyner, it was rumored, had £100,000 at hand when the run began, but he could hardly refuse the demands of government treasurers, and when the news spread about that even one of the Treasury Commissioners, the Duke of Albemarle, had withdrawn £12,000 from Vyner, the panic grew and demands for cash taxed even his resources.[168] On the eighteenth of June, Charles II took command of the situation by issuing a proclamation guaranteeing repayment of all Exchequer debts to bankers,[169] and the immediate crisis was over; but he was forced to make peace at once with the Dutch, dismiss the Navy Treasurer, Sir George Carteret, reinstate the popular Duke of Buckingham in his various offices, and eventually agree to the impeachment and banishment of Lord Chancellor Clarendon, before private and public credit recovered from the summer's excitement.

In February, 1667, Parliament had voted an Eleven-Months' Assessment estimated at £1,250,000. Money had come in but slowly; two days before the Dutch raid Vyner could only be prevailed on to lend £10,000 on the fund.[170] In August the King was advertising openly to pay 10 per cent for all loans on the Act,[171] but still lenders remained shy, feeling with Pepys that there was "no delight in lending money now, to be paid by the King two years hence."[172]

[167] *Pepys' Diary* (Braybrooke), III, 103, 107–108. The commissioners were the Duke of Albemarle, Lord Ashley, Sir Thomas Clifford, Sir William Coventry, and Sir John Duncomb, with Sir George Downing as their Secretary. *Cal. St. Papers*, 1667, p. 115; *Pepys' Diary* (Braybrooke), III, 107.

[168] *Pepy's Diary* (Braybrooke), III, 121, 126.

[169] *Cal. St. Papers*, 1667, p. 204.

[170] *Cal. Treas. Books*, 1667–68, p. 8.

[171] *Stowe MSS.*, 489, f. 173; *Pepys' Diary* (Braybrooke), III, 203.

[172] *Ibid.*, p. 208.

Vyner's stake in the national revenue was, in fact, by now staggering. For the Navy, Guards, Household, Jewel House, etc., since the Restoration he had lent at least £1,550,000, and a substantial part of this was still drawing interest with no immediate prospects of repayment,[173] although, his "credit, which is dearer than life, being at stake," he petitioned the King and Treasury Commissioners frequently.[174] In June, 1668, he was owed by the Crown £35,000 for plate alone; even so, relying on the promise of the Commissioners to pay, he fashioned a present for the wife of the Swedish ambassador, and by October his bill at the Jewel House had increased to £46,000.[175] On the Royal Aid which had now run its three-year course, Vyner had advanced to Sir George Carteret as Treasurer of the Navy £105,000,[176] but it was not until February, 1669, that the Treasury Commissioners made any practical effort to deal with this obligation, and then only by ordering that £5000 be paid him monthly from Customs, beginning seventeen months thereafter.[177] In June of 1669, the Commissioners paid to Vyner the remainder of a loan he had made to the Navy in July, 1662;[178] but in the main all they had to offer was the advice that the bankers "must have patience a little, and my Lords doubt not but the Parliament will provide for their debt."[179]

The prospects were not encouraging, for the general indignation at the mismanagement of the disgraceful Dutch War demanded scapegoats, and the bankers who had lent money at high rates of interest came in for their share of castigation by investigating committees. A committee to consider the decay of trade, which met in 1669–

[173] *Cal. St. Papers*, 1667, p. 148.
[174] *Ibid.*, p. 113.
[175] *Cal. Treas. Books*, 1667–68, pp. 345, 450.
[176] *Ibid.*, p. 444.
[177] *Ibid.*, 1669–72, pp. 1, 17.
[178] *Ibid.*, pp. 230, 243.
[179] *Ibid.*, p. 102.

1670 with full panoply of "a formal Board with Green Cloth and Standishes, Clerks good Store, a tall Porter and Staff . . . and a huge Luminary at the Door," [180] investigated "the causes of the depression" at length, and arrived at the conclusion that "large individual profits are a national loss." [181] Despite such disapproving dicta, scant repayment, and dubious promises, however, Vyner continued to loan to the government, presumably in the attempt to protect his earlier investments — £21,000 on Customs and unspecified funds in 1669 to the Exchequer,[182] £12,000 to the Treasurer of the Chamber, £62,169/10/4 for the Tangiers garrison.[183] In June, 1670, £10,661 for interest and reward on these loans was as yet unpaid him.[184]

Parliament, meeting in the autumn of 1670, had been confronted with a request from the King that they supply him with £800,000 for outfitting the Navy,[185] and that they pay off the debts he owed the bankers for which he was paying interest on a principal estimated at £1,314,000.[186] The bankers were generally unpopular, however; debate in the Commons recalled earlier sessions which had dubbed them "Cheats, Bloodsuckers, Extortioners, and loaded them with all the Reproaches which can be cast upon the worst Men in the World," [187] and eventually Parliament voted only a subsidy of £800,000 — the sum needed for the Navy — £300,000 by an additional excise on imported beer and ale, and an inconsiderable stamp

[180] Roger North, *Examen* (London, 1740), p. 461.

[181] *Hist. MSS. Comm. Reports*, VIII, *House of Lords MSS.*, p. 134.

[182] E. 401/1943–4 — Receipt Books (Pells').

[183] *Cal. Treas. Books*, 1669–72, I, 592.

[184] *Ibid.*, p. 486. £1500 in interest had already been paid.

[185] Andrew Marvell, *Letters* (Margoliouth ed., Oxford, 1927), p. 107.

[186] £1,000,000 at 10 per cent; £300,000 at 6 per cent. Marvell, *Letters*, p. 107; *Hist. MSS. Comm. Reports*, VI, *Ingilby* MS, p. 369.

[187] Clarendon, Continuation of *Life*, p. 314.

tax on legal documents.[188] Not only was the total painfully inadequate to pay off the debts, but the subsidy was to be raised partly by a tax of 15 shillings in £100 on all loans made to the King by bankers at interest above 6 per cent.[189]

The Customs Farm in which Vyner held a large share was due to expire at Michaelmas, 1671, and in November, 1670, he and his partners sought to renew their contract; but, although they advanced £26,000 towards their new undertaking,[190] another group was awarded the tentative contract;[191] they too, in the end, however, were denied the confirming indenture when their arrogant attempt to lower the annual rent of the Farm drove the King to put the Customs in commission.[192]

The whole situation was fast drawing to an inevitable conclusion — the repudiation of some, at least, of the debts of the Crown. This act was precipitated by the anticipations on revenue which had piled up much more than a year ahead, and, immediately, by the fact that the disappointed Customs farmers were too powerful to permit repayment of their advance of £207,400[193] to be ignored or postponed, and by the imminence of war with the Dutch, growing out of recent treaties of alliance with France, which made the outfitting of a war-time Navy immediately essential.[194]

The original plan for the repudiation had included all debts of the Crown except orders on subsidies granted by

[188] Marvell, *Letters*, p. 133.

[189] *Ibid.*, p. 119.

[190] *Ibid.*, p. 112; E 401/1945.

[191] Lord St. John, Sir John Bennett, brother of Secretary Arlington, Sir William Bucknall and his brother Ralph who farmed the Irish Revenue and controlled most of the Excise Farms of the Kingdom, Alderman John Bence, Hearth farmer.

[192] *Hist. MSS. Comm. Reports*, *Fitzherbert MS.*, p. 6.

[193] *Cal. Treas. Books*, 1669–72, II, 1122, 1163.

[194] *Hist. MSS. Comm. Reports*, *Ingilby MS.*, p. 368.

Parliament and Fee Farm rents, but this was, in the end, modified to include only advances made on paper orders which had come into general use by the Treasury. These orders, originally issued as receipts for actual loans made on definite security,[195] had come, in the past five years, to be perverted into printed paper orders, issued to department treasurers in large denominations, on which they were expected to raise what money they could.[196] Since, however, the orders were drawn against any money available in the Exchequer or against such income from one of the branches of the revenue as had not been otherwise assigned, and since such money was increasingly rare, redemption of the orders became more difficult, interest rates for loans on orders rose, advances on such security were increasingly hard to secure — and the "Stop of the Exchequer," voted by the Privy Council on January 2, 1672,[197] was the logical result.

An account drawn up in July, 1674, placed the debt of the government to Vyner on these orders at £147,446/6/2,[198] but the entire amount seems to have been even larger; and besides, Vyner had bought speculatively from the original holders at least £6638/6 more.[199]

At first, after the Stop, the bankers had entertained some hopes of an immediate arrangement which would at least ensure regular interest payments on the sums owed them, especially as the King had exacted a promise from the bankers to honor their obligations to their depositors;[200] but at the end of the year first prescribed for

[195] E 407/123 includes such a printed order, dated 7 Nov., 1667.

[196] W. A. Shaw, "The Treasury Order Book," *Economic Journal*, XVI (Mar., 1906), 39. Such an order, from E 407/120, dated 26 June, 1671, is printed *in extenso* in Richards, *Early History of Banking*, p. 63.

[197] The royal proclamation was issued January 5.

[198] E 407/33 — mainly on Hearth Money, Customs, Royal Aid, and Fee Farms.

[199] *Cal Treas. Books*, 1672–75, p. 306.

[200] Bishop Burnet, *History of My Own Time* (London, 1833), I, 551 note.

the Stop, a six months' prolongation was announced, and by the end of that, in May, 1673, most of the bankers' orders had expired.[201] Nor was there any help from Parliament, despite the King's commendation of the debt to their "care and consideration";[202] and after the prorogation in November, 1673, it was observed that "the Bankers are extremely disheartened, and now apprehend they shall never get their moneys. Amongst them all poor Sir R. Vyner is the most pitied and perhaps the most deserves it."[203]

He had, indeed, suffered especially, because many of the royal tax-receivers had deposited tax money with him, and these funds, due upon demand, the Treasury Commissioners had forced him after the Stop to pay at once. This he had done without demur, but it had led to suits by which the tax receivers sought to recover the principal on money from taxes which they had loaned to Backwell at interest; and although the Treasury Commissioners refused to "give any Encouragement to ym to detayne his Matyes Treasure in their hands for the Lucre of Interest,"[204] such suits were disturbingly recurrent.[205]

But the Lord Treasurer, Thomas Osborne, Earl of Danby, who had come into office at Midsummer, 1673, did what he could to keep the bankers from bankruptcy. For Vyner he ordered the immediate payment of the three years' arrears on a £1000 pension which Charles II had granted him,[206] gave sympathetic ear to the "hum-

[201] W. A. Shaw, Intro. *Cal. Treas. Books*, 1669–72, I, li.

[202] Arthur Bryant, *Letters of Charles II* (London, 1935), p. 271.

[203] *Cal. St. Papers*, 1673–75, p. 5.

[204] P. C. 2/66, 198.

[205] *Wynn Papers*, p. 411; *Cal. Treas. Books*, 1672–75, p. 756; *Hist. MSS. Comm. Reports*, IX, Pt. II, 68; P. C. 2/66, 193, 198; *House of Lords MS.* I, 273 (26 Mar., 1681).

[206] *Add. MS.* 28077, f. 24 (17 Nov., 1673).

ble desires" of Vyner and Backwell,[207] and reaped his reward in a £10,000 loan from Vyner in March, 1674, toward paying off the seamen being disbanded now that the war with the Dutch was ended.[208] There had been no question of repudiating what the King owed Vyner for plate. His account for March 1671/72 was accepted as usual,[209] and Danby seems to have issued in January, 1674, an order from which Vyner's plate charges were paid for the next few years.[210]

Whatever Sir Robert may have lost from the Exchequer Stop and its reverberations, he did not suffer such an eclipse as that which seems to have befallen Backwell — this in part, perhaps, because the clientele of the Vine was more diversified than that of the Unicorn and not confined so strictly to government officials and merchants of London. Nor was Sir Robert entirely dependent on his banking business and his goldsmith-shop. He was a member and stockholder of the Royal or "Guinea" Company,[211] which exploited the gold mines on the west coast of Africa; he was one of the original investors in the Hudson's Bay Company, although his £300 brought him no returns until a dividend of 50 per cent was declared in 1684;[212] and he was a member of the East India Company,[213] although, unlike his uncle, he seems to have been content to draw his dividends without taking part in active ventures.

It is difficult to say whether Sir Robert Vyner savored

[207] *Add. MS.* 28094, f. 35; *Add. MS.* 28077, f. 56.

[208] *Add. MS.* 28078, f. 150–151.

[209] *Cal. St. Papers*, 1671–72, p. 260.

[210] E 403/3062, f. 73; *Add. MS.* 28077, f. 100.

[211] Blome, *Britannia*, p. 161. He was a member of the Court of Assistants in 1672.

[212] Names and Stocks of Hudson's Bay Company — Nov., 1673; Douglas MacKay, *The Honourable Company* (Indianapolis, 1936), pp. 41, 339.

[213] Sainsbury, *op. cit.*, 1671–74 — list of stock transfers.

the irony of his erection of a statue of Charles II on a newly-completed conduit near Lombard Street, only a few months after the Stop, but Andrew Marvell soon pointed out to the world at large that

> "As cities that to the fierce conquerors yield
> Do at their own charge their citadels build,
> So Sir Robert advanced the King's statue, in token
> Of banker defeated and Lombard-Street broken." [214]

And at best the gift was something of a farce, since the statue had originally represented the Polish hero, John Sobieski, trampling on the recumbent Turk, and Vyner, buying it for a song, had had Sobieski's head replaced by a likeness of Charles II, and had trusted that the general hatred of Cromwell would condone the Oriental features and turban of the fallen enemy.[215]

In September, 1674, Sir Robert Vyner was elected Lord Mayor of London. There was a tense moment following his election, for a commission of bankruptcy was in the courts against him and the officials were loath to permit his escape into the year of immunity from arrest conferred by his new office. He was accordingly taken into custody at once by a Westminster bailiff, but Charles II intervened to order him freed, and he became Lord Mayor without further hindrance.[216]

Money with Vyner might be scarce, but the Goldsmiths' Company was determined to do their member full honor by providing a spectacular Lord Mayor's show. One of the floats included plate to the value of £1500, and the Artillery Company of which Vyner was

[214] "The Statue in Stocks-Market," *Poems* (Margoliouth ed., Oxford, 1927), p. 179. This was written in 1674 or 1675 when the statue was evidently repaired.

[215] *Vyner Family History*, p. 70.

[216] *Calendar of Wynn Papers*, p. 411.

a member, marched 350 strong and was very brave in buff with helmets of "massy Silver," all adorned with green scarfs or ribbons.[217] At this distance, "The Goldsmiths Jubile" appears only a stupid variation on the pageant which the reigning versifier, Thomas Jordan, annually composed, but no doubt the words were music in the ears of Sir Robert as he heard himself described as

"One meanly Descended, and weakly attended,
By Fortune befriended, in this City plac'd;
From pence unto crowns, & frō crowns unto pounds,
Up to hundreds, and thousands has risen at last.
In chain of Gold and treasure untold,
In Skarlet, on Horse-back, to boot;
(To th'Joy of his Mother) when his elder Brother
It may be, has gone a foot." [218]

No account of Vyner can ignore the oft-told tale of such a great feast at the Guildhall as always succeeds the Lord Mayor's Show. King and courtiers and City dignitaries were dining together, and when the pitch of joviality was rising rapidly, King Charles, who did not number drunkenness among his vices, slipped out early, and he hoped unobserved. But Sir Robert Vyner followed him in hot pursuit. "Sire," he cried with an oath, "you shall stay and take t'other bottle"; and Charles, quoting a line from an old song,

"He that is drunk is great as a King,"

graciously complied.[219]

The end of Vyner's immunity as Lord Mayor brought

[217] Thomas Jordan, *Goldsmiths Jubile*, p. 2; Anthony Highmore, *History of the Honourable Artillery Company* (London, 1804), p. 97.

[218] *Ibid.*, p. 11.

[219] *Spectator*, No. 462. Sir Richard Steele was an eye-witness of the incident.

further suit against him, this time in King's Bench, but he was able to evade it on the plea that it was "in contempt of his privilege as one of His Majesty's sworn servants in ordinary with salary, having been for fourteen years his Majesty's goldsmith by patent."[220]

The question of the debt to the bankers originating with the Exchequer Stop dragged on, unsettled. In the spring of 1674, Danby had agreed to begin the payment of interest the following year and he had, accordingly, assigned £140,000 from the Excise to serve proportionately as far as it would go, as 6 per cent interest for two years on the principal debt. This was, he freely acknowledged, but a palliative, and as soon as a complete account of their debts could be certified by Exchequer auditors, he promised a permanent arrangement. Over these details, bankers and departmental officials wrangled for many months,[221] until the final settlement was reached in May, 1677. An annuity of 6 per cent was to be paid out of the hereditary Excise on the principal, plus 6 per cent interest compounded annually since the date of the Stop. Vyner's share was £25,003/9/4 on a principal of £416,724/13/1½,[222] but he was also accorded a privy seal for special additional sums — 2 per cent per annum for the £250,000 he had advanced on the Hearth Money in 1665, 2 per cent on money he had lent the Navy Treasurer after May, 1665, during the Plague and the Dutch War, and 10 per cent on £27,842/12/8½ unpaid at the Exchequer Stop but based on securities which were not repudiated by it.[223] These so-called "bankers' annuities" were awarded with the explicit understanding that the sum was to be distributed proportionately to all the bankers' creditors, but

[220] *Hist. MSS. Comm. Reports*, IX, Pt. II, *House of Lords MSS.*, p. 68.
[221] *Cal. Treas. Books*, 1676–79, I, 36.
[222] E 403/2510, f. 129.
[223] *Cal. Treas. Books*, 1676–79, 432, 594.

since Vyner still owed the Crown for taxes deposited in his hands by tax-receivers, he was obliged to reserve £100,000 of his annuity until he had met these obligations.[224]

Sir Robert's relations with Lord Treasurer Danby, originally amicable enough, suffered a decided change during their controversy over the person and fortune of Lady Vyner's daughter, Bridget Hyde — indeed "a detestable and most ignominious story." [225] The unfortunate child possessed not only her mother's remarkable beauty [226] but an income of £4000 a year,[227] and among the suitors who clustered around her, was Peregrine, Lord Dunblane, son of Lord Treasurer Danby. It was a suit that Lady Vyner favored, and although she declared her twelve-year-old daughter too young for marriage, a preliminary contract was drawn up.[228] During Lady Vyner's last illness, however, Bridget lived with her uncle, William Emerton, who seems to have inveigled the girl into a secret marriage with his son, John, only a year older. Whether or not Sir Robert had actually connived, with the hope of keeping some part of Bridget's fortune in his own hands, as soon as the Emertons brought forward their claims after Lady Vyner's death in January, 1675, he hastened to contract with them for a share in Bridget's estate should they be able to prove their case.[229]

But the Lord Treasurer did not intend that his son should lose his wealthy betrothed without a struggle. For eight years, therefore, the case dragged on in the ecclesiastical Court of Delegates while Vyner increased

[224] *Cal. Treas. Books*, 1679–80, p. 625.

[225] Marvell, *Letters*, p. 146.

[226] Judging by her portrait in the Vyner family group reproduced in London Survey Committee, *Swakeleys*, plate 2.

[227] Smyth, *Obituary*, p. 104.

[228] Marvell, *Letters*, p. 146.

[229] *Add. MS.* 28072, f. 64–69.

his stake in the Emertons' claims and in the same breath added to the advantageous terms of the betrothal agreement with Danby and his son.[230] Bridget, in the meantime, was kept close prisoner by her uncle, but her life was enlivened, occasionally by the attempts which the Emertons made to kidnap her,[231] and frequently by Lord Dunblane who conducted a more effective wooing by bribing Bridget's maid to unlock the door.[232] At length, when time and largess had brought the Court of Delegates to annul the Emerton marriage, Bridget had been secretly wedded to Lord Dunblane a year since[233] and had borne him a son; John Emerton had reached his majority and sold out his claims to Danby; and Sir Robert Vyner, who had finally staked his whole lot on the Emertons' success, had lost out entirely.

But by then the providence which had variously intervened to protect Sir Robert Vyner from his creditors in the eleven years since the Exchequer Stop had deserted him completely. The details of his downfall are missing. As early as the end of March, 1678, he had moved to Coleman Street which runs between Lothbury and London Wall, having leased his great house on Lombard Street to the government for the General Post Office,[234] although he evidently continued to maintain an office at the old Vine.[235]

He had done what he could to bring his affairs into order by collecting his large outstanding debts. The Duke

[230] *Add. MS.* 28050, f. 13.

[231] *Add. MS.* 28072, f. 1; *Cal. St. Papers*, 1676–77, p. 546; *Add. MS.* 28094, f. 138.

[232] *Add. MS.* 28050, f. 15.

[233] *Ibid.*, f. 42.

[234] *London Gazette*, No. 1287, 21 Mar., 1687. The Post Office had been on Bishopsgate Street.

[235] In December, 1683, his creditors were summoned to the Vine on Lombard Street. *For the Creditors of Sir Robert Vyner, that have not yet Sign'd his Proposals.*

of Ormonde, for example, was much occupied in 1680 in paying off the £13,000 he owed to Vyner;[236] and in 1683 the Earl of Anglesey assigned to him over £2000 worth of rents in Ireland.[237] But Vyner had lost £60,000 since the Exchequer Stop,[238] and his accounts at the Exchequer were in confusion. The Treasury Commissioners in 1679–1680 were endeavoring to bring him to account for the Hearth Farm which had ended in 1672 and in which he had had a very large share; and in November, 1681, they had resorted to threats in order to clear accounts which had been carried in the Exchequer in the name of his partner, Richard Stratford;[239] but it is not clear whether his bankruptcy was actually precipitated by Treasury officials or by private creditors.

London Gazettes late in March, 1683, carried notices of a meeting of his creditors at the Cock Tavern, Lombard Street, "to consider the best way for the satisfaction of their debts."[240] His offer was one-fifth of his debt in cash and four-fifths in the form of assignments on his Excise annuity; but only part of the creditors accepted the proposal,[241] and the wisdom of those who refused appeared subsequently, when it was evident that the last payment by the Treasury on the bankers' annuities had been made in that month.[242] Another circular to his creditors, dated 12 December, 1683, urged their acceptance of the same terms, lamenting that the negotiations had already dragged on two years;[243] but his exhortations

236 *Hist. MSS. Comm. Reports, Ormonde,* N. S. IV, 320.

237 *Cal. St. Papers,* July-Sept. 1683, p. 387.

238 *For the Creditors of Sir Robert Vyner* — 22 Mar., 1684.

239 *Cal. Treas. Books,* 1681–85, I, 298.

240 *Vyner Family History,* p. 71.

241 Article on Sir Robert Vyner — *D. N. B.*

242 Henry D. Macleod, *The Theory and Practice of Banking* (London, 1923), I, 442.

243 *For the Creditors of Sir Robert Vyner, that have not yet Sign'd his Proposals.*

were in vain. The next month he was outlawed for debt at the suit of William Edwards,[244] and declared bankrupt, but although his country house, Swakeleys, and another house and lands at Ickenham and Hillingdon, were forfeited to the King, they were not actually seized until April, 1687. Ten months later they had come into the hands of John Russell, physician,[245] who for twenty-seven years had been bringing periodic suit against Vyner.[246]

In June, 1688,[247] Sir Robert's "hopefull son," Charles, barrister of the Inner Temple, died at the age of twenty-two,[248] and Sir Robert "fell into a deepe and reasonable greife for his loss . . . and . . . finding his calamities compleat," himself died at Windsor Castle the second of September,[249] thereby avoiding, had he but known it, all the stress and strain inevitable to the advent of a new king and the exile of the old with which less fortunate men than he were confronted a few months later at the coming of William and Mary. And with Sir Robert's death the Vine came to an end. His executor[250] struggled manfully to settle the estate — to that his tombstone bears witness: "in which Imployment meeting with great difficulties . . . he so much Impaired his health that for the Recovery thereof he travelled into Italy and died at Rome," in 1707;[251] but whether or not Sir Robert's creditors were ever satisfied, Vyner himself was long past caring, and history is silent on the subject.

[244] *Cal. Treas. Books*, 1685–89, III, 1748.
[245] *Ibid.*, 1685–89, III, 1748; IV, 2031, 2045.
[246] *Ibid.*, 1660–67, p. 146; *Hist. MSS. Comm. Reports*, VIII, *House of Lords MSS.*, p. 125.
[247] Brooke and Hallen, *op. cit.*, p. 255.
[248] London Survey Committee, *Swakeleys*, p. 14.
[249] *Hist. MSS. Comm. Reports*, *Laing*, I, 458; Brooke and Hallen, *op. cit.*, p. 255.
[250] His nephew, Thomas Vyner.
[251] London Survey Committee, *Swakeleys*, p. 15.

DOROTHY K. CLARK.

THE RECONCILERS AND THE RESTORATION (1660-1662)

DURING the winter of 1659–1660, as the restoration of Charles II to the English throne began to seem ever more probable, a group of London clergymen played a significant rôle. They displayed an activity in the negotiations which preceded the Restoration quite out of proportion to their number; while one minister, in particular, assumed a prominence the more surprising in that he had hitherto been a country minister. This clergyman, Richard Baxter, chronicling their activities called them "Reconcilers, of no Sect or Party, but abhorring the very name of Parties."[1] The term undoubtedly applies to a few of the group, if not to all of them, although a more accurate one would have been the old name Puritan. For they were the spiritual descendants of the men who had conferred with James I at Hampton Court; and they themselves had been active supporters of the Long Parliament.

Yet if they had championed the parliamentary cause in its early days, during the past ten years they had atoned for their error, if it were one. Almost to a man they had protested against the trial and execution of Charles I.[2] Some of them had been involved in the plots

[1] Richard Baxter, *Reliquiae Baxteriana* (hereafter referred to as *Rel. Bax.*) (London, 1696), Part II, 387. In his *Second True Defence . . . against Stillingfleet* (London, 1681) he spoke of them in the Preface as combining the beliefs of Erastians, Episcopalians, and Presbyterians as well as being so far inclined to Independency as to "wish to keep the discipline in the parish."

[2] Cornelius Burges and others, *Vindication of the Ministers of the Gospel in, and about London . . .* (London, 1648), declared that the proposed trial of Charles I was not only against "the Fundamentall Constitution and Government of this Kingdome," but against the "Word of God," p. 5; John Price, *Clerico-Classicum . . .* (London, 1649), p. 55, said that the Presbyterian min-

of the 1650's to bring about the restoration of his son. Jealous of Independency, hostile to the political ideas of the Commonwealth, they favored the restoration of the Stuart line, while at the same time they hoped for the triumph of Calvinism, if not Presbyterianism, in the restored church.

The temper of the group is seen in the fact that of the old "Smectymnuus" group of pamphleteers, who had sounded the Calvinist note of the Long Parliament, with its hostility to the prelacy, three were "Reconcilers": Edmund Calamy, his brother-in-law Matthew Newcomen, and William Spurstowe. Other members included the aged and gouty Simeon Ashe, who as friend of such early Puritans as Arthur Hildersham may be regarded as the link between Jacobean Puritanism and the Restoration dissent; Thomas Manton, the plump, jovial preacher at St. Paul's, Covent Garden; Anthony Tuckney, Thomas Case, and Thomas Jacombe.

The outstanding members were Edward Reynolds and Richard Baxter. Reynolds represented the right wing of the group. He was one of the first to support General Monck when he appeared in London and if he was, as Anthony à Wood called him, "the pride and glory of the Presbyterian party," his early rallying to Monck's side must have influenced the weaker and more impressionable members of his party. He was described by a contemporary as a man "of singular affability, meekness and humility, of great learning, and a constant preacher." [3] Although, like Calamy and the others, he had belonged to the Westminster Assembly, he had always advocated moderation. He had not been a chaplain in the parlia-

isters, now that episcopacy had been abolished, wished the restoration of the king.

[3] Anthony à Wood, *Athenae Oxonienses* (4 vols., London, 1813), III, 1085.

mentary army like Spurstowe; he had not become involved in plots, as Calamy and Case had; nor had he openly preached the funeral sermon for an avowed enemy of the Commonwealth, as Manton had for Christopher Love. He was a preacher rather than a man of action. By his refusal to take the Engagement, however, he had shown that he had courage.

His writings had always breathed a conciliatory spirit. As early as 1639 he had urged churchmen to maintain a spirit of unity and love,[4] and throughout the stormy years of the rebellion and Commonwealth he had continued to counsel moderation. Preaching before Parliament in 1657 and again in 1658 he had urged churchmen of all sects to forget their differences. There were three fundamentals upon which true Christians could agree, he declared: "Fundamentals in Faith, that (common) knowledge of God and Christ . . . Fundamentals in Practice, . . . and Fundamentals in Worship, to worship God in Spirit and in Truth."[5]

As early as August 1659 it had been recognized by the royalists that these clergymen would be "the best instruments" for the King's restoration.[6] And so it came about that when early in 1660 the titular Lord Chancellor — Sir Edward Hyde as he was then — felt the time was ripe for renewed activity, he turned to these clergymen. It was not only the restoration of the King which was at stake — it was the restoration of the Anglican Church, too. For during the past two decades the Church of England, with her distinctive ritual and government and sacraments, had existed only clandestinely. The use of the Prayer Book had been forbidden, bishops driven from

[4] Edward Reynolds, "Meditations on the Holy Sacrament . . .," *Works* (6 vols., London, 1826), III, 31–32.

[5] Reynolds, *Works* (London, 1679), pp. 931–943.

[6] *Clarendon State Papers* (3 vols., Oxford, 1767–1786), III, 546.

their sees, and the cathedral chapters dissolved. Of the pre-Restoration establishment only the fabric of the church buildings and the church wardens had preserved the historic continuity of parish life.

During Cromwell's rule Baptists had shared with Independents and Presbyterians the pulpits of the church, while a host of schismatics — Boehmenists, Seekers, Ranters, Quakers, — drew the extremely pious or the emotionally unbalanced from the places where their ancestors had worshipped. There had grown up a generation which knew not the Prayer Book, which had been ministered to by men who had in many cases not been ordained by bishops; a generation which if not hostile to Anglicanism at least was indifferent from sheer ignorance. Little wonder, then, that the Lord Chancellor as he viewed the situation should fear the ruin of the church and that he should endeavor to win moderate Presbyterian clergymen to his cause.[7]

Reynolds and his fellow ministers, it was therefore felt, might be vital factors in the rebuilding of the church. Educated at Cambridge or Oxford, duly ordained, they must possess a certain innate loyalty to the Anglican Church. That they were not entirely without a conciliatory spirit had been shown by their response to Cromwell's scheme for a national church, and one of the group, Matthew Newcomen, is said to have been the author of a plea for unity, *Irenicum*.[8]

These Presbyterian divines had more to hope for from a national church established on a broad basis than from toleration. A general indulgence would mean that they would be only one of many sects. The advantage that

[7] Letter of Clarendon to Dr. Barwick, in Peter Barwick, *Life of . . . John Barwick* (London, 1724), p. 465.

[8] *Rel. Bax.*, Part I, 193–197 *et passim*; Henry Rogers, *Life and Character of John Howe* (London, 1836), pp. 79–81, 83–93.

they had retained throughout the Commonwealth from the fact that in the 1640's they had either kept their livings or succeeded to sequestered benefices, would be lost. If the church were made sufficiently broad so that with free consciences they could return to it, from the point of view both of worldly gain and of increased power to do good their position would be better even than it had been under Cromwell. Before the rebellion they had conformed. There was behind them a tradition of churchmanship. Upon this they themselves placed too much reliance; but the Lord Chancellor and his advisors, as they made plans for the future, erred even more, as they trusted that this tradition would insure the moderate Presbyterians' adherence to the church.

In this hopeful spirit Clarendon sent George Morley over to England to negotiate with them. Morley was a wise choice. As a Calvinist and as a member of the old anti-Laudian party he would be personally acceptable to those who had hated Arminianism. Had he not, indeed, voiced sentiments acceptable to the House of Commons when he preached before it in 1640?

The problems confronting him in his new task were set forth in a letter to him written by Clarendon in January 1660:

"He that hath either his Eyes or Ears open, must needs know the Confusion to be great, and the State of it [the Church] most lamentable; and that not only in Regard of the wild Schismaticks, but even of those who would be own'd, and may pass for the better part. . . . Amongst those that either are, or would be thought loyal Subjects to the King, and obedient Sons of the Church, there is great Diversity of Opinion and Practice about Prayer, and the publick Worship of God. . . . The Persons thus divided in Judgment are Men of Worth; there being on all Sides some most to be valued, both for their Piety and Learning; and therefore not hastily to be condemn'd. . . ."[9]

To win these "Men of Worth" Clarendon instructed Morley to walk warily. Men who loved faction for its own sake were not to be sought after. But to those who seemed amenable preferment should be offered, the mastership of the Savoy, for instance, or such an influential pulpit as that in an Inn of Court.[10]

Morley first sought out Edmund Calamy and Edward Reynolds. Calamy, rector of the influential St. Mary's Aldermanbury Church, and his colleague, vicar of St. Lawrence Jewry, seemed responsive enough. He was able to write quite definitely to Clarendon that a limited episcopacy would be acceptable to both.

As the winter wore on, his task became the more difficult because of several unforeseen factors. The King's agent, Lord Mordaunt, Morley wrote to Clarendon, had complicated the situation by leading the Presbyterians to believe that they should have "all granted to them that was granted to those in Scotland."[11] They therefore were becoming "high in their demands and exalted in their hopes." Then, too, the fact that General Monck on arriving in London had openly declared himself in favor of a "moderate Presbyterian government"[12] had encouraged them to feel that there might be no need for compromise. Furthermore, a party in the Presbyterian sect refused to consider any departure from the Scottish form of government; its influence was to become stronger as time passed.

9 Barwick, *op. cit.*, pp. 539–540.

10 *Ibid.*, p. 525.

11 *Clar. State Papers*, III, 722.

12 John Price, *The Mystery and Method of his Majestys Happy Restoration* (London, 1680), pp. 117–118; Monck, according to Price, thought the "Temper of the Nation" was against the bishops.

Morley, too, felt himself handicapped because he had no authority to make definite proposals. He could only promise that a synod, or convocation, and Parliament would act. Upon the question of the bishops' power he found himself confronted on all sides with the fear that the Restoration would bring back the old tyranny of Laud and of the High Commission. "If the bishop transgresses," he would say, "he is answerable for it to a free Synod." But many of his questioners still doubted, although he found a useful ally in the Earl of Manchester, "one of the chief Pillars of the Presbyterians," who promised to use his influence to make the ministers accept episcopacy.[13]

While Morley was struggling with these problems Richard Baxter arrived in London from his rural parish in Worcestershire. Baxter was well known as a champion of church unity. He had impressed Cromwell with his zeal for union, while his efforts in Worcestershire had led to the formation of an association which included Baptists, Independents, Presbyterians and even a few Anglicans. On his arrival in London he threw himself heart and soul into the discussions.

The influence which Baxter exerted was tremendous. Yet to an outsider its source must have seemed difficult to find. For he was from an obscure parish; he was not even a University graduate; he had received only deacon's orders. He had not been a prominent royalist; indeed he had not at any time before this veered from a policy of neutrality in the conflict. He had no powerful friends among the laity, as Calamy and Manton had.

His strength lay in his aggressive personality. During the 1650's he had kept in touch with affairs in London,

[13] *Clar. State Papers*, III, 727–728.

both by correspondence and by frequent visits.[14] He was consulted by clergymen of all sects. As a young man in 1640 he had led the revolt in Worcestershire against the newly enacted canons — a significant act for a young man not yet in priest's orders — and he had grown steadily in influence. At this particular time, however, his strength lay in the fact that he alone of his party had a definite plan, his Worcestershire Association. That organization had evidently been a success and had been imitated in other shires. That the Worcestershire Association could not be the model for a national church was not appreciated: for its system of admitting to communion only those who in the Calvinist sense felt themselves elect and were so regarded by the clergyman, instead of admitting all who were baptized, as the Anglican church did, must inevitably lead to the creation of a church within a church. This aspect, however, of Baxter's scheme for unity was at the time overlooked. What mattered was that he, and he alone of his party, had a definite program.

At first, nevertheless, Morley and the others did not recognize in this enthusiastic new recruit an obstacle to their hopes. His presence in London seemed indeed an asset.

Another advantage, this a more real one, proved to be the temper of many Anglican clergymen. As early as February, for instance, John Gauden had advocated a policy of gentleness and healing in the settlement of the church. In his sermons before Parliament[15] and in conferences with the Puritans he strove for unity. The pronouncements of the Presbyterian clergy at this time too seemed

[14] Baxter's correspondence in the Dr. Williams Library, London, shows that he was constantly in touch with both Independents and Presbyterians in London and in the country, and was consulted about matters of policy, such as the conduct of pamphlet controversies.

[15] John Gauden, *Gods Great Demonstrations* . . . (London, 1660).

to promise well. Edward Reynolds, for instance, in two sermons before Parliament late in April urged that it bring "healing Resolutions" for the reconciliation of all Christians. "The Breaches are not so wide," he pointed out, "but that if Animosities and Prejudices are removed, they might by fraternal Debates be closed up again." [16] Baxter too, as he later pointed out, "preach'd for peace to the Parliament and City in publick Sermons." [17]

Indeed, Baxter, overlooking the previous efforts of Morley to unite Presbyterians and Anglicans, gives to one of his own sermons sole credit for causing negotiations between the two groups. The sermon was preached on the day of thanksgiving for the restoration of Charles II. It came directly to the point: "As for the Concord now wish'd in Matters of church government, I told them it was easy for Moderate Men to come to a fair agreement, and that the late Reverend Primate of Ireland and myself had agreed in half an Hour." "The moderate Episcopal Divines," he informs us, were greatly stirred by this bold statement. Dr. Gauden and several others sought him out and "all professed their great Desires and Hopes of Concord upon such terms."

A conference was then arranged by Dr. Gauden between members of each party at Dr. John Barnard's lodgings in Gray's Inn. Barnard, as chaplain to the late Archbishop Ussher, had published the archbishop's book on "primitive" or modified episcopacy and might be expected therefore to do his best to win over the Presbyterians. But only the host, Dr. Gauden, Manton, and Baxter appeared at the conference. Nevertheless, they discussed points of difference, the chief of which was the Book of Common Prayer. It was at this meeting that Baxter delivered his

[16] Reynolds, *Works* (London, 1679), pp. 987–1008.
[17] Baxter, *Penitent Confession* (London, 1691), p. 34.

famous pronouncement on the Prayer Book: "That I found little or nothing in the doctrinal Part of the Prayer Book which was not sound, having but as favourable an exposition as good men's writings usually must have." Cautious as this statement was, Baxter was to find it a boomerang in later negotiations, when Gauden, angry that Baxter had attacked the Prayer Book, published the statement leaving out the words "doctrinal part." The episode, seemingly unimportant, is of significance as showing the real difficulties to be encountered in a scheme for a comprehensive church. Baxter acidly dismissed it as proving that "Men were every day talking of Concord, but to little Purpose." [18]

Hitherto Morley had not conferred with Baxter; but now hearing from Manton of Morley's conciliatory attitude, Baxter asked for an interview to find "whether really Concord was intended." Opening on this note of suspicion, the meeting of the two men came to nothing. Morley of course could not be explicit, a fact which Baxter resented, and while the Anglican spoke vaguely of "Moderation in general," he seemed to disregard Baxter's own opinions. The question of formal prayer, as opposed to extemporary praying, came up and here the two men definitely disagreed. A mutual antagonism probably arose from this meeting, for they were never on friendly terms after that.[19]

That Baxter did not accompany Calamy and Reynolds and other "Reconcilers" when they crossed the Channel in May to interview Charles II may be ascribed to the unfavorable impression he made upon Morley. The inclusion of these clergymen in the party, along with com-

[18] Baxter, *A Defence of the Principles of Love . . .* (London, 1671), pp. 28–29.

[19] *Rel. Bax.*, Part II, 218.

missioners from Parliament and representatives of London, seems to indicate that Clarendon had been successful in his efforts to win them to his side. In audience with their King the clergy assured him of their loyalty and of the efforts they had made to restore him to his throne. He in turn replied with his usual graciousness. Parliament, he assured them, must settle religious matters. And, as they remembered the temper of the Convention Parliament, they must have been quite willing to have it so.

Upon their pressing him to discontinue the use of the Book of Common Prayer and to have his chaplain cease wearing the surplice, he rather lost his equanimity. "He would not be restrain'd Himself," he declared, "when he gave others so much Liberty."[20] In spite of this slight disagreement, which however is extremely significant as showing the real temper of the Reconcilers, they returned with an excellent impression of their monarch. As for Charles II, he informed the commissioners that he would "make it his care that both Episcopall Divines and Presbyterians should mutually agree."[21]

All was now ready for the Restoration. The Presbyterian clergy, if they had not received definite promises, could at least look forward to a conciliatory policy on the part of King and chancellor, and must trust Parliament. The Declaration of Breda, although its vague wording hinted at toleration, not comprehension, promised that Parliament, not the bishops, would direct the religious settlement.

As Charles II rode triumphantly through London the city ministers awaited him in St. Paul's Churchyard,

[20] Clarendon, *A History of the Rebellion . . . in England* . . . (3 vols. in 6, Oxford, 1727), III, 770.

[21] *The Flemings in Oxford* (2 vols., Oxford Historical Society, 1904), I, 133.

where Arthur Jackson, on behalf of the other clergy, presented the monarch with a "rich adorned" Bible. Charles received it graciously, assuring his hearers that it "should be the rule of his actions," and declared that their past services to the monarchy — "their Prayers and Endeavours" — which had made possible his return from exile had not been forgotten.[22]

The high favor in which these moderate Presbyterians stood was shown by the appointment of ten of them as chaplains to His Majesty. Of these, as the nonconformists pointed out later, only five ever preached before the King — Baxter, Calamy, Spurstowe, Benjamin Woodbridge, and Reynolds; yet the significance of their accepting the appointment cannot be overlooked, implying as it did their tacit acceptance of the Book of Common Prayer, which was of course regularly used in the King's Chapel. Baxter, it is true, aroused some consternation when he refused to wear a stole on the occasion of his preaching; but he later explained his refusal on the ground that he thought it should be worn only by holders of the Doctor of Divinity degree, which he had not received. The story, however, was circulated as proof of the ungraciousness of the Puritans, and the words "I'll none of your Toyes" ascribed to Baxter.

The attitude of Anglican clergy is illustrated by a tract published in May by Thomas Pierce. Speaking of the past disorders created by the church's enemies, he said: "I think our noblest way will be, to confute their fears with our moderation, and so to pull them unto us by cords of love." He even went so far as to express the hope that "perfect Liberty of Conscience, as well as of Person" would be granted; yet he wished "Unanimity and Uni-

[22] *Rel. Bax.*, Part II, 218; S. Palmer, *Calamy's Nonconformist's Memorial* (2 vols., London, 1775), I, 20.

formity in Religion." "Our breaches as well of judgment as of charity," he trusted, would be made up in order that "we may all be held together by the bond of unity in the truth." [23] With "Moderate Presbyterians" he had "ever had Communion and very affectionate Commerce." The fact, however, that he then proceeded to attack the views held by extreme Calvinists on sin, shows how difficult it was after all to lay aside differences and secure the much wished for unanimity.

Throughout June the conferences between the moderate Presbyterians and Anglicans continued. The fact that several eminent Presbyterians either had not been invited to confer, or had not wished to, made more difficult the task of Calamy and Reynolds. Under the leadership of William Jenkin and Lazarus Seamen, the first of whom had been involved in the plots of the 1650's for the King's restoration and the second of whom was renowned as a scholar, they stood aloof. Only if Scottish Presbyterianism were introduced would they conform.[24]

Clarendon, however, continued his efforts to win the Presbyterians to conformity. In his policy "by degrees [to] recover what cannot be had at once," [25] he had the coöperation of the new Lord Chamberlain, the Earl of Manchester. This staunch friend of Calamy's could be relied upon to use his influence for harmony and to give helpful advice to the clergymen, who were unused to the subtleties of court life.

As the first step in building a broad national church a

[23] Thomas Pierce, *An Impartial Inquiry into the Nature of Sin* (London, 1660), dedication, p. 4.

[24] *Rel. Bax.*, Part II, 229; White Kennet, *Register and Chronicle . . .* (London, 1728), p. 172. Baxter declared that the Jenkin group remained aloof "not as being unwilling, but because the Court did give them no Encouragement."

[25] *Clar. State Papers*, III, 732.

liberal policy was followed in the bestowal of livings and preferment. Except in cases where the former incumbent appeared, Presbyterians and Independents and, it is evident from Calamy's *Nonconformist's Memorial*, even Baptists, were confirmed in their livings. The large exodus two years later after the passage of the Act of Uniformity shows how many clergymen of nonconformist tendencies were permitted to retain their pulpits in these early years of conference and compromise. Anthony Tuckney, for instance, who had been Master of St. John's College, Cambridge, and Regius professor during the interregnum, but who was now superseded in these posts by the former incumbents, was given another living and a pension of one hundred pounds a year, a compromise which the Earl of Manchester urged him to accept. Clarendon himself intervened at times to aid those in danger of being dispossessed. The case of the Puritan John James of Ilsley, Berks, is of particular interest in this respect. A neighboring clergyman having taken steps to incorporate this parish with his own, James came in haste to London to ask Manton's aid. The good divine obligingly went out into the rainy night to seek Clarendon. By an extraordinary coincidence the official was at that very moment about to stamp the document which would rob James of his living, and Clarendon was able to intervene and to assure Manton that his friend would not be disturbed.[26]

More significant, however, as a step in compromise was the offer of preferment to leading Presbyterians. Baxter was offered the bishopric of Hereford, Calamy that of Lichfield and Coventry, and Reynolds that of Norwich. Bate and Manton were not overlooked, the former being offered the deanery of Lichfield and Coventry, and the

[26] Palmer, *op. cit.*, I, 206–207.

latter that of Rochester.[27] Although only Reynolds finally accepted preferment, — and the envious said that he did this only because of the ambition of his wife (whereas Calamy refused because of the piety of his wife)[28]— the fact cannot be overlooked that long and serious consideration was given to the offers.

Meanwhile, as has been said, conferences between Presbyterians and Anglicans continued. To prepare a statement of their position Baxter, Calamy, and the others, with the assistance of country clergymen, worked in Sion College. Liberal Anglicans, such as Gauden and Morley, were appointed by Clarendon to confer with them. Sometimes they met in Clarendon's lodgings in Worcester House, but the informality of their meetings is seen in the fact that at least once they gathered in a bookseller's shop.[29]

The fruit of these conferences was a declaration of indulgence issued by Charles II on October 25. It was more than a promise of toleration. Clarendon had earlier explained its purpose to Parliament as an attempt to bring "the Church, as well as the State . . . to return to that Unity and Unanimity, which will make both King and people as happy, as they can hope to be in this world." [30] In reality it was a summary of the papers which the Reconcilers had handed in to the King; furthermore it was a tacit acceptance of the spirit of compromise by the liberal Anglican clergymen. Morley regarded it as a document

[27] *Rel. Bax.*, Part II, 281 ff.; Wood, *op. cit.*, III, 1134–36, 1083–85; George Vernon in *A Letter to a Friend* . . . (London, 1670), p. 39, declared that the "fat Doctor" refused a "fat Deanery."

[28] Wood, *op. cit.* It seems quite possible that it was really the pressure of Calamy's brother-in-law, Newcomen, which led to the refusal.

[29] *Rel. Bax.*, Part II, 231–259; Clarendon, *Continuation* . . . (3 vols., Oxford, 1759), II, 140 ff.; George Morley, *The Bishop of Winchester's Vindication* . . . (London, 1683).

[30] *C. J.*, VIII, 174.

which would end faction and make "all honest and peaceably minded men . . . unanimously to joyne against the common enemy the Papists."[31]

The declaration promised modification of the church government. The power of the bishops was to be checked; as Clarendon explained it in a conference, in weighty matters they "should have the assistance of the Presbyters."[32] Those ceremonies so repugnant to Puritans — the use of the sign of the cross in baptism, bowing at the name of Jesus, wearing of the surplice — should not be forced upon the people, while the use of the Book of Common Prayer was to be left to the discretion of the clergy until it was "reviewed and effectually reformed." The power of the minister over communicants was increased: a change which shows that the principles of Baxter's Worcestershire Association had had some influence. These concessions had been worked over by a committee, as has been said, of both parties; but both Baxter and Bates were disposed to regard the conciliatory tone of the final version as Clarendon's work.[33]

The Convention Parliament, foreshadowing the uncompromising tone of the Parliament which was to follow, rejected the declaration by twenty-six votes. But even if it had not done so, it is doubtful whether many Presbyterians would have conformed. For their leaders, it was found, were found in the group of irreconcilables, not among those whom Clarendon had been courting. It became clear that Calamy and Baxter and the other Reconcilers had been speaking as individuals, without the authority of

[31] T. H. Lister, *Life and Administration of Edward, Earl of Clarendon* (3 vols., London, 1837), III, 110.

[32] William Bates, *Works* (London, 1700), p. 815.

[33] *Rel. Bax.*, Part II, 281–282; Bates, "Funeral Sermon for Richard Baxter," *Works*, pp. 815–816; Kennet, *op. cit.*, p. 283; Gilbert Burnet, *History of My Own Time* (2 vols., Oxford, 1907), I, Part I, 315–317.

their party. And, when with the exception of Reynolds all these clergy refused preferment, it began to appear that the efforts toward conciliation had been in vain. Furthermore, the Presbyterian ministers began to petition for further favors; they also sent letters to country ministers, urging them to "persist in the Use of the Directory," the form of service adopted during the rebellion. It was hoped, the letters stated, that the King might be won to even greater concessions than he had promised in the Declaration.[34]

The winter of 1660–1661, and indeed all the period leading up to the time when the Act of Uniformity went into effect, saw constant struggle within the church. Certain Presbyterian clergymen, although the Declaration had not been enacted into a law, regarded it as in effect. They therefore avoided using the Book of Common Prayer. The bishop of London found his task particularly difficult. In the previous June he had pleaded for a generous spirit which would forgive past injuries and inspire men to conciliation,[35] but now he found division among his people and a defiant spirit in many of the ministers. In some parishes the clergyman wished to use the Anglican liturgy, while his parishioners objected; in others it was the clergyman who did not wish to conform, while in still others the people were divided. Thomas Jacombe, who had been regarded as one of the Reconcilers, refused to use the Book of Common Prayer, although some of his parishioners wished to have it read; Bates attempted to get around the difficulty by having the Psalms and two lessons read, and the Ten Commandments and creed repeated.[36] Baxter,

[34] Clarendon, *op. cit.*, II, 141–143.

[35] *Certain Considerations tending to Promote Peace* (London, 1674), p. 1; Vernon Staley, *The Life and Times of Gilbert Sheldon* (London, 1884), pp. 261–263.

[36] *Cal. S. P. Dom. Car. II, 1660–1661*, pp. 539–540.

forced to give up the Kidderminster living to its former incumbent, was preaching in London churches. Manton, although he had refused preferment, was permitting the Common Prayer to be read in his Covent Garden church.[37] The policy of the bishops seems to have been a moderate one; Morley, now bishop of Worcester, for instance, advised his dean not to insist on his clergy wearing the surplice.[38]

As if the situation were not already sufficiently complicated, the question of ordination had to be considered. Unlike the others, Baxter and Manton had not received priest's orders and they found themselves confronted with the problem of whether they, having already been ordained according to Presbyterian usage, should now submit to the episcopal laying on of hands. Other clergy, ordained by presbyters during the interregnum, were in this dilemma. The question struck at the very root of the church. For, reasoned Anglicans, if the ordaining power of the bishop were done away with, he became little more than an administrative official; his sacrosanct character was disregarded. Such pamphlets as that by Giles Firmin, *Of Schism and Ordination by Imposition of Hands*, might regard episcopal ordination as having "some accidental corruptions adhering to it," but being "for the most part true," yet the majority of the Presbyterian clergy withstood the demands of the bishops that they submit to re-ordination. It is noteworthy that both Morley and John Cosin, when they became bishops of Worcester and Durham respectively, showed themselves very conciliatory in this respect. Cosin urged the ministers to submit to the laying on of hands with the statement inserted in the ceremony: "If thou hast not been ordained, I ordain thee."

[37] *S. P. Dom., Car. II*, P. R. O., 29/32, # 109.
[38] *Cal. S. P. Dom., Addenda, 1660–1670*, p. 680.

Reynolds, when he became bishop of Norwich, succeeded in winning over several Presbyterians by permitting them to indicate that they were entering the church because of the promises made in the King's declaration. Another clergyman active among the Presbyterians under the Commonwealth, who like Reynolds accepted a bishopric, John Wilkins, also followed a conciliatory policy in his diocese of Chester and won over many ministers to the church.[39] Despite their examples, Manton and Baxter did not submit to re-ordination, a refusal which makes the more extraordinary their steadfast and loyal efforts during their lives to secure a comprehensive church.

At the present, however, they were hard at work with the other Reconcilers upon the question of revising the liturgy. The Convocations were to meet in 1661; before that event, there was to be a conference of Puritan and Anglican clergymen at which the "exceptions" to the liturgy were to be considered.

As time went on, the Puritans found themselves steadily losing ground, so that by the end of the winter of 1660–1661 they were in a much less favorable position than in the preceding October. Reynolds and Wilkins alone of their party had accepted the restored Anglican church without waiting for changes. Furthermore, the Venner uprising in January had involved the Presbyterians in ruin almost as much as the "fanatic" sects. For the cavalier who had been in exile was not likely to draw any distinction between moderate Presbyterians and Anabaptist republicans. All were tarred with the brush of treason. The aid the Presbyterians had given in the Restoration was forgotten, as the fear of renewed civil war made

[39] John Cosin, *Correspondence* (2 vols., Surtees Society, 1869–1872), II, xliv; Palmer, *op. cit.*, I, 169; A. G. Matthews, *Calamy Revised* (Oxford, 1934), p. lxi; Kennet, *op. cit.*, pp. 804–814.

men irrational and suspicious. But even if there had been no Venner insurrection, nearly a year had passed since the King returned and those who disregarded the conscientious withdrawal of many dissenters from the church and saw only the enthusiastic conformity of those who welcomed back the historic church or the compliance of others because of fear or ambition, felt that in time all scruples would die away and that these Puritans were merely factious quibblers. The clock, many felt sure, could be turned back to 1640.

The failure of Jenkin's group to coöperate weakened the position of those who wished to compromise. The absence, too, of Independents from the council table — and the presence of as astute and pious a man as John Owen would have been indeed an asset — made the Presbyterians less representative of moderate dissent and, what is more important, meant that all Independency was hostile to comprehension.[40] For, as the nonconformists were aware, the adoption of a scheme which included only one group of nonconformity within the church would weaken the position of those left outside the church. Finally, the Duke of York's party preferred a toleration which would include Roman Catholics. Thus, a public opinion which could not but influence the course of events was growing up, hostile to comprehension and eager to prevent its adoption.[41]

This trend was reflected in the elections for Parliament. The cavaliers were in the saddle. Whether the support thus assured to a non-conciliatory policy by a House of

[40] Dr. Owen's protest to Clarendon against the omission of Independents from the conferences is recorded in James Ralph, *History of England* (2 vols., London, 1744), I, 52–53.

[41] In *Rel. Bax.*, III, 100–101, Baxter has listed the reasons why in 1672 comprehension was less popular than toleration; many of them existed in 1661–1662.

Commons of such a temper influenced the bishops is a question hard to answer. It has been stated that the bishops now opposed comprehension, feeling certain that they were firmly in power. Yet time was to show them to be more moderate than the laymen in their treatment of dissenters; and certainly the House of Lords with its quota of bishops was later to show itself in favor of modifying the strict Act of Uniformity. It is true, of course, that a party in the church was hostile to any who had shared in the rebellion. Peter Heylyn's *History of the Presbyterians*, although it was not published until 1670, reflects the animosity felt towards the sect.

Thus it came about that when the twenty-four commissioners met at Savoy House in April 1661, the outlook for comprehension was less promising than it had been the previous October. The purpose of the conference, as the King's warrant explained, was "to review the Book of Common Prayer" and "to make such alterations therein as should be thought most necessary and supply some additional forms in the Scripture phrase, . . . avoiding as much as may be, all unnecessary alterations of the forms and liturgy wherewith the people are already acquainted and which they have so long received in the Church of England."[42]

The ablest men of both parties were represented. On the side of those desiring changes in the liturgy were, of course, Reynolds, whom the bishop of London appointed as leader of the group,[43] Calamy, Newcomen, and the other Reconcilers; while John Wallis and John Lightfoot, the

42 *Documents relating to the Act of Uniformity* . . . (London, 1862), pp. 107–111.

43 William Harris, *Memoirs of . . . Thomas Manton* (London, 1725), pp. 26–27; the letter which Reynolds sent to Manton, telling him of his appointment and asking him to meet with the others at Dr. Calamy's house to "advise together" is printed here.

most scholarly of the group, although they were Puritan commissioners, took a much less active part. Robert Sanderson, bishop of Lincoln, acted as moderator, while Gilbert Sheldon, in whose lodgings the conference was held, presided. On the Anglican side were, as might be expected, Bishops Morley, Gauden, Gunning, Cosin, along with others.

At the first meeting Bishop Sheldon instructed the Puritan party to bring in a written statement of the changes it wished made. The Anglicans, he explained, saw no need for revision of the Prayer Book, but they were willing to hear the Puritans' requests. This move, which threw all responsibility upon those who wished changes in the church, has been condemned as a strategy which would throw all the blame upon the Puritans if the conference failed,[44] although it may not have been intended as one. At any rate, if it was a trap, the Puritans fell into it.

It is regrettable that Baxter, whose services in the past had indeed won him the reputation of a conciliator, now let himself and his party be carried away by his zeal for "alterations." Indeed, he thrust aside Reynolds, who had been appointed leader of the group, and carried the majority of the group with him in opposition to the wishes of the "sober party". These were willing to compromise, but found themselves helpless in the face of the "more fiery Party", led by Baxter.[45] For it came about that Baxter not only overruled Reynolds about the proposals brought in, but in the debates he took a leading part.

The greatest tactical error from which Reynolds sought to save his party was in respect to the liturgy. All the Presbyterians, Baxter informs us, admitted "the Lawfull-

[44] Norman Sykes, *Church and State in the Eighteenth Century* (Cambridge, 1934), p. 10.

[45] Kennet, *op. cit.*, p. 516.

ness of a Liturgie, and desired the Reformation of that which they had." So far, so good. Baxter's enthusiasm, however, led him to devise a new liturgy, which he described complacently as "seeming entire of itself." The faults of the Prayer Book, he felt, were "chiefly disorder and Effectiveness . . . a true Worship, though imperfect." His own liturgy was taken entirely from the Bible, except for the rubrics and should thus appeal to those who frowned upon the "man-made" nature of the Prayer Book. But it lacked smoothness and craftsmanship; the hand of the joiner was everywhere apparent. Bishop Reynolds objected to it; he "disliked the displeasing the Bishops by such large additions, and a Liturgie seeming entire of it selfe, instead of some additional prayers to theirs." [46] He was, however, overruled by the others.

The Puritan commissioners also drew up a list of objections to the Book of Common Prayer. Their piety cannot be questioned — but their zeal for reform led them to stress unimportant matters as much as important. Thus, for instance, while from the Calvinists' point of view much was to be gained by revision of the rite of baptism so that it did not imply that all infants when baptized were forthwith regenerate, yet to reword the litany's prayer for preservation "From battle, and murder, and sudden death," to read: "From battle, and murder, and from dying suddenly and unprepared" was mere quibbling which spoiled the rhythm and beauty of the petition. The power of the presbyter would be greatly increased. Not only could he refuse the sacraments to adult sinners, or

[46] *Rel. Bax.*, Part II, 306–333; Baxter, *Defence of the Principles of Love*, pp. 29–30. Possibly Baxter had been encouraged in his scheme by Giles Firmin, who wrote in 1660 (*Presbyterial Ordination Vindicated* (London, 1660)) that as far as the liturgy went, "We have Divines in England, endued with Grace and Gifts, able to compose one, for the matter agreeable to the Worde, and Forme, and less offensive, than to be beholding to the Popish Puddles."

indeed to any whom he deemed not sufficiently in a state of grace, but he could deny the rite of baptism to the children of atheists and such lost souls. The substance of their demands was that Calvinistic doctrines be introduced into the liturgy. The dead hand of Baxter's Worcestershire Association was seen here.[47]

The answer of the bishops to the thirty-four pages of "Exceptions" was at once a protest against the harshness of the Calvinists and a defence of the liturgy. "It is better to be charitable, and hope for the best," it observed in response to the request that the burial service be revised to take away words of comfort, "than rashly to condemn." Seventeen changes were conceded. Some were important, but most of them referred to changes in wording; all of them, however, may be regarded as not dealing with doctrine but as tending to liberalize the Prayer Book.

The Puritans at once recognized the refusal of the Anglicans to make any other than "verbal and literal concessions." In a lengthy rejoinder, of one hundred and forty-five pages, they defended the changes for which they had petitioned. In conclusion they warned the churchmen that "if these be all the abatements and amendments you will admit, you sell your innocency and the church's peace for nothing." [48]

In response to this threat of separation Bishop Cosin came forward with an attempt of conciliation, asking "whether there be anything in the doctrine, discipline, or the Common Prayer, or ceremonies, contrary to the word of God." If the Puritans could find anything definitely

[47] Baxter MSS. in Dr. Williams' Library, Letters, I, f. 249; Baxter, *A Treatise of Conversion* . . . (London, 1657), pp. 109–132; Baxter, *Humble Advice* . . . (London, 1655), pp. 4 ff.

[48] *The Grand Debate between the Most Reverend the Bishops and the Presbyterian Divines* (London, 1661); the documents relating to the conference are reprinted in *Documents relating to the Act of Uniformity* . . ., pp. 146–378.

unscriptural, he advised, "let them be satisfied"; but if not, he suggested that they "propose what they desire in point of expediency." These proposals should be acted upon by convocation, whose findings should be acquiesced in by all; for, Bishop Cosin declared, "they ought not to disturb the peace of the church under the pretence of the prosecution of expediency, since the division of the Church is the greatest inexpedient." Baxter replied that his party had already presented "alterations and additional forms . . . the adoption of which would end all our differences about matters of worship." Bates and Jacombe, who began to realize that their colleague's management of the controversy was not conducive to peace, succeeded in toning down his answer, but even then it resolutely asked "Whether the granting of what you cannot blame be not now the shortest and surest way to a general satisfaction."

Most of the conference was carried on "in writing *ex tempore*," in order, as Bishop Morley explained, "to prevent jangling and all other the aforesaid inconveniences interlocutory Disputes are subject to; as likewise that each party might have time to consider what they were to stick to, and abide by." [49] Oral debates, however, concluded the meetings. "Through want of Order, frequent Interruptions, and personal Reflections," Echard commented, these were "turn'd to little or no account." [50] Bishop Gunning and Baxter carried on a heated debate on the meaning of the terms "lawful" and "expedient". Indeed Baxter acted as chief spokesman for his party; the others, except for a few interruptions by Bates and Manton,

[49] Morley, *op. cit.*, p. 112.

[50] Lawrence Echard, *The History of England* . . . (3 vols., London, 1726), III, 46–49. Echard is useful to counterbalance the Whiggish Oldmixon and Kennet.

seem to have been inactive. Clarendon later chided Baxter for the uncompromising spirit he showed at the conference, jokingly regretting that he had not possessed the plump geniality of Manton.[51]

While both sides wished peace, neither knew how to attain this end. And so the conference accomplished nothing at all. Historians as a whole have cast the blame for its failure upon the bishops. Had the prelates been willing to make a few concessions, it is said, the grim ejections of 1662 need never have taken place. It is a debatable point. The changes which the Puritans wished to make in the liturgy would have opened the door to the introduction of a most uncompromising Calvinism, in which the variety of opinion and interpretation allowed under the old Prayer Book would have disappeared. For as it was then worded, Calvinist, Arminian, or neo-Platonist could interpret it as he chose. Had the proposed changes been adopted, the priest would have been even more powerful than the Scottish presbyter in his power to refuse the sacraments to those whom he deemed sinful. By rejecting such demands the conference at least preserved the catholic character of the church.

Under Baxter's leadership the Reconcilers prepared for the press the papers which had passed between them and the bishops. The plan was to present these to Charles II with a petition "for his promised help yet for those alterations and abatements which we could not procure of the Bishops." First they sought the alliance of Clarendon. The Lord Chancellor, who had hitherto been their constant ally in their efforts, was angry at Baxter because of his uncompromising attitude at the Savoy Conference; but he promised that if they drew up such a petition,

[51] *Rel. Bax.*, Part II, 364–365.

they should present it to him for his opinion. Their hope was that the Declaration of the past October should be made into the law.

The petition, drawn up by Baxter and approved by the other Puritan commissioners, was given to Clarendon. Some parts of it he criticized as "too pungent or pressing," but he did not advise that they be removed. However he told the Lord Chamberlain of his disapproval and when the petition came into Manchester's hands he agreed and urged that the offending sentences be blotted out. Sir Gilbert Gerard, "an ancient godly Man", joined Manchester in urging Baxter to make the petition less defiant in tone and Baxter much against his will consented.[52] Then came the news, heart-breaking to Baxter, that Lord Manchester felt that the petition should be presented to the King by Reynolds, Bates, and Manton because Baxter was out of favor at court. The three stoutly refused to go without their comrade, and finally after Baxter had declared that he must absent himself, he allowed himself to be overborne by their pleas and all went in together to the King's presence. Reynolds first made a brief address; Manton presented the petition, which Charles II graciously received. In the discussion which followed Baxter, unabashed by Manchester's advice, resolutely took his part in explaining to the King the Puritans' views on church government.

All efforts for conciliation by conference having failed, the Puritans now awaited the decision of Convocation and Parliament. London nominated two delegates from the Reconciler group, Calamy and Baxter, but the bishop of London, whose duty it was to select a few delegates from

[52] *Rel. Bax.*, Part III, 364–365. The sentences omitted (*Documents relating to the Act of Uniformity* . . ., pp. 381–382) declared that the efforts for conciliation had failed because of "uncharitable mistakes."

the total number of candidates nominated by the whole diocese, chose representatives from parishes outside London. The bishop of course was within his rights; and the fact that Baxter was not beneficed, but was now associated with William Bates in his parish, St. Dunstan's in the West, may explain his exclusion. The Anglicans, moreover, could point out to critics that both the delegates had had the opportunity to sit in the House of Bishops and had refused.

The synod, dominated by the High Church party, naturally revised the Prayer Book in such a way as to emphasize its catholic character. The exceptions so painfully listed by Baxter and his group were ignored. The inclusion of lessons from the Apocrypha — which the Puritans called the victory of Bel and the dragon over the righteous — and the rubric stating that baptized infants were saved, and the use of the word "priest" not only asserted the determination of the Church of England that she was not to become Calvinist but at the same time made it impossible for the rigid Calvinist to conform.

The House of Lords fought valiantly to make the new Act of Uniformity less drastic, but nevertheless the Act, as it finally was passed, indicated that the Restoration church was to be less inclusive than the pre-Restoration church. For, according to the Act, to retain his living the priest must solemnly "assent and consent" to the new Prayer Book in its entirety: this meant that whereas in the past the candidate for Holy Orders might interpret it in its broadest sense, henceforth a more literal acceptance was required. He must, furthermore, take the oath of canonical obedience, abjure the Solemn League and Covenant, and subscribe to an oath declaring the illegality of taking arms against the Book. The Cavalier Parliament, not content with making conformity difficult and nonconformity inevitable for the rigid Calvinist, was next to proceed to smite the conscientious for being conscientious.

So it came about that the majority of the Reconcilers left the church. Reynolds, it is true, stayed in it and strove manfully, by sermons and by his conduct of his diocese, to make the church truly a comprehensive one. Confronted with the necessity of separation, the London ministers gathered in prayer at St. Bartholomew's on Thames Street. They next proceeded to petition their earthly monarch. Charles listened to them with his usual suavity, promising to do what he could to gain at least delay in the operation of the Act. But in the council meeting the legalists declared that by non-performance of the service according to the Prayer Book the incumbent must forfeit his living. Even Bishop Sheldon, departing for a time from his conciliatory policy, insisted that the Act should not be suspended. He had already removed the ministers who refused to use the Prayer Book, he declared, and by so doing "he had so provok'd their anger and hatred that if they were again restor'd, he should not live henceforward in a Society of Clergy, but in the Jaws of his Enemies."[53] Clarendon felt that because the King had promised that he would suspend the Act, he should do so; nevertheless he declared that a policy of firmness would make many stay in the church who, if a lenient course were followed, would hope to gain their end by nonconformity.[54]

On "Black Bartholomew," as the dissenters called it, some eighteen hundred ministers left their livings. It must be noted that all were not Presbyterians, so that concessions to that party would not have kept them in

[53] Samuel Parker, *Bishop Parker's History of His Own Time* (London, 1727), pp. 31–32.

[54] Clarendon, *op. cit.*, II, 299–305; Burnet, *op. cit.*, I, 341.

the church. Some, like Dr. Daniel Dyke, were Baptists, others were Independents. "To keep their case in Heart and Life," a group of London ministers published their farewell sermons. Calamy, Manton, Baxter, Case, Bates, Ashe, and Newcomen were in this group, which included also Seamen, Jenkin, and a number more. The sermons, which brought forth the tears of their hearers, went into at least three editions, a third edition being necessary in 1663 because the others had been "so much used by private families in city and country." Most of the sermons were devoted to instructions to continue in godliness; Baxter's, however, is noteworthy in that he strove for unity. He urged his hearers not to fall into schism, but to "keep Communion with the Universal Church of Christ." Matthew Newcomen recalled how when he was young, his predecessor Mr. Rogers "was taken off from his Ministry in this kind." He pointed out that the present measures were taken not by a single bishop, as then, but by Parliament — "which makes the Wound the wider". Some godly ministers were conforming, he informed his hearers, and he warned against censuring those who did or did not conform.[55] The sermons, better than any other contemporary document, show where the strength of nonconformity lay.

Although ejected from their livings the London ministers voted to conform as laymen, as did many in the country. Baxter received from the bishop of London a license to preach in his diocese. Manton continued to serve as chaplain to the Dowager Countess of Exeter. Calamy became very active as a leader of dissent in Lon-

[55] Edmund Calamy *et al.*, *The London-Ministers Legacy to their Several Congregations* . . . (London, 1663). Kennet pointed out (*op. cit.*, p. 805) that the pictures of the ministers were "set before their Sermons, just as they looked from the pulpit, wrapped in their reverend black and white Caps, like the twelve Apostles."

don. Like other ejected ministers, they held conventicles; it was ironic that they who had upheld the power of Parliament now found themselves without the law through the action of that body. They were aided by powerful friends — the Earl of Bedford, the Earl of Manchester, the Earl of Anglesey; while Calamy and Jenkin gathered together "a publicke stocke for the encouragement of those Ministers turned outt". [56] Manton and Bates and Baxter still dreamed of comprehension and in after years were to prove themselves quickly responsive to conciliatory gestures from the Church of England. But their days of service to the church were over; henceforth they were to minister to little groups in private.

It was of these ministers — Calamy, Manton, Baxter, the leaders of nonconformity — that Milton must have been thinking in his lament in *Samson Agonistes*:

"But such as thou hast solemnly elected,
With gifts and graces eminently adorned,
To some great work, thy glory. . . .
Yet towards these, thus dignified, thou oft
Amidst their height of noon
Changest thy countenance. . . .
Nor only dost degrade them, or remit
To life obscur'd. . . .
But throw'st them lower than thou didst exalt them high. . . .
Oft leav'st them to the hostile Sword. . . .
Or to the unjust tribunals, under change of times,
And condemnation of the ungrateful multitude. . . ."

[56] *S. P. Dom. Car. II* 29/167, # 54.

ETHYN WILLIAMS KIRBY.

ENGLISH PARTY POLITICS (1688-1714)

THE history of English party politics in the period 1689–1714 has been written and rewritten, most recently by Mr. Keith Feiling and Professor Trevelyan.[1] Much attention has been given to the rival Whig and Tory philosophies, but numerous questions concerning party groupings remain obscure. Definitions of Whiggism and Toryism and interpretations of parliamentary manoeuvres in terms of a conflict between these rival philosophies do not explain the actual workings of the party system. What is needed is a thorough examination of the party groups in Parliament and an analysis of the votes of the individual Members who made up those groups. In this essay we hope to sketch the outlines of such an analysis and indicate a few tentative conclusions; but first, a word about definitions.

In order to avoid metaphysics and premature generalizations we shall confine the discussion to parties within Parliament itself, and we shall define the term "party" as "one of the parts into which a legislative body may be divided by questions of public policy or elections of public officers".[2] With such an empiric definition we shall not be tempted to assume the existence of two parties and only two. Our task will be to discover which individual Members of Parliament made up a distinct group, associating

[1] Cf. Keith Feiling, *History of the Tory Party, 1640–1714* (Oxford, 1924); and G. M. Trevelyan, *England under Queen Anne*, 3 vols. (separately subtitled), (London, 1930–34).

[2] This is the definition used by Professor Holcombe in his article on "Political Parties" in the *Encyclopedia of the Social Sciences*, except for the substitution of "legislative body" for "state or municipality."

and voting together, and how many such groups there were. If we discover that there were many such groups, each maintaining an independent existence and following an independent political course, clearly we must face the question of how far and how completely they were integrated in a Whig or a Tory party or in similar entities with other names.

The definition of party which we have adopted suggests an obvious first line of inquiry: examination of actual divisions of Parliament on specific issues, some of which were recorded in published division lists. Though not as frequent, as complete, nor as reliable as one could wish, such published lists do exist for twelve crucial divisions between 1688 and 1714, and they give a very good idea of how individual Members voted on the most controversial issues of the period.[3] Since there was presumably a "Whig" and a "Tory" position on each of these issues, the House should have divided along the same lines time after time. Unfortunately the lists do not square with this theory. The "Tory" side in any one division usually includes many who at other times voted "Whig," and *vice versa*. If we assume that Parliament was split between those owning allegiance to Whig principles and Whig leaders and those following Tory principles and Tory leaders, we will attribute these inconsistencies to the independence, the wavering, or the desertions of individual Whig or Tory Members. On the other hand if we assume that the Whig or Tory majority in any particular division is made up of groups united only on that particular issue or for that session, we may attribute the inconsistencies to the movement of groups from one coalition to another.

[3] See my article on "Division Lists of the House of Commons, 1689–1715," printed in the *Bulletin of the Institute of Historical Research*, vol. XIV, number 40 (June, 1936), pp. 25–36.

We submit that the latter assumption is more nearly correct.

During this period, before the advent of central committees and campaign chests, party organizations must have been held together by more primitive methods, by simpler and more personal ties. To some extent membership in the same class or the same profession would serve; but the personal relations between neighbors or between the members of a family connection, between the dependents of a territorial magnate or between politicians who, once associated in office, afterwards elected to stick together — these would furnish a more effective basis for a cohesive group. We suggest that many such groups, small personal and family connections, did exist within the larger parties. Further, it is possible to identify them by correlating innumerable data on the antecedents, economic interests, family and personal relationships, and political affiliations of individual Members; but first we must hit upon some method for fixing the political position of the individual groups which we shall identify.

We could, of course, characterize a group simply as "Whig" or "Tory"; but this leaves no room for groups whose political actions can not be accounted for in such simple terms. Realizing this, Feiling and Trevelyan both speak of "extremists" and "moderates," of a "Tory right wing" and a "Centre Party." According to them parliamentary parties lined up somewhat as follows:

Whig		Centre		Tory
Left Wing Whigs	Moderate Whigs		Moderate Tories	Right Wing Tories

This concept, though apparently logical, is misleading; since Members who do not vote regularly Whig or Tory are lumped together in the Centre Party despite the fact that they are divided into two radically different groups. Member A who has voted with both Whigs and Tories but usually *with* the Court is classed with his political opposite, Member B, who has voted both Whig and Tory but usually *against* the Court. In order to fix the position of such men and that of the groups to which they belong we need additional labels, signifying their attitude toward the administration *qua* administration. Not only must we know whether a group is "Whig" or "Tory"; we must also know whether it is "Court" or "Country," to adopt the contemporary terms for those who consistently adhered to the government, or, on the other hand, to the permanent opposition.

In order to map the political position of party groups we shall use both sets of terms: "Whig" and "Tory" as the "East" and "West," "Court" and "Country" as the "North" and "South" points of our political compass. Schematically we may represent Parliament as a circle that may be divided into an indefinite number of segments called parties, and in any one session we may expect to find it divided by different issues into different segments. Thus on a straight party issue, for example a contest between a Whig and a Tory candidate for the Speaker's Chair, we should have an "East-West" division into Whig and Tory segments; but on a standard opposition issue, such as a Place Bill barring royal servants from the House, we should have a "North-South" division into Court and Country segments, the first opposing, the second favoring the bill. Actually Parliament was divided into at least four segments, combining both these divisions: one segment faithfully voting Whig, a second voting Tory equally faithfully, a third voting more consistently with the administration than with either of these groups, and a fourth voting as consistently against the Court no matter who held office. Finally we should expect to find subdivisions within each of these major groups. In each case we might expect to find a nucleus of stalwarts — courtiers who always voted with the government or Whigs who always voted Whig — plus marginal groups — "administration Tories" or "Country Whigs" — which occupied some intermediate position. It will be our task to test the truth of this interpretation, and if we find it valid, to sketch in the details of the hypothetical outline we have suggested by identifying individual groups and tracing their connection with a Whig or Tory party, with the Country or the Court.

Working out our hypothesis let us turn first to the Court party in Parliament. Was there, in fact, a group of Members who can be described as pro-administration throughout the party vicissitudes of the period? There can be no doubt that such a group existed, its nucleus a bloc of "government Members" who owed their seats to government influence and who voted with the administration as a matter of course. In Anne's first Parliament there were some thirty such Members, among them Admiralty officials returned for the dockyard towns, military governors and their aides from the garrison towns, the Lord Warden's nominees for the Cinque Ports, Duchy of Lancaster officials elected at Preston, Post Office officials at Harwich, and Treasury officials returned through the influence of that Department in various seaports. An official class drawn from no single social stratum, this semi-professional group included full-time civil servants (later barred from the House), professional politicians, and various officers of the Services.

Less closely identified with the administration, yet connected with the government rather than a Whig or Tory party, was an important section of the trading community. The House of Commons in 1702 included some fifty Members engaged in trade or banking. Of these a dozen were local merchants from the outports, usually more interested in local than in national affairs. Normally of Nonconformist background they voted, as often as not, against the Court. No partisans of the government, either, were the brewers who often represented Westminster, Southwark, and Maidstone. The majority of the trading-element in Parliament, however, were London merchants and bankers. To label these men "Whig," as is so often done, is a mistake. Their politics were largely a matter of business, to be governed by the attitude of the government toward their particular activities. Thus the private goldsmiths were courtiers while Charles II used their services, but opponents of the government when it chartered their rivals as a National Bank. Similarly, representatives of the "Old" and "New" East India Companies fought each other in the 1701 election, not over "Whig" or "Tory" principles, but for privileges for their particular group. Perhaps half the London merchants in Parliament held government contracts or received lesser economic favors. The important fact is that almost all of them had relations with the Treasury and followed its lead in Parliament, no matter whether it was headed by a Tory or a Whig.

With these two groups, professionally or economically tied to the administration, were associated an important number of territorial magnates. The English aristocracy, one must remember, did not act as a political unit. Of the 180 members of the House of Lords only a fraction concerned itself with politics. In general, families with comparatively ancient titles, few acres, and moderate income were indistinguishable from the squirearchy, of whom more will be said below. It was the newer families, chiefly, that used their wealth or professional abilities to further territorial and political ambitions. This group naturally centred around the Court and normally supported the government of the day. To them must be added the heads of three or four families of more ancient and distinguished lineage who seem also to have felt the lure for titles, honors, and political prestige.

An examination of the division-lists and signed protests of the Lords shows which titled families acted with the Court, while other scattered information enables us to identify their dependents and nominees in the Lower House. Chief among these oligarchic groups were those headed by the Dukes of Newcastle and Somerset and by the Earls of Lindsey and Radnor, while lesser groups were led by the Earls of Derby and Pembroke. Master of the Horse throughout the ministerial changes of a dozen years Somerset was undoubtedly a courtier rather than a Whig. Through his wife, heiress of the Earls of Northumberland, he controlled the great Percy estates, which, together with his own lands in Wiltshire, enabled him to influence elections in three counties and as many boroughs. This electoral influence lent him an importance irrespective of his abilities. "Both he and his son may be managed so as to be of use," Godolphin once wrote,[4] and successive ministries found it true; for the votes of Somerset's "mob" [5] supported the government or the government-to-be. Significantly Somerset's group was one of the first to "rat" in 1709–1710, deserting Godolphin for Harley, his prospective successor, in the midst of the Sacheverell affair.[6]

[4] *Add. MSS.* 9107, f. 97.

[5] Marlborough's term. Cf. *Add. MSS.* 9107, f. 119.

[6] This was evident to Marlborough and Godolphin (see their correspondence for this period in *Add. MSS.* 9282–3 (Coxe transcripts)); the fact that Somerset voted the Doctor "not guilty" is further proof, if any were needed.

Another "mob" worth gaining was the Duke of Newcastle's group. Inheritor of huge estates from the Holles and Cavendish families, the Duke dominated Nottinghamshire elections, naming half the Members from that county, while two pocket-boroughs in Yorkshire he owned outright.[7] As for the politics of the Newcastle group, it followed the pattern of Somerset's. Allied with the Whig Junto while they were at the height of their power, Newcastle, like Somerset, swung his group over to Harley in 1710 and remained friendly with the new administration, in which he held office until his death in 1711.[8] Somerset and Newcastle quite eclipsed the other Court peers, but some of the lesser lights deserve mention. Lindsey in Lincolnshire, Pembroke in Wiltshire, Derby in Lancashire, and Radnor in Cornwall each returned four or five Members who voted consistently with the Court. Lord Radnor, for instance, having found seats for Whig politicians in 1708, was offering to return Tory candidates in 1710.[9] Hence the families of Robartes, Herbert, Bertie, and Stanley continued to hold office and receive honors throughout the party changes of the period.

This list of oligarchic groups led by magnates identified with the Court is by no means complete. There were many similar groups, but in most cases the politics of the leaders are not so readily apparent as those of Somerset and Newcastle. We have reached the penumbra of the Court party, the shadowy region between the sunshine of Court

[7] Adequate evidence for this account of Newcastle's electoral interest will be found in Newcastle's correspondence (*Hist. MSS. Comm. Reports, Portland MSS.*, II, 173–230, *passim*); in election correspondence regarding Aldborough and Boroughbridge (printed in *Records of a Yorkshire Manor*, ed. Sir Thomas Lawson-Tancred); and in evidence on Nottinghamshire elections given before the Committee on Elections (compiled in Carew's *Historical Rights of Elections*, 1755, *sub* Nottingham, Newark, and East Retford).

[8] Cf. note 6, above.

[9] *Hist. MSS. Comm. Reports, Portland MSS.*, II, 204; IV, 565.

politics and the full shadow of Whig-Tory party politics. Let us turn, then, to the two historic parties and, continuing the analysis, try to discover if the Whig and Tory parties do not consist, like the Court party, in a nucleus of party stalwarts, allied with peripheral groups connected on the one side with the administration, on the other with the permanent "Country" opposition.

The Tory party of this period, discussed in detail by Keith Feiling, is treated by him as an entity with a definite set of principles and leaders. Granted that there was a Tory philosophy, what parliamentary leaders did, in fact, attempt to carry those principles — respect for the throne and the prerogative, championship of the Church of England, and encouragement of the landed, as against the commercial, interest — into effect? Further, what parliamentary support could these leaders muster, and was this parliamentary following loyal to the Tory leadership as such, or to individual chieftains who incidentally embraced part or all of the Tory creed? To ask these questions is to suggest some of the answers. Certainly there was a host of leaders claiming to represent the Tory party, yet differing among themselves. Whom shall we select as the paladins of Toryism: Nottingham and his friends who best represented the High Church viewpoint and enjoyed the support of many upright Country members; Rochester and his following of somewhat tarnished henchmen, who voiced High Church slogans yet often sacrificed principle for place; Harley and St. John who, Feiling believes, forged and led a new and stronger Toryism only to fall out when victory was won; or Marlborough and Godolphin, who certainly headed an administration admittedly Tory for half a dozen years, though later overturned by the very Tory leaders who, earlier, fought and served beside that pair?

Let us turn first to Marlborough and his close associate Godolphin. Were these men Tories? Their careers would seem to indicate they were not. Both served Charles II, James II, Queen Anne, and even William, usually as members of Tory administrations, but often with Whigs. Both have been labeled Tories, but, while more Tory than Whig, they were never party chiefs. It was during William's last years that they were closest to the Tories, and even then their allegiance was primarily to the Court — not of William, but of the Princess Anne. As a young girl at Court, Sarah Jennings early won the affection of, and gained unusual influence over, the future Queen. With her marriage to Colonel Churchill, himself an accomplished courtier, her husband's family came to be included in the Princess' circle, and Anne and her consort, George of Denmark, heaped honors and favors upon them, going so far as to ask William for the next vacant Garter for their protégé, now Lord Marlborough.[10] Other members of the family profited as well. Marlborough's two brothers were given places in the Prince's Household, and their royal connections no doubt assisted their rapid rise in the army and navy, their respective professions. Marlborough's brother-in-law, two nephews, and his secretary also benefited. Like Charles and George Churchill they held seats in the House, representing the Churchill connection.[11]

The parliamentary interest of Lord Marlborough would have been slight, however, were it not for his alliance with Godolphin, an alliance dating from the Revolution and

[10] Sir John Dalrymple, *Memoirs of Great Britain and Ireland* (London, 1790), III, 255–256 (letters of the Princess Anne to William).

[11] Cf. *Dictionary of National Biography* for General Charles and Admiral George Churchill and Marlborough's secretary, Adam Cardonnel. Marlborough's brother-in-law, Charles Godfrey, and his nephews, Edmund Dunch and Francis Godfrey, are not separately noticed, but see *D.N.B. sub* "Hugh Boscawen."

cemented in 1698 by the marriage of Marlborough's eldest daughter to his friend's eldest son. As a result the parliamentary following of the Churchill faction was doubled, for Godolphin had considerable electoral interests in Cornwall. In addition to Helston, where he himself was patron and which returned two members of his family, he could count on seats for Tregony and Truro, boroughs controlled by Hugh Boscawen, who was a nephew of both Marlborough and Godolphin. Acting at first as borough-manager for his two uncles, Boscawen later enlisted with the Whigs and ended his career as Viscount Falmouth.[12] The addition of this Cornish contingent, and a few scattered henchmen, raised the parliamentary strength of the Churchills to about a dozen Members.

During William's reign this group represented primarily the interests of the Princess Anne with which its own future was so intimately connected. Most of its members held posts in the Princess' Household and acted politically not as Whigs or Tories, but as courtiers owing allegiance to the sovereign-to-be. With the accession of their mistress this group formed a perfect nucleus for a body of "Queen's Friends," and such it undoubtedly became. The appointment of Marlborough as Commander-in-Chief entrusted with the conduct and diplomacy of the war and the appointment of Godolphin as Lord Treasurer in charge of domestic affairs was no Tory triumph, but the beginning of eight years of rule by the Queen's favorites. Later we shall discuss the politics of the Churchill connection and its relations with the Tory groups. At this point we need only state that the policy which the duumvirs followed was not a Tory policy, but one inherited from William. The successful continuation and financing of the struggle with France, union with Scotland, and domes-

[12] *D.N.B.*, article "Hugh Boscawen."

tic unity unimpaired by factional or religious strife, these were the objects of the Godolphin ministry, and not one of them was a plank in the Tory platform.

That Marlborough and Godolphin were not "Tories" is admitted by Feiling.[13] The true Tory party of this period, he believes, was a coalition engineered by Robert Harley, and he recognizes two elements: a "Country" wing, Whig in origin, led by Harley; and a "Church" wing, by origin Tory, led by Rochester and Nottingham and their lieutenants in the Commons.[14] Whether this coalition was ever effectively maintained except for the years 1698–1702 may be doubted. There is some question, also, whether the Church wing of the "new Country Party" (as Feiling calls it) was as unified or as stable in its leadership, its parliamentary following, or its principles as Feiling and Trevelyan imply; for it seems to have included two distinct groups that acted only occasionally in concert. These questions are raised by way of introduction and will be dealt with later, but first we must analyze the "Country" wing, of which Robert Harley was the acknowledged leader.

The nucleus of this group was the Harley family connection, and its strength lay in its electoral influence in the Welsh border counties. William III's grant to the Harleys of a lordship in Radnorshire plus the site of Radnor Castle gave them the control of that county and borough, but the real source of their electoral influence lay in their connection with the Foleys. This family, founded in the seventeenth century by a wealthy ironmaster of Stourbridge, later retired from trade and invested its great wealth in land. By 1688 the Foleys were well established as territorial magnates in the counties of Stafford, Here-

[13] Feiling, *Tory Party, 1640–1714*, pp. 282–283, 366–367.
[14] *Ibid.*, pp. 286–288, 291–292, 314–316.

ford, and Worcester; and they controlled the return of at least five borough Members plus a considerable voice in the election of knights for three counties.[15] This was the family with which the Harleys became doubly allied when Robert and his brother Edward married two Foley sisters, granddaughters of the great ironmaster.

The Harleys and Foleys made up a bloc of some eight or ten Members, which was swelled by other friends and connections. One of Harley's intimates, Thomas Mansell, controlled both seats for Glamorganshire. Another friend and neighbor, Judge Robert Price, had great influence in the only Herefordshire borough not controlled by the Foleys. A close political friend, Lord Poulett, had influence in Somerset, amounting almost to nomination at the borough of Ilchester.[16] Finally Simon Harcourt, onetime schoolfellow, later friend and political associate of Harley, had influence, both as Recorder and neighboring landowner, at Abingdon in Berkshire, which he usually represented.

These kinsmen, personal friends, and neighbors were the nucleus of Harley's following. Enlisted somewhat later but only a little less closely identified with Harley was a group led by Henry St. John, later Viscount Bolingbroke. Entering the Commons in 1701, St. John immediately made a name for himself by brilliant attacks on Whig courtiers. Most famous politicians begin their careers in opposition, and St. John joined the new Country Party — but which wing? He acted with the High Church Tory

[15] Viz. the boroughs of Stafford (Staffs), Hereford and Leominster (Hereford), Bewdley and Droitwich (Worc.). Cf. W. R. Williams' parliamentary histories of these three counties, and *Hist. MSS. Comm. Reports*, *Portland MSS.*, III–VI (Harley Papers), *passim.*

[16] Cf. for Somerset and Ilchester, Poulett's letters to Harley, *Portland MSS.*, IV, 176–177, 200, 315, sqq. For Glamorganshire, W. R. Williams, *Parliamentary History of Wales*; and his volume on Herefordshire for Price's influence at Weobley.

extremists, but his letters show that he attached himself particularly to Harley.[17] St. John brought his "Master," as he called him, not only his own vote and interest at the family borough in Wiltshire, but also important recruits from among his cronies: his cousin James Brydges, the "Princely Chandos"; Tom Coke of Derbyshire; the "Silver-Tongued" Anthony Hammond; the poet George Granville, later Lord Lansdowne; and the notorious Jack How.[18] These half dozen young rakes plus his other personal adherents were the core of Harley's following. He has been credited as well with a following among the country squires and independent back-benchers. At various times a large number of such Members followed his lead, but only when he was opposing the Court. Later we shall review the course followed by the Tory groups and show that the Harley connection was a flying squadron relatively small in numbers rather than a wing of the Tory party.

It may be argued, however, that the Harleians are a special case. Surely in turning to the Church Tories we shall find a party of the type we have been led to expect — a large and cohesive group acting according to established principles under unified leadership. Upon analysis, however, the Church Tory wing proves similar in many respects to the groups already discussed. Like the Court party it had its complement of allies and its core of stalwarts. The Harleians and the Churchills might possibly be included among the allies. They were certainly not of the inner circle, which was composed of two central groups, both based, like the Harley and Churchill connections, on

[17] Cf. St. John's letters to Harley in *Portland MSS.*, IV, 176, 180, 223, *et seq.*

[18] The close relations between these men and St. John are best shown in their letters in *Hist. MSS. Comm. Reports*, *Cowper MSS.*, II, 32–66, *passim.* Cf. also articles on each of them in the *D.N.B.*

family relationship. The Church Tory party, to a surprising extent, was a family affair, the particular preserve of four great houses: the Hydes, the Granvilles, the Seymours of Berry Pomeroy, and the Finches. They and their friends and relations provided the party with most of its leaders. With their nominees and dependents they made up a phalanx of regulars who could be counted upon in every test of party strength.

The ascendancy in Tory circles of the Hydes is easily explained. Edward Hyde, founder of the family, was early the trusted friend and councillor of both Charles I and his son. He was made Earl of Clarendon and Lord Chancellor by Charles II, and though he was later driven from office the family influence continued. His daughter, although a commoner, had married the future James II and was the mother of the Princesses Mary and Anne. Both his sons were active advisers of their royal brother-in-law; but with James' deposition the elder son, the second Lord Clarendon, retired from politics, refusing to accept the new order. The leadership of the family thereupon passed to his younger brother, who had been raised to the peerage in his own right as Earl of Rochester.

It was Rochester who saw to the publication of his father's *History of the Great Rebellion*, and the posthumous appearance of this famous work increased the prestige that Rochester enjoyed as uncle of two Queens. He had considerable parliamentary influence as well, based largely on his connections with leading Restoration houses, like the Granvilles and the Gowers, with whom Rochester arranged an alliance by marrying his son and heir to a Gower.[19] The three related families together mustered a numerous and compact following in Parliament. As owner of the pocket borough of Christ Church in Hampshire,

[19] Cf. the genealogical diagram below, p. 98, note 28.

Rochester returned two Members, while a Hyde cousin was virtually permanent Member for Wiltshire. Two or three other kinsmen, with seats of their own, and one or two followers recommended at Huntingdon by Rochester's sister-in-law, brought the total of Rochester's own group to seven. The electoral interest of the Granvilles, less scattered than the Hydes', was concentrated in Cornwall. Lady Hyde's[20] grandfather, the first Granville Earl of Bath, was known as "the Great Elector", and James II could well rely upon him as Court manager for Cornish elections. This great family interest was being managed after 1688 by Colonel John Granville, Lady Hyde's uncle. In Cornwall and five of its boroughs Granville had a hereditary family interest, and these half dozen constituencies usually returned Granville nominees.[21] Sir John Leveson-Gower, Granville's nephew and Lady Hyde's brother, could be counted upon for another Member or two, for the Gowers controlled Newcastle in Staffordshire.[22] All told, the Hydes, the Granvilles, and the Gowers returned some fifteen Members, and the Tory party owed much of its cohesion to these related clans, which managed their electoral interests in concert.

Another family that coöperated with Rochester, though not at first allied by marriage, were the Seymours of Berry Pomeroy in Devon. Descended in the elder line from the Protector Somerset, Sir Edward, the fifth baronet, rather looked down on his kinsman, the "Proud Duke" of Somerset, as a descendant in the junior line. A Member of Par-

[20] Rochester's heir-apparent bore the courtesy title of "Lord Hyde," and his wife was known as "Lady Hyde."

[21] Cf. *Official Return of Members of Parliament* (vol. LXII, Parliamentary Papers, 1878). Of the M.P.'s for Bossiney, Grampound, Launceston, Penryn, and Michel in the 1701 parliament there was one Granville, Lord Hyde, and five kinsmen or henchmen of Granville.

[22] Cf. Wedgwood's *Parliamentary History of Staffordshire* (*Collections of the William Salt Archeological Society*, 1917, 1920–1922).

liament for more than forty years, sometime Speaker of the House and a Lord of the Treasury, Sir Edward was a veteran of unequaled experience, who in the course of a long career had built up a formidable electoral interest which Defoe called "Tsar Seymskie's Western Empire."[23]

Sir Edward usually secured a seat for himself and a friend at Exeter, where he was Recorder, and had two seats to spare at his pocket-borough of Totnes, near by. He could count on additional seats at Taunton and Wells, where his brother had estates and electoral influence inherited from a Somerset kinsman; plus two seats at St. Mawes, which was controlled by Sir Edward's brother-in-law.[24] Finally there was his first cousin, Sir Jonathan Trelawny, Bishop of Exeter, who could "muster up a squadron"[25] of about ten Members from the five Trelawny boroughs in Devon and Cornwall.[26] Unfortunately the Bishop was an unreliable ally. He had become a Tory hero by opposing King James in the Seven Bishops Case, but after the Revolution he went over to the Court. With an eye on a fatter bishopric, his first thought was to oblige the administration; and the Seymour cousins that Sir Jonathan provided with seats were apt to be thrown over once they put the Bishop's squadron out of step with the Court.

[23] *Hist. MSS. Comm. Reports*, *Portland MSS.*, IV, 222. For Sir Edward Seymour, cf. *D.N.B.*

[24] For Exeter cf. *Hist. MSS. Comm. Reports*, *Portland MSS.*, IV, 177, 270, 420; the list of Totnes M.P.'s shows Totnes was in Seymour's pocket; at Taunton and Wells Henry Seymour-Portman, who adopted the Portman surname on inheriting the Portman estates, was M.P. for seventeen years, and a cousin usually held another seat for these boroughs; as for St. Mawes, Seymour's brother-in-law, Sir Joseph Tredenham, represented it for forty years, from 1665 till his death, together with another Tredenham, such as his son John, M.P. 1690–1711 (died).

[25] Cf. Godolphin's letter to Harley, 1701, in *Portland MSS.*, IV, 28.

[26] Viz. Bodmin, Liskeard, and East and West Looe, in Cornwall; and Plymouth in Devon.

An important and far more reliable ally was Sir Christopher Musgrave. Since the days of Charles II's "Pensioners' Parliament" Musgrave and Seymour had worked together, and in William's last Parliament Sir Christopher sat for Seymour's borough of Totnes. Having to take refuge there must have been galling to one who had represented Oxford University for three years, Westmorland for six, and Carlisle for thirty! Head of a clan prominent in the northern counties, and sometime Governor of Carlisle, Sir Christopher usually won two or three Cumberland and Westmorland seats for his own nominees.[27] Including them Seymour could count on a dozen satellites in the House, which explains his importance as an associate of Rochester, with whom he formed a close alliance, dating from the Revolution and afterwards cemented by the marriage of Rochester's daughter to Seymour's son.[28] Later we shall trace the progress of this alliance, but first

[27] Cf. R. S. Ferguson's *Cumberland and Westmorland M.P.'s from the Restoration to the Reform Bill of 1867* (London, 1871), *passim*.

[28] The Granville-Hyde-Gower-Seymour relationships may be charted:

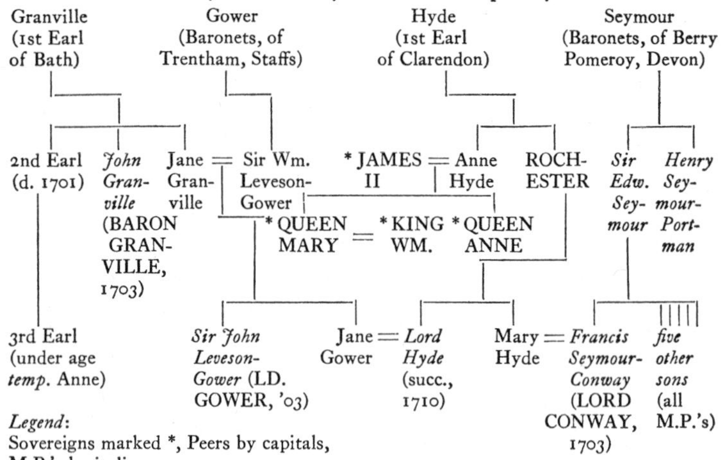

let us turn to that other family connection, the important Church Tory group led by Nottingham.

Daniel Finch, second Earl of Nottingham, had a compact band of followers like Rochester, based on his own family connection, the "whole flight of Finches," as Feiling calls it. Nottingham's family had played as great a rôle in English politics as the Hydes and had as honorable a place in Tory tradition. Nottingham's great-grandmother, heiress of an Elizabethan favorite named Heneage, was made Countess of Winchilsea in her own right, and from her eldest son descended the Earls of Winchilsea, an undistinguished line except for Nottingham's cousin, the second Earl, who served his monarch well throughout the Civil War. From a younger son descended the more important junior line. This son, the first Heneage Finch, and Nottingham's grandfather, was a great lawyer and became Recorder of London and Speaker of the House in the early years of Charles I. His son, the second Heneage Finch and Nottingham's father, was a greater man. A lawyer like his father he managed to stay neutral during the Civil War, achieving fame under Charles II as a Tory leader and champion of the Church. Member for Oxford University in the Cavalier Parliament he subsequently became Lord Chancellor and first Earl of Nottingham.

By his wife, daughter of a London merchant named Harvey and niece of the celebrated Dr. William Harvey, Nottingham left six sons, two of whom concern us. Heneage Finch (III), the second son, lived up to his name and carried on the family tradition at the Bar and as Member for Oxford. A leading Tory politician, he was made Solicitor-General by Charles II, created Lord Guernsey by Anne, and Earl of Aylesford by George I. His more famous elder brother Daniel succeeded as second Earl of Nottingham. Following in his father's footsteps the second Earl became a leader of the Church party and played an active part in the politics of five reigns, serving as an Admiralty Lord under Charles and James II, as a Secretary of State under William and Anne, and as Lord President under George I. A year before his death he inherited the Winchilsea earldom from his kinsman, the last of the senior line, adding a third earldom to the two which the cadet line had already won through their own ability.[29]

His political prominence Nottingham owed partly to a compact parliamentary following based on the family connections. He himself had little electoral influence except in Rutland, which chose his son upon Lord Finch's coming-of-age. Many of his relatives, however, had seats in the House. His brother Heneage represented Oxford University for a dozen years until his elevation to the peerage and had some electoral influence in Surrey, which his son later represented for nineteen years. Moreover he had in-laws in politics: his son-in-law Dartmouth, who usually followed Nottingham's lead in the Lords; another son-in-law, Robert Benson, a Member of Parliament and a follower of Nottingham till 1710; and finally Dartmouth's son-in-law, who occupied a safe Hampshire seat and voted with Nottingham's group. These last two Members were less important, however, than those grouped around Nottingham's own son-in-law, Sir Roger Mostyn, who headed a knot of able Members, most of them related and representing Flint and Cheshire constituencies.[30]

Other important family groups were allied with Not-

[29] For sketches of important members of the Finch family cf. the *D.N.B.*

[30] Mostyn sat for Flintshire or Cheshire; his brother Thomas was M.P. for Flint, 1698–1705; his first cousin, Sir Thomas Hanmer, at various times represented Flint, Flintshire, Thetford (where his wife, the Dowager Duchess of Grafton, had influence), and Suffolk; Hanmer's uncle, Sir Henry Bunbury, was M.P. for Chester, 1701 till death (1723); and his colleague, Peter Shakerly (M.P. Chester, 1698–1715), was another of the group. All were staunch followers of Nottingham.

tingham. His second cousin Winchilsea, a rather mediocre figure, was inclined to put place and profit ahead of Tory principles, but he had relatives who were abler and more useful. His uncle, Thomas Thynne, Viscount Weymouth, was one of Nottingham's lieutenants in the Lords and had electoral interests in Wiltshire and at Weymouth and Tamworth, which usually returned Thynne nominees.[31] Another useful ally was Charles, Lord Bruce, Winchilsea's second cousin. Heir apparent of the exiled Jacobite, Lord Ailesbury, Bruce was acting head of a family with interests in three Wiltshire boroughs. Three Bruces sat in the Commons in Anne's reign, voting with the Finches, with whom they were related through the marriage of Lord Bruce to Nottingham's granddaughter.[32] Another ally of importance was Robert, third Lord Bulkeley, an Irish peer who was Nottingham's first cousin. Head of an influential Welsh family, Bulkeley controlled both Anglesey constituencies, and his uncle, Thomas Bulkeley, represented another Welsh constituency near by.[33] The three Welsh Members returned on the Bulkeley interest must also be included in Nottingham's group.

One other Tory house connected with Nottingham remains to be considered: the Berties. The senior branch of this great family, led by the Earl of Lindsey, profited greatly by its close relationship to Danby, and on Danby's retirement held on to its places and profits by going over

[31] Weymouth's son, Henry Thynne, represented both Weymouth and Tamworth, 1700 to 1708 (died); Weymouth's brother-in-law, Sir Richard How, represented Tamworth, 1685, and Wilts, 1701–27, both on the Thynne interest. William Harvey, M.P. Weymouth, 1710–15, a kinsman of Nottingham, and Joseph Girdler, M.P. Tamworth, 1705–15, and a Nottingham follower, were probably Thynne nominees.

[32] For the borough interests and politics of the Bruces cf. *Hist. MSS. Comm. Reports, Ailesbury MSS.*, pp. 188–205.

[33] Cf. W. R. Williams, *Representative History of Wales, sub* Anglesey, Beaumaris, Carnarvonshire, and Carnarvon.

to the Court.[34] The younger line, on the contrary, were zealous Church Tories. Their chief, the second Earl of Abingdon, was an ally of Nottingham, and the alliance was given a family angle by the marriage of Abingdon's sister to Nottingham's first cousin, Lord Bulkeley. This Lady Bulkeley had a surprising number of Bertie relatives in the Commons. Her brother sat for the Bulkeley's Welsh borough for some twenty years, but most of the Berties owed their seats to Abingdon. This nobleman, with extensive estates in Wiltshire and Oxfordshire, controlled the return of half a dozen Members: two from the family borough in Wiltshire, plus three or four from Oxfordshire; while his Bertie uncle had a firm hold on one seat for Stamford in Lincolnshire.[35] If we add the seven Bertie seats to the three controlled by the Bulkeleys we find that this family connection could return ten Members pledged to Nottingham. The Bruce family contributed another three; the Thynnes, three also; Nottingham's son-in-law Mostyn, five; and his brother, Heneage Finch, three, making a total of two dozen M.P.'s, in addition to the five peers — Nottingham, Winchilsea, Dartmouth, Weymouth, and Abingdon, tied to the Nottingham connection.

The Nottingham and Rochester groups together mustered some sixty Members and undoubtedly formed the backbone of the Church Tory interest. Since they often acted together they have been treated by historians as a single group, but with this interpretation we cannot agree. We suggest that the very real differences between the various Tory groups have been under-emphasized. In

[34] Danby married the 3rd Earl of Lindsey's sister. For Lindsey's politics cf. above, pp. 87–88.

[35] Both M.P.'s for Westbury (Wilts) and four of the nine Oxfordshire M.P.'s can be identified as kinsmen or dependents of Abingdon in almost any Parliament of this period.

analyzing the composition of the Marlborough-Godolphin, Harley, Rochester, and Nottingham connections we have treated each group as an independent unit, led by one or two individuals, and we have ignored the relations which the separate groups bore toward each other and toward the "Tory party." It remains to determine whether these groups did in fact form a single parliamentary party, a question that can best be decided by tracing the politics of the various groups.

In the period before 1688 the Tory party had not yet taken the form it was to have in 1700. It included Jacobite and Catholic elements which steadily gained influence up to the Revolution, only to be driven from politics into exile or retirement, while it did not include the Harleys and Foleys, who were still voting with the Whigs. The steadier section of the party was still commanded by elder statesmen like Halifax and Danby, but it already included many Nottingham and Rochester Tories. The new Tory party was to be built around them, yet between these two groups there were important differences from the first. The principal allegiance of the Rochester Tories was to the King; that of the Nottingham Tories, to the Church. Moreover they differed in character. Few of the Nottingham Tories could be accused of time-serving or venality, while no such strict virtue marked the Rochesterites.[36] Thus the Rochester Tories were led to connive at some of the most questionable policies of Charles II and James, in contrast to the Nottingham Tories, who took the lead in championing the Church against the machinations of the Court.

[36] Seymour, for example, was involved in an unsavory East India Co. scandal, with his client Thomas Coulson; Musgrave was suspected of foregoing opposition to William's government for a bag of sovereigns; and there were many other somewhat tarnished politicians among the Rochester group (cf. the *D. N. B.* articles on Seymour and Musgrave).

More active in their constitutional opposition the Nottingham Tories were at the same time less hasty in deserting their rightful monarch when rebellion came. In the Revolution it was the Hydes, the Seymours, and the Granvilles who went over with Danby to Orange, while Nottingham and Halifax stayed with James, urging to the last the necessity for reform. When James finally fled and forfeited the crown the Tory groups drew together. In the debates over the Revolution settlement Nottingham, Rochester, and Churchill Tories joined to argue against changing the succession and in favor of a regency for William, stripping James of every vestige of kingship except the title. Overborne by a Whig majority all three groups moved that Mary alone be named queen, but this too failed. A Whig settlement was eventually carried and perforce accepted by the Tory groups, but their attitude toward the new order was not the same. The Churchills and some of Rochester's group accepted the settlement with reservations and maintained contacts with the exiled Court, but the Nottingham Tories never wavered in their allegiance to the Protestant Succession.

This loyalty to "the conqueror" was rewarded. Appointed Secretary of State, Nottingham served William for five years, and he and his followers voted with the government against the Place and Triennial Bills. In so doing they set themselves squarely against a new Tory current. In 1689 Robert Harley entered Parliament and started the Harley-Foley connection on a new course. This group, originally Whig and Nonconformist in its sympathies, had voted with the Whigs in the debates over the Revolution Settlement and had joined the Whig extremists in voting for the Sacheverell clause.[37] Now, under Harley's leadership, it coöperated with the Rochester

[37] The list of the Whig majority on the Sacheverell clause (in J. Oldmixon's

Tories in opposition to William's first ministry. Calling itself the "New Country Party" this coalition championed measures which the Country groups had always pushed: reduction of the army, Place and Triennial Bills, a negative on royal grants, and so forth. From this combination, more Country than Tory, many Tories held aloof. Nottingham's group in particular refused to join it, siding instead with the government until 1694. In that year the Junto Whigs won office and forced Nottingham out. For the remainder of the reign he and his followers were in opposition and may be called a wing of the New Country Party; but in the party battles against the Junto they took a much less active part than the Harley or Rochester group, and it was not they, but Rochester and his henchmen who won office for a time in 1701.

The accession of Anne, one year later, is supposed to have marked a revolution in party politics. For the first time since the Revolution all the Tory leaders won office. It was the Churchills, however, that actually took over the government, and we have already suggested that Marlborough and Godolphin were Tories neither in principle nor in practise. Why, then, did they allow Nottingham and Rochester such generous representation in the ministry? [38] Rochester, of course, was the Queen's uncle, and Nottingham's zeal for the Church suited Anne's pious Anglicanism; but the principal reason for their promotion was surely their combined parliamentary following, which the Churchills desperately needed. Rochester and Not-

---

History of England (London, 1735), III, 36–37) includes three Foleys, two Harleys, one Mansell, and Jack How.

[38] Nottingham and his disciple, Hedges, became Secretaries of State. Weymouth, Dartmouth, and Abingdon got places. All five became Privy Councillors. Rochester got the government of Ireland. Seymour, Granville, and Gower got places and became Privy Councillors. In the first batch of peerages Nottingham's brother, Seymour's son, Granville, and Gower got baronies.

tingham were enlisted to win votes for the government and cashiered because they failed to deliver. Appointed and dismissed at the same time the Rochester and Nottingham Tories apparently acted as a single party, but the fact that both groups disagreed with the Churchills' policy toward the war and the Church does not mean that they agreed among themselves.

How best to carry on the war against France was a question on which all three groups disagreed: Marlborough favoring mainland campaigns in the Lowlands; Rochester, naval operations in the Atlantic and West Indies; and Nottingham, joint naval and military attacks in Spain and the Mediterranean. The moderate success of an expedition to Spain, commanded by Nottingham's cousin, Admiral Rooke, and Rochester's son-in-law, Ormonde, was naturally cited as proof of the superiority of Tory strategy and leadership; and the questionable victory at Vigo Bay was magnified by the Rochester and Nottingham Tories, some of whom pointedly disparaged Marlborough's simultaneous triumph at Blenheim. The relative merits of the two engagements became a party issue, and the disagreement between Marlborough and the Tory leaders was embittered by the injection of personalities into the dispute.

Other disagreements worked to widen the breach. The Churchills were unalterably opposed to the revival of party warfare, which by dividing Parliament might jeopardize the successful prosecution of the war; but the Rochester Tories refused to bury the hatchet. By reviving the impeachments of the Junto Lords, by threatening to resume all of William's grants, by using every means to prove the ex-ministers corrupt, and by fighting to the finish an election squabble between the Junto Lord Wharton and one of Rochester's henchmen,[39] no matter what the cost, Sey-

[39] This famous case, known as "Ashby v. White," arose from the efforts

mour, Musgrave, Granville, and the other Rochesterites precipitated a bitter quarrel with the Lords which virtually paralyzed public business. This was bad enough, but the Rochesterites made matters worse by their unyielding conduct in still another, more personal affair. Soon after her accession the Queen asked the Commons to extend a generous grant to Marlborough's family, out of consideration for the Duke's services. The way was smoothed by private conversations with Tory leaders, and when the question came before the House, Nottingham's brother and son-in-law spoke dutifully for the Duke. Seymour and Musgrave, however, led the successful opposition to the grant, speaking with scant respect.[40] All this made it easier for the Churchills to dismiss Rochester and his crew.

In the affair of Marlborough's grant the Nottingham Tories behaved well, and they played a less prominent rôle than the Rochesterites in the party battles against the Whigs; but they, too, offended by adopting extremist measures in regard to the Church. Religious issues, like party quarrels, the Churchills wished buried. Nottingham, hereditary champion of the Church, refused; and he had a bill introduced in the Commons, imposing drastic penalties on Nonconformists who received the Sacrament solely to qualify for public office. Sentiment for "the Occasional Conformity Bill" was so strong that the Court did not venture to oppose it outright; but as the Lords failed to

---

of Sir John Pakington, who married Rochester's cousin, to capture the borough of Aylesbury, where he was Lord of the Manor, from Wharton, the great Whig magnate, who usually wooed the Aylesbury electors with complete success.

[40] The preliminary conversations are mentioned in Godolphin's letter to Harley, Dec. 10, 1702 (*Portland MSS.*, IV, 53). The debates are reported in the letters of Thomas Johnson, M.P. for Liverpool, to Richard Norris, Dec. 10, Dec. 12 (in *The Norris Papers*, ed. for the Chetham Society by T. Heywood, 1846, pp. 103–107).

pass the bill, session after session, open warfare broke out between the Houses over this question, culminating in an effort, initiated by the Nottingham Tories, to "tack" the bill to the Land Tax, so that the peers must either swallow it or starve the war. The "tack" was defeated, but it cost Nottingham his office, and every Tory placeman who voted for it was ousted.

This somewhat detailed discussion of the political course followed by the Nottingham and Rochester Tories shows quite conclusively that the two groups did not follow identical policies and were not ousted for the same reasons. On the conduct of the war the two groups disagreed, but united in stressing naval operations and deploring the costly Netherlands campaigns. In violent anti-Whig tactics it was the Rochesterites who led, and the Nottingham Tories who followed; in the fight for Occasional Conformity and the Tack it was the Nottingham Tories who led, and the Rochesterites who followed; while in the matter of Marlborough's grant the two groups took opposite sides. As if to emphasize these differences Rochester was dismissed a year earlier than Nottingham, and his lieutenants ousted before Nottingham's henchmen.

By 1705 the ministry was purged of Rochester and Nottingham Tories, who thereupon went into opposition. The next few years are a strange commentary on Tory party unity, with the two Church Tory groups arrayed against the rival Tory groups led by Godolphin and Harley. It was the Harleians that filled the gaps left by the displaced Church Tories, Harley succeeding Nottingham as Secretary of State, Mansell replacing Seymour, and St. John becoming Secretary at War. From 1704 to 1708 the Harleians and Churchills coöperated, simultaneously fighting off the attacks of their former Tory associates and the shrewder attacks of their future Whig allies. In 1708 the Whig groups at last won their battle for office, and the Harleians were dismissed. Refusing to concede the necessity of alliance with the Junto, Harley had intrigued against his colleagues, trying first to undermine the moderate Whigs who entered the government after 1705, then to supplant Marlborough and Godolphin themselves. Driven finally into opposition, the Harleians rejoined the Church Tories, and for two years the three wings of the Country Party were once again united.

Unanimity in opposition did not signify a united Tory party, however, and the alliance again broke up in 1710. The fall of the Godolphin ministry and its disastrous defeat in the general election was engineered by Harley, with the help of numerous allies — Tory, Church, and Country groups of every shade, disaffected Whigs, Court peers who recognized a bandwagon, and, above all, a sovereign alienated from the Churchills. Yet only a fraction of these groups supported the new government. The new ministry was Harley's own creation and was staffed mainly with his satellites. Harley, in fact, occupied much the same position as the Churchills had held in 1702. His government, like Godolphin's, could rely at first only upon the chief minister's personal following plus the government Members and a number of oligarchic groups like Newcastle's and Somerset's. To be effective it needed the cooperation of the other Tory groups, but this Harley could never obtain. Rochester and his followers enlisted, but most of the Nottingham wing refused. Allying with the Whigs the Nottingham Tories opposed the peace and the commercial treaty with France and showed themselves increasingly hostile to the ministry, which, under Bolingbroke's leadership, seemed bent on setting aside the Act of Succession. For thus bolting the government and rallying to the Hanoverian cause Nottingham's group of

"Whimsicals" was rewarded upon the accession of George I, and their leader ended his political career as Lord President in a ministry overwhelmingly Whig.

Another cause of Tory dissension arose from the uncompromising Toryism of certain young Members, first returned in 1710. Organized in the "October Club" these newcomers pressed for extremist measures and rebelled against Rochester and Harley as too lukewarm. For a while they found a leader in Bolingbroke, but their hopes of a Tory millennium were blasted by the Queen's death. The existence of this group furnishes one more evidence of the lack of harmony among Tories, of the difficulty of forging a Tory party from the separate blocs led by individual Tory chieftains. Surely the record shows that the Churchill, Rochester, Nottingham, Harley, and St. John Tories were distinct groups which could never successfully be merged into a united party. The Tory Members made up approximately a quarter of the House, but this segment, we submit, was not a party but a collection of smaller Tory segments, ranging from the Churchill bloc, which was less closely identified with its Tory associates than it was with the Court, to the independent Members who voted with the other Tory groups only when these were in opposition and who were thus more "Country" than "Tory." Somewhere in between came the Harleians, the bloc which started as Whig, adopted the Country program, and ended by following a course of action which was only a little more "Tory" and less "Court" than that of the Churchills. The two remaining Tory blocs, marked by less deviation from "true Toryism," formed the heart of the Tory aggregate; and one could make out a case for a Tory party composed of the Rochester and Nottingham groups. Such a party, numbering well under a hundred members and thus a much smaller group than the Tory party of Mr. Feiling, would nonetheless be a coalition rather than a party, for we have seen how these two groups during several important periods divided against each other. The record of the Tory groups, in other words, seems to prove our hypothesis. The Tory segment of Parliament was not a party but an aggregation of at least four distinct blocs organized under individual leaders and intent on pursuing independent policies rather than joining in a common Tory course of action.

The concept of a united Tory party does not stand the test of detailed analysis, but perhaps the theory of a united Whig party will fare better. Certainly the Whigs possessed a more consistent and better formulated philosophy. In their attitude toward the Revolution, toward the Protestant Dissenters, and toward the commercial interest the Whigs were fairly well agreed, in contrast to the Tories who could never unite on a formula for reconciling their conflicting loyalties to Church and King. Moreover in the five lords of the Junto the Whigs had a leadership far more unified than the loose confederacy which at different times included different Tory chieftains. Before we assume that all the Whig Members followed the Junto leaders, however, we must make as thorough an analysis of the Whig segment of Parliament as we made of the Tory segment. In view of our previous findings we should expect to discover a number of Whig groups — a nucleus of Whig stalwarts flanked by other Whig groups allied more closely with the Country or the Court. That the Junto group formed the Whig nucleus seems indisputable, but other important questions remain. How many Members could the Junto muster, and how was their following held together — by modern methods of party organization, or by family and personal relationships, as was the case with the Tory groups? For the answers to these questions we must examine the electoral interests and parliamentary following of the Junto leaders: Somers, Orford, Halifax, Wharton, and the younger Sunderland.

The careers and personalities of the Junto lords have often been described, but their parliamentary influence has never been given the detailed treatment it deserves. From the point of view of parliamentary influence, John, Lord Somers, was the least important. Son of a Worcestershire attorney Somers used his great talents to win brilliant success at the Bar. Entering Parliament he became one of the leading Whig statesmen, ultimately attaining the office of Lord Chancellor; but lacking noble connections and large estates his electoral influence was slight. A grant by William III of the manor of Reigate in Surrey gave him control of a seat for that borough; but this was the extent of his electoral interest aside from the natural respect accorded him by the voters of his native Worcester. A distinguished product of the Middle Temple, Somers named two lawyers of that Inn as his candidates for Reigate and Worcester,[41] and counted among his followers other Middle Temple barristers, including his two brothers-in-law, Charles Cocks and Sir Joseph Jekyll. He was on close terms as well with such notable Middle Temple barristers in Parliament as Spencer Compton, later Lord Keeper and Prime Minister; Peter King, later Lord Chancellor; and William Cowper, another future Lord Chancellor. But these men, though friendly, cannot be counted among Somers' followers, since they belonged, as we shall show, to Whig groups outside the Junto's orbit.

[41] Viz. Stephen Harvey, M.P. Reigate, 1698 till death, 1707 (for whom see the anonymous *Memoirs of Lord Somers*, 1716, p. 41; and W. R. Williams, *Welsh Judges*, pp. 112–113); and Thomas Wylde, M.P. Worcester, 1701–27 (for whom see *Middle Temple Records*, III, 1495, and W. R. Williams, *Representative History of Worcestershire*, p. 100).

Somers' influence with the Bar was equaled by Lord Orford's influence with the Navy. Born Edward Russell, Orford was of the ducal house of Bedford; but, younger son of a younger son, he had to make his own way. Entering the navy, he rose soon to high rank, helped by royal favor. A signer of the invitation to William of Orange, Russell accompanied the Prince from Holland to England, and William subsequently rewarded him with an admiral's flag, the lucrative treasurership of the Navy, and after Russell's victory at La Hogue first place at the Admiralty Board and a peerage. In the course of this career Orford built up an important following of naval officers and administrators, many of whom sat in Parliament, occupying seats which they owed originally to Admiralty influence, but which they often retained long after they and their chief left office.[42]

This professional influence was augmented, as Somers' was not, by family connections and landed wealth. An important landowner in the county, and Lord Steward of the borough of Cambridge, Orford usually managed to name one knight for the shire and exercised a lesser influence in the borough.[43] This local influence added less to Orford's importance, however, than the fact that he was "supported by so many relations and strong alliances,"[44] that he was connected with the great Whig houses of Russell, Cavendish, and Manners. Orford was a nephew

[42] Such were Philip Papillon, Orford's secretary and cashier of the Victualling Office, 1693–98, and M.P. for Dover, 1701–20; Admiral Aylmer, Admiralty Lord, 1694–99, 1709–10, and M.P. for Dover, 1697–1713, 1715–20; and Admirals Shovell, Jennings, and Byng, who all held admiralty posts at various times and sat for admiralty boroughs (cf. the articles on these men in the *D.N.B.*).

[43] Cf. "The Representative History of the County, Town, and University of Cambridge," unpubl. thesis by D. Cooke, deposited at the Institute for Historical Research, London.

[44] Arthur Maynwaring to Lady Marlborough, in *The Private Correspondence of Sarah, Duchess of Marlborough*, 2nd ed. (London, 1838), I, 205.

of the first Duke of Bedford and doubly allied, by marriage as well as blood, with the Duke's children. The eldest of these, William, Lord Russell, died on the scaffold for his part in the Rye House Plot, leaving a son who inherited the title. Unfortunately the second Duke strayed from the Whig fold, and until he "recovered from his infatuation" with the Tory leader, Granville, and "returned to the principles of his family," the Bedford interest in Devonshire was lost to the Whigs.[45] The county and borough of Bedford, however, continued to return candidates acceptable to Orford; and the loss of two Devon seats was offset by the electoral interest of two other nephews of Orford, the Marquesses of Hartington and Granby. Their respective fathers, the Dukes of Devonshire and Rutland, were Court Whigs rather than Junto adherents; but they themselves were protégés of Orford and inclined to place their family electoral interest at his disposal, so that Cavendish candidates for Derby and Manners candidates for Leicestershire and Grantham were usually friends of the Junto.

Charles Montague, Lord Halifax, belonged like Orford to one of the leading noble families, but he too was the younger son of a younger son. Choosing politics as a career he soon made his way to the top. Appointed Chancellor of the Exchequer and first Lord of the Treasury, Montague carried through the recoinage, the founding of the Bank, and the funding of the National Debt, showing a talent for finance which won him a peerage and the friendly respect of most of the merchants and bankers in Parliament. The parliamentary influence which Halifax

[45] For the quotation, cf. *Private Correspondence of Lady Marlborough* I, 206; for the Russell interest in Devon, cf. J. J. Alexander's article on "Tavistock as a Parliamentary Borough" in *Devonshire Association Reports*, XLIII, 370–377. Lords Edward, James, and Robert Russell, M.P.'s for Tavistock before 1702, failed to get returned after that date.

enjoyed as a financier was strengthened by the electoral influence of his family. His own branch controlled one seat for Northampton, five miles from their estate at Horton;[46] and the neighboring county of Huntingdon was the preserve of his Montague cousins, the Earls of Manchester and Sandwich. Lord Manchester, head of the Kimbolton Montagues, was a stepson as well as first cousin of Halifax, which meant that the Member returned for Huntingdonshire on the Kimbolton interest was usually a Junto nominee. The other three Huntingdon Members were usually named by the Montagues of Hinchinbrooke, Earls of Sandwich. Their interest, built up by Pepys' boss, the first Lord Sandwich, was supposedly managed in this period by Halifax's cousin, the second Earl; but since he was physically incapacitated, it was taken over by his two closest relatives, who sacrificed Lord Sandwich's influence in county elections by quarreling over the control of Huntingdon borough, just outside the gates of Hinchinbrooke. Here the Earl's mother, Lord Rochester's sister-in-law and a Tory sympathizer, worked successfully to return Tory candidates until 1705, when the Earl's uncle, Sidney Wortley-Montague, taking advantage of his position as trustee and mortgagee of the family estates, ousted mother and son and occupied Hinchinbrooke himself. This turned the balance, and henceforth till the heir's coming-of-age in 1713 Huntingdon was represented by Junto candidates attached to Halifax and set up by Wortley-Montague.[47]

[46] Halifax's brother, Christopher Montague, was M.P. for Northampton, 1695–1702; Halifax's nephew and heir, George Montague, was M.P. for Northampton, 1705–1715 (cf. *Parliamentary Return*).

[47] Cf. Matthew Prior's remark to Lord Manchester, 1700: "My Lady [Sandwich] is gone to Hinchinbrooke, I hear, in order to set up Charles Boyle [her Tory cousin] against Mr. Wortley's interest at Huntingdon" (*Court and Society from Elizabeth to Anne*, edited from the papers at Kimbolton by the Duke of Manchester (London, 1864), II, 85). For Huntingdon elections see the

The electoral interests of Halifax and Orford were extensive, but added together they did not equal Lord Wharton's. Head of a family established in the North in the reign of Edward I, Thomas, fifth Lord Wharton, had inherited large estates in half a dozen counties. In Cumberland and Westmorland the family interest, based on land wrested from the monasteries during the Reformation, was strengthened by the purchase of "burgages"[48] at Cockermouth and Appleby. The Duke of Somerset had the paramount interest at one of these boroughs, and Lord Thanet, at the other; but Wharton could usually win seats for two or three of his friends, particularly at Appleby, where "my Lord Wharton's instrument is a tricking attorney, clerk of the peace, and alehouse keeper all in one."[49] Wharton was equally successful at returning his friends for Richmond and Northallerton in neighboring Yorkshire, boroughs where he had similar interests, based on family estates and the possession of numerous burgages.

In the South Wharton's interests were even more impressive. From his mother he had inherited considerable Buckinghamshire property, and the boroughs of Aylesbury, Wycombe, and Marlow, which bordered upon his estates, inevitably came under his influence. To return candidates for the shire and the remaining Buckinghamshire boroughs was more difficult, but with the assistance of strategically placed henchmen even this was possible. At elections for Buckingham "my Lord Wharton and several others of his Gang appear'd there and made interest,"[50] and usually

account, based on papers at Hinchinbrooke, in *The Victoria History of the County of Huntingdon*, II, 22–38.

[48] A burgage was a piece of property which carried with it a vote in parliamentary elections, a vote at the owner's disposal.

[49] *Hist. MSS. Comm. Reports, Portland MSS.*, IV, 578. See also R. S. Ferguson, *Cumberland and Westmorland M.P.'s, passim.*

[50] *Remarks and Collections of Thomas Hearne*, ed. for the Oxford Historical Society by C. E. Doble, and others, 1885–1918, I, 117. For a revealing light

the thirteen electors returned his Lordship's friends. At Wendover the trick was turned with the help of the Hampdens, whose estates lay close by; while in county elections the "crew that herded with Lord Wharton" [51] helped him return his nominees. Amersham, the pocket borough of a Tory family, was the only Buckinghamshire constituency that resisted his efforts; and Wharton made up for this defeat by successful attempts on Lord Bridgwater's borough of Brackley, close by in Northamptonshire [52] Wiltshire elections tell much the same story, for there, too, Wharton had estates and faithful henchmen. At Malmesbury he named both Members; and by concerting measures with his Wiltshire "gang" he was able to influence elections at Chippenham, Cricklade, and Calne. He lacked the power, unfortunately, to name candidates for the county, but he was always unflagging in his efforts to return gentlemen who were friendly to the Junto, whether standing for Wiltshire or Yorkshire, for Cirencester or Devizes.[53]

The success with which Wharton managed this great amalgam of "interests" was a tribute to his skill no less than to the length of his purse and the excellence of his horses at election time. No such superlative manager was Charles, Lord Spencer, last and youngest of the Junto lords. Heir-apparent of the Earl of Sunderland, he was

---

on Bucks elections cf. *Verney Letters of the Eighteenth Century from the MSS. at Claydon House*, ed. Lady Verney (London, 1930), I, 159 ff.; and the anonymous *Memoirs of the Life of . . . Thomas, Late Marquess of Wharton* (London, 1715).

[51] *Verney Letters*, I, 164.

[52] Cf. Sunderland's remarks to Lady Marlborough, in *Private Correspondence . . .*, I, 35–36.

[53] For Wharton's rôle in Wiltshire elections see the interesting correspondence between Wharton and his friends printed by Lord Lansdowne in his article, "Wiltshire Politicians *circa* 1700" in *The Wiltshire Archeological and Natural History Magazine*, XLVI, 60 ff. Cf. also *Hist. MSS. Comm. Reports, Portland MSS.*, II, 95; IV, 175.

first returned to Parliament upon attaining his majority in 1695. Unlike his father, who was known as the shiftiest courtier of the age, Spencer proved a steady follower of the Junto, zealous even to rashness. A bibliophile and a classicist he affected a patrician republicanism, but he was no dilettante in politics and was soon accepted by the Junto as one of themselves. In 1702 he succeeded as third Earl of Sunderland and inherited considerable electoral influence. His Northamptonshire property gave him some voice in the county elections, but the oppositon of the High Church gentry was usually too much for him. In Coventry in Warwickshire he had a better interest, based on alliance with the wealthy and influential Hopkins family, who helped him win some notoriously turbulent elections there.[54] The twenty-six corporators of Tiverton in Devon were more easily managed. Having returned Spencer from his coming-of-age till his removal to the Lords, they continued to return Junto candidates, apparently charmed by the young Earl, who presented the town with a "large Fire Engine."[55]

The electioneering of Spencer and the other Junto lords was remarkably successful. Usually they managed to return some forty-five to fifty Members, but this did not constitute the whole of their following. We must also take into account the nominees of Bolton, who was practically a sixth member of the Junto. Charles Powlett,[56] second Duke of Bolton, was head of a great landed family settled

[54] Cf. "Memoirs of Edward Hopkins," comprising selections from his MS. autobiography, edited by M. D. Harris, in the *English Historical Review*, XXXIV (1919), 495 ff.; also T. W. Whitley, *The Parliamentary Representation of the City of Coventry* (Coventry, 1894), pp. 110–146.

[55] Cf. W. Harding's *History of Tiverton* (Tiverton, 1847), vol. II, book iii, p. 224.

[56] The name is spelt variously "Paulet," "Pawlett," "Poulett," "Powlett," &c. For sketches of various members of the family see the articles in the *D.N.B.*

in Hampshire since the time of Henry VII. His broad estates Bolton owed chiefly to his ancestor William Powlett, a Tudor politician who was rewarded with huge grants of monastic land by Henry VIII, managed to stay in favor under Edward VI, Bloody Mary, and Elizabeth, and ended his career as Lord Treasurer and Marquess of Winchester. A later Marquess of Winchester won fame in the next century by his heroic defense of Basing, the family seat, which was finally razed by Cromwell after a celebrated three-year siege. His successor was neither a Loyalist nor a Catholic, like his father. A follower of Shaftesbury, he avoided trouble during James' reign by counterfeiting insanity, conveniently regaining his senses in time to support William of Orange, who made him a Privy Councillor and Duke of Bolton. This eccentric peer was succeeded in 1699 by his son Charles, who as "Marquess of Winchester" had served a political apprenticeship of eighteen years as Member for Hampshire plus a year as a Lord Justice in Ireland. A close friend of the Junto lords he proved to be a valuable associate. In alliance with a local Whig family he controlled the Hampshire borough of Lymington. At Winchester, Whitchurch, Petersfield, and Andover in the same county, and at St. Ives in Cornwall, he recommended Members with considerable success; and he could usually count on securing one or both seats for the county.[57]

Two peers less closely identified with the Junto than Bolton should also be included as Junto allies. Charles, head of the Naworth Howards and third Earl of Carlisle, frequently coöperated with Wharton and Sunderland,

[57] Evidence for Bolton's electoral interest is largely indirect; but we can identify three Powletts, two kinsmen, and a number of political henchmen of Bolton among the M.P.'s for these constituencies. At Lymington the case is clear; cf. Sidney Burrard, *Annals of Walhampton* (London, 1874), particularly the letter from Paul Burrard to Lord William Powlett, printed on p. 31.

helping them to return Junto candidates for Yorkshire, Cumberland, and Westmorland; and Carlisle's nominees at Morpeth, the family borough in Northumberland, and at Carlisle, where the Earl was Governor and had electoral influence, usually included important Junto henchmen as well as the inevitable Howards.[58] In the same way we can identify Junto Whigs — Somers' brother-in-law, for example — among the Members for the Cornwallis' pocket borough of Eye in Suffolk,[59] indicating that Charles, fourth Lord Cornwallis, was likewise an ally of the Junto. Finally we must add to the dozen Members returned by Bolton, Carlisle, and Cornwallis at least six Yorkshire Members who had seats of their own and required little help from the Junto, who but acted and voted with the Junto group as consistently as the regular Junto nominees.[60]

This whole following of nominees and allies the Junto managed to hold together by constant and effective effort. Leading members of the group and their friends met constantly at one another's houses and at the Kit Cat Club, a convivial gathering of *littérateurs*, politicians, and wits. The chief significance of the Kit Cat was social rather than political, however; for in addition to the Junto leaders it included aristocrats who were noted for conviviality and a lack of interest in politics, as well as politicians who were not identified with the Junto. Marlborough and Godol-

[58] For Carlisle's electoral influence cf. *Hist. MSS. Comm. Reports, Carlisle MSS.*, pp. 15–30; Ferguson's *Cumberland and Westmorland M.P.'s*; and W. W. Bean, *Parliamentary Representation of the Six Northern Counties of England* (Hull, 1890), pp. 53, 540–563.

[59] Cornwallis bought the Honor, castle, and borough of Eye in 1698. Cf. W. A. Copinger, *Suffolk Records and MSS.* (London, 1904), II, 343.

[60] Detailed documentation is impossible in a footnote. It is certain, however, that such Yorks M.P.'s as Sir Wm. Strickland, Sir Wm. St. Quintin, Sir Chas. Hotham, and at least three others, followed the Junto and were given places by the Junto Lords.

phin, for example, at one time belonged, as did the courtier Somerset.[61] Included also were representatives of a large and important group which stood midway between the Junto and the Court. It is this group which we must examine next.

Up to this point we have narrowed our discussion of the Whigs in order to show how the Junto managed to secure the election of some sixty Members, bound to them through personal ties. We have suggested that these Members formed the backbone of the Whig segment of Parliament, but we cannot ignore the existence of other Whig blocs. Continuing our analysis we can identify a number of important Whigs who were not tied into the Junto network, but were connected instead through a common relationship with the Duke of Newcastle. Included are: Newcastle's second cousin, Lord Rockingham, who had two members of his family in Parliament; his first cousin, the Marquess of Dorchester, who also had two relatives in the House; his brother-in-law, Sir Thomas Pelham; and Lord Townshend, who married Pelham's daughter, the Duke's niece. All of them had political influence; all were allied with Newcastle and the Court and, to a lesser extent, with the Junto Whigs; but Pelham and Townshend were easily the most important.

Sir Thomas Pelham, the fourth Baronet, headed a prominent family which had electoral interests in Sussex. At their borough of Lewes, and at Seaford, Hastings, and Rye the Pelhams had sufficient influence to effect the return of five Members; and they usually managed to keep one of the seats for Sussex in the family.[62] Pelham's electoral interest in Sussex was exceeded, however, by the

[61] For a list of members cf. Oldmixon's *History of England*, III, 478–479. For the best account of the Kit Cat cf. R. J. Allen's *Clubs of Augustan London* (Cambridge, Harvard University Press), 1933, pp. 33–54, 230–250.

[62] For an excellent account of the Pelhams' interest in Sussex cf. S. H.

influence which his son-in-law Townshend enjoyed in Norfolk. As the only peer of any consequence in Norfolk and for thirty years its Lord Lieutenant, Charles, second Viscount Townshend, naturally influenced elections in that county, particularly at Norwich and Yarmouth. He was closely connected, moreover, with the Walpoles, the one family that had a comparable interest in Norfolk elections. Inheriting the title as a child, Townshend had Robert Walpole's father for a guardian. He and young Walpole were together at Eton and King's College, Cambridge, and their early association developed into a friendship which was strengthened by Townshend's subsequent marriage to Walpole's sister.

In 1698, soon after Townshend took his seat in the Lords, Walpole unexpectedly became head of his family and left college to enter politics, abandoning all thought of the Church, for which, as a younger son, he had originally been destined. Entering Parliament was the first step and an easy one, for the Walpoles had a choice of seats in Norfolk. At Castle Rising, a borough which belonged originally to the Dukes of Norfolk, the Walpoles had bought an interest which gave them control of one, and later, both seats. Walpole's father represented Castle Rising from the Revolution to his death, and Walpole took his place in the last Parliament of William III, handing on the seat to his uncle Horatio Walpole when he himself became Member for King's Lynn in the next Parliament. This large seaport Walpole was to represent for some forty years, together with his brother-in-law, Sir Charles Turner, head of an influential family of Lynn merchants. Turner's uncle had represented Lynn ever since 1679, and he, since 1695. The retirement of the elder

---

Nulle, *Thomas Pelham-Holles, Duke of Newcastle: His Early Political Career, 1693–1724* (Univ. of Penn. Press, 1931), chapters 1 and 3.

Turner in 1702 opened the way for another member of the family, and Walpole was elected. Thereafter, until Sir Charles Turner's death and Walpole's removal to the Lords, the brothers-in-law never failed of reëlection.

Walpole and Townshend together dominated Norfolk politics,[63] but Walpole's friends and followers were not all Norfolk men. At Westminster he was soon closely associated with a group of influential Members. Henry Boyle, younger brother of the Earl of Burlington, Chancellor of the Exchequer and later Secretary of State; Lord Coningsby, Harley's great rival in Herefordshire and a perennial officeholder; and John Smith of Hampshire, Speaker of the House, 1705–08, were the oldest members of this circle. The others were contemporaries of Walpole. Spencer Compton, brother of the Tory Earl of Northampton and later Earl of Wilmington, and William Pulteney, protégé of a rich politician who left him a fortune and a seat in Parliament, were close friends of Walpole in Anne's reign, though both became famous later as opponents of Sir Robert.[64] Lord Hartington was one of the group for a time, and in 1702 Walpole gave him a seat at Castle Rising; but Hartington was the nephew of a Junto lord and followed Orford's lead rather than the course set by Walpole and his friends.[65] Even without Hartington,

[63] For the influence of the Townshend and Walpole families cf. *The Letters of Humphrey Prideaux to John Ellis*, Camden Soc. Publ., new series, XV (1875), 166–200, *passim*. For Townshend's electoral interest, *Hist. MSS. Comm. Reports, Townshend MSS.*, pp. 329–340. For Walpole's and the Turners', H. L. Bradfer-Lawrence's essays on "Castle Rising and the Walpoles" and "The Merchants of Lynn," in *A Supplement to Blomefield's Norfolk*, edited and published by Clement Ingleby (London), 1929.

[64] Cf. the *D.N.B.* articles on these men, and Walpole's early correspondence in William Coxe's *Memoirs of the Life and Administration* of Sir Robert Walpole (London, 1798), II, 1–10.

[65] Marlborough calls Hartington "a very honest man", but goes on to say that "lord Orford has too much power with him." Cf. Marlborough's letter to his wife, printed in William Coxe's *Memoirs of John Duke of Marlborough, with his Original Correspondence*, 2nd ed. (London, 1820), IV, 365.

Walpole and his five associates exercised an influence out of all proportion to their numbers. Members of the Pelham and Townshend delegations looked to them for leadership, and other related groups followed suit. Together with Walpole and his friends they made up a bloc which functioned almost as effectively as the Junto Whigs.

Most historians who have written of the Whig party assume that there was no distinction between the Junto and the Walpole-Townshend Whigs. In analyzing the composition of the two groups we have already discovered certain obvious differences. If we should find that they differed as well over parliamentary tactics, repeatedly refusing to coöperate, we might well conclude that the Junto and Walpole-Townshend Whigs were distinct. We cannot follow the political manoeuvres and alliances of the Whig blocs, however, without dealing briefly with the so-called "Country Whigs." The name gives a somewhat misleading picture of this very miscellaneous group. It did include a number of independent Members who distrusted the Court and never held office; but the most prominent "Country Whigs" were quite willing to take office, and equally willing to accept a seat in Parliament from some friendly peer. Sir Peter King and Sir John Hawles were perhaps the leading members of the group; and Hawles sat for a long string of pocket boroughs, including Old Sarum and three little Cornish constituencies, while King owed his seat to Lord Stamford. At Stamford's borough of Bere Alston King's colleague was William Cowper, a Whig of the same stripe. Another of the group was Sir Richard Onslow, who usually represented Surrey, a county in which he enjoyed an influence comparable to Pelham's in Sussex, but was quite willing to take refuge in a small Cornish borough.

The careers of these men are a curious commentary on

the "Country Whigs." Onslow was a Treasury Lord under William, Speaker of the House under Anne, and Chancellor of the Exchequer under George I, who made him a peer. Cowper was made Lord Chancellor by Anne and re-appointed by George, who made him an earl. His successor on the woolsack was Sir Peter King, who became Recorder of London in Anne's reign and then a judge. The least famous was Sir John Hawles, and he reached the office of Solicitor-General, which he filled for seven years under William III. "Country Whig" seems a curious term for these men; but there is some justification. On any issue that clearly lined up Court and Country against each other, they sided with the Country Members, or at most were persuaded by their friends in office to abstain from voting.[66] Furthermore the group as a whole cared very little for party discipline, whether imposed by the Junto lords or by Walpole's group. This made them satisfactory compromise candidates for office, for when the Court, the Junto, and the Walpole Whigs could not agree on an appointment, they often compromised on some Country Whig. Such compromises were not uncommon, for the Whig groups were frequently at odds. A brief history of the Whigs will serve, perhaps, to make this clear.

The Whig party was largely Shaftesbury's creation, and under his leadership it enjoyed a brief period of success, only to be routed by Charles II in 1681. The seven years of conspiracy and crisis which followed nearly wrecked the Whigs, but they were saved by Charles' successor. By alienating every important group James paved the way for William. The Revolution of 1688 could not have succeeded without the help of the Tories, but they

[66] Cf. Cowper's account of his efforts in 1706 to induce leading Country Whigs to forego opposition to a clause revoking certain sections of the Act of Settlement, particularly one barring placemen from the House (*The Private Diary of William Lord Cowper* (Roxburgh Club), London, 1823, pp. 10–11).

played their part reluctantly; and of course it was the enthusiastic Whigs who gained by the new régime, for 1688 gave them a platform and a monarch that they considered their own. On fundamentals the Whigs were agreed, but not until 1694 did they develop a unified leadership and persuade William to give them a real share in the government. By that time the Junto lords had perfected their organization and gained office. For three or four years they managed domestic affairs with great success, only to be driven from the government by a powerful combination of opposition Country Members, Harleians, and Church Tories. There followed a succession of shifting coalitions, as William turned to the Rochester Tories and then to various Court Whig groups in an effort to find reinforcements for the regular courtiers who were having serious difficulties with Parliament; but he was still searching for a satisfactory combination when he died.

With the accession of Anne the task of managing Parliament fell to Marlborough and Godolphin. For the necessary allies they turned first to Rochester and Nottingham, and then to Harley; but we have already seen how difficult and eventually impossible it was for them to rely on these groups. After two or three stormy sessions the Church Tories left the ministry and went into opposition. Their place was taken by Harley and his friends, but the Churchills still lacked a majority. If the government was to survive it must enlist support from the Whig part of the House. In general the Whig Members approved the Churchills' conduct of the war, their proposal for a union with Scotland, and especially their dismissal of Rochester and Nottingham; but this did not mean that every Whig group was anxious to join the ministry, nor that the Churchills wanted all of them as allies.

The groups that stood nearest the Court were enlisted

first, and in 1705 the Churchills began with Newcastle. By making the Duke Lord Privy Seal and by finding places for his cousin Rockingham and his brother-in-law Pelham the support of Newcastle's important group was secured. This gave the Churchills a link with the Townshend-Walpole group, who were soon brought into the coalition. Henry Boyle, Chancellor of the Exchequer at the end of William's reign, had been kept on by Godolphin, together with Somerset and the Court Whig Devonshire. Boyle was now joined by his friend Walpole, who took a place at the Admiralty; and half a year later two more of the group took their place with him. A coalition of Court and Whig Members in the new House managed to elect Jack Smith as Speaker and Spencer Compton as Chairman of the important Committee of Privileges and Elections. For the next three years these gentlemen did yeoman service, and when Harley and his friends broke with the government they got their reward. Boyle succeeded Harley as Secretary, Smith took Boyle's place at the Exchequer, and Walpole succeeded St. John as Secretary of War. At the same time Compton got a place at Court, Coningsby and his father-in-law were made Privy Councillors, and Townshend, who had already been made a Privy Councillor, was now sent on an important mission to Holland. By 1708 every one of Walpole's group had been given office by Marlborough and Godolphin.

There was no such close coöperation between the Churchills and the Junto. The Junto leaders were quite willing to lend their support in return for a major share in the government, but their terms were refused. The Queen disliked them, and Marlborough distrusted their partisan tactics; so the Court kept them at arm's length, hoping to secure their unwilling support by playing them off against Harley. In this they were not unsuccessful, for the Junto lent their support to Smith, Compton, and Cowper, none of whom were Junto Whigs, in order to keep Harley's friends out of the Chair of the House and the Committee of Elections and, above all, off the woolsack to which they had hoped to elevate Somers. Support from the Junto, begun in this reluctant fashion, also enabled the government to carry through supply and particularly the Regency Bill, which set up a provisional government to take charge automatically on the Queen's death and govern until the arrival of the Hanoverian successor. For this assistance the Junto demanded a place in the ministry, and after a titanic struggle they did get Sunderland made Secretary of State. They had to be given a real share, as well, in framing the Union with Scotland. Nine of the Junto leaders were included in the commission and were largely responsible for the framing of the Treaty and its passage through Parliament. In return they demanded a larger share in the government, but failed to get it. Sunderland remained their sole representative in the ministry, and it is doubtful if he would have been included had he not been Marlborough's son-in-law.

With the dismissal of Harley in 1708 the Junto redoubled their pressure on Godolphin, threatening to oppose him absolutely, if their demands were not met. On occasion they made good their threats, opposing the Court in the 1708 Scottish elections and leading an attack on the Admiralty, which was run by Marlborough's brother. By such means they finally got the Presidency of the Council for Somers, and Ireland for Wharton; but they did not capture the Admiralty for Orford until late in 1709, and they never did get an important post for Halifax. Throughout this struggle for office they received very little help from Walpole's group, whom they nicknamed "Treasurer's Whigs." They accused the Court of trying "to make Mr. Smith and Lord Coningsby, &c. great men among the

Whigs," who normally "would never consider them at all," but "fall naturally under their old leaders" of the Junto.[67] Coningsby, on the other hand, explained to George I that the moderate Whigs "under the influence of Lord Carlton [Henry Boyle], Mr. Smith then Chancellor of the Exchequer, and myself, had carried on the publick business with the greatest success, in opposition to the wild embroilments attempted by the Junto."[68]

Under the circumstances the storm of religious and Tory enthusiasm which the government brought down on its head in 1710 by impeaching Dr. Sacheverell found the Whigs sadly divided. Refusing to stand together, they fell one by one before Harley's shrewd attacks. In secret favor with the Queen and already allied with Shrewsbury, Newcastle, Somerset, and other important Court peers, Harley managed to keep the Treasurer's Whigs at odds with the Junto and drive the Junto leaders from office. When it had become too late to make a stand, the Churchills were removed, together with the Walpole Whigs, who were treated with significant tenderness until all efforts to attach them to Harley's government proved vain. Eventually all the Whig groups joined in opposition to Harley, and for the last years of the reign they were admirably united; but Whig unity, like Tory unity, seldom survived a return to power. Back in office under George I, the Whigs divided again. Walpole and Townshend, backed by the Pelhams, quarreled with Sunderland, the only Junto lord alive in 1716 and the acknowledged leader of the Junto Members as well as the important connection built up by Sunderland's father-in-law, the Duke of Marlborough. For six years the Whig party was torn by the struggle between these two groups.

67 *Private Corresp. of Lady Marlborough*, I, 152.

68 "Lord Coningsby's Account of Parties, 1702–15," British Museum, *Lansdowne MSS.* 885, f. 62.

Walpole, of course, was the victor. Become chief minister he proceeded to build up the formidable coalition of government and Whig supporters through which he ruled for twenty years, leaving it virtually intact for his allies, the first Pelham Duke of Newcastle and his brother.

It has been possible to get a fairly clear picture of the Whig groups, but the fourth and last segment of Parliament admits of no such satisfactory analysis. Nearly two hundred Members in the average House of Commons were unconnected with the peerage, the Court, or the various organized Whig and Tory groups. Landed gentry, some of them were shire-knights sent up to Westminster by the local squirearchy, while others sat for their own private boroughs. Both types looked upon attendance at the House as an honorary and not very important duty, and they frequently missed divisions, seldom spoke, and played almost no part in ordinary parliamentary business. In their politics they ranged from Country Whig to Country Tory, a few more active Members at one extreme voting with the Whigs, so long as they steered clear of the Court, while those at the other extreme gave the Tories the same qualified support. Comprising perhaps a fourth of the Country Members, they acted as a make-weight. When the organized party groups joined with the government, they lost the votes of their Country supporters while gaining allies from the Court; regaining their Country following when they lost their Court allies and left the government. The rest of the Country Members were not so active. Lacking any organization or leadership worthy of the name they left the work of government to the politicians, rousing themselves only rarely to vote against some ministry rash enough to tamper with the economic system or fundamental "Old English" institutions like the Church.

Our survey of parliamentary groups concluded, we can restate our original hypothesis. The English House of Commons was divided not into two parties, but into four major segments: Country, Whig, Tory, and Court. Each of these segments was composed in turn of groups of stalwarts together with various border-groups. It is possible, in other words, to read the roster of party groups as though we were boxing the compass: courtiers, Court Tories, Churchill Tories, Harley Tories, Rochester Tories, Nottingham Tories, October Club Tories, Country Tories, Country Members, Country Whigs, Junto Whigs, Walpole-Townshend Whigs, Court Whigs, and so back to the courtiers. The architects of parliamentary majorities worked within this framework, seeking to combine as many allied groups as possible. Godolphin started with a Court-Churchill-Harley-Rochester-Nottingham coalition, and ended eight years later with a Churchill-Court-Townshend-Walpole-Junto combination. Examples could be multiplied, but the general interpretation must be fairly clear. Party organization in the period 1688–1714 has been explained so often in terms of the two-party system that the many striking similarities between it and the later eighteenth-century political structure have been overlooked. Yet we venture to say that the description of party organization under William and Anne which Trevelyan suggested in his Romanes Lectures on the two-party system is less applicable to our period than the detailed picture of eighteenth-century politics which emerges from Professor Namier's volumes on the Age of Newcastle.[69]

[69] Cf. G. M. Trevelyan, *The Two-Party System in English Political History* (Oxford, 1926); and L. B. Namier, *The Structure of Politics at the Accession of George III*, 2 vols. (London, 1929); and *England in the Age of the American Revolution*, 2 vols. (London, 1930).

ROBERT WALCOTT, JR.

SOME SIDELIGHTS UPON THE GENERAL ELECTION OF 1715[1]

HISTORIANS have consistently ignored one of the most interesting and significant general elections in eighteenth-century Britain. Some half-dozen of the more detailed accounts of the period devote only a page or two each to this election, which fortified the position of the Hanoverian dynasty and fastened the Whigs' grip upon political power for more than half a century. Only certain aspects of the election, and those in but a few shires and boroughs, can be discussed here. This will be done, — with the aid of the English periodical,[2] a source hitherto generally neglected in such studies, — in an attempt to recreate the atmosphere in which appeals to the country were held in the early eighteenth century.

At her accession the invalid Queen endeavored to reign with the help of Tory ministers, whose position was strengthened by the election of 1702. Their power was reduced by the election three years later which paved the way for the admission of some moderate Whigs into the Ministry. Marlborough's continued diplomatic and military successes increased the pressure of the Whig Junto, who, early in 1708, encompassed the dismissal of Robert Harley, the moderate Tory leader. Ministerial changes, coupled with the abortive Jacobite expedition of 1708, produced considerable Whig gains at the election in May

[1] The preparation of this article was made possible by grants-in-aid from the Social Science Research Council and Indiana University.

[2] Miss Mary Ransome's interesting article on "The Press in the General Election of 1710" (*Cambridge Historical Journal*, 1939) devotes less than two pages to periodical materials. Usually the numbers of periodicals are given; when they are not numbered, or in case the number refers to more than one issue, the dates are given, which range from October, 1714 to April, 1715.

of that year. The Junto immediately increased its representation in the Ministry, which presently became almost entirely Whig, except for its head, the Earl of Godolphin. The Whig leaders then went too far, in forcing the hand of the Queen, who was highly reluctant to admit into her councils men whom she suspected of harboring designs against her prerogative, if not against the monarchy itself. These leaders made their fatal misstep when they impeached the fatuous Dr. Henry Sacheverell for his sermon attacking the doctrines underlying the Glorious Revolution of 1688.

Harley, one of the shrewdest political managers the English race has produced, quickly sensed his opportunity in Sacheverell's prosecution. The clergy considered it a personal attack upon their order, and this would certainly awaken misgivings in the mind of a Queen so deeply devoted to her Church. With the whole-hearted assistance of the Tory Highfliers, the clergy and the Queen were thoroughly aroused. Relying upon the latter, Harley displaced the leading Whigs in the Ministry, and finally ousted even the moderate Tory, Godolphin; while his appeal to the Anglican clergy helped produce a Tory landslide in the election of 1710.

The new ministerial leader soon discovered that it was easier to secure the support of the Tory zealots, than to control them. Meanwhile he endeavored to make as much capital out of negotiating a peace, as the Whigs had made in waging a successful war against the most powerful monarch in the world. Facing attacks from the Highfliers, from the Whigs and from the Allies who resented his under-handed attempts at peace-making, he prevailed over all of them, not only in making a peace with France, but in securing its ratification by Parliament.

From that time onward Harley, now Earl of Oxford,

lost power, partly because of the jealousy of his colleague, Henry St. John, Viscount Bolingbroke, partly because of his own declining physical powers. He was unable, or unwilling, to secure Parliamentary sanction for the commercial clauses of the Treaty of Utrecht. The Queen's health was declining even more rapidly than his own; the Pretender was taking fresh courage; and the Hanoverian dynasty was displaying increasing petulance towards him. Although the election of 1713 was a Tory victory, the Whigs regained some of the ground lost three years before. The Tories in the Commons now began to show a preference for the more dashing policy of Bolingbroke, the statesman who had already bought off Lady Masham — formerly Oxford's other pair of ears in dealing with the Queen. This female favorite helped turn the tiring sovereign against Oxford and he was compelled to resign.

The *coup d'état* of 1714 still remains to be explained. A definitive account of it cannot, in truth, be written until the pamphlets and periodicals have been more carefully studied. The final weeks of the reign were nerve-racking to the Tory ministers. Whether any of them actually planned the restoration of the Stuarts, cannot yet be stated with any degree of certainty. For our present purpose, it does not matter. What matters a great deal, however, is that the Whig Leaders, convinced that the Tories were making such preparations, acted accordingly. The most curious fact about the *coup d'état* is that the initiative, which should have rested with the Ministry in power, was seized by the Whigs.

Once in the saddle, the Whig leaders never looked back. During the weeks prior to the arrival of George I, the key men of the late ministry were either laid aside, or ignored. Sir Robert Walpole, a Whig, became Paymaster General, "to get some meat on his bones," as the replacing of Tories by Whigs in various administrative posts went rapidly forward. Whether the new sovereign ever seriously contemplated a coalition Ministry is extremely doubtful, although it was reported that Sir Thomas Hanmer and William Bromley declined important posts.[3] In order better to supervise preparations for the forthcoming election of George I's first Parliament, the Whigs saw to it that Charles, Viscount Townshend immediately displaced Bolingbroke as Secretary of State. The new reign also brought to an end the tenure of the lords lieutenants, places of great dignity and of some importance in the elections, which for the most part were now filled with Whig dignitaries. Likewise, the selection of sheriffs for the ensuing year was hurried on, for they acted as returning officers for the shires, and handled the precepts for the borough elections.

The pamphlets and periodicals of these months clearly suggest that the Whigs were seriously alarmed over the possibility of a Jacobite reaction, and the "Fifteen" proves that their fears were well founded. The Whigs, indeed, had ample reasons to expect the worst. A nearly contemporary writer described the tenseness of feeling:

> "There never was a Juncture, within the Memory of any who are now living, when the Rage of Parties ran higher than at this Time . . ., and, consequently, there never was a Time when public Interest suffered more from the Spirit of Party." [4]

One recent writer has also wisely observed:

> "For three-quarters of a century before 1714, England had been a byword for political instability. She

[3] See W. Coxe, *Memoirs of . . . Robert Walpole* (London, 1798), II, 47–49.

[4] *Memoirs of the Life and Ministerial Conduct of . . . Bolingbroke* (London, 1752), p. 280.

had passed through the crucible of Civil War, executed her King, abolished and then restored the monarchical government, expelled the restored dynasty and repudiated its hereditary right to the throne, and placed first a Dutch and then a German sovereign on a throne held by a purely Parliamentary title."[5]

This feeling is also clearly revealed by the broadsides and ballads in the weeks immediately before and after George I's accession, and caused the Government, whether Whig or Tory, to carry on an active prosecution of daring journalists and pamphleteers.[6]

Throughout this exciting period the Whig leaders displayed more foresight than their rivals. In addition to preparing for the elections, they surrounded George I with advisers, who saw to it that their foreign-born monarch should reign rather than govern. They capitalized the King's ignorance and inexperience, in order the more quickly to establish cabinet government — in other words to carry out to their logical conclusion the principles inherent in the Revolution Settlement. For the moment, however, everything hinged upon their success at the polls.

The fate not only of the Revolution, the Protestant Succession, and the Union with Scotland, but — what was far more important to the Whig leaders — the immediate future of their party seemed to be at stake. The mercantile interests behind the Whigs were deeply concerned, for another Stuart restoration might mean the end of the Bank, and of some of the leading joint-stock companies. The Highfliers regarded these great corporations as Whig institutions, definitely in league with the stock-jobbers,

[5] D. L. Keir, *Constitutional History of Modern Britain* (London, 1938), p. 288.
[6] *Monitor*, No. 2.

who had nicely feathered their own nests during the quarter century of war, while the Tory aristocracy was being bled white by the land tax. Whig merchants and manufacturers, on their side, still reflected with horror upon how narrowly they had escaped disaster through the commercial clauses of the Treaty of Utrecht, which they considered a knock-out blow aimed at Whig interests by the Tory landed aristocracy.

Whig writers argued eloquently that only anarchy would result from a Tory triumph at the polls, accompanied by their complete subjection to Louis XIV, should the Pretender be restored by French arms. Britain, they urged, would become a political and economic satellite of France. A Tory triumph, in short, would mean Popery and wooden shoes. The late Tory Ministry, they continued, had almost succeeded in selling England out to the French, and were only prevented by the defeat of the commercial clauses, and the providential death of the Queen. They urged, furthermore, that a restoration spelled humiliation for the Anglican clergy, disgrace for their wives, bastardy for their children, and the end of the Church of England.[7]

The Tories in turn insisted that a Whig victory would bring about the extinction of the Established Church as then understood, for the King was at heart either a Lutheran, or a Calvinist. If the former, his Lutheranism might mean, because of its similarity to Catholicism, the return of England to the Roman fold; if the latter, his Calvinism might cement an alliance with the Dissenters and Low Churchmen. In either case the end would be put to all the authority and dignity which surrounded the Church. Dr. Francis Atterbury, Bishop of Rochester, prophetically insisted that this was Toryism's last chance, unless it

[7] *Flying-Post*, Nos. 3531, 3584. See also Steele's *Crisis* (Dublin, 1714), p. 64.

capitalized its opportunities to the uttermost.[8] The High-Church Tory leaders were quite successful in arousing the fears of the country clergy, who were mainly of the Laudian persuasion. Sacheverell was once more their hero, but they found to their cost that he was a horse that had run superbly well once, but was not likely to keep the course a second time. Whig journalists meanwhile made Sacheverell the spearhead of their attack upon the Jacobites and Highfliers, whom they always bracketed together.[9]

The Whigs complained of the action of the late Ministry in spreading rumors that the Church was in danger, while at the same time they abandoned the Protestant interest everywhere in Europe in favor of France, welcomed such Jacobite emissaries as Sir Patrick Lawless at St. James's, and even allowed Dr. Thomas Brett to preach Popish doctrines before the Queen.

> "'Tis plain, that this clamour is rais'd and spread to influence the next election for members of Parliament, and such members may be returned as will hang on the wheels of his Majesty's administration, as the faction did in the reign of King William; but the eyes of the nation seem in a great measure to be opened, and that London, our capital, has, notwithstanding the intrigues of faction, baffled them in the late choice of a sheriff and lord mayor, 'tis hoped this good example will be universally followed, and that all loyal electors will exert themselves, to choose such as will support his Majesty's title, and demand justice (as some of our noble addressers have already done) upon those who had advanced the enemies of his succession, so high in

[8] *English Advice to the Freeholders of England* (1714).

[9] *Flying-Post*, No. 3589.

power at home and abroad, and nothing but the immediate hand of God could have brought his Majesty to the throne, without a deluge of blood." [10]

Large numbers of loyal addresses were presented to the King from all parts of Britain, and even from Ireland.[11] Although they appear at first sight to have been spontaneous, a closer reading reveals a certain sameness in many of them, both in sentiment and phraseology, which suggests that the majority may have been inspired by the Whig politicians. This impression is greatly strengthened by the mild riots in many places against the new dynasty which served as a sort of epilogue to the Coronation Day ceremonies.[12] At Frome, the disaffected were both clever and bold. They dressed up an "ideot" named George "in a fool's coat, with a hat chalk'd instead of lace, and gave him a wand to carry with a turnip on it." [13]

[10] *Flying-Post*, No. 3551. Brett explicitly denied that he was a Catholic. See *Dr. Brett's Vindication of Himself* . . . (1715).

[11] The number in the Nichols Newspaper Collection at the Bodleian is impressive, and they are especially numerous in the weeks immediately preceding the election. Many have been reprinted in Abel Boyer's *Political State of Great Britain*, VIII, 308–323, *passim*. See also *Flying-Post*, Nos. 3567, 3569.

[12] There were riots, so-called at least, at Bedford, Birmingham, Bristol, Canterbury, Chippenham, Coventry, Frome, Norwich, Reading, Taunton, and several other places. See *Dawks' News Letter* (hereafter cited as "*Dawks*'), *Weekly Packet*, *Evening Post*, and *Flying-Post*, for the fortnight after October 20. The most serious disturbances occurred at Bristol. The Whig Government sent three judges forthwith to try the rioters, several of whom were promptly convicted. *An Historical Account of the affairs of Great Britain* (London, 1714), pp. 95–100. *Post Boy*, No. 3054; *Add. MSS.* (Bodleian) A 269, f. 35; *Flying-Post*, No. 3571. Others concerned in riots elsewhere were brought to Westminster in custody of the King's Messenger. *Dawks*', Nov. 27, 30; *Weekly Packet*, Nos. 124–125; *Ev. Post*, Nos. 829–830; *Polit. State*, VIII, 530. On Coronation day Oxford University conferred, *nem. con.*, the honorary degree of D.C.L. upon Sir Constantine Phipps, whose Jacobite activities as Lord Chancellor of Ireland had been most objectionable. *Weekly Packet*, No. 121. As an aftermath to the Coronation, London witnessed an attack on Reverend Joseph Acres, for his sermons in Whitechapel, lauding William III and Marlborough as the architects of the Revolution. *Flying-Post*, No. 3567; *Annals of King George* (London, 1716), p. 308.

[13] *Flying-Post*, No. 3562.

Judging entirely by the number of these riots, and the attention devoted to them by Whig newspapers, we might conclude that George I was very unpopular, and that the Pretender would have found a warm welcome had he come alone to England and cast himself upon the mercy of the British people. Such a conclusion, though not shared by one recent writer, might not, moreover, be so far from the truth.[14]

These riots were partly responsible for three proclamations issued in November and December: one for suppressing riots; another for enforcing existing laws against Papists and Non-jurors; and a third ordering the clergy to abstain from discussing political affairs in the pulpit.[15] Throughout these trying weeks at the beginning of the reign, the Whig ministers were unusually cautious, as is shown by their careful attention to those suspected of Jacobitism. One little known English periodical frankly commented upon such disloyalty:—

> "There has been a studied concerted design, both by the French abroad, and the faction at home, to subject and betray our country to Popery and Slavery, and an arbitrary Prince, by the bringing in and establishment of that Idol Bastard of theirs, the Pretender." [16]

From the City of Gloucester came a letter attacking the political activity of Jacobite excise officers, who had in

[14] Basil Williams, *Whig Supremacy, 1714–1760* (Oxford, 1939), p. 144. After reading a large number of the pamphlets and periodicals for these years, the writer is compelled to disagree with Professor Williams' conclusion that the majority of the people favored George I over the Pretender. On the basis of the Austrian minister's dispatch from London to Vienna, Professor Wolfgang Michael wrote: "In the summer of 1715, it was estimated that two-thirds of the nation were hostile to the new dynasty." *England under George I* (London, 1936), p. 131.

[15] *London Gazette*, No. 5284; *British Mercury*, No. 488; *Post Boy*, No. 3042; *Histor. Account*, p. 85.

[16] *Patriot*, III, No. xvi.

many cases been appointed by the late Ministry, and asking for the enforcement of 3 & 4 William III, c. 1, which forbade such efforts:

> ". . . its being well-known that those officers have a great influence on maltsters, brewers, distillers, alehouse keepers, &. to vote in electing Parliament-men as they direct them, for fear of vexatious informations and prosecutions by those fellows." [17]

The Whig journals and the Government meanwhile kept an eye upon the Highflier periodical publications. The rejuvenated *Examiner* was presented by the Middlesex Grand Jury, which stated that it was:

> "spread in the coffee-houses, and other places of resort, to poison the minds of the people with seditious stories, traitorous insinuations, and very scandalous expressions highly reflecting on the pious memory of the late Queen, and the wise and just administration of his Majesty." [18]

The *Flying-Post* (No. 3567) insisted that those the *Examiner* attacked,

> "never sacrificed the trade and honour of their native country to its enemies, for French gold, and a Popish Pretender. They never prostituted, and made a stalking horse of the Church, to carry on trayterous and villanous designs in the state. In short, they were never guilty of rebellion and murther, by bullying and fright-

[17] *Flying-Post*, No. 3580. It was reported, however, that an exciseman at Creefe, Scotland, who refused to drink to the health of a Jacobite nobleman, had an ear torn off. *Patriot*, No. xviii.

[18] *Post Boy*, No. 3057; *Eve. Post*, No. 834; *Histor. Account*, p. 86. There had been for months many complaints against certain "clubs and coffee-houses, where they [Jacobites] buffoon the Government they live under, bully the ministers of state, and make the Queen the subject of their most filthy, obscene, and unmannerly railings." *Patriot*, No. 33, quoting the *Monitor*.

> ening their Queen into fits, by which she lost her life, as are the *Examiner's* masters."

In a similar manner, a letter from Hampshire bitterly attacked Dormer's Letter (in manuscript), claiming that Dormer's insidious doctrines were being swallowed by the Jacobites, and tended to alienate the affections of the people from George I.

> "There's scarce a town of any note in England but what has one or more of those letters, and some have three, four, five, or six of them; and after the first day's reading in public houses, they are by agreement sent to neighbouring gentlemen's houses and adjoining villages." [19]

Nor did the Whig leaders stop with the appointment of civil officials in a day when Church preferments were avowedly considered a part of the patronage. By the close of 1714 three vacant bishoprics were filled. William Fleetwood, of St. Asaph, was translated to Ely; Dr. John Wynne, Principal of Jesus College, Oxford, became Bishop of St. Asaph; and Dr. Richard Willis, Dean of Lincoln, Bishop of Gloucester.[20] Fleetwood was a "zealous Whig"; Willis was a "good Whig," and Wynne had given offence by his "unblushing Whig propagandism," although he probably owed his see to the Earl of Nottingham.[21]

Thus slowly, but thoroughly, and methodically, the Whig leaders prepared for the election. About the middle of November it was rumored that Parliament would be dissolved in a fortnight; soon thereafter it was said that the writs calling a new Parliament would bear the *teste* of

19 *Flying-Post*, No. 3592. Dormer's paper succeeded *Dyer's News Letters*.
20 *Polit. State*, VIII, 452; *Brit. Mercury*, No. 490.
21 *D.N.B.*; *Add. MSS.* (Bodleian), A 269, f. 36.

December 10.[22] Such reports were a trifle premature, since the proclamation for dissolving Parliament and speedily calling another, was not ordered in Council until January 5.[23] Some days later, another paper accurately prophesied that the writs would bear the date January 17, although this proclamation was not issued until January 15, with the writs returnable March 17. The Tories very properly objected to the tone of the latter proclamation, which openly attacked the actions of the late Ministry.[24]

The open canvass, therefore, extended over two months, although preparations were in train in many places long before. In fact, the Whig leaders began their campaign almost with the death of the Queen, not only by replacing Tory ministers and placemen with Whigs, but by keeping a watchful eye upon the Tory press, and proceeding promptly at the first suggestions of riots and tumults against the new dynasty. Two days before the announcement of the election, the King in Council ordered the impounding of the papers of the Earl of Strafford, one of the British plenipotentiaries for negotiating the Treaty of Utrecht.[25] No action, significantly enough, was taken against Dr. John Robinson, Bishop of London, the ranking plenipotentiary, either at this time or later, although Strafford was impeached. The Whig leaders apparently remembered the Sacheverell case, although on the very day they ordered the seizure of Strafford's papers, a proclamation was issued for the discovery of the author of *English Advice* (a pamphlet actually written by that arrogant Highflier, Bishop Atterbury).[26]

[22] *Weekly Packet*, Nos. 124–125; *Dawks'*, Nov. 27.

[23] *Lond. Gaz.*, No. 5292; *Post Boy*, No. 3068; *Dawks'*, Jan. 8.

[24] *Weekly Packet*, No. 132; *Lond. Gaz.*, No. 5295; *Ev. Post*, No. 850; *Flying-Post*, No. 3595; *Dawks'*, Jan. 18; W. Cobbett, *Parliamentary History* (London, 1811), VII, 24–25; *House of Commons Journal*, XVIII, 14.

[25] *Postman*, No. 11050 (Jan. 11–13).

[26] *Daily Courant*, Jan. 13.

Ten days after the Coronation it was reported that the Whigs would support General William Cadogan and Paul Methuen as candidates for Westminster against the sitting members.[27] Three weeks later came news from Malton (Yorkshire) of the method employed by Sir William Strickland, to nurse his constituency. Making use of the Coronation day, he

> "prepared the effigies of Pope and Pretender, which he caused to be burnt, and entertained the townsmen at his own charge, with large bonefires and quantities of drink, to plege his Majesty's health; and on both of these occasions he was accompanyed by a considerable number of gentlemen." [28]

From the county of Norfolk, came reverberations of a political deal. Sir Jacob Astley, one of the sitting members, having refused

> "to stand by that interest he has so often chosen, this is to certify, that Erasmus Earle . . . is prevailed on . . . to join Sir Ralph Hare as candidate, . . . and [they] do accordingly desire the votes and interest of all honest gentlemen and freeholders." [29]

In Somersetshire the Tories were active and "at a general meeting of the principal gentlemen of the county" nominated Sir William Wyndham, Bt., called "Wildfire" by his political opponents, and William Helyar, "for whom your vote and interest is desired, they being gentlemen *heartily well affected to the present Constitution*, *both*

[27] *Applebee's Weekly Journal*, Part XLIV, 267.

[28] *Flying-Post*, No. 3569. One of the other candidates did likewise with somewhat better results. *Ev. Post*, No. 816. See also *Parliamentary Register* (London, 1741), p. 152.

[29] *Ev. Post*, No. 825; *Post Boy*, No. 3048.

in Church and State." [30] The italicized words above seem to be almost a formula, for they reappear in substantially the same form in the case of the Tories of Middlesex, where at a meeting of a "great number of gentlemen and freeholders . . . it was unanimously agreed" that James Bertie [brother of the Earl of Abingdon] and Hugh Smithson, should be the candidates, having "very faithfully served those they represented in the last and foregoing Parliaments, and are persons of such honour and worth that their characters cannot be tainted." [31]

More than a month before the dissolution, the Kentish Whigs met in the interest of Mildmay Fane and William Delaune, "gentlemen well known to be zealously affected to his Majesty . . . and present Constitution." The "very considerable number of gentlemen and other freeholders" present decided that they

> "would come on Monday next . . . to the King's Arms Tavern in Southwark, at 4 a clock in the afternoon to meet their friends of London and Southwark, there where all such as are well-wishers to that interest are desired to be." [32]

A fortnight later, the Tories complained that it was "very industriously reported" that Percival Hart, one of the sitting members, "was dead, as also that he had declined to stand as a candidate." Hart personally protested that both reports were "false and malicious, and that it hath been unanimously agreed at several meetings by a great number of gentleman freeholders," that both the sitting members should appear as candidates, "being

[30] *Post Boy*, No. 3061; *Ev. Post*, No. 839; *Weekly Packet*, No. 129.

[31] *Post Boy*, Nos. 3054, 3075; *Weekly Packet*, No. 133.

[32] *Flying-Post*, No. 3578 (Dec. 7). The Tories held a final meeting to perfect their arrangements a few days before the poll. *Post Boy*, No. 3079.

gentlemen well-affected to . . ., King George, and the present establishment, both in Church and State." [33]

Some weeks before the campaign officially opened the Whig *Flying-Post* (No. 3580) felt constrained to describe the duties of a member of Parliament who

> "is both particularly to watch upon, and guard, to the best of his power, the weal and benefit of the place, for which he serves, and also of the weal, benefit, safety and honour of the Prince of the Kingdom, and every particular subject therein."

This statement of political morality is, perhaps, significant, coming it as does from a highly partisan journal, even though it was more observed in the breach than in the performance.

Just before Christmas, a Tory complaint came from Sussex that it was "industriously reported" that Sir William [?] Ashburnham and Charles Eversfield had declined to stand for knights, a rumor branded as untrue "and entended only to prejudice them in the said election." [34] In Wales a similar attempt was made earlier to queer the pitch of the Duke of Bolton's heir as candidate for Carmarthenshire.[35]

The canvass, however, did not gain any momentum until after the holidays. In Somerset the Whigs followed up their action of a month earlier by preparing a formal address to the freeholders, containing an indirect slap at the Highflier candidates:

> "At a general meeting of the High Sheriff, and other principal gentlemen . . . it was unanimously resolved to set up John Figott, and George Spoke, . . . for

[33] *Post Boy*, No. 3062 (Dec. 21).
[34] *Post Boy*, No. 3062.
[35] *Ev. Post*, No. 836. This was the titular Marquis of Winchester.

whom your vote and interest is desired, they being persons that always express'd their affection for the Church by their zeal for the Protestant Succession." [36]

A letter from Windsor dated early in October provided an interesting prophecy as to the election:

"We have no news in this place, but that both sides are eating and drinking for the Parliament. And if Oxford Inn-Keepers maxim holds good, that that is the freest Parliament where most money is spent, we of this town are like to have the freest election we have ever yet had." [37]

The London election this year was of unusual importance. The City's wealth and population were both greatly under-represented by its four members. Because serious irregularities, which had taken place at the previous election, had aroused Whig ire, the sheriffs served notice, before the election began, that such actions would be put down with a heavy hand.[38] The Whig leaders decided, moreover, to make it one of the test elections by going to the polls as early as possible.[39] As champions of the commercial clauses of the Treaty of Utrecht, the Tories were in bad odor among the powerful mercantile classes in the City, who had already scored a victory in the selection of the Lord Mayor and sheriffs. The Whigs immediately put up the four eminent merchants who had been defeated in 1713, but the Tory leaders had such difficulty in finding suitable opponents, that the Whigs gleefully reported that

[36] *Postman*, No. 11050 (Jan. 6–8). "Figott is probably a misprint for Piggott, knight of the shire, 1705–1708. *Py. Register*, p. 221.

[37] *Dawks'*, Oct. 29, 1714.

[38] *Daily Courant*, Jan. 24.

[39] *Dawks'*, Jan. 18; *Polit. State*, IX, 82; *Lond. Gaz.*, No. 5295; *Ev. Post*, No. 850; *Flying-Post*, No. 3595.

the election would be uncontested.[40] When that rumor proved to be the product only of their wishful thinking, they still hoped that the Tories would not insist upon a poll. But in that, too, they were disappointed, for the Tories stubbornly demanded one.[41]

The Whigs published *A Short Advice to the Citizens of London*, which was intended to neutralize the efforts of the High Church clergy:

> "Be not influenced in your choice by the advice of such hot-headed clergymen, who sharpen their tongues like serpents, and have the poyson of adders under their lips, which on all occasions they pour forth to blacken the Revolution and his Majesty's succession, which is founded upon it, since it is very well known that these men's tongues are set on fire of Hell, and that they have done what they can, not only to set the course of nature, but the whole nation on fire." [42]

Both parties indulged in political "rallies," or "love-feasts." On January 22, 1715, *Dawks' News Letter* proudly announced:

> "That the world may see what a noble spirit the citizens of London begin to exert in the choice of members, . . . who are the likeliest persons to preserve their precious liberties, and take care to advance trade, we can now acquaint our correspondents, that last night, by appointment there was a meeting of some

[40] *Flying-Post*, No. 2583; *Postman*, No. 11050 (Jan. 6–8). The Treaty of Utrecht, "delivered up Europe in chains" to France, and the "Tories had so fair a prospect of ruining the trading by getting the 8th and 9th articles of commerce ratify'd." *Flying-Post*, No. 3584.

[41] "The poll will begin at 9 a-clock this morning, and continue till 4-a-clock in the afternoon precisely." *Post-Boy*, No. 3076.

[42] *Flying-Post*, No. 3597. About the same time appeared another pamphlet, *Some Cautions offered to the Consideration of those who are to chuse members to serve in Parliament* (London, 1715).

> thousands (the greatest meeting ever known) of the Livery Men at the Crown and at the Swan taverns behind the Exchange, where it was unanimously agreed [to nominate four Whig candidates, who] always abhorred the Pretender and his adherents."

The briefer Tory statement was equally challenging as to a general meeting, "where were present the greatest number of eminent citizens that ever appeared on a like occasion." [43]

The Whig appeal claimed that "these four worthy merchants" were in "every way qualified for that honour, and zealously affected to his Majesty . . . and to the present happy Constitution." [44] The Tories maintained that their candidates were

> "of known loyalty to his Majesty . . ., and who have been always for supporting, and preserving the Protestant Succession, our happy Constitution . . ., *and rights, privileges and welfare of this City*, and for whom your interest, vote and poll (if needful) are desired." [45]

The Whigs were annoyed at the Tories for demanding a poll, since "there was such a vast appearance of citizens for the four merchants at Guild-Hall, that they were declared to have a majority." [46]

This tedious polling lasted some days. The Whigs published *A Letter to the Livery Men of London*, which

[43] *Daily Courant*, Jan. 19; *Post Boy*, No. 3074. The Whigs also boasted: "Last night there was a very great appearance at the Crown Tavern, . . . of many eminent citizens, much greater than was ever before known to meet on such an occasion (and as far exceeding the number of those who met on Wednesday last)." *Postman*, No. 11050 (Jan. 20–22).

[44] *Daily Courant*, Jan. 20.

[45] *Post Boy*, No. 3074; *Daily Courant*, Jan. 19. In the *Postman* the underscored words are changed to, "and for preserving the rights and privileges of their fellow citizens." No. 11049 (Jan. 25–27).

[46] *Polit. State*, IX, 87.

condemned the "pernicious and destructive treaties of peace and commerce with France and Spain," the decline in stocks, and the enlisting men for the Pretender. This pamphlet also accused the Tories of irregularities and violence during the election of 1713, and of having "raised little rebellions throughout the kingdom . . . to carry their elections this Parliament." The letter very sigficantly continued:

> "For who should represent a trading City but Traders? . . . that the honour of a Trader cannot, properly, be applied to any but merchants who are concerned in exports and imports. That all other Traders are only subordinate to them, and are no other than the mechanicks, who either prepare our manufactures for the exportation of the Merchant, or are dispersers of foreign commodities, when imported by the Merchant from abroad, in exchange for those of our own growth. . . . It is a Merchant only that has the science, and sees trade in its naked principles, and in the first causes. . . . The Merchants are like so many Centinels placed in all the nations of the world to watch over and defend her." [47]

This creed of the bustling commercial bourgeoisie may sound slightly naive, but it is only one of many bits of evidence that indicate the activity and interest of London merchants in elections. Many of them were candidates for Parliamentary seats from other parts of England.[48] The same initiative is manifested in the instructions drafted by the citizens of London for their elected repre-

[47] *Polit. State*, IX, 82–86, *passim.* This was probably a broadside hawked about the streets.

[48] Among others, Sir William Humphreys, Lord Mayor of London, was elected at Marlborough, and Samuel Shepheard for Cambridge town. *Py. Reg.*, pp. 43, 153.

sentatives, discussed below.[49] The Whigs were entirely successful, winning by some six hundred votes in a total of more than six thousand.[50] This important victory, coming so early, served as a tonic to the Whig stalwarts.

The candidates in the City were saved one of the worries of those standing for the shires and boroughs immediately adjacent to London — that of getting electors to the polls. This problem of course concerned all active candidates throughout the kingdom, but not to the same degree as in the region around London, whose wealthy classes were moving rapidly into the surburban areas near by. Many of the voters for Middlesex, Surrey, Hertfordshire, Kent, and Essex lived in the metropolitan area, and transportation (as well as refreshments) must be provided, presumably at the candidates' expense.

The Surrey polling was at Guildford, thirty miles from London. The Tory candidates, Heneage Finch, nephew of the Earl of Nottingham, and Edward Harvey, "two very loyal gentlemen, and stedfast friends to the Church of England upon all occasions," [51] advertised that

> "coaches will be ready for those freeholders that live in London and Westminster, at the Rainbow Coffee-House by Temple-Bar, and in the Old Palace Yard, and in Southwark at the 3-Tun-Tavern, on Wednesday morning the said 26th instant, at 7." [52]

The only Whig candidate asked his supporters going on horseback to meet "at the Hand-Inn against St. Mary

[49] *Annals*, I, 353–357. See especially *Flying-Post*, No. 3608.

[50] *Whalley's News Letter* (Dublin), No. 64; *Daily Courant*, Jan. 26–29, *passim*; *Ev. Post*, No. 853; *Dawks'*, Jan. 25; *Postman*, No. 11050 (Jan. 26).

[51] *Weekly Packet*, No. 133. Finch, as Nottingham's nephew, was acceptable to the Whigs, who did not contest his seat. His father had been created Earl of Aylesford just before the Coronation.

[52] *Post Boy*, Nos. 3074–3075. See also *Postman*, No. 11050 (Jan. 20).

Magdalen Church in Bermondsey to Morrow Morning at Six exactly." [53]

The difficulties encountered by the Middlesex candidates were greater than those for Surrey. Although the distance to Brentford, the polling place, was only ten miles, the number of electors to be transported was greater. The Whig candidates, Sir John Austin and Henry Barker, were supported by a great number of Livery Men of the City, who were also freeholders of the county.[54] They desired that their friends, and

> "the freeholders in the Tower-Hamletts and the parts adjacent . . . meet on Tower-Hill, at seven a-clock in the morning to go from thence to Lincoln's Inn-Fields to meet Sir John Austen, who will proceed from thence to St. James's Square, and afterward to Turnham Green to joyn Henry Barker, Esq. Note, barges will be ready at seven . . . at Old-Swan, Still-Yard, Black-Fryers, and Whitehall-Stairs, for those that please to go by water." [55]

The Tories advertised that the electors favoring Bertie and Smithson, "supporters of the trade of the nation," who planned to ride to Brentford, should meet at the same hour, at White-Chapel Bars

> "to proceed to Hatton-Gardens to meet Mr. Smithson in order to join the Honourable James Bertie at Hanwell-Heath. And for those that intend to go by water barges will be ready for them at the 3 Cranes, the Tem-

[53] *Postman*, 11049 (Jan. 25–27). One enterprising election agent incurred the displeasure of the authorities, being "committed to the Gate-House Prison the very morning as he design'd to carry down his Gang in Coaches to Guildford, to vote in the election in the County." *Whalley's News Letter*, Supplement, No. 70.

[54] *Flying-Post*, No. 3597; *Postman*, 11050 (Jan. 21).

[55] *Daily Courant*, Jan. 24; *Postman*, 11050 (Jan. 25–27). The *Courant* also announced (Jan. 26) the poll would be completed in one day.

ple Stairs and Hungerford Stairs in order to convey them to the 3 Pidgeons in Brentford. Any that want conveyance are desired to enquire at the following taverns, viz, at the Bell in Westminster, the Mitre in Fleet-street, the Feathers in Cheapside, the Rummer at White-Chappel Bars, and the Ship at Ratcliff Cross." [56]

The trials and tribulations of the candidates and their agents were probably greater for Hertfordshire than for either Surrey or Middlesex, because of the difficulties of travel in midwinter over very bad roads. One candidate was Sir Ralph Radcliffe, Kt., a

> "person well-affected to our present Constitution . . ., which he has shown by his early and constant adherence to the Protestant Succession, . . . being zealously affected to his Majesty . . ., and a person every way qualified for that great and honourable trust."

He announced that the election would be held February 3, and desired his supporters in or near London "to meet without the bar at Bishopsgate Street, next Thursday between 6 and 7. The poll will be ended in one day." [57]

Maidstone, the polling place for Kent, though forty miles from London, was easy of access by the main highway to Dover. The Tory agents provided a "rendezvous at the Catherine-Wheel in the Borough of Southwark by 7-a-clock on Monday [or Tuesday] morning," [58] whereas the Whigs preferred to meet an hour later at the Green-Dragon in Bishopsgate-Street.[59]

The polls for the shire of Essex at Chelmsford were probably the most difficult to reach of all the counties in the

[56] *Post Boy*, No. 3076.
[57] *Daily Courant*, Jan. 26, 31.
[58] *Post Boy*, No. 3081. The poll was to last two days.
[59] *Daily Courant*, Feb. 4; *Postman*, No. 11050 (Feb. 1–3).

metropolitan area. The Whigs announced that any of their electors

> "That want the conveniency of coaches to carry them to and from the election, are desired to enquire at Tom's Coffee-House in Cornhill, the Amsterdam Coffee-House in Threadneedle-Street, and at the White-Lyon in Whitechapel, where tickets will be delivered them. N. B. Those that go in coaches are desired to be at Tom's Coffee-House . . . or at the White-Lyon by 5 of the clock Tuesday morning."[60]

It required real fortitude to set forth on a thirty-mile journey long before daybreak on a winter morning, even when fortified by the good-cheer for which the White-Lyon and Tom's were probably famous.

Due to the dangerous illness of one of their sitting members, the Tories decided to set up William Harvey, Sr., to "joyn with Sir Richard Child, Bart.," who were "both gentlemen of known zeal for supporting the Constitution."[61] The Tory voters must have been built of even sterner stuff than those of the Whigs. They might secure tickets at the Rummer Tavern in Whitechapel, the Garter Coffee-House behind the Royal Exchange, the Legg Tavern in Fleetstreet, or the Bull Head Tavern in Southwark, but "all persons that go in coaches are desired to be at Batson's Coffeehouse in Cornhill, or the Rummer . . . by 4 a clock on Tuesday morning."[62]

[60] *Daily Courant*, Feb. 4.

[61] *Post Boy*, No. 3079; *Postman*, No. 11050 (Jan. 29–Feb. 1). See also *Ev. Post*, No. 856.

[62] *Postman*, No. 11050 (Feb. 1–3, 1715). See also *Post Boy*, No. 3080; *Ev. Post*, No. 857. Another advertisement stated that, "there will be horses taken into the meadow grounds behind the town at 6*d*. per head. Also outhouses there convenient enough for setting up horses at hay or otherwise at reasonable price. Attendance will be given at a private house against the Crown and Mitre over the bridge." *Postman*, Feb. 1–3.

The necessary expenses for such transportation and entertainment of electors was a drain on the purses of candidates and political patrons. We have, fortunately, an itemized statement of expenditures for such purposes in this election for Sussex, with a total of £173 8*s*.[63]

As in all other British elections of the eighteenth century, the elections were purely a matter of form in a large number of the constituencies. Pocket boroughs already abounded. Numerous places either went uncontested, or never proceeded to a poll. Several elections this year, however, were decidedly lively; some of them both entertaining and enlightening as to the ways and wiles of politicians in the early eighteenth century. That held in Hertford Borough involved two questions: the validity of the Last Determinations Act (1696), and the right of honorary freemen to vote. The Whigs criticised the mayor's arbitrariness in polling honorary freemen, "as also great numbers of . . . strangers and no housekeepers, and by refusing legal votes, and polling those who had no colour of right to vote contrary to law." [64]

The Whigs further complained that the Tories had earlier created a hundred and fifty honorary freemen, "some of whom are parsons, some country gentlemen, and some tag-rag, and bob-tail." They also accused the Tories of hiring "a gang of poor scoundrels from other towns, to take parlours of them the night before the election, and the next day took their votes" for the Highflier candidates. They testified that one man voted for a bath-room, another for a stable, and a third elector for a "house of office" [privy].[65]

[63] Newcastle Papers, *Add. MSS.* 33,058, ff. 223–228, *passim*; S. H. Nulle, *Thomas Pelham-Holles, Duke of Newcastle: his Early Political Career* (Philadelphia, 1931), pp. 61–62.

[64] *Flying-Post*, No. 3599.

[65] Letter from Hertford to *Flying-Post*, No. 3604 (Feb. 3).

In attempting to check up on these "out-voters," the Whigs discovered that many of the sixty odd who had voted Tory, were not to be found, and offered a "good reward" for knowledge of their whereabouts. These Whigs reflected particularly on the actions of Charles Cesar, one of the Tory candidates:

> "There came the morning of the election about 600 persons from Mr. Cesar's of Bennington, . . . who had maintained them with victuals, drink, and gave them more than the Common wages for labouring men for more than two months. They spent it in playing at hat-farthing, carding, ringing the bells, and going a-shooting, when sometimes they killed the fowls and sheep of the neighbourhood. This noble crew made their entry by beat of the drum, and streamers flying . . .; their usual cry was, No Presbyterians, High Church and Sacheverell, Low Church and the Devil; and some of the gang were heard to cry in the night, No Presbyterians, no King George."[66]

The mayor incurred the serious displeasure of the Commons, which declared him guilty of behaving

> "in an illegal and arbitrary manner . . . in contempt of the act to prevent false and double returns . . . and ordered [him] . . . for the said breach of priviledge [to] be taken into the custody of the serjeant at arms."

The House likewise unseated Cesar and his colleague in favor of the Whig petitioners.[67]

[66] *Flying-Post*, No. 3601. Cesar lost his lucrative post of Treasurer of the Navy soon after George I came in. *Histor. Account*, p. 122.

[67] *Commons Journal*, XVIII, 136; *Polit. State*, IX, 417. See [J. C. Small?], *Orders and Resolutions of the . . . Commons on Controverted Elections* . . . (2nd. ed. London, 1736), pp. 109–110; Reg., p. 114. Although heard at the bar, the question of the last determination of December 6, 1705, requiring honorary

The election of knights for Leicestershire also involved the returning officer in serious difficulties. The reports are detailed and highly conflicting, consisting mainly of accusations and recriminations between the Tory candidates and the Under-Sheriff, the returning officer. The Whigs accused the Tory zealots of being responsible for so much violence at the polls that the Under-Sheriff [John Baresby], despairing of an honest vote and fearing for his life, rode to Westminster to lay his case before the King and Council. Most unfortunately for him, he failed to file a proper return before Parliament opened.

The Tories put up two baronets, Sir Thomas Cave, one of the sitting members, and Sir Jeffery Palmer, who were opposed by George Ashby, and Thomas Byrd, "firm friends to the present happy establishment." The Whigs said that

> "A mob appeared for the two former, and abused and wounded, with hangers and swords, several friends of the two latter, who refused to take the money that was offered them to vote the other way. The Under-Sheriff was assaulted and threatened to be stabb'd if he did not immediately make a return of the two knights. This was before the poll was half ended, there being at least 2,000 freeholders to pool. The Under-Sheriff with great difficulty escaped their fury, was forced to abscond, and afterwards privately to leave the town. Some of the knights friends offered £5 next morning for a sight of him, and swore they would be his death whenever they saw him. The Sheriff, 'tis probably, will make a double return, and there is no doubt but the Parliament, will

freemen to be resident at the time of their being made such, and which contradicted that of January 27, 1701, does not seem to have been discussed. J. C., *The Candidates Guide, or Electors Rights decided. . . .* (London, 1735), p. 22.

take cognizance of such notorious and scandalous offenders against the laws and libertys of their country."[68]

The Whigs, likewise, bewailed ecclesiastical partisanship:

> "There was a mighty appearance of the clergy for . . . [the Tories], and the Church was said to be in danger, if they were not elected. We had the most mobbish doings that ever was known, which lasted two days."[69]

Tory delegations marched about the town, presumably to encourage members of their own party, and intimidate the Whigs, who stated that their voters were kept from polling. Such a contingent of six to seven hundred, marched with

> "thirty-five parsons ranked four and four in front . . . [and] twenty-two squires," with the main body having "cockades in their hats, of guilt leather or paper, stamped with the Mitre, to shew their pretended zeal for the Church."[70]

[68] *Flying-Post*, No. 3604. The *Political State* added that Baresby had "part of his cloathes and periwig burnt" IX, 162. Several days later a letter to the High Sheriff, accused the Tory agents of putting fire to Baresby's clothes "in the open court; pulled the chair from under him, and threaten'd to cut his throat," when he refused to declare the baronets elected. *Flying-Post*, No. 3610. The Tory version is given by Mrs. Mary Lovett (*née* Verney). "We hear from London yesterday that the Sheriff has been before the King and Councell, in a Coat and Wig all burnt, which he said was done by Combustable matter that the Barronets party put to him and set on fire; there was never any such thing heard of nor done to him, but a young woman in the Town has made Oath that he came into her Father's house, and fell A Kissing and Pulling of her, at which she gave him A Push and he fell against the fire and singed his coat." Lady Verney, Editor, *Verney Letters of the 18th Century* (London, 1930), I, 327.

[69] Letter to *Flying-Post*, No. 3607.

[70] Letter to High-Sheriff, *Flying-Post*, No. 3610.

Whig leaders insisted, furthermore, that the agreement among the candidates not to poll copyholders had been openly violated by their opponents, who saw to it, nevertheless, that no Whig copyholders voted. Many, they said, were permitted to vote for the Tories, with

> "no freehold nor any title to house and lands in the world, . . . while gentlemen of prime quality were insulted by scoundrels, and a reputed Jacobite's suffrage accepted, without taking the Abjuration oath,[71] tho' at the same time 'twas tendered to him."[72]

The Tories on the other hand, although distrustful from the first of the Sheriff and scornful of the efforts of "Canary" Byrd, insisted that the election "was carry'd on with great peace and calmness, and without the least riot, disturbance of the peace, or the insult offer'd to the said Under-Sheriff, or any other person."[73] This counterblast was answered by the *Flying-Post*, which accused some of the clergy of drinking the health of Louis XIV, and insinuating that they "would muffle the gentleman that kept the Turks." The *Examiner* by joining in the defense of the Leicestershire Tories, led the *Flying-Post* to link the *Weekly Packet* and *Examiner* together as "two of those brothers in scandal . . . sons of Belial! known advocates of Rome! the most abandoned scribblers for a Popish Pretender."[74]

The Tories encountered difficulties in putting their case before the public. Sir Thomas Cave wrote Ralph Verney:

[71] Statutes: 4 Anne, c. 8; 6 Anne, c. 7.

[72] *Flying-Post*, No. 3610. Although the baronets polled the greater number, the Whigs maintained that only the use of violence prevented their candidates from winning by some five hundred votes, as only half the freeholders voted.

[73] *Weekly Packet*, No. 138. Their statement was signed by some seventy gentlemen and freeholders, including the sitting members for Leicester town. See also *Verney Letters*, I, 325–327.

[74] *Flying-Post*, Nos. 3611, 3613.

"A printed relation of this matter I have sent to London and to the Coffee Houses there. We endeavour'd to insert our Case in the *Evening Post*, *Post Bag*, and *Post Man*, but they all refuse us, tho' we have offered Security for the proof of our insertions; this makes good the saying that Truth is not at all times to be spoken."[75]

The Whiggish House of Commons curiously enough was not greatly concerned about the charges of Tory violence,[76] but immediately noted Baresby's failure to make a regular return, initiated sharp enquiries into the reason therefor, and commanded Baresby to attend the House. Petitions, meanwhile, had been lodged by both political parties. Upon the Sheriff's appearance at the bar, witnesses were heard for and against him. The House thereupon moved that Baresby, "having neglected to return two knights . . . is guilty of a great breach of privilege of this House," and was ordered "committed to the custody of the serjeant-at-arms." After a month's imprisonment, he petitioned for his release, which was refused because he had not acknowledged his fault. Having made the necessary submission, a week later he was formally reprimanded by the Speaker, and dismissed, paying his fines,[77] which must have been heavy for six weeks' incarceration.

The Cambridgeshire election was a bit out of the usual run, particularly because of the interest taken in it by university students. The Whig candidates,

75 *Verney Letters*, I, 329. This "printed relation" was probably a broadside, *A Certificate for Leicester*, which the *Flying-Post* described as being without stamp, printer, or publisher. No. 3613.

76 This may have been due to their jealousy of the Council, to which Baresby had appealed.

77 *Commons Jour.*, XVIII, 21–22, 58, 117, 125; *Polit. State*, IX, 290. See

"for want of time to write particularly to their friends in London, and in distant parts of the county, give this publick notice, that they continue to stand candidates, notwithstanding the unsuspected declaration of Granado Piggott, Esq., to stand against them." [78]

Despite the Vice-Chancellor's edict confining the students to their respective colleges, some college heads apparently encouraged their protégés to disobey it. The noise and tumult of the election was prodigious. The Whigs complained particularly of

"A wise and valiant Lord [who] came into the town at the head of a squadron of ragamuffins; and then to show he would stand by the Church, and partly to prevent any desertion of his tater'd troops, he took up his station near Round-Church, and there, bareheaded, with a great deal of left-handed complaisance, reviewed his party as they marched to poll." [79]

Samuel Shepheard, a wealthy London merchant, a candidate for Cambridge town,[80] was particularly objectionable to the students, who placed themselves at the best vantage points from which to insult the Whig supporters on their way to the polls.

"From these softer degrees of malice, they betook themselves to stones and brickbats, whereby many honest gentlemen were bruised or knocked down as they ran the gantlet thro' this learn'd mob." [81]

---

also *Verney Letters*, I, 332; Samuel Heywood, *A Digest of the Law respecting County Elections* . . . (2nd ed., London, 1812), p. 578.

[78] *Ev. Post*, No. 859.

[79] *Flying-Post*, No. 3611. Pigot was elected for the shire in 1702.

[80] This controverted election consumed much time in the Commons. See C. H. Cooper, *Annals of Cambridge* (Cambridge, 1852), IV, 126–137.

[81] *An Account of the Riots and Tumults, and other Treasonable Practices* . . . (London, 1715), pp. 19–20.

The High Sheriff failed to keep the peace, even when accompanied by the rival candidate. After attempting to arrest a rioter, he was forced to seek sanctuary in his own coach, much to the amusement of his guest.

Interest and excitement at the polls increased as the day wore on.

> "About noon, the street leading to the place of poll, was lined with townsmen and gownsmen bespangled with Dr. B——y's blue Guards and square caps of other colleges; the windows crowded with shoals of non-resisting damsels, encouraging their dear scholars to throw dirt, and spit at any that should presume to oppose the tacker. It was common to see those little sprigs of divinity dip their sleeves in the dirt and bespatter their antagonists." [82]

The pace still further quickened as darkness approached.

> "In the evening, when this peaceable company perceived their idol could not be exalted, they grew more enraged than ever, and formed two dangerous designs against the newly elected [Whig] members. There was a party placed on the bridge, whose rails are low, and over which the new elects were oblig'd to come, riding in chairs from the polls; their business was to toss 'em over, with their chairs, into the river; and lest that design should fail, a right body of passively obedient Johnians were mounted on their college leads (under which the members were to pass), with a goodly store of brickbats to discharge on their heads."

Having been warned of the plans of the playful undergraduates, the members substituted coaches for chairs. Nevertheless these youthful enthusiasts

[82] *Flying-Post*, No. 3611.

> "discharged whole vollies of brickbats, &c. at the coaches of the members, thirteen brickbats being taken out of the coaches. . . . After this insolence, 'twill be needless to mention the glasses being all broken and the leathers slit in several places." [83]

Although the Whigs carried the election by nearly two hundred, they insisted that it would have been much larger,

> "had not many been terrify'd by the danger from the young fry in black and blue, who like the Hudubrastick Saints,
>
> Would fight as mad or drunk
> For Mother High-Church, or for punk
> Whose honesty they all did swear for
> Tho' scarce a soph of 'em knew wherefore.
>
> In sober sadness, these caddies of the Church militant, acted with rudeness and insolence, as would have made the vilest of a London mob to blush for 'em." [84]

Of the borough elections, that at Bristol was among the more interesting. Just before the election began, the authorities arrested one person for dispersing Atterbury's stimulating pamphlet.[85] A few days later, the Whigs complained that Sir William Wyndham, the Jacobite candidate for Somersetshire and Minehead

> "contrary to established rules among the gentry here, appeared to raise votes, attended by Coll. Cod——ton, and Mr. Pr——r; he invited his friends to an entertainment at the Rummer; among his company was one John Hopton, a piece of a linnen draper, bound over last

[83] *Account of Riots and Tumults* (1715), p. 20.
[84] *Flying-Post*, No. 3611.
[85] *Flying-Post*, No. 3598.

assizes for abusing the grand-jury, and was one of that Gloucester jury that found the bill against Mr. Bull, the clergyman." [86]

Sir William Daines, and Joseph Earl,[87] were the Whig, and Thomas Edwards, Jr. and Philip Freke the Tory, candidates. When the poll ended, it was thought Freke and Edwards "had a majority of forty or fifty, but the books being sealed, the parties are not certainly known.[88] The polling was tame, due largely, perhaps, to the mayor's precaution in swearing in "eighty new constables to attend the poll from day to day." Daines and Earl, however, "having had a plain Demonstration of foul Play, by Oath against some, and by the Confession of another, who offered themselves to poll a second time," demanded a scrutiny, which was most vigorously opposed by the agents of the rival candidates, who

> "immediately leapt upon the Table where the Clerks were writing, and in a very riotous and tumultuous manner insulted the Sheriff, and abused the first nam'd Candidates, crying out, No Scrutiny, No Scrutiny, Declare, Declare." [89]

The Sheriff, despite Tory efforts to intimidate him into returning their candidates, agreed to the scrutiny, which was to begin a fortnight later.[90]

[86] *Flying-Post*, No. 3599. These leaders were termed Jacobites, although it was conceded that their agents were quiet.

[87] Daines represented Bristol from 1700 to 1710, and Earl from 1710 to 1727. *Py. Reg.*, p. 37.

[88] *Postman*, 11,050 (Feb. 17–19). Letters from Bristol said that "when the books were shut, all the candidates had polled above 1900, and Mr. Freak and Mr. Edwards had carry'd it by forty." *Flying-Post*, No. 3609.

[89] *Flying-Post*, No. 3618.

[90] The Sheriff, "by reason of the length of time, which the scrutiny is likely to take up, is resolved to return all four candidates, and leave the decision to the House." *Weekly Packet*, No. 140.

"In that Interval, all imaginable Industry and Dilligence was us'd by the Hanoverian Party, to detect the Illegal Voters, in the Prosecution of which, such a Scene of Villany was disclosed, that 'tis impossible for me to give you a just idea of it, without entering into a more particular Relation than the Design of this Letter will allow. Some by raising the Sheriff's Mark out of their Copies, had prepared themselves to Poll several Times, others were raised out of their Graves, to appear in the Cause of the Church, as they profanely and impudently call'd it; some swore to Freeholds which they never had in Possession, and others to show their Zeal against the present Government, voted both in the Quality of Freemen and Freeholders. . . .

"These Discoveries made such a Noise about the Town, that the Sheriffs thought themselves oblig'd in Justice to the Legal Voters of this City, to be very exact and critical in the Scrutiny, being sensible of the Inconveniencies that would ensue, if it was carry'd on with too much Popularity, appointed with the consent of the Candidates four Scrutineers of a Side to controvert all Points relating to the Qualification of the Persons who should be objected to." [91]

It soon appeared that Daines and Earl "will have a fair majority, they having but two false votes, when Mr. Freke and Mr. Edwards had sixty-three." [92] The dissatisfied Tory faction spirited up a mob to delay, if not prevent, the completion of the scrutiny, so that "nothing was heard in the Council-House but Cursing and Swearing, Scandal and Scurrility." The Sheriff, finally convinced that it was impossible to continue the scrutiny, or at least

[91] "N. W." in a letter to Editor of *Flying-Post*, Mar. 7 (No. 3618).
[92] *Dawks'*, Feb. 26; *Flying-Post*, No. 3612.

finish it, before the opening of Parliament, dropped it, and returned the Whig candidates.[93]

The bitterly contested election for Shaftesbury was accompanied by that most frequent of all complaints — the partiality of the returning officer. The Whigs maintained that William Benson had a great majority, but the mayor "declared that he would not return him, and that he was to have £1000 bond to bear him harmless," and consequently returned Edward Nicholas and Samuel Rush, "but we do not doubt that this return, which is one of the most notorious that ever was known, will soon be set right in Parliament." [94]

Benson and Henry Andrews, the fourth candidate, demanded a scrutiny, which was granted. This soon revealed that

> "the mayor had allow'd twenty-six bad votes . . . tho' they had all been objected against, and refused seventeen good ones. . . . But a petition being lodged, 'tis not doubted that justice will be done to petitions, and upon the mayor." [95]

John Bennet, the said mayor, promptly replied:

> "that the above Accusations are groundless, scandalous, and malicious, the Majority of the legal Votes, both at the close of the poll and on the finishing the Scrutiny

[93] *Flying-Post*, No. 3618. The Tory petition complaining of the Sheriff's partiality, was referred to the Committee on Privileges and Elections, March 31 but there was no determination. Consequently the Whig attempt to establish that "the right of election is in the freemen, and freeholders who always produced their copies at the time of the poll" failed. *Commons Journal*, XVIII, 40; T. H. B. Oldfield, *Representative History of Great Britain* . . . (6 vols., London, 1816), I, 415; *Py. Reg.*, p. 37; *Return of Members of Parliament* (London, 1878), II, 40.

[94] *Flying-Post*, No. 3602.

[95] *Flying-Post*, No. 3603. This organ sought to show that with these changes the Whig candidates would have a majority.

(which was managed by the Council and Agents of each candidate) having fallen upon Edward Nicholas, and Samuel Rush, Esqrs., as is underneath inferred, who were accordingly returned and therefore confides in the Justice of a British Parliament to vindicate his innocence." [96]

This election petition dragged its way through the Commons. The hearing at the bar resolved itself into a duel between the counsel for the petitioner and that for the sitting member. The former leveled his attack upon the mayor, seeking to disqualify several persons, who had been admitted to vote for the sitting members.[97] The counsel for the latter sought to show bribery by the petitioners, and that, according to a recent statute, neither was qualified to sit in Parliament.[98] Much time was spent by the House not only upon the question of the franchise, but also upon the qualifications of the petitioners and in discussing the act of 1711. Since the House did not specifically charge bribery, or interpret the statute, we can only surmise that, by unseating both sitting members, they objected to the mayor's action, and that they were dissatisfied with the qualifications of Andrews, by their ordering a new writ for one of the seats, after they had seated Benson.[99]

[96] *Post Boy*, No. 3085. The *Flying-Post* (No. 3066) retorted that "our Mayor has at last thought fit to return William Benson, Esq., with Mr. Nicholas and Mr. Rush for this borough; and 'tis not doubted but Mr. Andrews will also have justice done him." The Town-Clerk indignantly denied that Benson had been returned. *Post Boy*, No. 3085.

[97] *Commons Jour.*, XVIII, 26; *Polit. State*, IX, 292.

[98] 9 Anne, c. 5. Knights of the shire must have an income of £600 a year from a copyhold or freehold, and borough representatives an income of £300 from the same source. See Sir William Blackstone, *Commentaries on the Laws of England* (2nd ed., London, 1844), I, 182.

[99] *Polit. State*, IX, 295–298, 379; *Commons Jour.*, XVIII, 66–69, 74, 161; *Orders and Resolutions*, pp. 103–106, *Candidates Guide*, p. 37.

It may be significant that just before the Commons completed this case, it decided, *nem. con.*, to give leave to bring in a Bill "for the more effectual securing and preventing the Abuses of Sheriffs and other returning Officers, in not returning the Writs of Summons in due Time, and for preventing Bribery and Corruptions in the Elections." [100]

The election at Minehead (Somersetshire) also seems a bit complicated, partly because it raised the questions as to the electoral qualifications in a householder borough, and as to the proper returning officer. The Tory candidates were Sir William Wyndham, Bt., who had represented the shire since 1710, and Sir John Trevelyan, Bt., who had sat for the borough since 1708. Their Whig rivals were Samuel Edwin and James Milner. One report of the results was: Milner, 178; Edwin, 173; Trevelyan, 161; Wyndham, 156. Another one ran: Trevelyan, 177; Wyndham, 172; Milner, 124; Edwin, 119. A third stated that the Whig candidates were declared elected by the principal burgesses and inhabitants, but "the Constables who pretended to be the returning officers, in a most riotous and partial manner, have declared the majority" for Trevelyan and Wyndham. [101]

Though petitioned against, the last two were apparently accepted as the sitting members.[102] Few election petitions crept so slowly through the Commons. The petition of Edwin and Milner was received March 30, 1715, and was ordered to be heard at the bar May 31 — two months later. It was put off eight times before being heard on September 3rd, 6th, 8th, and 9th. Finally, on

[100] *Polit. State*, IX, 379; *Commons Jour.*, XVIII, 72.

[101] *Postman*, No. 11050 (Feb. 5–8); *Ev. Post*, No. 864; *Flying-Post*, No. 3604.

[102] *Return of Members*, II, 43. It could have been for a very brief period, however, as Wyndham was returned for the shire, and must have waived for Minehead, which he does not appear to have done.

September 10, the election was declared void, but no warrant was to issue for that Parliament.[103] More than two years passed before the Commons passed upon the double return in the ensuing by-election, and seated Trevelyan and Milner, and it was six weeks later still, before the indenture by which the other two candidates were also returned, was taken off the file.[104]

Eventually they adjudicated the issues raised in both the general and by-elections. During the hearing, they admitted as a witness a person charged with having distributed bribes. As to the returning officers, they decided June 13, 1717, that "the precept ought to be directed to the two constables, and they to make the return." On February 24, 1718, they declared that the franchise lay "in the Parishioners of Minehead and Dunstar, being Housekeepers in the borough of Minehead, and not receiving Alms." [105]

The instructions issued to their representatives by the electors of Buckinghamshire and London were a rather novel feature of the election. Complaining of the Treaty of Utrecht, the French fortifications at Mardyke, and of the extravagant expense of previous elections, that from Bucks suggested an examination into the late ministry's responsibility for such conditions

> "the peace was no sooner finish'd, and produc'd, but we found ourselves in worse Circumstances than at the Beginning of the War. We saw Spain and the West Indies (the very Prize we were contending for) deliver'd

[103] *Commons Jour.*, XVIII, 33, 149, 185, 222, 239, 261, 274, 284, 296, 299–303.

[104] *Return of Members*, II, 43 — April 11, May 23, 1717; *Py. Reg.*, p. 161.

[105] *Candidates Guide*, p. 29; *Commons Jour.*, XVIII, 592, 751. While the result of this election was pending, the Commons passed both the bill relating to Sheriffs and another for limiting the number of officers sitting in the Commons. *Commons Jour.*, XVIII, 183–234, *passim*. Neither apparently passed the Lords.

up to a French Prince. The strong Towns we had won with much blood and treasure, given back to France; our Allies most perfidiously abandon'd and betray'd. . . .

"We earnestly importune you to consider of, and provide some severer Law for preventing the great Expence and Corruption in electing Members of Parliament. This is every Day growing to that Excess, that those honest Gentlemen wno are left qualified to Represent us, will soon grow weary of the Burden, and decline standing. Elections are now become meer Markets, where the highest Bidder is sure to carry it: If some Stop be not put to this wicked and mercenary Practice, it must end in the Ruin of our Constitution; for they that Buy us, will not fail, one time or other, to Sell us." [106]

The London representation, as published, contains twenty-five articles. It asked the City's representatives to make inquiries as to the behaviour of the late ministry in certain specific instances. Its main interest, perhaps, lies in its preamble: —

"We the Citizens of *London*, who have chearfully elected you to represent us in Parliament, and thereby committed to your Trust, the Safety, Liberty, Property, and Privileges of us and our Posterity, think it our Duty, as it is our undoubted Right, to acquaint you, what we desire and expect from you, and what we take to be your Duty, as our Representatives." [107]

The election results were a great tribute to the industry, alertness and organizing ability of the Ministry. "So

106 *Polit. State*, IX, 164, 166.

107 *Flying-Post*, No. 3608; *Polit. State*, IX, 166–170; *Annals* I, 353–357. The Commons, of course, never conceded that such instructions had any legal force, though they had been used as early as 1680. See John Chamberlayne, *Magnae Britanniae Notitia* . . . (London, 1716), p. 96. [Defoe's?] *Some Reasons offered by the late Ministry* (1715) complained of these instructions.

many Whiggs have not been returned since the Revolution," wrote James Stanhope, Secretary of State, to Lord Stair.[108] A contemporary periodical, just before the election closed,[109] estimated: — Total chosen, 495; Whigs, 299; Tories, 195; double return, 1; Court Tories, 12; Whigs chosen in place of Tories, 144; Tories in place of Whigs, 4.

The Whigs even made considerable headway in the shires, the fortresses of Toryism, capturing about half these seats throughout England.[110] In the boroughs, the Whigs secured about twice as many members as the Tories. The Government gained thirty-two of the forty-four in Cornwall,

> "chiefly owing to the great interest and indefatigable industry of Hugh Boscawen, Esq., Comptroller of his Majesty's Household.[111] Of sixteen Barons of the Cinque-Ports, one only avow'd Tory was chosen; and though in Wales the Elections were almost equally divided between both Parties, yet 'tis remarkable, that the Earl of Oxford's interest, which some Time carried all before it, was now fallen so low, that his son, Lord Harley, lost it at the town of Radnor."[112]

The Whigs gained some seventy seats in the four south-western counties, and in Wiltshire the trend continued to

[108] F. O. 90/14 (Feb. 2, 1715); W. Michael, *England under George I*, p. 116. "Little more than a year had elapsed since . . . the freeholders and burgesses had returned . . . three Tories to one Whig." Sir H. E. Bunbury, *Correspondence of Sir Thomas Hanmer* (London, 1838), p. 61.

[109] *Whalley's News Letter*, Supplement, No. 70. William Nicolson, the militant and politically-minded Bishop of Carlisle, estimated a fortnight earlier that the Whigs had 244 and the Tories 151: Tories in posts at Court, 11; Whigs for Tories, 117; Tories for Whigs, 3; Whigs in two places, 3. *Lonsdale Papers* (*Hist. MSS. Comm, Reports*, 1893), p. 249.

[110] *Polit. State*, IX, 160; *Whalley's News Letter*, No. 70.

[111] Boscawen was a nephew of the late Earl of Godolphin, and controlled the boroughs of Tregony and Truro. *D. N. B.*

[112] *Polit. State*, IX, 161. Thomas Harley, his cousin, also lost in Radnorshire, *Py. Reg.*, p. 200.

favor them. Tory losses were rather general throughout England, while in Scotland likewise the Whigs made notable gains, largely through the influence of the Dukes of Argyle, Montrose and Roxborough. The young Earl of Clare (later Duke of Newcastle) was responsible for the presence of eighteen representatives in the House of Commons. James Craggs, Sr. together with his son and namesake, were patrons of an equal number, while the Earl of Sunderland and General William Cadogan sponsored nine each, James Stanhope eight, and George Treby six.[113] The Whigs secured a safe margin of more than a hundred, without taking into consideration the large number of controverted election cases that remained to be decided.[114] Early in June, 1715, there was a party vote on the report of the Committee of Secretary, appointed to inquire into the actions of the late Tory Ministry. The result was an easy victory for the Whigs by a vote of 280 to 160. With such backing, the Whig cabinet proceeded apace with the impeachment of Bolingbroke and Oxford.[115]

The four vigorous Whig leaders, who averaged only about forty years of age, never gave the Tories a chance to rally their forces after this decisive defeat at the polls.[116] Immediately a victory was assured, the Whigs speeded up their policy of punishing their political enemies and rewarding their friends, until nearly half of the total membership of the Commons were office holders, pensioners or sinecure holders. Before the pollings were quite ended, the

[113] Memorandum in Cragg's Papers, *Stowe MSS.* (Brit. Mus.), 247, ff. 193–199; Nulle, *op. cit.*, p. 65. The first reference is due to the courtesy of Dr. Robert Walcott, Jr., of Harvard University, who kindly sent me a copy of his transcript.

[114] These numbered one hundred and twelve. *Polit. State*, IX, 120.

[115] *Commons Jour.*, XVIII, 166.

[116] *British Weekly Mercury*, No. 508; *Weekly Packet*, No. 142; Sir Thomas Erskine May gave the number of officeholders as two hundred seventy-one. *Constitutional History, 1760–1860* (N. Y., 1891), p. 298.

Earl of Nottingham received a pension of £3500 during his Majesty's pleasure; Lord Wharton, £2000 during his Majesty's life; the Duke of Shrewsbury a pension of £3000, and Lord Somers an additional pension of £2000.[117] Within a few weeks inexorable Whig pressure drove Viscount Bolingbroke into exile and, a few months later, the Duke of Ormond, darling of the people, was impeached and fled to France, as Oxford was being sent to the Tower to await trial. Almost at once, the Ministry rewarded the mercantile interests for the energy and money they had expended in the election, by passing two laws which further strengthened "the bonds between the State and the Bank," whereby the latter "began its management of the National debt."[118] The bourgeoisie thus encouraged, soon cast discretion to the winds, as the South Sea Bubble sufficiently attests.

The Tory leaders were gradually rendered desperate by the firmness of the Whig Ministry and were literally goaded into a rebellion in which they had slight chance of success. The victory at the polls greatly strengthened the prestige of the Whig Ministry in Continental diplomacy. The aging French monarch was reluctant to give further cause for offence to a Government which was bitterly denouncing the Tories for having conceded so much to the Bourbons by the Treaty of Utrecht. The lack of French aid

[117] Charles Leslie, the Highflier journalist, was most cynical: — "The Exchequer has purchased a Parliament that is to fall in with the measures of your pretended King and his Ministry, and when the blood is drawn which they are hankering after, if an army should be required (under the pretext of an invasion) by him that has a prior title to the Crown, you have no great reason to believe that it would be refused; but if they should hesitate upon that demand, the Treasury that bought a Parliament of the country, may buy an army of the Parliament, and when a bargain is struck, Dutch bottoms can bring in more Prussians and Hanoverians." *Somers Tracts* (London, 1815), XIII, 699.

[118] R. D. Richards, *Early History of Banking* (London, 1929), p. 192; 1 George I, chaps. 19, 20.

financial and military, made the Jacobite adventure a rash one, particularly since the Dutch stood ready to aid Britain with 8000 troops. The collapse of the Stuart cause at Sheriffmuir and Preston furnished the astute Whig leaders with sufficient pretext for the passage of the Septennial Act, three months after the Pretender's flight. This measure successfully fortified the Whig position, which was strengthened by each succeeding general election for a generation.[119]

One of the most fundamental successes of the Whig leaders, after the defeat of the "Fifteen," was in associating Jacobitism with the Church. The Church was somewhat quiescent during the election. It thus overlooked its last great opportunity, for another never came. In 1710 it drove the Whigs into political exile; at the beginning of 1715, these same Whigs dared not move against the ranking plenipotentiary at Utrecht because he was a bishop; nor proceed against Bishop Atterbury, for his *English Advice*; only five years later, however, this brilliant and popular Churchman was sent to the Tower, and soon thereafter both deprived and banished.

During the closing hours of July, 1714, not only Queen Anne but the Old Tory party became the victim of an apoplectic stroke; the Tories' second stroke resulted from the election of 1715; the third and final one was the Jacobite Rebellion; and the Septennial Act marks its interment. A fragment of the old party wandered more than the Biblical forty years in the political wilderness, before it managed to reëstablish itself in power, by the aid of a new political philosophy and the cordial support of the third Hanoverian King. A broadside forecast such results immediately after the election:

119 L. Hanson, *The Government and the Press* (London, 1936), p. 3.

"Farewell Old Year, for thou canst ne'er return,

No more than Our Great Queen for whom we mourn.

. . . .

Farewell Old Year, for thou with Broomstick hard
Hast drove poor Tory from St. James's Yard.
Farewell Old Year, Old Monarch, and Old Tory.
Farewell Old England, thou has lost thy Glory." [120]

[120] Reprinted in *Verney Letters*, II, 21.

WILLIAM THOMAS MORGAN.

ACADIA AND THE BEGINNINGS OF MODERN BRITISH IMPERIALISM[1]

IN APPROACHING the study of British colonial history from that of the Maritime Provinces of Canada, one may raise the question of the relations of this region to the beginnings of modern British imperialism as distinguished from the earlier British mercantilism. When did Great Britain turn from her earlier preoccupation in acquiring and controlling possessions for the furtherance of mercantilistic ideals to acquiring and governing them for the furtherance of imperialistic ideals?

While something may be said in favor of the position that the successful revolt in America of the thirteen colonies represents the collapse of mercantilism as a leading experiment in British statecraft, one is confronted by the fact that in many respects the policy of the government toward overseas possessions continued to be much the sort of thing after 1783 that it had been before the Revolutionary War. It will be noted in this connection that the navigation laws of the Restoration period, culminating in the comprehensive Act of 1696, constituted the chief vehicle for the realization of mercantilistic ideals. These laws were reënforced in the eighteenth century by numerous statutes regulating trade and industry. And, in spite of the influence of Adam Smith's *Wealth of Nations* against the interference of government with the course of trade, it was only in 1823 that there appeared a frank repudiation of the old British trade and navigation system in the pas-

[1] This paper under title "The Approach to the Study of Colonial History from the Maritime Provinces" was presented at the Washington meeting of the American Historical Association in 1934.

sage of the free-trader Huskisson's reciprocity duties bill. But by that year the so-called New British Empire was well on its way, with practically all of what is now India and Ceylon under firm political control, together with the Cape of Good Hope, the Straits Settlements, Malta, British Guiana, and Australia — not to mention other acquisitions of perhaps less importance secured subsequent to the Peace of 1763. In other words, the transition from seventeenth-century mercantilism to full-fledged nineteenth-century imperialism was undoubtedly very gradual. For example, the delicate negotiations culminating in the Jay Treaty of 1794 indicate to what extent mercantilistic conceptions still possessed vitality.

Two dates have been suggested by American scholars as most significant in marking the transition under consideration and each, it may be noted with interest, precedes the American Revolution. Professor Charles M. Andrews in the first volume of his *magnum opus*, *The Colonial Period of American History*, stresses the importance of the year 1763 [p. xiii], while Professor Stanley M. Pargellis in his *Lord Loudoun in North America*, fastens upon the year 1757, that is, the year in which Pitt took office [p. 1]. Accepting the importance of these dates, to the writer the year 1749 appears to be even more significant. For it seems to mark a decided shift in British policy in favor of employing modern imperialistic methods both in the region to the south of the St. Lawrence and in that of the upper Ohio. By imperialism as against mercantilism, one has in mind of course the policy of comprehending through conquest or diplomacy large bodies of land either occupied or unoccupied by people. In this connection one thinks of government as by no means passive with groups of patentees exploiting the opportunities for private gain, but on the other hand aggressively employing whatever means may be necessary to achieve the desired ends as envisaged by the state, with centralization of power. One thinks also in terms of systematized efforts to control dependent races or nationalities in order to further the purposes of the dominant group and of government-promoted immigration for the consolidation of political power. Trade and immediate profits with the political and economic philosophy embodied therein, in other words, becomes secondary to power politics, empire-building and future prospects.

It is not without significance that the Treaty of Aix-la-Chapelle was the last entered into by Great Britain — at least before the days of Gladstone — that voluntarily sacrificed empire for trade. In turning back to France the two strategically located islands of Isle Royale (Cape Breton) and Isle St. Jean (Prince Edward) in the Gulf of St. Lawrence in order, among other things, to secure the restoration to the East India Company of its trading post at Madras, British diplomats were following the sound mercantilistic principles that guided them in the Treaty of Utrecht.[2] For it must be understood that up to 1748 the relations of England with India were based fundamentally upon reciprocal trade advantages. At Madras the British East India Company faithfully paid its annual rental of 1200 pagodas for the ground occupied by the post of St. George up to the time of its capture by the French in 1746; the struggle in that year with the French Compagnie des Indes, while in a sense a phase of the War of the Austrian Succession, was primarily one over the trade of the Deccan and the Carnatic and continues after the conclusion of the Peace. Even the so-called sovereignty

[2] While the Treaty of Utrecht brought extension of the empire, the great motivation guiding the English in the various stages of negotiations that led to its ratification was that of immediate trade and commercial advantage. For an excellent brief analysis of these negotiations see A. W. Ward, "The Peace of Utrecht," *Cambridge Modern History* (Cambridge, 1908), V, 439–445.

of Bombay was a purely commercial asset of the Company and was confined until 1756 to the narrow limits of the island of that name. Indeed, after a century and a half of important activity in India, the directorate of the now United Company of Merchants of England Trading to the East Indies could write in 1752 to those in charge in India, that " . . . a solid and durable peace is the sole end at which you should aim . . . the object of the Company is not to become a land power." [3] Thus it seems clear that at Aix-la-Chapelle the British government retreated from the daring imperialistic project of the conquest of New France with which it had toyed from time to time, and especially in 1746. In spite, therefore, of the influence of such thorough-going imperialists as William Shirley, the British turned back into what seemed to them to be the comparative quiet and also comparative security of traditional mercantilism.

But this hoped-for tranquillity was not to be. Indeed, all available evidence points to the fact that the French authorities were in no mood after 1748 to emphasize mere economic development and trade penetration in North America. From the time of the signing of the treaty of peace the governors of New France ceaselessly promoted enterprises aggressively imperialistic in nature and for reasons that are not difficult to understand in following the official correspondence. In 1749 Céleron de Blainville was sent by the Comte de la Galissonière to the upper Ohio region with French troops to take possession of the country in the name of His Most Christian Majesty and to drive out the British fur traders; Boishérbert was ordered to the St. John with a detachment to reassert French control over the region west of the Bay of Fundy. Not

Quoted by V. A. Smith, *The Oxford History of India* (Oxford, 1919), p. 478.

only was he to protect the Abenaki Indians from British interference, but also the Acadians living about the river who were disinclined to renew their oaths of allegiance to the British Crown, now expected of them with the restoration of peace; [4] later in the year the Chevalier de la Corne appeared in the Acadian settlements at the head of the Bay of Fundy with another force,[5] announcing to the people of Shediac (Chedaique), Petitcodiac, Memaramcook, and Shepody that they also were not to renew their oaths of allegiance to King George since they were not only Frenchmen in language and ways of life, but French subjects, however much they had been neglected as such during the previous thirty-five years.[6] By that year, in

[4] With respect to the region to the westward of the Bay of Fundy, it may be pointed out that in 1718 the Marquis de Vaudreuil in a letter from Quebec to the British governor at Annapolis Royal protested the presence of English vessels in the St. John River which he claimed was within the French dominion; he also encouraged the Acadians to withdraw from the Peninsula, promising them lands along the St. John, which they might receive by applying to the French missionary to the Abenaki Indians, Loyard. As a result, a number of families removed thither. However, during the period that Jean Pierre Danielon was acting as priest at Medoctec, the Governor at Annapolis Royal, taking cognizance of the Acadian settlements on the St. John, ordered the heads of families to come to the fort in order to take an oath of allegiance. Apparently a number of them living at St. Anne thereupon complied in 1736 and agreed to hold their land of the British Crown. By 1733 the Acadian families on the St. John numbered, according to a census taken in that year, twenty — in all one hundred and eleven souls. (W. O. Raymond, *The River St. John* (St. John, 1910), pp. 162–164, 167.) With respect to the Acadian settlements about the head of the Bay of Fundy, it is clear that land disputes were appealed to the Council at Annapolis Royal and that its decisions were accepted. For a discussion of this see John Clarence Webster, *The Forts of Chignecto* (Shediac, N. B., 1930), p. 22.

[5] Boishérbert's detachment that came to the St. John in the spring of 1749 was small, but de la Corne who left Quebec for Baie Verte in October of that year had a considerable force and was placed in general command of operations to the west and north of the Bay of Fundy. *Canadian Archives, Report* (Ottawa, 1905), II, 288, 295.

[6] It is estimated that at the time of the expulsion there were some three thousand Acadians living beyond the Peninsula in what is now New Brunswick. W. O. Raymond, "New Brunswick," *Canada and Its Provinces* (Toronto, 1914–1917), XIII, 127–128.

fact, it is now clear that the governor general of New France was acting upon a settled policy which had in view nothing less than the regaining, if possible, of all Acadia.[7] Naturally, the movements just described compelled a drastic change in British policy toward this region and elsewhere in North America, thus effectually preventing the anticipated relapse back into mercantilism with its emphasis upon trade interests, individual initiative, and a passive type of government regulation — such as was presaged in the Treaty of Aix-la-Chapelle.

In other words, the history of British policy with respect to the region comprehended within the present Maritime Provinces, may be divided into two distinct periods. During the first, extending to 1749, this policy is quite in harmony with seventeenth-century mercantilistic conceptions; during the second, from 1749 onward, with nineteenth-century imperialistic conceptions. From the time of the cession of Acadia in 1714, to 1749, a weak garrison at old Port Royal, renamed Annapolis Royal, kept alive British claims to Acadia under title to Nova Scotia; a governor and council equally weak made gestures in the direction of asserting control over the rapidly multiplying French-speaking inhabitants dispersed in settlements about the Bay of Fundy, while tactfully temporizing over such serious issues as were involved in the oath of allegiance and land-holding and in unauthorized land appropriations on the part of the Acadians.[8] Under this policy of neglect the inhabitants multiplied, scattered, and

[7] Maurepas, writing to de la Galissonière on June 3, 1748, gave him *carte blanche* to take whatever measures he desired for the purpose of drawing the Acadians to Isle Royale and Isle St. Jean. *Canadian Archives*, *Report* (1905), II, 282. By July of the following year the latter, it is clear, was designing the recapture of the entire Acadian Peninsula. *Ibid.*, II, 303.

[8] This has been treated in a most illuminating manner by J. B. Brebner, *New England Outpost* (New York, 1927).

prospered. From the beginning of the third decade to the capture of the Island of Canso in 1744 by the French, another weak garrison watched over the British interests in the Canso fisheries which were almost entirely in control of New England men who came in the spring and departed in the fall, leaving behind their fish staging and cook houses.

The great change of the year 1749 in British policy affected not only Acadia but the region of the upper Ohio.[9] However, it is with the former that we are particularly concerned. At last the Crown, after a third of a century of neglect, determined — as the designs of France upon this region became ever more apparent — to assert an effective control at least over the Peninsula by promoting the colonization of it by disbanded British troops and their families and by foreign Protestants and by erecting two or more strongholds at strategic points supported by powerful garrisons made up of regular soldiers.[10] This would discourage, it was felt, any further French interfer-

[9] This is indicated by the granting in 1749 to the Ohio Company of a royal permit to patent a large body of land about the forks at the Ohio under condition that it would settle the same, and also by the sending of cannon from the royal arsenal in 1753 for the manning of one or more forts to be constructed by the Company for the purpose of repelling the French. Subsequently, with the outbreak of hostilities at the forks, there took place the dispatch of regiments from Ireland under General Braddock for active service in the Ohio Valley previous to a declaration of war.

[10] At this point it may be well to point out that the settlement of Georgia, while having certain things in common with the settlement of Nova Scotia, as, for example, the setting up of a buffer colony to guard against the encroachments of a rival nation, was conceived and carried out in a very different spirit. It was, to begin with, primarily a philanthropic enterprise fostered not by the Government itself but by an association whose aims were so far removed from those involved primarily in the extension of the power of the state, which characterizes all really imperialistic enterprises, that a charter was issued that placed immediate authority for the realization of the plan in the hands of a body of trustees whose chief interests throughout the entire history of its activities, as the minutes of its meetings disclose, were fundamentally charitable and benevolent. See "An American Arcadia," in the author's *The British Empire before the American Revolution* (Caldwell, Idaho and New York, 1936, 1939), II, chap. vi.

ence with the inhabitants, would also permit the government to bring adequate pressure to bear upon the latter to take an unequivocal oath of allegiance to King George, and would break the French alliances with the Acadian Indians, especially two powerful tribes, the Micmac and the Abenaki. The project had been strongly urged upon the Board of Trade, not only by Governor Paul Mascarene at Annapolis Royal,[11] but by Governor William Shirley of Massachusetts Bay, whose influence with the ministry was very great indeed at this juncture on account of the success of his plan during the late war for the capture of Louisbourg.[12]

In gathering support for his plan Shirley turned to the Massachusetts Bay Assembly. On April 6, 1749 — some two months after his first letter to the Secretary of State for the Southern Department, in which he had first set forth this program, and almost a month after his second letter on the same subject — he sent a message to the Assembly in which he made clear not only the dangers to New England of the French "encroachments" at Crown Point and the importance of erecting a fort near that place, but also the necessity both of a stronghold at Chebucto Harbour within the Province of Nova Scotia to guard against the menace of Louisbourg which the French were preparing to re-occupy, and of the colonization of the Peninsula "with good Protestant subjects." The Assembly a fortnight later drew up resolutions in which it concurred heartily with the Governor in his proposals for safeguarding the frontiers.[13] The British government, however,

[11] Governor Mascarene to the Board of Trade, Oct. 17, 1748. Nova Scotia State Papers, *Public Archives of Canada*, A. 32, 1748, 231–244. These papers will hereafter be designated by the letters *N.S.S.P.*

[12] See, for example, Shirley's letters to Bedford of February 18 and March 3, 1749, *N.S.S.P.*, A. 33, 1749, 148–149, and 198–199.

[13] The resolutions are to be found in *N.S.S.P.*, A. 33, 1749, 231–233.

before Shirley could communicate the desires of the Assembly, had determined to act.

Thereupon, with vast expenditure from the public treasury [14] and with the concentration of a powerful force of regular troops, which no immediate commercial advantages could possibly justify, this strongly imperialistic enterprise was pressed toward fulfillment under the supervision, in turn, of Governors Cornwallis, Hopson, and Lawrence. This appears to be not merely a New England enterprise, nor even primarily a New England enterprise.[15] Granting the influence of the Governor of Massachusetts Bay, who was not a New Englander either by birth or adoption, in furthering the undertaking, one may suggest that Shirley's point of view at this period was, quite apart from his official New England connections, distinctly that of an extremely aggressive British official, really an arch-imperialist, determined to advance the interests of the British Crown at the expense of the great rival of the latter, His Most Christian Majesty, the King of France.[16] In fact, Shirley's detachment with respect to peculiar Massachusetts Bay interests is evidenced not only in his refusal to support the claims of that province to lands claimed by New York when this bade fair to hamper the working out of the British imperialistic program in North America,[17] but also in his efforts, at the height of his popularity in New England, to secure a transfer to the governorship of

[14] The amount expended from 1749 to 1763 was £613,969. 1. 8½. This is quoted by J. B. Brebner from *Chalmers MSS.*, folio 29. (*New England Outpost*, 187.)

[15] For a very able defence of this thesis that the new policy in Nova Scotia can be laid at the door of New England consult again Brebner, *New England Outpost*.

[16] For example, see his letter of February 18, 1748/9 to the Duke of Bedford, *N.S.S.P.*, A. 33, 1749, 136–159.

[17] E. B. O'Callaghan, *Documentary History of New York* (Albany, 1849–51), III, 801–803.

either New York or Jamaica.[18] As to the New Englanders themselves and the new policy, it is evident that in some respects at least they felt highly gratified with it — especially as to those phases relating to the protection of their Canso fisheries and the control of the Acadian Indians, both of which they had so much at heart. In other respects they must have had reason to feel apprehensive of the unprecedented extension into North America of the active, military authority of the Mother Country in time of peace in a region adjoining their own through the setting up of a régime quite out of sympathy with New England republicanism.[19]

While the foundations of Halifax were being securely laid in Chebucto Harbour and a strong fort at Beaubassin was likewise taking form, a joint Anglo-French Commission was meeting in Paris for the purpose of attempting to settle definitively not only the ownership of St. Lucia and other West India Islands but also the limits of the territory ceded to Great Britain by France in 1714 at Utrecht under name of *Novam Scotiam quoque sive Acadiam totam limitatibus suis antiquis comprehensam ut et portus regii urbem, nunc Annapolim regiam dictam* — "Nova Scotia, otherwise called Acadia, in its entirety, conforming to its ancient limits, together with the town of Port Royal, now called Annapolis Royale." [20] In this connection it is of interest to note that Great Britain and France, in making appoint-

[18] *Correspondence of William Shirley*, ed. C. H. Lincoln (New York, 1912), I, 508–550; II, 1–3.

[19] The problem involved in the establishment in Nova Scotia of a representative form of government at this juncture is clearly developed by Professor Brebner in his *New England Outpost*, Chap. ix, "The Rights of Englishmen."

[20] On October 31, 1749, the Duke of Bedford wrote to the Board of Trade signifying His Majesty's command that a commission and instructions be prepared for William Shirley and William Mildmay nominated "as commissarys for settling all Points in dispute in America between the Crowns of Great Britain and France as well in relation to the Limits in North America as to the four disputed Islands in the West Indies" (C. O. 323, O. 22. 3). The commission there-

ments to this commission, each selected perhaps the most extreme advocate of imperialistic measures in North America in the persons, respectively, of Governor Shirley and the Marquis de la Galissonière, men who had, indeed, already clashed in North America over rival expansionist plans before they met face to face across the green baize in Paris during the years from 1750 to 1753.[21] In emphasizing this point, one may say that it is not without significance that early in 1749 before his appointment, Shirley in a letter, previously mentioned, to the Secretary of State for the Southern Department, the Duke of Bedford, had set forth claims respecting the true limits of Nova Scotia which were magnificent in their sweep. On this occasion he affirmed that should Crown Point be recognized to be within the limits of Canada and also Gaspé near the mouth of the St. Lawrence, "of which the French have been possessed upwards of twenty years," it might greatly affect the boundary of Nova Scotia as the French would naturally claim that this province was limited to lands east of a line connecting the two places "which would bring above half that Province within the French Limits." He, therefore, urged that it was absolutely necessary for commissioners to be appointed "to run Lines between His Majesty's Colonies and Canada." [22] But Shirley was over-optimistic respecting the limits that such Frenchmen as Galissonière were prepared to assign to Nova Scotia or Acadia, for the latter in July of the same year, and also previous to his appointment as a "commissarie," had expressed to the French minister his views that "*l'Acadie*

---

upon issued is dated April 14, 1750. It is in Latin and is among the old Plantations General Papers: C. O. 323, O. 49. 4.

[21] See, for example, the letter sent by Galissonière to Governor Mascarene dated January 15, 1748/9 which was sent to Governor Shirley for reply. *N.S.S.P.*, A. 33, 1749, 18–19.

[22] His letter is dated February 18, 1748/9. *N.S.S.P.*, A. 33, 1749, 141–142.

suivant ses anciennes limites est la presqu'ile bornée par son isthme," by which he meant that Canada extended up to the Acadian Peninsula.[23]

The selection of these men on the part of Great Britain and France, respectively, is indicative, not only of the wide divergency in point of view of the two governments, but also that neither was in a mood to make extreme concessions in the midst of promoting its own imperialistic program. It is, however, perhaps only just to point out that the French ambassador in London, the Duc de Mirepoix, was still convinced, after the negotiations had been going on between the powers for over two years, of the devotion of the English ministry in seeking a basis for peace and of its unwillingness to commit aggression.[24]

The instructions prepared for Shirley and his associate, Mildmay, in the spring of 1750 make clear that such issues as those involving the Great Lakes region, or the Ohio Valley, or the neutral islands in the Caribbeans, were quite secondary in importance to those respecting Acadia or Nova Scotia. It was declared that "nothing is of so much importance or can tend more immediately to the preservation of the good Harmony which at present so happily subsists betwixt the two Crowns, as the speedy determination of the Disputes relating thereto." The commissaries were therefore directed "to insist that this point be the first discussed, and you are not to treat upon any other Point until this be finally settled and concluded." [25]

[23] His letter is printed in the *Canadian Archives*, *Report* (1905), II, 304.

[24] This is emphasized in a letter sent by M. Rouillé, the Minister, to M. Galissonière, August 15, 1752. Referring to the possibility of a peaceful termination of the negotiations he writes: "Il [the Duc de Mirepoix] est toujours dans le mesme opinion ou vous l'avès vu sur la sincérité des dispositions que le ministère Britannique fait paroître pour les terminer." *Archives des Colonies*, Canada, B. 96, 45.

[25] For the instructions see *N.S.S.P.*, A. 39, 1750, 263.

As to the boundaries, the British commissaries were called upon "to insist that Accadia, part of which has since been called Nova Scotia, was actually deemed and understood by both nations to be bounded by the following limits": on the west a line from the mouth of the Penobscot (Pentagoet) River northward to the St. Lawrence River; on the north, the southern bank of that stream eastward to Cape Rozier; on the east, the shore line of the Gulf of St. Lawrence, but excluding Cape Breton; on the south, the Atlantic Ocean back to the Penobscot, but including the Cape Sable Islands. They were advised that it was this region with the general limits indicated above that France repeatedly claimed under the express name of Acadia and which she finally, under the terms of the Twelfth Article of the Treaty of Utrecht, handed over to Great Britain, while reserving Cape Breton and the islands lying within the mouth and the Gulf of St. Lawrence. With respect to the region along the Atlantic between the Penobscot and the Kennebec and stretching northward to the St. Lawrence, they likewise were instructed to insist that — in spite of claims put forward by the French at an earlier period that Acadia included the same — "the said Lands and Territory did then and so now belongs to the Crown of Great Britain." [26] Further, they were to

[26] With respect to the region between the Kennebec and the St. Croix River, as early as 1673 the General Court of Massachusetts Bay presumed to set up the County of Devonshire and appointed commissioners among the so-called proprietors of these lands to hold a county court and courts for small causes. Subsequent to this effort at colonization other attempts were made to settle this region, particularly between 1714 and 1720, and rather large sums were laid out for improvements. For in the second Massachusetts Bay charter it was expressly placed under the jurisdiction of the colony. The enterprises, however, came to naught by reason of the incursions of the Indians, particularly in 1723. In 1731, a dispute having arisen between rival proprietarial groups over the lands to the eastward of the Kennebec, the matter was referred to the Attorney and Solicitor General, P. Yorke and E. Talbot, who handed down an opinion that was favorable to the continued claims of jurisdiction on the part of Massachusetts Bay. This opinion, with supporting evidence regarding earlier efforts

press "that necessary orders be dispatched for the due execution of the aforesaid Article of the Treaty of Utrecht according to the true Intent and meaning thereof, and for removing any settlements made by the subjects of his most Christian Majesty, if there be any such within the Limits aforesaid." Finally, they were to insist that the French, who, contrary to the express terms of the treaty, had taken upon themselves to fish upon the coast of Acadia or Nova Scotia, had no right or title to carry on this activity anywhere within thirty leagues of any part of the coast of the said Province, thus denying the legality of the French fisheries on Isle Percée.[27]

However, in addition to these instructions, the British commissaries were furnished with a general plan of compromise comprehending both Nova Scotia and the neutral islands of the Caribbean Sea. This involved the recognition on the part of His Most Christian Majesty of the British claims as to the true limits of Nova Scotia and a pledge to demolish all forts erected by him on the Peninsula or the coast of the mainland southward of the St. Lawrence River, with the recalling of all his subjects who did not desire to take an oath of allegiance to the King of Great Britain. In consideration of this recognition, the latter was prepared to promise that no settlements should be made, or forts erected, on any part of the coast or shores of the Gulf of St. Lawrence or the St. Lawrence River "whereby the free Navigation of the subjects of his most Xtian Majesty in & upon the said Gulf & River may

---

of colonization, is embodied in Edward Northey's *Legal Opinions*, an annotated manuscript copy of which is in the Library of Congress. For Massachusetts Bay's interest in the Kennebec region in 1754 see Governor Shirley's letter to the Board of Trade of February 20, and the letters of the Board of Trade of May 24 and July 2 to Sir Thomas Robinson, Secretary of State for the Southern Department, C. O. 5: 754, 6, 32–34, 35.

[27] *N.S.S.P.*, A. 39, 1750, 264–275.

be any ways interrupted, molested or annoyed, saving to His Majesty the King of Great Britain all Right & Priviledge of Fishery by virtue of the Treaty of Utrecht & of any other Treaties." Again, with respect to the neutral islands, the British commissaries were permitted to agree that if his British Majesty "shall have & enjoy the quiet & peaceable possession of the Island of Tobago in consideration whereof His most Xtian Majesty shall have & enjoy the quiet & peaceable possession of the Island of St. Lucia." Finally, it was proposed, "That the Islands of St. Vincent & Dominica shall be declared Neutral with Liberty to the subjects of either Crown to Trade or Settle thereon." [28]

Thus, it is evident that while the British government was at last determined to press its claims to all of the region stretching from New England eastward and northeastward to the St. Lawrence River and the Atlantic Ocean, it was not oblivious of the fact that the French must have an unimpeded access to Canada and were quite prepared to grant this. Indeed, it is quite apparent that no threat against the latter province was intended during the period of negotiation.[29]

When the British commissaries set forth the above claims respecting Nova Scotia these were flatly rejected by those representing the French crown. As a result, both made their appeal to history. In discharging at one another rival memoirs as to the true limits of ancient Acadia supported by skilfully edited collections of documents,[30] the

[28] *Ibid.*, A. 39, 1750, 276–279.

[29] In the final reply of the French, issued in 1757 in the midst of war, the English were accused of setting forth exorbitant pretensions as to the limits of Acadia for the purpose of invading Canada. *Mémoires des Commissaries du Roi et de Ceux de sa Majesté Britannique* (Paris, 1755 and 1757), IV, 36.

[30] These are embodied in *Mémoires des Commissaries du Roi et de Ceux de sa Majesté Britannique* (Paris, 1755 and 1757), I–IV; *Memorials of the English and French Commissaries Concerning the Limits of Nova Scotia and Acadia* (London,

strength and weakness of each side to the controversy appeared. The British were accused of confusing both in their arguments and in their maps the limits of ancient Acadia with those of ancient Nova Scotia; as for the latter, the French commissaries insisted that at best it was only a dream province never having enjoyed reality.[31] The former were also accused of confusing the limits of ancient Acadia with those of the Acadia of the year 1710 which was not "ancient Acadia" at all but "modern Acadia." [32] The French, on the other hand, were accused of distorting the plain meaning of the Treaty of Utrecht; of attempting to accomplish by diplomacy something that they had failed to achieve by war.[33]

From the viewpoint of the present-day student of international law the French diplomats undoubtedly labored under certain fatal handicaps in attempting to sustain the thesis, to wit: that all that France surrendered or ever intended to surrender in 1714 under title of Acadia with its ancient limits, was a narrow strip of land along the eastern littoral of the Peninsula extending from Forked Cape at the southern end to Cape Canso — a region almost utterly devoid of Acadians; and that beyond this ancient Acadia the only other possession surrendered was the town

1755); and *All the Memorials of the Courts of Great Britain and France Since the Peace of Aix-la-Chapelle Relative to the Limits of the Territory of both Crowns in North America; And the Right to the Neutral Islands in the West Indies* (The Hague, 1756).

[31] They said that the Nova Scotia granted to Sir William Alexander by James I was and remained "purement ideale." *Memorials of the English and French Commissaries*, p. 152.

[32] ". . . il port la cession de l'Acadie, non suivant ses limites actuelles, mais suivant ses anciennes limites," declared the French commissaries in their memorial. *Ibid.*, p. 180.

[33] The French commissaries, for example, insisted that if Sieur de Subercase, who was governor of Acadia in 1710 with his headquarters at Port Royal (that is, the later Annapolis Royal), placed that stronghold in Acadia in surrendering it to the English, this was the result of an improper extension that had been given to the limits of that province. *Ibid.*, p. 172.

of Port Royal in New France, with its environs.[34] This thesis quite ignored the fur trading monopoly granted to Sieur de Monts by the French King as early as 1604 to cover all the region stretching from what is now Pennsylvania to the St. Lawrence under title of Acadia (La Cadie) and which, therefore, made it the most ancient of Acadias to be recognized in French law; this thesis also ignored the fact that the most ancient of Acadian settlements was on an island in Passamaquoddy Bay and that, after the failure of this, the second most ancient of these was at Port Royal, both quite removed from the eastern shore yet both considered at the time by Frenchmen to be in the midst of Acadia. Further, it ignored the fact that the French diplomats in the negotiations just preceding the signing of the Treaty of Utrecht, but after the words "Acadia with its ancient limits" had been inserted at the request of the English, sought to persuade the latter to restore this possession to France for certain considerations, under the agreement that in that case its western limits would thereupon be the St. George River, rather than the Kennebec to the westward as the French had claimed in previous negotiations.[35] This, of course, affords the

[34] The French in these negotiations leaned heavily upon Champlain's *Voyages* (Paris, 1613) in making a distinction between the district of ancient Acadia and the districts of *Etchemins*, of *Almouchiquois*, and of *la grande rivière de Saint-Laurent. Ibid.*, pp. 571–575. They declared in this connection that the issue before them had nothing to do with the *jurisdiction* of governments established within the region under dispute but with the *limits* of the different provinces which sometimes had recognized one governor, as in the time of Subercase, and at other periods several, as in the time of Denys. In 1662, when M. le Comte d'Estrades was in this region, the predominant usage, they affirmed, was to call not only Acadia proper "Acadia" but also the neighboring regions that had been reunited under the same government. But these latter were not really in Acadia. *Mémoires des Commissaries du Roi et de Ceux de sa Majesté Britannique* (Paris, 1757), IV, 88, 302.

[35] *Memorials of the English and French Commissaries* (London, 1755), p. 679. It is true that on occasions the westward boundary of Acadia was not pushed to the Kennebec by the French. For example, in a memorial presented by the

strongest possible presumption that the French crown expected to yield in good faith the region westward to New England under title of Acadia,[36] and also that they would do this without attempting to engage in the diplomatic legerdemain of subtle distinctions that, for example, Sir Thomas Temple and Sieur du Bourg were guilty of in 1668, but rather by following the laudable example of Charles II who in 1671 brushed aside all specious and partial reasoning and turned back to France Acadia with the specific limits demanded by His Most Christian Majesty, which carried its boundaries westward to the Kennebec.[37] The French interpretation in 1750 of the Treaty of

---

French ambassador to the King of England on January 16, 1685, reference is made to "La Côte de l'Acadie, qui s'étend depuis l'isle Percée jusqu'a celle de Saint-George," somewhat to the east of the Kennebec (*ibid.*, pp. 614–615). Also on April 29, 1700 the French ambassador set forth certain proposals in which it was suggested that the boundary of Acadia under certain circumstances having to do with concessions by England elsewhere should be the St. George River, otherwise it would be the Kennebec. *Ibid.*, p. 622.

[36] In this connection it should be noted that in the memorial presented by Henry St. John to the Marquis de Torsi and dated May 24, 1712, the point was stressed that to help end all disputes between England and France arising over North America, Nova Scotia or Acadia according to its ancient limits, should be yielded by His Most Christian Majesty (*ibid.*, p. 662). This same request was embodied in the final proposals sent to the French King and signed by him on June 5, 1712. Further, in his reply Louis XIV agreed to the cession of Acadia according to its ancient limits "as it is demanded by the Queen of Great Britain" (*ibid.*, p. 667), implying thereby, according to all accepted rules of legal interpretation, that the territory surrendered was the territory that the Queen had in mind as Acadia and which in the preliminary negotiations was regarded by both sides to the treaty as being embraced within the general term of Acadia.

[37] By the act of cession of Acadia to France, February 17, 1667, as the result of the Treaty of Breda concluded the preceding July, it was provided that Charles "grant, quit, transfer, succeed all that country called Acadia, lying in North America which the said most Christian King did formerly enjoy, as namely the Forts and Habitations of Pentagoet (Penobscot), St. John, Port Royal, la Héve and Cape Sable." It is of interest that the specific places thus enumerated as lying within Acadia were written into the deed of recession by M. de Ruvigny. Temple argued in 1668 that Acadia was but a small part of the country of Nova Scotia and lay in the eastern part of the Peninsula. Du Bourg, representing the Campagnie Françoise des Indes Occidentales in North America at this juncture, was just as emphatic in insisting in retort that Cape Sable and

Utrecht was in fact preposterous, if not totally lacking in sincerity, for it was, as has been stated, an interpretation that adroitly excluded all the lands then considered the most fruitful from the cession, as well as most of the Acadians.[38] This interpretation placed upon the shoulders of His Most Christian Majesty a tremendous responsibility for the continuance of peace in North America.

As to the position of the English that the northern limit of Acadia was the St. Lawrence, two things may be said in support of this interpretation of the Treaty of Utrecht: First, the commissions of the French governors of Acadia before 1714 generally gave them jurisdiction from the St. Lawrence to the Kennebec.[39] Second, after the surrender of Acadia it is not without significance that the French officials who came to Annapolis Royal from Cape Breton in 1714, hoping to make arrangements to move the Acadians to French soil, not only assumed that those who were settled about Beaubassin at the upper end of the Bay of Fundy were within the ceded territory but would not encourage the inhabitants to settle at any place north or west of the peninsula on the mainland. They, in fact, bent all of their efforts, though unsuccessfully, to placing them upon either Isle Royale or Isle St. Jean, islands, it is to be

la Héve, that is, the eastern part of the Peninsula were not in Acadia at all but in Nova Scotia. For the act of cession of Acadia to France and the definite order of Charles II for the surrender of Pentagoet "in the countries of Acadia," see *ibid.*, pp. 581–585, 588–591, 601–603, and 606–610.

[38] In 1749, as has been previously pointed out, even de la Galissonière insisted that "l'Acadie suivant ses anciennes limites est la presqu'ile bornée par son isthme." *Canadian Archives, Report* (1905), II, 304.

[39] For example, the commission given to Sieur d'Aulnay Charnisay to be governor and lieutenant general of the country and coast of Acadia in New France, placed under his jurisdiction the region from the St. Lawrence River to the Virginias. (For the letters patent see *Memorials of the English and French Commissaries*, 573.) That given to Sieur de Subercase was in some respects less definite respecting the assumed limits of Acadia. His title was "Gouverneur de l'Acadie, du Cap Breton isles et terres adjacentes, depuis le cap des Rosiers de fleuve Saint-Laurent, jusqu'a l'ouverture de la rivière de Kinibequi."

noticed, specifically awarded to France in the Treaty of Utrecht.[40] Although it is true that Governor Vaudreuil sought to preserve after 1714 some semblance of influence in the valley of the St. John to the west of the Bay of Fundy by reason of seventeenth-century concessions granted by the French Crown, he felt impelled to act covertly through the French Indian missionary Loyard, whom he authorized to make grants of land to those Acadians who might be persuaded to leave the Peninsula. Yet even some of these who came, later on obeyed the summons of the English governor to appear at Annapolis Royal for the purpose of acknowledging that they held their lands of the Crown of Great Britain.[41] Indeed, even so late as 1749 the Intendant of New France, M. Bigot, in writing to the ministry regarding the possibility of colonizing the Acadians within the limits of New France, was obliged to confess that they could not with confidence be placed in any part of the region between "Gaspe" and "Boston" by reason of the fact that the limits of Canada in these parts had not been established.[42] Where, in fact, south of the St. Lawrence and east of Lake Champlain after 1714 and before 1744, the year King George's War began, was there a single military post above which the King's *fleur-de-lis* was flying as a sign of possession of the land? Had the representatives of the Crown of France in America really believed that any part of the mainland south of the St. Lawrence belonged to them, why did they not boldly assert their rights after Utrecht?[43] French

[40] For details regarding this see *N.S.S.P.*, A. 5 (1714), 14, 33–38.

[41] W. O. Raymond, *op. cit.*, pp. 162–164.

[42] See Bigot to Puyzieulx, Oct. 13, 1749. *Mémoires et Documents, Amerique*, 9, pp. 1, 146–153.

[43] The French commissaries asserted that the Sieurs de Vaudreuil who had a patent to a large part of the land of the St. John River had appointed judges and notaries and that the people on the River had always recognized the governor-general of Canada as their commander. (*Mémoires des Commissaries du Roi*

policy in North America, it should be kept in mind, was characterized by the setting up of posts wherever the Crown had important regional claims.

Indeed, outside of the settlements of the Acadians about the Bay of Fundy and other adjacent places the French commissioners in 1751 could only point to Isle Percée, an island fishery in the Gulf of St. Lawrence near the mainland, as settled by Frenchmen.[44] In 1752 a memorandum was issued at Quebec with reference to the possible colonizing of Canadians within the region between the mouth of the St. Lawrence and Baie Verte (Green Bay); those who prepared it could find that only one Canadian family was settled on the mainland and this poor family was cultivating but two arpents of land on the Restigouche River that flows into Chaleur Bay.[45] In addition, there were within these limits, it may be pointed out, two Indian missions, in each of which a French priest was established.

In attempting to account for the seeming indifference of France to the region on the mainland from the St. Lawrence to the Kennebec after 1714, it would appear that the ministers of His Most Christian Majesty were convinced that the Crown had lost all legal claim to this region; it would also appear that they looked forward hopefully to some change in fortune which would bring about the restoration of Acadia, peopled, as it was, only by French-speaking inhabitants. They may well have felt

et de Ceux de sa Majesté Britannique, IV, 37.) Yet Galissonière in writing to the minister July 25, 1749, before leaving for France, asserted that the inhabitants of the St. John were *demi-sauvages* who knew no other Frenchmen than those of the Peninsula of Acadia; that, having obeyed the French governor at Port Royal before the Treaty of Utrecht, they had been led to understand by the English governor that they were to obey him in the same manner. *Canadian Archives, Report* (1905), II, 304.

[44] *Mémoires des Commissaries du Roi et de Ceux de sa Majesté Britannique*, IV, 37–38.

[45] *Mémoire sur les Terres que bordent le Golfe St. Laurent*, Arch. Nat., Col., C[11] A. 98, 441.

that it was, therefore, to their interest not to attempt to juggle with the terms of the Treaty for the purpose of narrowing the limits of whatever they might some day demand back as old Acadia, especially in light of their seventeenth-century pretensions as to westward sweep of that province. But, with the news of the British plans for the colonization and the fortification of the Peninsula and their unfoldment, whatever optimism they had had that Acadia might, as it were, drop into the lap of the French King faded away, and was replaced by deep apprehensions as to the ultimate purposes of the English even with respect to Canada.

Nevertheless — granting the existence of this fear — in determining to limit British rights to the environs of Annapolis Royal and to the eastern part of the Peninsula, the French ministry assumed in this connection responsibility for two series of overt acts, both of which must be regarded as serious violations of international law and amity. The first was the establishment, as was previously made clear, of military posts in the heart of the very region that their predecessors had claimed and received back as Acadia in 1671, and had surrendered and vacated in 1714. The second was the approval accorded to the carefully formulated plans entered into by the Intendant of New France, M. Bigot, and the French missionary to the Micmacs, Le Loutre.[46] These plans called for the spreading of terror throughout all parts of Acadia, among all — including even Acadians as well as the new settlers — who might be disposed to recognize British authority.[47] This

[46] Bigot to the Minister, Oct. 18, 1750. Arch. Nat., Col., C[II] A. 96, 51.

[47] In an unsigned letter from New France written in the spring of 1749 and read to the French King on August 29, means were suggested for preventing the English from consolidating their position within the Peninsula. According to this, the Indians were to be engaged to oppose them openly and the Acadians were to be excited to support the hostile activities of the Indians. It was de-

was done by the simple means of driving the Micmacs and Abenaki into motion; who, incidentally, at this juncture were showing every inclination to enter into friendly relations with Governor Cornwallis at Halifax.[48] By this and other types of pressure, perhaps less terroristic but severe in the extreme, brought to bear upon the Acadians who had lived for forty years peacefully, even if rather independently, under English rule, it was expected that they would be impelled to refuse to take the unqualified oath of allegiance now expected of them and, if need be, leaving behind their bountiful farms, betake themselves in flight out of the Peninsula. In pursuit of his aims, it is quite clear, as evidenced in the French documents, that Le Loutre, although a priest of the church, did not hesitate to put a price in time of peace upon the scalps of all those loyal to the British Crown. What is more, he paid his Indians in person for bringing in these bloody souvenirs.[49] Indeed, it may be affirmed that the Bigot-Le Loutre project of stirring up the Acadians by means of the Indian terror and otherwise, supported as it was by Governor

---

clared that the missionaries to each of those groups had received orders and were disposed to conduct themselves accordingly. (*Canadian Archives*, *Report* (1905), II, 292.) On October 9 of that year La Jonquière, writing from Quebec to the French minister, stressed the necessity of acting with great secrecy so that the English might not suspect that the Canadian authorities were back of the Indians in their hostile moves. He declared that he was happy to say that the missionaries to the Abenaki and the Micmacs, "Le R. P. Germain et M. l'abbé Leloutre . . . ménageront leur intrigue de façon à n'y pas paroître." (*Ibid.*, II, 311.) However, it should be pointed out that not all of the French-speaking priests among the Acadians were involved in this plan to break the peace.

48 For Boishérbert's report from the St. John of August 29, 1749 on the accord of the Abenaki with the English see *ibid.*, II, 290.

49 See, for example, the letter of M. Prévost written from Louisbourg to the Minister of August 16, 1752. Arch. Nat., Col., C[11] B 33, 197. Other references relating to the terroristic activities of Le Loutre are presented by J. C. Webster in *The Career of Abbé Le Loutre in Nova Scotia*, pp. 10–11. Norman McL. Rogers, in his "Jean Louis Le Loutre" in *The Canadian Historical Review* for June, 1930, emphasizes especially the great devotion of the Abbé to the cause of his religion.

La Jonquière and the French ministry, made inevitable the final expulsion and dispersion as a war measure of this simple-hearted, ordinarily inoffensive people. In other words, the historic expulsion — an extreme, imperialistic act — was the direct result of the determination of the French authorities to undo by violent means the work of the statesmen at Utrecht. In condemning this procedure of the French authorities one must not forget, however, the dangers that seemed to threaten the Roman Catholic religion in face of the Protestant immigration and the desperate need of the Crown of France of reclaiming Acadia and the Acadians, especially after 1749. These people and their fertile lands possessed an importance out of all proportion to the numbers of the former and extent of the latter. The Peninsula was, indeed, the connecting link between Canada and the fortress of Louisbourg — in fact, the only link in winter, with the closing of the St. Lawrence to navigation. What is more, Louisbourg before 1750 was at most times quite dependent upon Acadia for food supplies and even after that year, in spite of all prohibitions, continued to receive from that source fairly large quantities of provisions. In fact it was Acadia, not Louisbourg, which was really the key to Canada. This was fully appreciated by the French authorities both in New France and at home.

The importance of maintaining at all costs the well-established route and indeed the only route by land between Quebec and Louisbourg by way of the St. John, Baie Verte, and the northern shore-line of the Peninsula doubtless helps to explain the unwillingness of the French ministers to consider favorably any such compromise as was apparently offered in the course of the negotiations by the English commissaries. According to this plan, a line should be run from the mouth of the Penobscot to its source and then due north to the St. Lawrence River, while another line should be run from a point twenty leagues up the Penobscot to a point on the Gulf of St. Lawrence twenty leagues to the northward of Cape Tourmentine, with the understanding that all lands to the southeast of the latter line should be in full sovereignty to the Crown of Great Britain, while all lands to the northwest of the same within the triangle should not be settled or possessed by the subjects of either crown.[50]

Curiously enough, the French Empire with all its resources could not feed itself in the middle of the eighteenth century. From Canada, Bigot sent reports of grain shortage and food riots;[51] France herself was an importer of bread stuffs and other staple food supplies in times of emergency; neither the French Sugar Islands nor Louisiana could live without succour; the Illinois settlements isolated in the heart of North America alone had at this period a constant surplus of food, but this was neither available nor adequate for supplying the great needs of the other French possessions beyond those of Louisiana and the scattered posts in the region of the Great Lakes. Acadia reclaimed, however, could not only support herself and the Louisbourg garrison but also aid Canada during the lean years. With the growing crisis between the French and British governments in the early 1750's, it is noteworthy that the former, in order to prepare for the outbreak of hostilities, felt under necessity to purchase enormous quantities of food stuffs from abroad for the provisioning of New France.[52] Ironically enough, most of

[50] This is set forth in the Newcastle Papers, *Add. MSS.* 33029: 291 and 299.

[51] See, for example, the letter written by de la Galissonière and Bigot to the French minister in 1748 (*Canadian Archives*, *Report* (1905), II, 281) and that by Jonquière and Bigot in 1752. (*Archives des Colonies*, *Canada*, B. 95, 40–43.)

[52] As to the extent of this commerce in grain in 1753, see the letter written by Raymond and Prevost from Louisbourg, July 17 and that by Prevost on the same date. *Archives des Colonies*, *Canada*, B. 97, 279–282, 308–310.

these supplies apparently came either from England after importation into France or from the English continental colonies.

In the light of all the factors involved, it is no wonder that the French Crown attached an incalculable value to the simple Acadian peasants and their fruitful marshlands as well as to the free access by land to Canada by way of the Acadian Peninsula. No wonder, perhaps, that His Most Christian Majesty was driven to embark upon a policy of extreme aggressiveness in hopes that it would bring elements of strength and permanence to his empire. But in doing so he risked his empire in America — and lost it. Under these circumstances Great Britain was thus led to make her first great move into the field of modern imperialistic enterprise, a move, however, that ended only with the conquest of Canada and the annihilation of French political power in India. The imperialism of Shirley and the Earl of Halifax of 1749 led to that of Pitt of 1757 with its even wider scope, and finally, following the Peace of 1763, to that of Grenville and Townshend, which came in answer to the demand for the internal reorganization of the expanded Empire.

LAWRENCE HENRY GIPSON.

THE ORGANIZATION OF GENERAL SULLIVAN'S ARMY IN THE RHODE ISLAND CAMPAIGN OF 1778

WHILE much has been written respecting the operations conducted by General John Sullivan in Rhode Island in 1778,[1] one aspect of the subject has been largely overlooked. I refer to the fact that Sullivan was obliged not only to command but to create an army. He was compelled to do on a small scale in the New England colonies what Washington was compelled to do on a large scale in all the colonies; viz. organize a fighting force out of scattered and scanty materials which had to be extracted from a group of states each of which claimed to be sovereign and independent and each of which by habit was more interested in securing its own welfare than in helping to promote that of its neighbors. Sullivan's achievement merits high praise and entitles him to rank not only as a capable general but as a capable organizer.

On February 21, 1778, the Continental Congress directed Washington to order a major-general to take command of

[1] Besides the general accounts in the histories of the American Revolution by Fiske, Trevelyan, Bancroft, Winsor, F. V. Greene, and C. H. Van Tyne, and in the histories of Rhode Island by S. G. Arnold and I. B. Richman, consult B. Cowell, *Spirit of '76 in Rhode Island* (Boston, 1850), G. W. Greene, *Life of Major-General Nathanael Greene* (3 vols., New York, 1871); T. C. Amory, "The Siege of Newport," *The Rhode Island Historical Magazine*, July, 1884; J. G. Rosengarten, "The German Soldiers in Newport, 1776–1779, and the Siege of 1778," *ibid.*, October, 1886; E. Field, *State of Rhode Island and Providence Plantations at the End of the Century* (3 vols., Boston, 1902); H. W. Preston, *The Battle of Rhode Island* (Providence, 1928). Several orderly books and diaries relating to the campaign have been preserved. Especially noteworthy are the *Journals* of Manasseh Cutler, ed. W. P. Cutler and J. P. Cutler (2 vols., Cincinnati, 1888), and the *Diary of Frederick Mackenzie* (2 vols., Cambridge, Massachusetts, 1930).

the troops in Rhode Island in place of Major-General Spencer, resigned.[2] Israel Putnam and William Heath were considered for the post, but since there was objection to them on the part of the committee which Congress had appointed to advise Washington, the commander-in-chief on March 10 appointed Sullivan.[3] Born in New Hampshire in 1740 of Irish parentage, John Sullivan had prior to the Revolution been a prosperous lawyer, mill-owner, and major of militia.[4] In December, 1775, when Paul Revere brought word to New Hampshire that the British were planning to remove the military stores from Fort William and Mary at Portsmouth, Sullivan with others rallied a band of men, captured the stronghold and made off with ninety-seven barrels of powder which were later used by the patriots with good effect at Bunker Hill.[5] He served in the first and second Continental Congresses. In 1776 he was appointed major-general. He took part in the siege of Boston, in the operations on the Canadian border, in the battles of Long Island, Trenton, Princeton, Brandywine, and Germantown, and shared the sufferings of Valley Forge. He was a man of overflowing energy, of ardent feeling, of exceptional bravery, and of resolute purpose. While quick to resent any imputation upon his character or capacity, he was also quick to return loyalty

[2] *Journals of the Continental Congress*, ed. W. C. Ford *et alia* (Washington, D. C., 1904–1936), X, 188.

[3] *The Writings of George Washington*, ed. J. C. Fitzpatrick (Washington, D. C., 1931–1934), XI, 1, 31.

[4] For biographical material relating to Sullivan, consult T. C. Amory, *The Military Services and Public Life of Major-General John Sullivan* (Boston, 1868); R. G. Adams' sketch of "John Sullivan" in *Dictionary of American Biography* (Washington, D. C., 1928–1936), XVIII, 192–193; *Letters and Papers of Major-General John Sullivan*, ed. O. G. Hammond (Concord, N. H., 2 vols., 1930–1931). The last mentioned work will be referred to in subsequent footnotes as Sullivan Papers. Volume I contains a sketch of Sullivan by Alonzo H. Quint. Major Hammond's prefaces abound in illuminating comment upon Sullivan's character and career and display appreciation of his ability as a military administrator.

[5] E. Taylor, *Paul Revere* (New York, 1930), pp. 123–126.

for loyalty. He was generous to the point of extravagance and drew heavily upon his private fortune to promote the success of the revolutionary cause.[6] He wielded the pen as effectively as the sword and woe to the soldier or politician who ventured to engage him in controversy, for he was a master of sarcasm and invective.[7] While hot-headed, he was not rash. Despite his impulsiveness, he often displayed on the field of battle a prudence and caution more characteristic of the Scotch than the Irish temperament. Like most gentlemen of his time he liked the flowing bowl.[8] Upon arriving in Providence to take charge of the American forces, one of his first acts was to address a letter to General Heath, commanding the Eastern Department with headquarters in Boston, inquiring of him where he could purchase a quarter-cask of the best port wine. In order to make certain of its quality, he requested Heath to have it tasted by one of his aides.[9] Upon arrival the wine failed to satisfy Sullivan's taste and despite the cares of newly-assumed office he sat down and addressed a letter to Heath in his own hand stating that "the wine is so Prick'd that it is Inferiour [*sic*] to Common Cyder." He added that he did not believe it had ever been tasted as requested.[10] Perhaps it was knowledge of this epicurean discrimination that caused Count D'Estaing, vice-admiral of the French fleet, upon his arrival off Newport, to make to the American general a present of pineapples and lemons and that led Lieutenant Pleville Le Peley to offer Sullivan a gift of cocoa-nuts.[11]

At the time of Sullivan's arrival in Rhode Island, the

[6] Amory, *op. cit.*, pp. 250, 255.

[7] Many illustrations are afforded in *Sullivan Papers*. See especially the controversy respecting Sullivan's conduct at Brandywine.

[8] Amory, *op. cit.*, pp. 251–252.

[9] *Sullivan Papers*, II, 38. Sullivan to Heath, April 24, 1778.

[10] *Ibid.*, II, 43. Sullivan to Heath, May 1, 1778.

[11] *Ibid.*, II, 171, 233.

British had been in occupation of Newport for two years and four months. On December 1, 1776, Howe had dispatched five fifty-gun ships and eight smaller vessels under Sir Peter Parker and six thousand troops under Sir Henry Clinton to take possession.[12] The reasons were both naval and military. The waters of Narragansett Bay flanked the line of communication between New York and England and thus afforded an excellent vantage point for attacks by American privateers and men-of-war upon British shipping. Such attacks could only be suppressed by the presence of a fleet.[13] From Rhode Island as a base, moreover, it was hoped that an army might be pushed into Massachusetts or Connecticut with a view to coöperating with the royal forces on the Hudson or Lake Champlain.[14] In the meantime the British were able to raid the towns of Rhode Island and southeastern Massachusetts with disastrous effect. They had the Americans at a disadvantage. The rebels were obliged to disperse their forces widely in order to guard one hundred and twenty miles of coastline, extending from Point Judith to Providence on the west and from Providence to Seaconnet Point on the east.[15] The British operating from Newport, which is centrally located, could select a point of attack on the shore and swoop down upon it before an adequate body of militia could be mobilized for its defence.[16] By the time local levies had assembled, the work of fire and sword had usually been completed and the invader was able to retire to his boats with

[12] J. W. Fortescue, *A History of the British Army* (London, 1902), III, 194.

[13] A. T. Mahan, *Major Operations of the Navies in the American War of Independence* (Boston, 1913), pp. 47–48.

[14] T. S. Anderson, *The Command of the Howe Brothers during the American Revolution* (New York, 1936), pp. 110, 112–113, 222–223, 246; Fortescue, *op. cit.*, pp. 194, 199.

[15] *Sullivan Papers*, II, 45. Sullivan to Washington, May 1, 1778.

[16] *Ibid.*, II, 46–47. Sullivan to Henry Laurens, May 3, 1778.

comparative safety.[17] Such raids were carried out against Warren and Bristol, Fall River, and New Bedford during the spring and summer of 1778.[18]

When Sullivan arrived at Providence on April 17 to assume command, the condition of affairs from the American point of view was gloomy. There were practically no troops on hand save a few bands of militia. On July 30, 1777, delegates from the New England states had assembled at Springfield, Massachusetts, to consider among other matters the defence of Rhode Island and had voted that four thousand and fifty men were to be raised for that purpose in the following proportions:

New Hampshire	300
Massachusetts	1500
Connecticut	750
Rhode Island	1500[19]

The decision of the convention had been approved by Congress in a resolution adopted January 13, 1778.[20]

Prior to Sullivan's arrival, however, little had been done to carry out the Springfield plan. Governor Cooke of Rhode Island reported to the general on March 26, "We have had no troops from New Hampshire since the 1st of January; or from Connecticut, since the middle of this month. The time for which the troops from Massachusetts were to serve expires to-morrow, when every man will leave us."[21] Thus the department of Rhode Island was "almost destitute of troops."[22] An army had to be

[17] *Ibid.*, II, 71. Sullivan to Meshech Weare, June 11, 1778.

[18] *Ibid.*, II, 57. Sullivan to Washington, May 26, 1778; *ibid.*, II, 63. Sullivan to Laurens, May 31, 1778; *ibid.*, II, 319–320. Silas Talbot to Sullivan, September 7, 1778.

[19] *Ibid.*, II, 31; B. Cowell, *op. cit.*, pp. 135–140.

[20] *Journals of the Continental Congress*, X, 46; XI, 759.

[21] *Sullivan Papers*, II, 31.

[22] *Ibid.*, II, 37. Sullivan to Governor Trumbull of Connecticut, April 22, 1778.

created. Sullivan at once began to shower appeals for men upon the neighboring states. These appeals were couched in strong though respectful language. The states were exceedingly touchy about their sovereignty and had to be handled with the utmost tact. In dealing with them Sullivan displayed an adroitness in diplomacy unusual in any soldier and especially surprising in a man of his temperament. The response to his appeals was laggard. There were many promises but little performance. On May 8, he wrote to Governor Bowdoin of Massachusetts that not a man had arrived from Connecticut, only sixty from Massachusetts, only fifty from New Hampshire, and two hundred and fifty from Rhode Island. "With this force," he added, "I am to Defend a Shore of nearly a hundred miles in Extent against an Enemy . . . who can bring all their Strength to a Point when and where they please." [23] On the 16th, he informed Henry Laurens, President of Congress, "The Troops come in So Slowly that I have now Less than five hundred." [24] In a report to Washington dated the 26th, he wrote, "I am sorry to inform your Excellency that notwithstanding my repeated solicitations, there is not A Hundred men sent here from Massachusetts, but Eighty from New Hampshire, & not a Man from Connecticut; . . . While we remain in this weak Situation, the Enemy will have it in their power to destroy the towns on the shore one after another, & retreat before any force can be collected to oppose them successfully." [25] The next two weeks witnessed only slight improvement in the state of affairs. Sullivan wrote to Meshech Weare, chairman of the New Hampshire Committee of Safety, on June 11 that he now had about six hundred men and expressed the hope that New Hampshire might be able to

[23] *Sullivan Papers*, II, 50. [24] *Ibid.*, II, 52. [25] *Ibid.*, II, 58.

furnish the troops which Connecticut seemed unable to provide.[26] On July 18, he reported to Heath that he now possessed a total of fifteen hundred men.[27] Despite earnest appeals and remonstrances, backed up by the authority of Congress, this was the utmost amount that he was able to extract from the states of New England during the first two months of his command.

What were the reasons alleged for the lack of coöperation? Meshech Weare declared that New Hampshire was hampered by the fact that Massachusetts had drawn off large numbers of volunteers by offering higher bounties than New Hampshire could afford.[28] Many patriots of the Granite State, moreover, found privateering more profitable than soldiering.[29] Connecticut complained that the military requirements of regions other than Rhode Island had absorbed her troops. Writing to Sullivan on June 5, Governor Trumbull declared that the state had recently dispatched six battalions of infantry and three troops of light horse to General Gates in New York. Two regiments had been detached to defend the exposed coastline. The demands of the Continental Army had further depleted the man power of Connecticut.[30] The season of the year was also pleaded as an excuse for failing to furnish troops. The Massachusetts Council affirmed that in the summer it was difficult to persuade farmers to enlist save for very limited periods: "This is the time for the farmers to reap & ingather the fruits arising from their labours, on which fruits they have their sole dependence under God for the support of themselves & families, the remainder of the year. This being the Case the Councill

[26] *Ibid.*, II, 70–71.

[27] *Ibid.*, II, 92.

[28] *Ibid.*, II, 61, 80. Weare to Sullivan, May 29, June 26, 1778.

[29] *Ibid.*, II, 131–132, Weare to Sullivan, July 28, 1778.

[30] *Ibid.*, II, 66.

[*sic*] fear that they shall not be able to procure many if any to serve during pleasure." [31] In Rhode Island the legislature voted to draft militia into service under Sullivan but large numbers refused to submit. Indeed, despite the fact that the state was partially occupied by the British, it was necessary to employ what were equivalent to press gangs in order to compel men to don uniform.[32]

With the arrival of the French fleet in Rhode Island waters and the possibility of joint military and naval action against Newport, a fresh impetus was given to the attempt to procure troops but with the same discouraging results. On July 23, Sullivan received instruction from Washington to raise an army of five thousand men inclusive of those already called to the colors.[33] On the following day Sullivan wrote to the authorities in Connecticut, New Hampshire, and Massachusetts, urgently requesting contingents of militia and volunteers.[34] The Massachusetts Council promised three thousand men; [35] Governor Trumbull five hundred in addition to those already raised; [36] the New Hampshire Committee of Safety agreed to do the best it could despite the demand for harvest laborers, the temptations of privateering, and the inroads of Massachusetts recruiting officers.[37] These pledges were far from scrupulously kept. About three weeks later, on August 18, Sullivan reported to Governor Greene of Rhode Island that out of 3000 men promised by Massachusetts only 1386 had appeared. Connecticut instead of sending 1500 had dispatched 412. Rhode Island, which boasted of

[31] *Sullivan Papers*, II, 112–113. Massachusetts Council to Sullivan, July 25, 1778.

[32] *Ibid.*, II, 83. Sullivan to Governor William Greene, June 30, 1778.

[33] *Ibid.*, II, 89.

[34] *Ibid.*, II, 105, 108, 110.

[35] *Ibid.*, II, 132–133. Massachusetts Council to Sullivan, July 28, 1778.

[36] *Ibid.*, II, 171. Trumbull to Sullivan, August 3, 1778.

[37] *Ibid.*, II, 131–132. Weare to Sullivan, July 28, 1778.

having put 3000 men in the field, had actually mustered only 1228.[38] Washington took alarm at the situation, writing to Sullivan on August 10 that the tardiness of the New England militia might frustrate the attempt to capture Newport and expose the French fleet to disaster.[39] Despite delays and discouragements Sullivan's tact and persistence eventually triumphed and he succeeded in mobilizing a force of five thousand men in accordance with the instructions of Washington.

Sullivan's candid opinion of the army was disclosed in a letter to a fellow officer wherein he spoke of it as a "Chaos of Militia," an "unwieldly body" which no "Power less than the Almighty fiat could reduce to order." [40] Desertions were so frequent that on August 16 the general was obliged to issue a proclamation urging the inhabitants of Rhode Island "to apprehend, secure, and return to Camp all persons . . . not having a proper Pass." [41] In a letter of the same date to the New Hampshire Council he pointed the finger of scorn at "the unsoldierlike Behaviour of those Militia who had engaged to serve for fifteen days and who could not be prevailed upon to remain One hour after the expiration of that time, tho' the establishing of American Independence had been their Reward." He besought the council to supply him with "*Men*." [42] It is generally assumed that the withdrawal of the French fleet was the reason for Sullivan's failure to assault the British lines at Newport. In a letter of August 31 to the President of Congress, he wrote, "I shoud [*sic*] have attempted carrying the works by Storm

[38] *Ibid.*, II, 229–230. William Greene, Jr. succeeded Nicholas Cooke in the governorship on May 6, 1778. See S. G. Arnold, *History of Rhode Island* (New York, 1878), II, 417.

[39] *Ibid.*, II, 195–196.

[40] *Ibid.*, II, 197. Sullivan to Heath, August 11, 1778.

[41] *Ibid.*, II, 220–221.

[42] *Ibid.*, II, 224–226.

. . . had I not found to my great surprize that the Volunteers which compos'd great part of my Army had return'd [home] and reduced my Numbers to little more than that of the Enemy. Between two and three thousand return'd [home] in the Course of twenty four Hours and other men still going off upon a supposition that nothing could be done. . . . His dependence must be upon a Reed who has faith in their . . . Support."[43]

Sullivan had not only to raise an adequate fighting force in Rhode Island but to arm it. With respect to this matter he also encountered many difficulties. On May 31, he wrote to Henry Laurens that the authorities in Rhode Island had no arms to place in the hands of the troops of the state. He requested that Congress furnish two thousand stand.[44] Despite the fact that the need was pressing, almost a month elapsed before he received a reply. On June 26 the Board of War informed him that Congress had voted to supply the arms requested; but the grant was so hedged by conditions as to be of doubtful value.[45]

The forts in Rhode Island were ransacked for available cannon. At Sullivan's request Heath dispatched to Tiverton Colonel Craft's artillery regiment with six brass four-pounders and two brass howitzers, Major Thomas Bumstead's company of Boston artillery with two brass field-pieces, a detachment of Continental artillery under Major Zaccheus Dunnel with two field-pieces, and a thirteen-inch marine mortar and bed.[46]

There was a serious shortage of flints and ammunition. The British during a recent raid had destroyed the powder magazine at Warren.[47] On July 25 Sullivan begged Heath

[43] *Sullivan Papers*, II, 281.

[44] *Ibid.*, II, 62–63.

[45] *Ibid.*, II, 81–82.

[46] *Ibid.*, II, 289; *Memoirs of Major-General William Heath*, ed. William Abbatt (New York, 1901), p. 174.

[47] *Ibid.*, II, 56. Sullivan to Weare, May 26, 1778.

to forward to Taunton as soon as possible for the use of the army in Rhode Island 140 ten-inch shells, two tons of cannon powder, and 40,000 flints.[48] Heath replied that apart from the flints he was unable to meet Sullivan's needs in the matter of ammunition, since there was no laboratory at Boston. He advised him to try his luck at the arsenal in Springfield.[49] From the latter place Ezekiel Cheever, commissary of stores, wrote to Sullivan that he had already sent to Providence all the musket cartridges on hand and two tons of powder. He had directed Captain Frothingham who was in charge of the laboratory to manufacture as many additional cartridges as possible. On August 1 he hoped to forward to Rhode Island ten tumbrils with seven or eight hundred canisters of cartridges.[50]

The historic storm of August 12 and 13, which played such havoc with the rigging of the French fleet that D'Estaing felt obliged to abandon the siege of Newport, proved equally disastrous to the ammunition of Sullivan's troops. A large part of it was destroyed by floods of rain.[51] According to Heath the disaster was due partly to the wretched cartridge boxes with which the men had been accoutered.[52] For a period Sullivan's army was practically defenceless and might have been driven from its works without the firing of a shot.[53] There followed a scramble to replenish the supply of ammunition. Governor Greene at once set on foot inquiries to ascertain the resources of

[48] *Ibid.*, II, 117.

[49] *Ibid.*, II, 119, July 25, 1778.

[50] *Ibid.*, II, 160, July 31, 1778.

[51] *Ibid.*, II, 205–206. Sullivan to Washington, August 13, 1778; Massachusetts Historical Society, *Collections*, series 7, vol. IV, "Heath Papers" (Boston, 1904), Part II, 250. Greene to Heath, August 13, 1778.

[52] *Ibid.*, II, 211. Heath to Greene, August 14, 1778. Heath overestimated the number of cartridges which he was able to send. The amount was later cut to 36,000. The amount of musket powder was increased to 1000 lbs. "Heath Papers," Part II, 252.

[53] E. Field, *op. cit.*, I, 493.

Rhode Island with respect to powder and ball. He discovered that the state could supply only twelve thousand cartridges and a half-ton of pistol powder.[54] At Sullivan's request he addressed fervent appeals to Heath and Governor Trumbull. The former agreed to forward out of his own magazines thirty-eight thousand cartridges and ten barrels of powder.[55] The latter generously dispatched one hundred barrels of musket powder and placed at Sullivan's disposal two hundred barrels located in Norwich.[56] A few bombs were obtained from the French fleet.[57] Without these supplies it is doubtful whether Sullivan could have fought the battle of Rhode Island on August 29.

The problem of provisioning the army likewise proved difficult. Among the Sullivan Papers in the New Hampshire Historical Society is a copy of a report on the state of the food supply, drawn up by the issuing commissary, Solomon Southwick, less than two weeks before Sullivan's arrival at Providence.[58] From this the General learned that there were practically no provisions on hand nor any cash with which to purchase them. This condition of affairs appears to have been chronic. On July 25, for example, after Sullivan had received definite instructions from Washington to coöperate with the French fleet in the reduction of Newport, he wrote to Heath that the plan seemed likely to fail owing to the absence of provisions. "Unless some extraordinary Exertions are made to forward Supplies, the Expedition must certainly fall through. It would be a dishonorable Reflection in the Annals of America to attribute the Failure to such Cause." [59] He

54 *Sullivan Papers*, II, 208–209. Greene to Sullivan, August 14, 1778.
55 *Ibid.*, II, 211. Heath to Sullivan, August 14, 1778.
56 *Ibid.*, II, 228. Greene to Sullivan, August 17, 1778.
57 *Ibid.*, II, 233. Lieutenant Pleville Le Peley to Sullivan, August 19, 1778.
58 *Ibid.*, II, 29–30.
59 *Ibid.*, II, 115–117.

begged Heath for fish, flour, and rice. A similar appeal was addressed to Governor Trumbull: "I am under the necessity of requesting you to forward with the greatest imaginable dispatch such quantity of provisions as you may have in your power. . . . Unless this is done, I shall be obliged to disband the troops, not having any provisions here . . . for their support."[60] Heath's response was prompt and generous. He agreed to ship four hundred barrels of flour, one hundred barrels of beef, "perhaps one hundred barrels" of salmon and mackerel, and a quantity of rice and pork. He added: "A little rum will not be amiss. If you have not a supply, and will order Teams for it, twenty hogsheads are at your service."[61] Governor Trumbull agreed to forward to Boston for delivery to Sullivan fifty barrels of pork and fifty barrels of beef.[62]

While Sullivan usually found Heath a loyal and willing collaborator in procuring provisions, friction occasionally developed between the two men, thereby adding to Sullivan's trials. For example, there had been collected at Westborough, Massachusetts, nine hundred barrels of salted provisions, which Sullivan on July 24 directed his men to appropriate for the use of the forces. Upon learning of this Heath took fire, contending that while Sullivan might take possession of public stores in Rhode Island, he had no right to do so in Massachusetts without Heath's permission, since that state constituted a department subject to Heath's jurisdiction. "I cannot construe your order," wrote Heath, "in any other light at present than offering me the highest indignity and Insult." He went on to say that he desired "an immediate explination [*sic*]."[63] Sullivan sought to defend his conduct on the

60 *Ibid.*, II, 122, July 25, 1778.
61 *Ibid.*, II, 118–119. Heath to Sullivan, July 25, 1778.
62 *Ibid.*, II, 130–131. Trumbull to Sullivan, July 27, 1778.
63 *Ibid.*, II, 122–124. Heath to Sullivan, July 26, 1778.

ground of emergency. His men were "on point of Suffering for want of provision." If he had waited to untangle all the red-tape with which the provisions were tied up, nothing would ever have been achieved and he would have been left "to find out by fasting and prayer where the great power of Delivering provisions lay." He added that he had no idea that Heath had any connection with the stores at Westborough.[64] Heath retorted that their earlier correspondence proved unmistakably that Sullivan was well aware that the provisions were under Heath's exclusive control — a fact which he declared sarcastically "must have totally sliped [*sic*] your memory."[65] After this acid exchange of views, the controversy was apparently suffered to slumber.

The procuring of foodstuffs was sometimes hampered by unpatriotic greed. Those possessed of supplies sought to take advantage of the distress of the army by charging exorbitant prices. Heath reported to Sullivan on August 14 that he had attempted to purchase a cargo of "salt provisions" at Boston, but had been prevented by the fact that the owners, seeking to capitalize the urgent needs of the troops, had raised the price to an unwarranted level.[66] With the arrival of the French fleet off Newport, Sullivan was obliged to supply not only his own requirements but those of D'Estaing. The latter wrote that he was completely dependent upon New England for foodstuffs, that he had provisions for only twenty days, and that his biscuit was nearly exhausted.[67] Sullivan at once sent out appeals to Heath and the Massachusetts

64 *Sullivan Papers*, II, 138–140. Sullivan to Heath, July 28, 1778.

65 *Ibid.*, II, 144–145. Heath to Sullivan, July 29, 1778.

66 *Ibid.*, II, 210.

67 *Ibid.*, II, 167. Sullivan to Jeremiah Powell, President of the Massachusetts Council, August 2, 1778; *ibid.*, II, 174, D'Estaing to Sullivan, August 4, 1778; *ibid.*, II, 180. Sullivan to Weare, August 4, 1778.

Council. He urged the former to send rice, and the latter to forward flour and salted provisions.[68] He also procured a quantity of bricks, lime, and wood to enable D'Estaing to construct ovens on board ship for the purpose of baking the flour obtained ashore into bread.[69] In such manner he undertook to help victual the French forces as well as his own.

The difficulties encountered by Sullivan in finding transport for his army on both land and water were numerous. In order to convey troops from the mainland across the East Passage to the island upon which Newport is located, flat-boats were required. General Spencer, who preceded Sullivan in command of the department of Rhode Island, had collected about seventy flat-boats in Kickemuet River, but unfortunately for Sullivan all of them except twelve were burned by the British during a raid on May 25. A new flotilla had to be created. Accordingly, ship-carpenters were assembled. Major Silas Talbot was dispatched to Tiverton to prepare eighty-six flat-boats each capable of transporting a hundred men.[70] Ten or eleven excellent boats built upon an English model were obtained in Massachusetts through the aid of Heath. These were brought by water from Boston to Weymouth Landing and laboriously hauled over-land to the Taunton River where they were launched and sent to the coast. Most, if not all, the boats employed by the army were directed by Marblehead and Salem fishermen drawn from Glover's brigade.[71]

[68] *Ibid.*, II, 167. Sullivan to Powell, August 2, 1778; *ibid.*, II, 168. Sullivan to Heath, August 3, 1778.

[69] *Ibid.*, II, 233. Lieutenant Pleville Le Peley to Sullivan, August 19, 1778.

[70] Field, *op. cit.*, I, 491; *Sullivan Papers*, II, 158. Nathanael Greene to Sullivan, July 31, 1778.

[71] Heath, *Memoirs*, p. 173; Field, *op. cit.*, I, 502; *Sullivan Papers*, I, 106: Sullivan to Heath, July 24, 1778; *ibid.*, II, 118: Heath to Sullivan, July 25, 1778; *ibid.*, II, 223: Heath to Sullivan, August 16, 1778.

To take charge of land transport, a "wagon-master general and a deputy were appointed, clothed with power to hire and impress teams." [72] Carts and wagons were sought over a wide area. When Sullivan decided to abandon the siege of Newport, an especially large number of vehicles were required for the transportation of stores and baggage to the northward. He dispatched agents "to all the farms as far north as Attleborough and from thence all along down to Taunton." [73] Vehicles were obtained in many towns in eastern Massachusetts and Rhode Island including Berkely, Rehoboth, Providence, and Swansey. Men were drawn from the ranks to drive the teams. The train was organized into sections, each in charge of a conductor.[74]

In seeking wheeled transport Sullivan became involved in controversy with Heath similar to the one which arose in connection with provisions. On July 26, Heath complained to Sullivan because the latter had issued warrants for the impressment of teams in Massachusetts. He declared that he had no objection to Sullivan's impressment of teams in Rhode Island but Massachusetts was his (Heath's) department. No warrants should be issued there save with the authorization of Heath or his deputy quartermaster general.[75] Sullivan replied (July 28) with warmth that he considered his authority to impress teams to be coextensive with the requirements of the army. "It ever has & Ever must be practiced for an officer to Extend his Authority So Far as his necessities may Extend." If to obtain transport it was necessary to issue warrants in Massachusetts, he had the right to do so, Heath to the contrary notwithstanding. "I beg you to consider," he wrote, "whether it would be Reasonable to

[72] Field, *op. cit.*, I, 491.
[73] *Ibid.*, I, 496.
[74] *Loc. cit.*
[75] *Sullivan Papers*, II, 122–124.

Suppose that I should be restrained from impressing a Boat Team or other article till I would send to Boston to obtain power for the purpose." [76] The conflict of jurisdiction remained to vex the relations of the two generals.

In his determined search for transport Sullivan ran foul not only of Heath but of the local authorities. On July 29, the Massachusetts Council called his attention to the "Extraordinary conduct of a certain person, calling himself a deputy Quartermaster General in your department, who assumed to himself power & Authority to Impress teams & Carriages within this State; and even within a few miles of the place where the Council was siting [*sic*], whose right alone it was to give directions and orders in the matter." The Council added a request that Sullivan "take the most effectual measures" to prevent a repetition of the incident.[77] The General replied tactfully, "I shall take Effectual care to See that nothing is done in future that may occasion the Least uneasiness. . . ." [78]

As one surveys the operations in Rhode Island in 1778, it seems clear that the mobilization of an army for its defence and for the capture of Newport was a striking achievement. It required on the part of the American commander a rare combination of moral and intellectual gifts: organizing ability, tactfulness in dealing with civilian authority, resourcefulness in supplying deficiencies in men and *matériel*, and patient persistence in the face of discouraging obstacles. Such qualities do not have a martial ring but it was by virtue of them as well as by virtue of personal bravery and tactical skill that Sullivan rendered a creditable, if not a brilliant, service to the cause of American independence.

[76] *Ibid.*, II, 137–141.

[77] *Ibid.*, II, 147–148.

[78] *Ibid.*, II, 163. August 1, 1778.

EDWARD ELY CURTIS.

THE PENOBSCOT EXPEDITION

In 1898, Charles Francis Adams, then President of the Massachusetts Historical Society, called the attention of that learned body to the almost universal silence which historians had maintained as to the Penobscot Expedition of 1779, conducted by Massachusetts against the British. "Bad in conception, bad in preparation, bad in execution,"[1] it had been allowed to sink into oblivion. The prodigious expense, ruined reputations, and total loss of fleet, equipment, and supplies, were excuse enough for this; yet abundant materials on the disaster are extant in the form of newspaper accounts, depositions at the court of enquiry, long letters from the leaders of the expedition, diaries kept by American and British participants, and numerous orders and letters of Council and House.

Prior to 1779, the major event of the Revolutionary War on the Maine coast had been the burning of Falmouth Neck, now Portland; thereafter hostilities had consisted of petty attacks and annoyances, of the unpleasant episodes of civil war, such as cattle stealing and house burning. Fort Pownall, at the mouth of the Penobscot, the only armed stronghold in that region, had been dismantled in 1775 by the British and burned by Americans later the same year. As the war continued, the British felt the need of a pied-à-terre along the Maine Coast. Not only would it supply refuge for their own ships in case of storm or distress, but it would serve as a base to prevent raids into Nova Scotia, and provide a timber supply for the royal shipyards at Halifax. At the end of the war it was planned

[1] *Mass. Hist. Soc. Proceedings* (1898), XXXII, 200–202.

to make the country a loyalist province, and call it "New Ireland." [2]

On the north side of Penobscot Bay, about twenty miles from the outer-most islands, and ten from the point which marks where bay merges into river, is a peninsula, now known as Castine, then as Majabigaduce. Towards the Bay it presented a mile of rugged and broken bluffs, in some places two hundred feet in height; a horn-shaped tip extended back about a mile and three quarters, and sloped gradually down to a large sandy beach along a harbor formed by the junction of the Bagaduce River with the Bay. The passage into this harbor was narrow, and defensible by a comparatively small number of ships. The only access from the mainland to the northern end of the horn lay across a marsh about a quarter of a mile wide and submerged at high tide. The peninsula was densely wooded throughout, the fir and spruce marching straight to the water's edge; even the face of the cliffs was covered with underbrush.

On the 16th of June, 1779, General Francis McLean landed at Majabigaduce with 450 rank and file of the 74th Highlanders, and 200 of the 82nd, a lowland regiment raised at the private cost of the Duke of Hamilton. On the highest point of the ridge which extended along the peninsula, almost in the center of the island, a fort was laid out in the shape of a square, and dubbed Fort George after the British monarch. The inhabitants of the surrounding region were called upon to take the oath of allegiance, and most of them, after holding a meeting to determine on defense or submission, accepted the situation. But loyalty was of the lip only, and they provided little assistance in building the fort.[3] Probably the cases were

[2] G. A. Wheeler, *History of Castine* (Bangor, 1875), pp. 64–65.

[3] *Samuel Adams Papers* (New York Public Library), VI, August 20, 1779. Majabigaduce Hospital.

frequent such as that described in the letter of an unknown Maine girl to her sister. When the three boys of the family were given their choice of taking the oath, "Natt did comply without hesitation. Jo and Ben both ran off the first chance they had & enlisted in the American army, and the latter was shott the very first boat that landed here, so that was his fate." [4]

The ships of war which had conducted the troops to Majabagaduce departed, leaving only three sloops of war, the *Albany*, *Nautilus*, and *North*, two of sixteen guns, one of eighteen, under the command of Captain Henry Mowatt, the same who had broken his parole and burned Falmouth Neck four years earlier.

News of the British landing flew southward, arousing the Maine towns to a frenzy of alarm. In a week the tidings had reached Boston. A joint committee of House and Council decided within twenty-four hours that a naval force should be despatched at once.[5] This resolve was strengthened by the appeals for assistance which began to pour in.[6] Haste was of the essence, but the preparation of such an expedition required ships of war and transports, sailors to man them, and soldiers for a land force, leaders to command them and artillery for the reduction of the fort, ammunition, food, clothing and supplies of all kinds, and, not least important, money to pay for them.

At first, alarm and resurgent patriotism lent wings to preparations. Newburyport offered four vessels to be ready for sea within the week. Three Continental ships, including the new thirty-two-gun frigate *Warren*, then in Boston harbor, were asked for and received.[7] New Hamp-

[4] *Loc. cit.*

[5] Cushing to Council, Pownalborough, June 19. Received June 23. *Maine Historical Collections*, ser. 2, XVI, 295–296.

[6] *Ibid.*, p. 296, Falmouth to General Court.

[7] Navy Board to Powell, June 30, 1779. *Ibid.*, p. 316.

shire tendered the *Hampden*,[8] Massachusetts supplied its own fleet, the brigs *Hazard*, *Tyrannicide*, and *Active*.[9] Authority was given the Council by the Assembly to hire or impress any vessels which might further be required. In consequence, two gentlemen were sent to Beverly to make sure that the *Black Prince*, built in 1777 to be the largest, fastest, and most heavily armed privateer ever launched from the Massachusetts shipyards, should join the expedition. Because she had just returned from an unsuccessful voyage her owners, desirous of greater financial returns, showed reluctance to surrender her.[10] The sheriff of Essex County was ordered to take possession, and also of her fellow privateers *Hector* and *Hunter*.[11]

In all, nineteen ships of war were gathered together, mustering more than three hundred guns. No fleet comparable in size was commissioned by the Americans during the War. But the number of guns was no true index of strength. Only the *Warren* was equipped with eighteen and twelve pounders. The *Vengeance*, the *Gen. Putnam* and the *Hector* had nines, the rest sixes. Twenty-four additional vessels of various types were procured for transports and supply ships.[12]

With every able seaman of Boston off privateering, the

[8] Resolves of General Assembly, June 29, 1779, as printed in *Magazine of History*, XXV (extra number 99), 183.

[9] The *Hazard* was noted for her stability and swiftness, and in the two years between her launching and her destruction she took many prizes. She was commanded by John Foster Williams, later commander of the *Protector*. Her first lieutenant was George Little, later with Williams on the *Protector*, and commander of the Continental Frigate *Boston*, years later. J. Winsor, *Memorial History of Boston*, III, 186.

[10] O. T. Howe, "Beverly privateers in the Revolution," *Colonial Society of Mass. Proceedings*, XXIV, 347–348.

[11] *Magazine of History*, XXV, 127.

[12] Among the transports were the sloops *Centurion*, *Defiance*, *Abigail*, *Britannia*, *Fortune*, *Sparrow*, *Sally*, *Nancy*, *Race-Horse*, *Dolphin*, *Hannah*, *Bethaiah*, *Industry*, *Job*, *Pidgeon*, *Safety*, and the schooners *Nancy*, *Allen*, and *Rachel*. *Maine Historical Collections*, XVII, 140–141.

Council well knew there would be trouble manning the ships, and a press was proclaimed, and guards placed at the town ferries and other outlets to prevent seamen or marines escaping until the task of collecting the unwilling victims was finished.[13] Marblehead was also combed for sailors. Particular difficulty was experienced in recruiting for the *Warren*, partly because of the rule of the Continental Navy that no enlistments should be made for a single cruise; but mainly because the opportunity for sharing in the prize money offered to the other crews was lacking. The Navy Board had to admit enlistments for the cruise and allow thirty able seamen to be taken from the other vessels before her complement was full.[14]

For the land force Lincoln and Cumberland counties, in Maine, being nearest the scene of operations, were each ordered to supply six hundred men for two months and York was to add three hundred more.[15] Troops, however, were collected with the greatest difficulty. A few joined voluntarily, some had to be taken by force, and some skulked in successful concealment. Many towns "sent Boys, old Men, and Invalids. If they belonged to the Train Band or Alarm List they were Soldiers, whether they could carry a Gun, walk a mile without Crutches, or only Compos Mentis sufficient to keep themselves out of Fire and Water." [16]

The Board of War figured on provisions for sixteen hundred men for eight weeks, and in this respect there was no scarcity. The supplies included rum, jack-knives, beaver shot, flints and corn for supplying a company of Indians

[13] Order of Council, July 3, 1779, quoted in *Magazine of History*, XXV, 187; *Mass. Archives*, CXLV, 399.

[14] *Maine Hist. Collections*, 2 ser. XVII, 386, Order of Council, July 13.

[15] *Magazine of History*, XXV, 180–181, Resolve of General Assembly, June 26, 1779.

[16] *Mass. Archives*, CXLV, 284–301.

on the spot.[17] A war belt of wampum had been sent to the Penobscots, and John Preble, captain of Indians, wrote there were already about sixty Indian braves at Passamaquoddy, "the greater part firce for War & wait only for Orders to march & assist their Brothers the Americans . . . they seem to be more & more Sensible of the diabolical intentions of the Enemy & the Justness of our Cause."[18]

Dudley Saltonstall, of New Haven, was appointed Commodore to lead the navy and hoisted his broad pennant on the *Warren*. His record had been good. In December, 1775, he had captained the *Alfred* in the squadron under Commodore Esek Hopkins, the first to hoist the American flag. Charges which had been preferred against him in 1776 were thrown out by the Marine Committee of the Continental Congress.

In charge of the land forces was Solomon Lovell, sometime farmer of Weymouth, who had begun his military services as colonel in the Second Suffolk Regiment of militia, and had served as brigadier on both Rhode Island expeditions of 1777 and 1778. Peleg Wadsworth of Duxbury, second in command, called him a "true old Roman Character, who never would flinch from Danger." [19] Another member of the expedition called him a very good sort of man, but shrewdly observed, "these good sort of men very seldom make good Generals. I recollect that I thought then, and I still think, that Mr. Lovell would have done more good, and made a much more respectable appearance in the Deacon's seat of a country church than at the head of an American army." [20] Wadsworth himself,

[17] *Mass. Archives*, CXLV, p. 11.

[18] *Maine Hist. Collections*, 2 ser. XVII, 395–396, Preble to Council, July 24, written from Clam Cove.

[19] *Ibid.*, II, 157.

[20] Narrative of Thomas Weld Philbrook, *Rhode Island Historical Society Proceedings* (1871–75), p. 76. This narrative was written some time after the expedi-

grandfather of the poet Longfellow, graduate of Harvard, and master of a private school at Plymouth, Captain of minutemen at Roxbury, aide-de-camp to Major General Artemas Ward, and brigadier on the Rhode Island expedition of 1778, proved himself a better soldier than his chief. Had he been in command the outcome might have been vastly different. Paul Revere, who formerly had carried the good news from Boston to Lexington, was promoted from command of the Castle in Boston harbor to be Lieutenant Colonel of the Expedition's artillery.[21] Saltonstall and Lovell were both middle-aged gentlemen of fifty, conservative in planning, cautious in tempting fate with sudden measures, unused to military responsibility, without trace of the dash, go, and personal magnetism which make forlorn hopes successful, and without the scientific knowledge of tactics and strategy which might make up for the lack of the former qualities.

Practically everybody expected an easy victory. Only an occasional note of doubt was heard, such as from a friend of William Heath who wrote, "all are generals and pretend to be perfect masters of these matters as well as the business of the Court."[22] The Council did what it could to ensure secrecy. An embargo was laid on all ports in the state, and guard boats were despatched nightly to make sure no boats passed out of Boston harbor before the sailing of the fleet.[23] The effort was futile, however. The British were warned of almost every step.

When it came to getting the ships away from the rendezvous at Nantasket Roads, there was delay after delay. Not until noon of the fifteenth did General Lovell go on

---

tion, and while the memory of the writer for facts was indistinct, there is no reason to doubt the genuineness of his opinion of General Lovell.

[21] Copy of order in *Revere Papers*, in Mass. Historical Society.

[22] Heath Papers, *Mass. Hist. Society Collections*, ser. 7, IV, 309. Seth Loring to Heath, July 7, 1779. [23] *Maine Historical Collections*, ser. 2, XVII, 380.

board the *Warren*. Even then there was a fresh wind from the North, and the fleet did not sail. The next day the wind veered into the northeast, blowing so fresh it parted the cable of the *Warren*, and the drizzle continued until Sunday, the eighteenth, when the weather broke in the morning and by afternoon the sun was out.[24] At three o'clock of the following morning the Grand Fleet finally got under way toward Townsend in Boothbay Harbor where the troops were to be embarked.[25] To Lovell's consternation he found only a thousand instead of the fifteen hundred troops expected. Nevertheless he ordered them embarked at once, but the task took two days, and not until the twenty-fourth when a fair breeze sprang up from the south southwest was the flotilla able to run up the coast before it. Several smokes on shore were sighted, which were correctly supposed "to proceed from Traitors hir'd by the Enemy to give them intelligence of our approach." [26]

Almost a week before, when the British garrison had first heard a fleet and army were preparing, the ground for the fort had been cleared and the first works commenced. No cannon were yet in position. Night and day the garrison toiled unflaggingly to raise an abatis around the fort and to build platforms for the guns.[27]

News kept coming in of the slow progress of the American fleet. Finally, towards late afternoon of the twenty-fourth, the Americans were sighted. To the British peering anxiously from their half finished ramparts, the enemy flotilla appeared "like a floating island with innumerable

[24] Journal of General Solomon Lovell, *Weymouth Historical Society Proceedings* (1881), I, 95.

[25] *Historical Magazine*, VIII (1864), 51. Journal of the Privateer Ship *Hunter*.

[26] Lovell Journal, *op. cit.*, p. 97.

[27] John Calef, "The Siege of Penobscot" (London, 1781). Reprinted in *Magazine of History*, III (extra numbers), 303–333.

trees."[28] At five o'clock an alarm gun from the *Albany* recalled the sailors from where they had been working on the fort.[29] All night the British guard boats kept watch on the enemy fleet at anchor in the Penobscot narrows. At seven, Sunday, the twenty-fifth, the Americans stood up the bay under a light breeze, the Continental brig *Diligent* leading the way. Three sympathizers who waved their hats from shore were taken aboard and eagerly informed Captain Brown the fort was not half finished. He took them to the *Warren* at once. Saltonstall, unable to make up his own mind, asked the Captain's opinion. Brown retorted firmly that there would never be a better time than right now to go in, to which Saltonstall, immediately adopting the contrary position, replied, "none but madmen would go in before they had reconnoitered, & it would be the Hight of madness to attempt it."[30] Colonel Brewer, who had been in the British fort the day before the arrival of the American ships, advised an immediate attack on the British fleet, telling Saltonstall that he could have everything his own in half an hour, upon which Saltonstall hove up his long chin and replied, "You seem to be damned knowing about this matter I am not going to risk my shipping in that damned hole."[31] That ill feeling which was so important in bringing on the final disaster was already apparent. Saltonstall told Captain Salter, of New Hampshire's *Hampden*, that his ship "would make a verry good prade ship." Salter responded with a woeful lack of the respect due his superior, "Sir I did not com hear for a prade Ship I come hear for sumthing Else."[32]

[28] Sir G. Collier, *A detail of . . . services . . . in America* (New York, 1835), p. 106.

[29] Calef Journal, *op. cit.*, p. 305.

[30] *Mass. Archives*, CXLV, 260. Deposition of Philip Brown, Commander of the Brig *Diligent*.

[31] J. Williamson, *History of Belfast* (1877), p. 176.

[32] *Mass. Archives*, CXLV, 44, Salter Deposition.

The commanders argued at length as to the strength of the British position, but about three o'clock nine ships, forming into three divisions, "stood towards the King's ships, and, as they advanced in the line, hove to and engaged." In spite of the superior weight of the American metal, the British ships received no damage beyond their rigging in a brisk cannonade, and as long as they defended the harbor neck, the fort appeared reasonably safe.[33] The population of Belfast, gathered on the heights on the eastern side of the harbor, watched the action.[34] This half-hearted attempt to silence the British ship was but the cover to an attempted landing of troops at a high head of land covered with brush and trees. But the British, thoroughly concealed in the thicket, opened fire. After an Indian had been killed, the first casualty of the expedition, the signal for retreat was given.[35] Whereupon the British garrison manned their works and gave three cheers for the men-of-war, which was returned by the sailors.

The next morning the American cannon again serenaded the British, doing practically no damage,[36] after which the marines attacked wooded Nautilus Island, two or three acres in size, off the mouth of the Bagaduce River, where the British had a small outpost with four guns. The twenty British marines beat a precipitate retreat, abandoning guns and ammunition and, in their haste, leaving behind their colors.[37] Revere and his mattrosses toiled all night setting up a battery. Mowatt prudently withdrew his little fleet out of the line of fire, and the Americans moved up.

33 *Mass. Archives*, CXLV, p. 266.

34 J. Williamson, *op. cit.*, p. 175.

35 Lovell Journal, *op. cit.*, p. 97. Revere Diary, printed in E. H. Goss, *The Life of Colonel Paul Revere* (Boston, 1891), p. 364.

36 Hunter Journal, *op. cit.*, p. 52.

37 Lovell Journal, *op. cit.*, p. 98.

At the Council of War which was henceforward to be a daily affair, the decision was finally made to attack. Since the British fleet commanded the harbor, and the isthmus connecting with the mainland was fortified, the only alternative seemed to be at Bagaduce Head where the bluffs were almost perpendicular, two hundred feet high, and thickly brushed.[38]

Between three and four o'clock on the morning of the 28th, the *Hunter* and *Sky Rocket* began firing into the woods "to scower them of the enemy." [39] A thick fog hung over the calm water. No sign of dawn had yet appeared in the East. The boats were lowered noiselessly and made for the rocky shore. The marines landed first, on the right, the militia on the left, the artillery and volunteers in the center.[40] A British picket fired from the top, but the shots went over the heads of the landing party as they formed into line. The order to scale the heights was given; a fifer boy set up his thin shrill tune. Catching hold of trees and shrubs, bracing themselves on rocks, taking advantage of every foothold, they clambered toward the top. Almost a third of the way up they began to feel the effects of the British fire, but they persisted until, within a few yards of the top, the British picket gave way, and the Portland company scrambled first over the top and reformed its ranks. The ascent had taken twenty minutes.[41]

The British picket under a captain of the 74th had been taken by surprise. Lieutenant John Moore, later the hero of Corunna, was among the last of the British to retreat.[42]

[38] *Boston Gazette*, Aug. 9, 1779.

[39] G. W. Allen, *Naval History of the American Revolution* (Boston, 1913), II, 416.

[40] Major William Todd Deposition, *Mass. Archives*, CXLV, 230–237.

[41] *Boston Gazette*, *loc. cit.*

[42] Letter of Sir John Moore quoted by J. Williamson, *op. cit.*, p. 177. Also B. Brownrigg, *The Life and Letters of Sir John Moore* (New York, 1925), p. 16.

Lovell was vastly complacent. He wrote in his diary, "I don't think such a landing has been made since Wolfe. When I returned to the shore it struck me with admiration to see what a Precipice we had ascended, not being able to take so scrutinous a view of it in time of Battle." [43] The troops apparently behaved with spirit on this occasion, but it was noted that there was little order or regularity, and after the heights were reached, difficulty was experienced in reforming the men.[44] About fifty Americans were killed, only a few British. Lovell decided not to push on. Entrenching tools were at once issued and rough covering thrown up about seven hundred feet from the Fort. The Commander of the Marines on the *Tyrannicide* thought if the ships had attacked at the same time to keep the British fleet occupied, the fort could easily have been taken.[45] Revere's opinion was that they could have taken the fort by themselves "and we to have marched on to the fort and stormed it; they not knowing our strength, and we being flushed with victory, I have no doubt they would have lain down their arms." [46]

Meanwhile, the battery from Nautilus harbor was energetically shelling the British ships; the fire was returned "with as good sulphur as Britons could give." At ten the *Warren* got under way and with three companions made an appearance of entering the harbor, but then "hauled

[43] Lovell Journal, *op. cit.*, p. 99.

[44] Jeremiah Hill Deposition, *Mass. Archives*, CXLV, 284.

[45] Downe Deposition, *ibid.*, p. 266–270.

[46] Revere to Heath, *Mass. Hist. Soc. Collections*, ser. 7, IV, 321. The account of the affair given by William Hutchings in his old age says McLean was standing ready with the pennant halliards in his own hands, ready to strike his colors if attacked. Col. Brewer, who went to see McLean after the rout of the Americans and was received politely, testified that McLean expressed surprise that he had not been attacked, saying he was in no situation to defend himself. He only meant to give the Americans one or two guns so as not to be called a coward, and then would have struck his colors, as he did not wish to throw away the lives of his men for nothing. Wheeler, *op. cit.*, p. 323.

by the wind at a long distance."[47] Her mainmast was hit in two places, the gammoning of her bowsprit cut to pieces, and the confusion on board so great she almost went ashore. She retired to a sheltered inlet where she remained two days repairing damages. It was a bad shock to Saltonstall's timid nature.

When dark came, Mowatt moved his ships still farther up the harbor out of reach of Nautilus Island battery, and thus ended the major action of the siege. Thereafter, no serious attempt was made to capture the fort. General Lovell, who had eagerly sought advice which he never took, finally wrote to the President of the Council that with the advice of the most experienced officers on the expedition it was impracticable to take the fort by storm and not probable it could be reduced by a regular siege. He must have regular disciplined troops and nine-inch mortars.

Hesitation and inaction, obstinacy and recrimination, typified the course of events during the succeeding two weeks. The days went by amid dissension and grumbling on the part of the Americans, feverish activity on the part of the British. The morale of the American troops, never excellent, became seriously impaired, and at the daily councils the captains of the privateers showed increasing uneasiness at the protracted delay in accomplishing anything. As one of them candidly expressed it, he "had rather all the ponobscot Expedition would go to hell, than he should Loose the Benefit of his Cruse."[48]

Unfortunately no time remained for Fabian policies. The British were daily making their fort more formidable,[49] for they continued to have an exaggerated idea of the

[47] Calef Journal, *op. cit.*, p. 308.

[48] Captain John Foster William Deposition, in *Mass. State Archives*, CXLV, 211–216.

[49] Calef Journal, *op. cit.*

American strength, 2600 on land and "by sea superior beyond every proportion." [50] But their "flying scout of 50 men . . . in particular distinguished themselves to admiration, marching frequently almost round the peninsula, both by day and by night, and with drum and fife playing the tune called Yankee, which greatly dispirited the Enemy, and prevented their small parties from galling our men at the works." [51]

General Lovell, on one occasion, had had the unpleasant experience of being cut off from his boat in a reconnaissance. He had had to "pad the hoof through woods, swamps, and briars" all night,[52] and not until sunrise the next morning was he sighted standing on the beach. He had become so unpopular he was hissed and hooted whenever he appeared and everybody united in cursing and execrating the Commodore. What made it worse for equipment and dispositions was the rain, cold, miserable, dispiriting, which began August 8 and continued thereafter, as Maine rains do, day after day.

Captain Hoysteed Hacker of the Continental Sloop *Providence*, hitherto conspicuous for taciturnity at council meetings, suggested an attack, the *Warren* to lead the ships in, the battery on Nautilus to keep up a constant cannonading, a hundred marines and three hundred militia to land and cut off the British fort from the British ships.[53] The captains unanimously agreed but reckoned without their men. When the news got about that the fort was to be stormed, only two-thirds of the men appeared when General Lovell ordered them paraded. Many had deserted during the night; many skulked in the woods to avoid

[50] Extract of letter from Penobscot, *Boston Gazette*, Sept. 27, 1779.

[51] John Calef, *The Siege of Penobscot*, *op. cit.*, p. 318.

[52] Thomas Weld Philbrook, Narrative in *Rhode Island Hist. Soc. Proceedings* (1875), pp. 73–81. See also Lawrence Journal, *op. cit.*, p. 317.

[53] *Mass. Archives*, CXLV, 88–89.

the attack. Jeremiah Hill, adjutant general, said Colonel Mitchell's officers were "so terrify'd at the Idea of storming, that they found fault with the Colonels nomination, and absolutely drew lots on the parade who should go to take the command of their men, and included those then on Guard, and reliev'd them if it fell to any of their turns." [54]

The afternoon of the 11th, Lovell sent half the troops he had collected, about two hundred, to the battery the British had evacuated August 1. According to the usual habit on these excursions, some small parties were sent out to decoy the enemy from the fort. Accounts differ as to what happened, but the British accepted the decoy, sent out a small party which approached back of the peninsula out of sight and through a cornfield until they came near the battery where the Americans were parading. The Americans started to retreat, whereupon the British emerged from concealment behind a barn and fired. The Americans took to their heels "in the greatest confusion imaginable — the officers damning their soldiers, and the soldiers their officers for cowardice, many losing their implements of war &c." The British party returned to the main fort "exulting with loud huzzas." [55] The master of the *Hazard*, who had gone to the breast work with the Americans, laid himself down prudently until the firing was over, and could hear the British damning the Yankees.[56]

The American officers were naturally much perturbed. They said their reputations would be ruined if they went into the field with such men, held another Council, decided unanimously the land force could not coöperate according

54 Jeremiah Hill Deposition, *Mass. Archives*, CXLV, 284–301.

55 Lieutenant William Downe Deposition, *Mass. Archives*, CXLV, 266–270.

56 Hunter Journal, *op. cit.*, p. 53.

to the plan of the day before.[57] Lovell wrote to Saltonstall to go ahead and destroy the navy, even at the cost of half the American vessels, although he could not conceive of failure. He said a deserter had informed him that the moment the American ships entered the harbor the British ships would be blown up. "I feel for the honor of America, in an expedition which a nobler exertion had long before this, crowned with success; and I have now only to repeat the absolute necessity of undertaking the destruction of the ships or quitting the place." [58]

But the Commodore was not to be hustled into action. He called another Council with his captains, and decided unless the general could get possession of the point near the British ships, it would not be advisable for the ships to go in under the fort and artillery fire.[59]

Lovell was in a predicament. He was afraid to raise the siege because of the obloquy his action would receive at home. He counted on the reinforcements which the Council was gathering. He thought he had a safe retreat up the river.[60] With winged words, he addressed his troops,

". . . we must ride triumphant over the rough diabolical Torrent of Slavery, and the Monsters sent to rivet its Chains. . . . Our Characters in the face of the whole World, must be our Conduct, in this Enterprise either rise or fall. . . . Is there a man able to bear Arms in this Camp? that would hide his Face in the day of Battle; Is there an American of this Character? is there a man so destitute of Honor? . . . let each man stand by his officer, and each Officer animated, press forward to the Object in view, then shall we daunt the vaunting Enemy,

[57] Lovell to Council, *Mass. Archives*, *op. cit.*, p. 163.

[58] Wheeler, *op. cit.*, pp. 310–311. Also introduction to Lovell Journal, *op. cit.*, p. 71.

[59] Hunter Journal, *op. cit.*, p. 54. Also *Mass. Archives*, CXLV, 97.

[60] Lovell Journal, *op. cit.*, p. 104.

who wishes to intimidate us by a little Parade, then shall we strike Terror to the Pride of Britain, we shall then return crown'd with Laurels, each being able to relate to his Children hereafter, when the Reverence of Old Age has spread a milky hue on the Locks of each by the Fatigues of War, and other Cares: I say then may we relate our Enterprises, our Attacks, and Conquests, and with pleasing Sympathy observe the listening Hearers attentive to our victory . . . let after Ages say pointing to the Heights of Majabigwaduce, there landed the American Troops, forced the Enemy for their out Posts, secured good Lines and openly attacked the hostile Bands of Georges Troops, there did they stand like men inspired, there did they fight, and fighting some few fell, the rest still victorious, firm, inflexible still fighting conquer'd." [61]

Friday the thirteenth was a desperate day. The British earthworks were now a formidable citadel. The American troops were frankly mutinous. One council after another had been held and nothing decided. Yet Lovell reiterated "I would rather die than consent to raise the siege or leave the Commodore any further excuse for not cooperating with me." [62] The question of raising the siege was put to a vote — Saltonstall and the Privateers were all for leaving. But there were ten for and thirteen against; it was decided to make a last attempt. Lovell led out 400 of his troops. The British greeted him with grape but remained behind their fortifications. In fog and low visibility the ships got under way. The British thought the great moment had come at last, called the marines on board their ships, strengthened the barricades, double-shotted the guns.[63] But the American fleet did not come

[61] *Maine Hist. Soc. Collections*, ser. 2, XVI, 453–455.

[62] Col. Samuel McCobb Deposition, *Mass. Archives*, CXLV, 310. Also J. Williamson, *History of the City of Belfast, 1770–1875* (Portland, 1877), p. 179.

[63] Calef Journal, *op. cit.*, pp. 316–317.

in; stood off and on uncertainly. The report spread that British reinforcements had been sighted. Some said it was only the trees on the island that loomed like a fleet in the fog.[64] A shower of rain dropped a curtain before their eyes, then as it lifted, now one, now another was sure he saw sails in the offing. At sunset the fog gradually withdrew and no doubt remained. Six British ships of war were standing up the Bay.

Hurriedly the American captains asked for orders from their Commodore which were not forthcoming.[65] The ships heaved up their anchors and stood uncertainly back and forth. Saltonstall sent word to Lovell the transports should be under way up the river at once. By three in the morning, McCobb's regiment with ammunition and provisions was at the water's edge, by four-thirty all were embarked and towed sluggishly off from the shore in a dead calm.[66] No progress could be made up river because the tide was at ebb; chafing at the delay, they had to wait for the turn.[67] The night was dark, and it was daybreak before the British in the fort discovered the American flight.

The British squadron took a long time moving up due to the light wind. Observers on the British fleet thought from the American position, drawn up in the shape of a crescent, that they meant to contest the day. But Saltonstall and his captains decided unanimously not to go out and engage the enemy, and, also unanimously, to go up the Penobscot River. There was no fight left in them.[68] From the *Rai-*

[64] Jeremiah Hill Deposition, *op. cit.*

[65] Captain John Foster Williams Deposition, *Mass. Archives,* CXLV, 211–216.

[66] Col. Samuel McCobb Deposition, *Mass. Archives,* CXLV, 54, Joshua Davis testimony. *Maine Historical Society Collections,* XVII, 312–317.

[67] Major William Todd Deposition, *Mass. Archives,* CXLV, 230–237.

[68] *Ibid.,* p. 130. There were present the Commodore, and Captains Waters, Thomas, Holmes, Williams, Cathcart, Carnes, West, Brown, Hallet, Burke.

sonnable[69] of sixty-four guns and five hundred men, far larger and more powerful than any vessel of the Americans, flew the broad pennant of Sir George Collier. With him were the *Blonde*, thirty-two, the *Greyhound*, twenty-eight, the *Galatea*, twenty-four, the *Camilla* and *Virginia* of twenty-four and twenty-eight, and the sloop *Otter*, two hundred guns and fifteen hundred men in all.

The Commodore, recovering from an attack of fever, was carried on deck in a chair. The wind was blowing directly into the bay; the Americans had to fight or be destroyed. As he watched, at two o'clock he saw the *Warren* hoist signals for each captain to shift for himself. "The enemy spread all their sails to assist their flight, and looked like a moving forest skimming over the waters. A universal shout from the British fleet was heard, and echoed from ship to ship."[70]

The transports, without a favoring breeze, and assisted only by a sluggish tide, were at Fort Pownal, some seven miles upstream, expecting fully that the war ships would contest the passage of the river. Consternation and surprise greeted the sight of the fleet standing up river with the sea breeze behind them.[71]

Meanwhile at the fort the off-side guns of the *Albany*, *North*, and *Nautilus*, were hastily hauled back from the fortress, taken on board, and the three British sloops slipped their stern moorings, hove up their bower anchors, and for the first time in months were off in the wake of the *Raisonnable*, from whose mainmast were fluttering the signals for battle and general chase.[72]

69 Sir George Collier, *A Detail of some particular services performed in America, 1776–1779* (New York, 1835), pr. for Ithiel Town.

70 Collier, *op. cit.*, p. 109; Captain Daniel Waters Deposition, *Mass. Archives*, CXLV, 238–245.

71 General Peleg Wadsworth Deposition, *Mass. Archives*, CXLV, 230–237.

72 John Calef, "The Siege of Penobscot" (London, 1781). Reprinted in *Magazine of History*, III (extra no.), 303–333.

The *Hunter*, which was supposed to be the "swiftest sailor in America," [73] had tried to slip through the western passage of Long Island, now Isleborough, but was cut off, stood for the shore and with all sails set went aground, her crew instantly tumbling over the side and taking cover in the woods. The British got her off without much difficulty. The *Defiance* hid in a small inlet, intending to push to sea when it was dark, but the crew decided not to risk it, and about midnight set her on fire, and she blew up.

Captain Salter, who throughout the siege had raged at the inaction of the Commodore, was doomed to be an early victim. The enemy cut away the rigging and stays of his ship, the *Hampden*, hulled him several times, wounded some of his men, and he had to strike his colors.[74]

The transports meanwhile had arrived at a place called "The Ledge," where the tide ran so rapidly that the light wind would carry them no farther. The armed vessels, calling out to clear the way and let them go by, soon began to pass them, "by which means many of the transports was Run a Shore, and the whole of the armed Vessels gone past finding our selves in this situation with the Enemy Ships within Shot we began to land our troops about 6 p.m. and at 7 had the whole of them on shore." [75]

Distracted, General Lovell wrote in his journal "to attempt to give a description of this terrible Day is out of my Power. It would be a fit subject for some masterly hand to describe it in its true colours, to see four Ships pursuing Seventeen Sail or Armed Vessells, nine of which were stout Ships, Transports on fire, Men of War blowing up. Provision of all kinds, & every kind of Stores on Shore (at

[73] Despatch from Commodore George Collier, quoted in Almon, *Remembrancer*, VIII, 352.

[74] Salter Deposition, *op. cit.*

[75] McCobb Deposition, *op. cit.*

least in small Quantities) throwing about, and as much confusion as can possibly be conceived." [76]

Had some of the heaviest ships been formed in line a little below the transports, something might still have been done. The wind was already dying away, as was usual towards evening, and the ebb tide was so strong the heavier British ships would have had to wait for the next tide. But the *sauve qui peut* made all considered action impossible. The Americans did set a sloop on fire and send her down with the tide, but the British ordered out boats and towed her to shore.[77] The transports were clustered on the westerly shore, a mass of flames. Ten were burned, nine were saved by the British.[78]

Meanwhile the army disembarked at a dozen different points along the river, camped out in the woods, "paraded round the roots of the trees & I tryed to get some of them to get up and go out to the House, told them General Wadsworth was there but all in vain. I ask'd them what they meant to do, they answer'd they meant to go thro the woods tomorrow for Kennebeck, Col. Tyler said it was the General orders for every one to take care of himself and that seemed to be the prevailing cry of all, officers and men." [79]

The narrative of this Sunday in mid-August is largely a tale of panic and the endeavors of each individual to save himself. The ships of war had begun to tow upstream early that morning, each one trying to get up as fast as possible. The *Providence*, *Tyrannicide*, *Hazard*, and *Diligent*, all regular vessels of war, arrived safely at the head of

[76] Journal of General Solomon Lovell, *Weymouth Historical Society Proceedings* (1881), I, 95.

[77] *Massachusetts Spy*, Oct. 7, 1779; copied from Rivington's *New York Gazette*.

[78] Wadsworth Deposition, *op. cit.*; Calef Journal, *op. cit.*

[79] Jeremiah Hill Deposition, *Mass. Archives*, CXLV, 284, 301.

the tide.[80] The width of the river was not more than a hundred yards; in some places even less. Collier said the yards of his ships were sometimes brushed at the same time by branches of trees on different sides of the river. It should have been an easy place to defend,[81] and so it might have been done had not the *Hector*, the *Black Prince* and other privateers pulled up in a mad panic, and done their best to bring on a general flight. The effect of the terror of their crews was so great that all the men determined to land the next morning rather than make a defense.[82] Revere reported to Lovell the ordnance brig *Samuel* was burned and all the entrenching tools had been on the transports, also burned. What was Lovell's surprise to find the *Samuel*, with all sail set, about three miles down stream aground about six miles above where she had been left. She had come off with the tide and drifted up. With some trouble she was freed and followed after the *Warren*.[83] Before they reached head of tide the wind failed, and two British ships appeared in sight. An hour later a puff came but not enough to move them; the British were drawing near slowly. Fearful, Saltonstall decided to burn his ship, although Lovell pleaded with him against this.[84] Saltonstall asked Lieutenant Little what he could do. Little replied rather abruptly he had done nothing as yet. Why did he not fire his stern chasers to cover the transports? Why did he not get springs on his cables, get his eighteen-pounders on one side, and defend the ship as long as possible "as its impossible for more than one ship to Engage you at a time and I would stay on board and assist". The second lieutenant of the *Warren* interposed, saying there were as good or better men already on board, and he had

[80] Capts. Hacker, Cathcart, Williams and Brown.

[81] Collier, *op. cit.*, p. 111.

[82] Todd Deposition, *op. cit.*

[83] *Ibid.*

[84] Little Deposition, *op. cit.*

orders to burn the *Warren*. Little retorted that if there were better men on the *Warren*, neither he nor his Commodore had yet shown themselves such, and he would see the lieutenant on shore where he would be as good a man as he was.[85]

General Lovell was a bundle of energy, raging back and forth up the river, entreating the captains to act together, to save the *Warren*, to fortify the banks, to cut a road through to the Kennebec and get in provisions, to save the guns, sails, and rigging. All the answer he received was that the enemy would be up the river in the morning, and they must be out of the way by then. Captain Williams of the *Hazard* was especially anxious to fortify, but the "Private Property ships had sot the Divell in his People . . ." Captain Cathcart of the *Tyrannicide* agreed this was so. He had had to put some of his men in irons for attempted desertion.[86]

A loud blast from down river proclaimed the end of the ordnance brig. A report that the *Warren* would come up put heart in the men for a time, but then rumor and fear again became busy. The crew of the *Hazard* told Captain Williams they had heard they were to stay, but if they stayed they would be made prisoners. That night Saltonstall abandoned the *Warren* and had her burned. The news arriving, a general conflagration was prepared. The *Vengeance* was already adrift and aflame.[87] Somehow, without orders, flames broke out on the *Black Prince*, spread to the *Monmouth*, and then to the *Hector*.[88] The guns on board the burning ships were loaded, and the remaining vessels only a ship's length away were in as much

85 Little Deposition, *op. cit.* Graphic account in testimony of Waterman Thomas, captain of volunteers, *Maine Hist. Soc. Collections*, ser. 2, XVII, 310.

86 Little Deposition, *op. cit.*

87 Waters Deposition, *op. cit.*

88 Philip Brown Deposition, *Mass. Archives*, CXLV, 260–265.

danger as from a general engagement.[89] The people on the *Hazard* were crying out "for god sake to fetch them off a Boat (to get ashore) an they had none alongside & expected every moment to be sett on fire by the two ships which were on fire." [90] When everybody was ashore orders were given to set fire to the ships still remaining intact. Captain Holmes of the *Charming Sally* was the last to apply the torch.[91]

Meanwhile the British ships remained below, becalmed in the fog. General Wadsworth made a last effort to rally troops but both men and officers "dismissed themselves & march'd off the parade faster than they could be brot on." [92] Finally he swung his own pack over his shoulder and headed for Camden, directing all he overtook to halt there. He arrived on the seventeenth, found some of the militia already gone through; others had sheared off to prevent being stopped, and the rest skulked off. The fortunate ones had got through in two days; some were as long as six or seven in the woods. Many of the Maine militia had been hunters, but did not remain to guide their more unfortunate fellows. Parts of five companies were ordered to Belfast, Camden, Townsend and St. Georges to protect the inhabitants from Tory raids.[93] Much apprehension was expressed over the attitude of the Indians who, having learned of the utter defeat of the Americans, had gone to their upper town, some ninety miles from the river mouth. General Lovell followed them there, thanked them for faithful service, assured them ill-fortune was but temporary. The chiefs replied a little misfortune would

89 Philip Brown Deposition, *Mass. Archives*, CXLV, 260–265.

90 *Ibid.*

91 Todd Deposition, *op. cit.*

92 *Mass. Archives*, CXLV, 135–138. Wadsworth to Powell, written from Thomaston, Aug. 19, 1779.

93 *Ibid.*

not make them change their hearts, and they would assist no one but their two fathers, General Washington and the King of France. They intimated, however, that certain material benefits would help them remember their agreements and they were promised a trading post on the Penobscot.[94]

The Council adjured Lovell to hold his ground in Maine, relying upon it that "God will not permit this his Professing peoples to be troden down by those who thurst for their blood."[95] A single disappointment should not be allowed to act as a discouragement, and it was hoped that "by the Smiles of Heaven our Enemies in that Quarter will yet be subdued."[96] The British, however, were satisfied with their retention of Majabigaduce and during the rest of the War limited operations to plundering raids.

The newspapers printed hardly a word about the fiasco, whether because of a policy of minimizing disaster, or because of intimations from on high that publicity would be inadvisable. A Court of Enquiry — four members from the house, four from the Council — sat at Faneuil Hall to consider on whom the blame should rest. All land officers and captains of armed vessels were summoned to appear. "What will arise from ignorant militiamen being examined by an ignorant court 'tis impossible to tell," wrote Israel Keith to General Heath.[97]

Saltonstall for some time refused "to give an account before white wigs. He said he was to be tried by other authority."[98] But the Committee, not to be balked of its

[94] *Maine Hist. Soc. Collections*, ser. 2, XVII, 12–14. Account of Lovell's conference with the Indians, Aug. 16, 1779.

[95] *Mass. Archives*, CXLV, 134. Powell to Lovell, Aug. 19, 1779.

[96] *Ibid.*, 144–149.

[97] Heath Papers, *Massachusetts Historical Society Collections*, ser. 7, IV, 318. Israel Keith to William Heath, Boston, Sept. 25, 1779.

[98] Keith to Heath, *op. cit.*, "Nothing is more natural than for an old soldier to despise men in civil life who have never smelled powder, and whom he looks

bird in hand, brought him before it. No testimony was given in his favor. Years afterward General Wadsworth, who had loaded the whole blame on Saltonstall, slipped in a word of apology for him. He did not think the Commodore was so much a coward, but rather "willful and unaccommodating, having an unyielding will of his own." The command of the fleet "did not set easy upon his shoulders." [99]

Most of Saltonstall's accusers were extremely bitter. John Preble, Captain of Indians, unable to be present, contributed his bit in writing. "I was the Commanders pilot ancored him a little above mash Bay, he never can answer for this Conduct he will have the curses of the people for ever upon him. . . . P.S. Hope you will Excuse the Incorrectness & Writing its wrote on my Knee with a bad pen & Inke & a heart full of Grief." [100]

The fleet captains testified that if they had gone in any time from July 25 to August 12 the British ships would have been destroyed. But Saltonstall had constantly preached caution, discouraged forward action. Nor did he, as a good commander would have done, prepare any plans for the future. Although constantly expecting British reinforcements, when the contingency which he had feared actually came about, he was totally unprepared. His one idea was to get away. He abandoned the transports and, when his own ship ran aground, put aside General Lovell's proffers of help, and burned her. He could not, perhaps, have fought the *Raisonnable* successfully, but the British flagship did not lead the pursuit up river, and had shortly to anchor for lack of water. The *Blonde* mounted no more

---

upon as cowards. But to be brought to answer for his conduct in the field before such men is intollerable."

[99] *Maine Hist. Soc. Collections*, ser. 2, II, 157. Wadsworth to Williamson.

[100] John Preble to Council, *ibid.*, XVII, 35–36.

guns than the *Warren*, yet the latter fired not a shot on the retreat. If Saltonstall had set the example, a line could have been formed across the narrows of the river, guns mounted on shore, and under these conditions a British attack would have been doubtful, especially with the light breeze prevailing. As Joshua Davis, agent of transports, remarked, "It was unpresidented for a Ship to go Stem on to the Enemy's Broadside."[101] Too irresolute to embark upon a decisive course himself, Saltonstall proved capable of an obstinacy that neither the threats nor persuasions of others could move to action.

Perhaps Lovell was not entirely guiltless, because he had definite orders to work with Saltonstall — orders he did not and probably could not carry out.[102] Moreover, Lovell was responsible to a certain extent for failure to notify the Council of the shortage of troops at Townsend. He knew General Gates, the Continental officer in charge of the New England district, was at Providence. He had not even asked his advice as to the expedition. A report was current that the proposal to call in Continental troops was met with the remark, "If but ten Continental soldiers are concerned, the Continent will take all the honor."[103] Not until August 2 did Lovell despatch the Reverend John Murray to the Council with urgent requests for reinforcements; then it was too late.

Another charge against Lovell was that he, like Sal-

[101] *Maine Hist. Soc. Collections*, ser. 2, XVII, 317. Testimony.

[102] His orders from the Council read: "You will consult such measures as shall appear to you most likely to affect the salutary purpose designed by the State in undertaking the expedition aforesaid. You will at all times study to promote the greatest harmony, peace and concord, between the land and sea forces engaged in the entire prize aforesaid. You will in all your operations consult with the Commander of the fleet, that the naval force may co-operate with the troops under your command, in endeavoring to captivate, kill and land." Orders dated July 2, 1779. Printed in Proceedings of General Assembly and reprinted *Magazine of History*, XXV, 184.

[103] Hazard letter, Mar. 22, 1780, in *Mass. Hist. Soc. Proceedings*, IV, 129.

tonstall, was too anxious to put things to a test. When the Heights were stormed the morning of July 28th, the troops were eager to go forward against the fort, yet he stayed them at the edge of the woods, and started to throw up earthworks without trying an assault. Then if ever was his great opportunity. He had landed at a place which the British had believed inaccessible, and had had all the advantage of surprise on his side.[104] The British had been almost entirely unprepared. Lieutenant John Moore said two bastions were only eight feet high, the other two sides entirely open.[105]

Nor did Lovell provide for a place of security if the British were reinforced. Wadsworth had urged it, but Lovell had countered with the claim it would dishearten the army and show them there was no real hope of success. But when the transports were standing up the river, "Oh, then how we wished for a place of Rendezvous." [106]

Saltonstall certainly expected British reinforcements; he kept some of his ships on scout duty looking for them. Lovell also knew his situation became more precarious each day he remained. Why then did he so steadfastly refuse to retreat before it was too late? His own reason was he expected reinforcements at any moment, and his orders were "of such a Tenor I did not consider myself at Liberty to retreat without an Order from Council." [107] With the mutinous spirit abroad, it was probable Lovell could not have stormed the fort after missing his first

[104] Sir George Collier, *Detail of Services Performed in America, 1776–1779* (New York, 1835), p. 107.

[105] Letter of Moore to his father, quoted in B. Brownrigg, *Life and Letters of Sir John Moore* (1923). He says a fascine work was afterwards thrown around the well which was in one of the open bastions, while the interval of the other was filled up with logs.

[106] Wadsworth to Williamson, Jan. 1, 1828, *Maine Hist. Soc. Collections*, ser. 2, II, 156.

[107] *Mass. Archives*, CXLV, 163–65. Lovell to Council, August, 1779.

golden chance. Though officially acquitted, he tendered his resignation, which was accepted, and he was never again employed in a military capacity.[108]

Other factors contributed to the failure. The vessels of the state navy, maintained primarily to guard against interference by Congress in matters of local defense, were jealous of the Continental ships. Moreover, the hurried impressment of seamen to fill up the crews of the ships did not tend to increase the fleet's efficiency. Finally the privateers were mainly interested in taking prizes, and the resultant profits in which officers and crews shared; all the private vessels were bound to go on cruise for prizes as soon as the Penobscot expedition was over.[109]

Even though one American militiaman, in his own opinion, might esteem himself the equal of two of the enemy, and in fact might have been had he met them in the forest, yet, in regular concerted operations of war, he proved inferior. The blame for not obtaining a leaven of Continental troops rests upon the Council. The fact that the American land force was not much larger than that of the British, while incomparably poorer in morale, was undoubtedly a major cause of failure. The delay in starting, delay in arriving, delay in attack, all contributed. Although the British were well aware of what was transpiring among the Americans, the Americans had apparently little idea of the precarious position in which their inaction placed them.

The British losses were surprisingly small. Collier in his report to the Admiralty cites twenty-three killed, thirty-three wounded, eleven missing. Even the American

108 *Massachusetts Soldiers and Sailors of the Revolutionary War* (Boston, 1905).

109 G. W. Allen, "State Navies and Privateers in the Revolution," *Mass. Hist. Soc. Proceedings*, XLVI, 170–191.

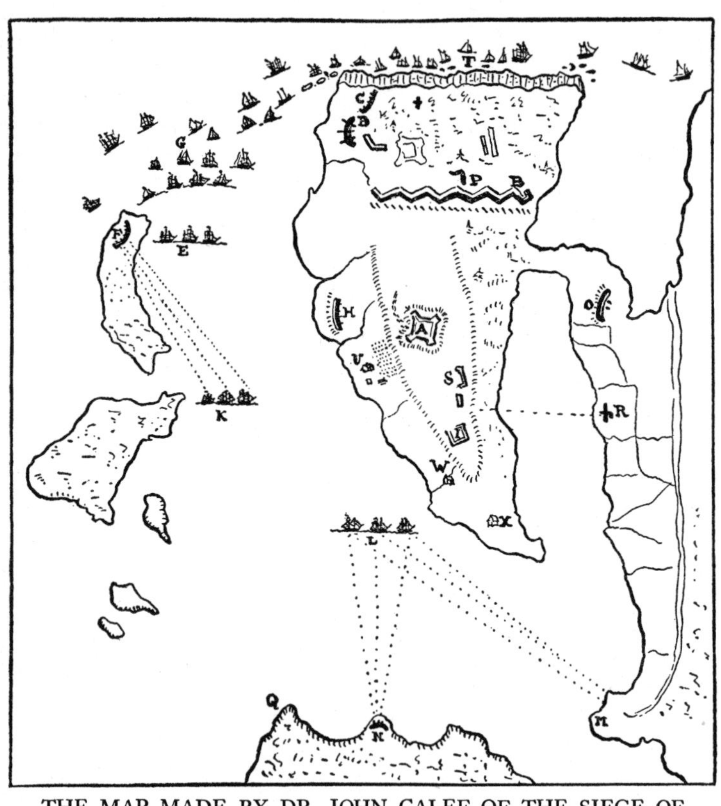

THE MAP MADE BY DR. JOHN CALEF OF THE SIEGE OF FORT GEORGE ON MAJABIGADUCE

A. Fort George, the n.w. and s.e. bastions were opened when the enemy appeared in the bay.

B. Rebel redoubt on height of Majabigaduce.

C. Rebel encampments.

D. Breastwork where three pieces of cannon which were mounted on the appearance of the fleet were taken by the rebels the morning they landed.

E. The King's ships Albany, North & Nautilus, lying at their 1st station & engaged with the Rebel Ships as their Divisions advanced.

F. Rebel Battery on Nautilus Island opened on King's Ships at their 2d station.

G. Rebel Fleet.

H. Half Moon Battery at Banks House — afterwards moved into the Fort.

I. Seaman Batteries & Redoubt.

K. Second Station of the King's Ships.

L. Third Station of the King's Ships.

M. Rebel Battery of 18 pnrs. at Westcott point opened at the King's Ships at their third Station.

N. Rebel Battery not Finished.

O. Rebel Battery not Finished.

P. Rebel Batteries & lines abbotised.

Q. Hainey's Point where the Rebel Piquet was drove by the Seamen.

R. Field Piece brought against the Seamen working at the Redoubt.

S. Encampment of the Troops before the Rebels appeared.

T. Here the Rebels Landed.

V. Joseph Perkins House.

W. John Perkins House.

X. Mark Hatch's House.

Y. A. Banks House.

Z. Dyce's House.

figures probably did not pass a hundred, most of these occurring at the storming of the heights.

Worse even than the recriminations, the disappointment, and chagrin, was the financial effect. Massachusetts was practically bankrupted by well over a million pounds of debts. Bills rained in. The town of Falmouth wanted to be repaid for furnishing provisions for the people returning from "Pernopskot."[110] The ferryman at Sheepscut wanted pay at 3d. a head for ferrying eight hundred and seventy-six returning soldiers over the Sheepscut River.[111] Eventually almost all claims were settled, but a half owner of the sloop *Pigeon* was not paid until ten years after his partner.[112] Massachusetts appealed to the Continental Congress for permission to retain its taxes, which was granted. Shortly the demand was put forth that Congress assume the entire expense of the expedition, and the claim was long pressed.[113]

The Court of Enquiry, pondering the evidence, tending perhaps to make the wish the father of the thought, unanimously ascribed the failure of the expedition to the "want of proper spirit and energy on the part of the Commodore."[114] The general whitewashing and making of Saltonstall the goat was not entirely satisfactory to everyone. "As he was a Continental officer, it was hoped his bulk would keep the smaller fry out of sight, and thereby the credit of the state would be saved, and a plea furnished for saddling the Continent with the expense."[115] The

[110] E. V. Smith, *History of Newburyport* (1854), p. 118.

[111] Speech to General Court, June 2, 1786, *Maine Hist. Soc. Collections*, ser. 2, XXI, 68.

[112] *Maine Hist. Soc. Collections*, ser. 2, XX, 404.

[113] *Ibid.*, XXI, 197.

[114] Proceedings of the General Assembly, *Magazine of History*, XXV (extra numbers), 202.

[115] *Mass. Hist. Soc. Proceedings*, IV, 129, Letter of Eben Hazard from Jamaica Plain, Mar. 22, 1780.

naval commanders in the service of the state were commended, General Lovell exonerated for not storming the enemy fort, Wadsworth complimented for his "great activity, courage, coolness, and prudence."[116] Revere was specifically exempted from praise or blame, and not until 1782 was he officially cleared. All those who had participated in the expedition were only too glad to have it forgotten. So little interest remained that when it came time to surrender the fort in 1784 the British commanding officer, after waiting in vain for someone from the Massachusetts government to be sent to receive the delivery, finally burned the barracks and departed.

[116] Proceedings of the General Assembly, *loc. cit.*

WALTER S. HAYWARD.

MADRAS IN 1787

On April 7, 1786, Sir Archibald Campbell landed at the sea-gate at Madras from the Honourable East India Company's ship *Earl Talbot* and received a governor's salute from the guns of Fort St. George. Sir Archibald, a Scotsman who had spent much of his military career in America,[1] was depended upon by His Majesty's ministers to assist them in inaugurating a new era in Indian affairs. His appointment and that of Lord Cornwallis, another American veteran, who was about to sail for Bengal as Governor-General, were dictated by those new considerations of policy which were enjoined upon the Company's directors by the Younger Pitt's India Act of 1784. In appointing able military men to the highest posts in India, Pitt and his chief adviser in Indian affairs, Henry Dundas, hoped to avoid in future the difficulties which were then confronting them as a result of Warren Hastings' rule in Bengal. In 1786, the King's ministers and the Company's directors were at one in their aims. They desired a lasting peace with both European and Indian powers to the end that commerce at home and abroad might prosper. They all looked to India to restore to Britain some of the power and prestige which she had lost in foreign eyes by her American disasters. Sir Archibald Campbell was accordingly expected to take strict account of stock at Madras and to place that settlement upon the soundest possible basis as an emporium of British trade and a bulwark of British prestige in the East.

[1] *Dictionary of National Biography*, III, 794. Sir Duncan Campbell, *Records of Clan Campbell in the Military Service of the Honourable East India Company 1600–1858* (London, 1925), p. 27. From February 1768 to December 1772, Campbell served the East India Company as Chief Engineer in Bengal.

In his examination of affairs at Madras, one of the things that may have surprised Sir Archibald Campbell most was the size and heterogeneous composition of the European community on the Coromandel coast. In the strict letter of the law, he should have found in the Presidency of Madras only the Company's military and civil establishment together with a few gentlemen who had received the license of the Company to reside within its Indian territories. In actual fact, the law requiring licenses was almost a dead letter, as Sir Archibald speedily learned during the course of his first year of government, when he asked every European not in the Company's or His Majesty's service to send in an account of himself.

These accounts give an unusually clear picture of what life at one of the Company's settlements in the late eighteenth century was really like. They show the presence in Madras of about one hundred seventy-five Europeans who had drifted to India in devious ways. By far the largest group among them were men who had come out as ordinary seamen or soldiers, had got their discharge by fair means or foul and then set up for themselves as petty shopkeepers or "punch-house" keepers in the Fort or in the Black Town at Madras or at the country commercial "factories" and military cantonments. Thomas Andrews,[2] for example, arrived as a midshipman in Sir Edward Hughes' squadron in 1780, was taken by the French under Suffren in 1782, delivered over to Hyder Ali, sultan of Mysore, with four hundred twenty other prisoners, and finally, on release, returned to Madras to set up a shop in the Fort. Daniel Palmer, who arrived in 1771, rose to be a sergeant-major in the Company's army, obtained his discharge in 1784, and opened a shop for the sale of

[2] See Madras Record Office, Public Department, Sundries, XLI, for all data concerning Europeans not in the Company's or His Majesty's service.

"Europe articles" at Masulipatam. John Gullett, who had earned enough as a shopkeeper in the Fort within three years to retire to the Danish settlement at Tranquebar, gave the Governor the clearest account of the way in which many seekers after fortune were arriving in India. His letter reveals the ease with which it was possible through the exercise of a little influence at home to come to India as a midshipman and then desert a Company's ship. He says that it was well known to Mr. Webster, the Company director who secured him a berth as midshipman, that he would desert the ship at Madras.

Shipping as a midshipman was obviously the easiest way for the ordinary man to get out to India if he could not get into the Company's army with the intention of deserting. Leaving a minor post in the army was apparently simple enough if a man could pay a substitute to take his place. Ill health due to the climate would often do as well as a substitute. James Barter, who arrived in India as a surgeon's mate in the army in 1782, was allowed for this reason without the slightest difficulty to abandon medicine for shopkeeping in 1785. There were also disabled soldiers among the shopkeepers. Patrick Scott who was injured by the breaking loose of a gun in a gale off the Cape of Good Hope was one of these. Another who deserted medicine for trade was Charles Lloyd, a Hanoverian Jew, who arrived in 1772 in a French ship *La Lion*, served for a time as a doctor with Hyder Ali's army, and finally settled down as a baker in Madras in partnership with a certain David Young, who had started his Indian career as a private soldier in 1768 and had subsequently failed as a merchant.

A common practice, also, was to come to India as a servant of a person of position and then stay on, if possible, to make one's own way in the world. Zachariah Polack, "by birth an Englishman, by education a Jew," arrived in 1777 as a clerk to a Calcutta merchant with the intention of setting up a shop of his own as soon as he could. Thomas Laney, who came as a servant in the family of Captain Dalling, threw himself on the governor's mercy, pleading that he would be utterly ruined if forced to close his shop at Trichinopoly. William Leamy, a former servant of Mr. Stone, a Company's chief factor, was taken into partnership by Peter Massey Cassin, an Irishman of Dublin who had secured Governor Macartney's permission in 1782 to engage in trade. William Brumage served a Mr. Hanky, until that gentleman unfortunately "fell in a duel," and forced him to open a retail shop in the Fort. The well established firm of Alexander and Britain, shopkeepers at Masulipatam, had a similar origin. Peter Alexander and Samuel Britain had become so inseparable that they never thought of sending in two letters to the Governor. They wrote to him jointly: "We came to India with Mr. Cotsford when He was appointed Chief at Masulipatam in the year 1778 as his servants on board the Southampton Indiaman, by the permission of the Honourable Court of Directors, and continued in his service until the beginning of the year 1781, when he left this settlement and returned to Europe." They added that they had begun to trade on their own account even before their master's departure.

Possibly the occupation easiest to enter, next to shopkeeping or punch-housekeeping at Madras, was that of captain or owner of a so-called "country" trading ship, *i.e.* a ship engaged in the port to port trade of the Indian peninsula and the adjacent lands. This occupation, which absorbed many Europeans who had been "bred to the sea line", was extremely lucrative. Captain Robert Middleton had come out in 1782 as chief officer of the *Myrtle* transport which proved so leaky she was condemned at Bencoolen in Sumatra. He then took over the Company's "snow" *Elizabeth* on which he served for a year until he left her to command a vessel belonging to Messrs. Alexander and Britain. Joseph Bagott, although he began life as a soldier in the Company's and Nawab of Arcot's service, was commanding a "country vessell" at Tuticorin in 1787. William Maddern, whose career in the Royal Navy was cut short by the French, returned from prison at Mauritius to enter the "country" shipping service. W. A. Gay was perhaps the best type of "country" commander, a simple man anxious to build a new life for himself in the East. He had come out in the *Nassau*, had entered the "country" trade after commanding the Company's snow *Nancy*, and had married and settled down at Negapatam. Anxious not to be disturbed, he wrote to the governor that he was "regular in discharging the Hon. Company's customs, paying my debts, going to Church and praying to the Father of mercies for the prosperity of King George and the Honourable East India Company."

Madras also had its share of Europeans who followed the more select occupations of jeweller, clock-maker, musician, and miniature painter. Her leading jewellers were of Swiss or French origin. Chief among them was John James Durand of Geneva who wrote to the governor under protest, for, as he said, he thought his having a brother and son in the Company's service "would shelter him from being on a par with unknown vagabond adventurers." He had come out under the protection of General Sir Eyre Coote and the "late Director Rous." He already presided over quite a large establishment which needed two assistants; one, an Englishman, John Wright, a jeweller who had come out in 1771; the other, a Swiss relative of the proprietor who had recently been shipped out from Geneva via Lisbon with the connivance of a British naval officer.

The other owner of a jewellery shop was César Boucher, a Frenchman born in Ceylon. The clock-makers were all English. This calling was represented by Messrs. Leathem and MacIntosh who had been given charge of "the Honourable Company's clocks" for some years. John Leathem and Angus MacIntosh had apparently first met by accident on board the *Nassau*, Captain Gore, in 1776 on the voyage out. Leathem was serving in her as a midshipman when MacIntosh came aboard at Madeira where he had been waiting some months for a chance to sail for India with the help of Mr. Murray, the British consul. Both men, having some knowledge of clocks, decided to join forces on arrival at Madras. After 1781 they had to compete with a rolling-stone named Samuel Crawford, who, after arriving on a Company's ship, was "pressed" and sent on board H. M. S. *Burford* at Negapatam. Having served in her at the sieges of Negapatam and Trincomalee and taken part in three actions with Admiral Suffren's fleet, Crawford was allowed to settle in Madras by Lord Macartney who "honoured" him "with the care of the Honourable Company's Town Clock." Perhaps because of his appearance in this capacity, Leathem and MacIntosh were obliged to sell "goods from the Europe ships without interfering with the Company's trade" in order to eke out their earnings as watch and clock makers.

Competition was likewise keen among the musicians, of whom there seem to have been too many at Madras. Not only did the Company employ its own organist, Eric Dieurstedt, but there were no less than four others, two of English and two of German origin. Samuel Dicker, Edward Miller, and Charles Jessel a Bohemian, teachers of music, apparently pursued no other occupation, but Anthony Frederick Franck, a German musician, who arrived in 1759 with Governor Pigott, had been obliged to go into retail trade. The only Madras artist in 1787 was John Smart, who wrote: "I had the Court of Directors' full assent to come out to follow my profession of painting, and bring my daughter with me. I sailed April 19, 1785 from England on board the *Dutton*, Captain West, and arrived at Madras the 6th September following, in the same vessell."

The less socially desirable occupations of hairdresser and farrier were followed by Samuel Chaplin and John Story. Chaplin had come to India with Sir Archibald Campbell's predecessor, Lord Macartney, in 1781 "as his lordship's butler and valet." His master had been so kind as to allow Chaplin to open a hairdressing shop of his own in the Fort to occupy his "leisure time." Chaplin was permitted to continue this business on the governor's return to England. John Story had entered his profession by the other route of release from the Company's army by means of paying a substitute "in his room." After he had served in India eleven years, Sir Thomas Rumbold in 1778 allowed him to set up a livery stable of his own and gave him the post of farrier to the Company's horses.

At a higher level in the social scale stood the teachers, the Company's printer, the handful of retired gentlemen of leisure, and the Europeans in the service of the Nawab of Arcot. The teachers are interesting because they also show the flexibility of Madras society. All were ex-soldiers who had chosen schoolmastering as a way of escape from difficulties in their own profession. Foremost among them was Benjamin Goard who arrived in 1765, served in the Company's army until 1770, and then entered the Nawab's service to remain until 1782, "when being two years in arrears, a large family to maintain, and not the least distant prospect of being paid or even getting a subsistence from his Highness," he was obliged to resign "even though a Captain of Infantry" and open a school in the Black Town. His rival was W. F. Rutter, formerly an "invalid bombardier" who had been discharged from the army in 1774 after eleven years' service with "an incurable disorder, gravel." In spite of this disadvantage, he was in 1787 supporting "a wife and seven children" on his earnings as a teacher. The only other teacher was James Porter, who, on return from a French prison in the island of Bourbon, was made "master of the Charity School" and "clerk of the Parish." The Company's printer was an unattractive character. Richard Johnston had left England in 1783, as a captain in the thirteenth regiment of foot with the intention of joining his brother-in-law Sir John Burgoyne at Madras. That officer exercised his influence at the Admiralty to gain Johnston permission to bring out his family. In August, 1785, Johnston obtained the sanction of the government "to publish a weekly paper and to establish a regular printing-office in Fort St. George." In this way the *Madras Courier* was born. Its editor became one of the most turbulent and quarrelsome citizens of his day, for he was a defendant in suits in the Mayor's Court no less than six times in a single year.

The number of persons who confessed to having "no employment" was naturally small. Anyone who had accumulated a competence ordinarily desired to go home to Europe. The only real retired "gentleman" was possibly John Parkison who came out properly licensed and had "no apparent occupation." Another respectable person was Nathaniel Bacon who "had retired with a wife and family" after many years in seafaring as an officer of the Company's ships. Less respectable, but more colorful, was John Charles Wilkins Box, a former clerk in the office of the Paymaster-General of His Majesty's forces, who in 1787 lived in the Black Town and "did nothing" except run up debts. César Boucher, the jeweller, sued him for a formidable amount in jewellery which he had apparently lavished on his Indian mistresses.

The officers in the Nawab's service were sometimes equally colorful and extravagant. Undoubtedly the most extraordinary career of an officer in the Nawab's service was that of James Woolley who happened to be living in Madras in 1787. He had arrived in 1772 in His Majesty's squadron with prospects of being employed in His Majesty's service in "an eligible line," but entered instead the Nawab's corps of artillery. Within a few months he became the Nawab's confidential secretary. In February, 1780, he resigned, "having through the bounty of my master acquired more than my deserts entitled me to." He was then "entrusted by this government with a commission to the Sherif of Mecca, and to the Basha and the Beys of Egypt, for opening a conveyance for paquets by way of Suez." Of this enterprise, he wrote: "I exerted all the zeal and perseverance in my power, but, from unexpected causes, my efforts terminated in four months imprisonment from which I escaped only with my life." On his escape he returned to England and came out to India again in order to save his property from ruin. He then continued his efforts on behalf of the opening of the overland route via Suez. He was succeeded as secretary to the Nawab by Charles Binney who became one of the founders of the great mercantile firm of Binney & Co. which still exists at Madras.

Of all the persons so far mentioned, none expressed a desire to remain in India permanently. They all requested permission to stay in the country until they had arranged their affairs in such a manner as to enable them to return to England. The three who did express a wish to remain in India for the rest of their lives deserve special attention. Josses Nevill, a lieutenant in the Nawab's service, had first come to India in 1755 as a Company cadet and had entered the Nawab's service in 1771. In 1787, he described himself as an old man with a large family who, after thirty-two years of faithful service, wished to remain in India "as long as I live." At Vizagapatam, lived Andrew Ferguson, a mariner in the "country" service since 1766, who wished to remain there "the rest of his days." George Baker was by all odds the most interesting old European resident of Madras in 1787. He first came to India in a Company's ship in 1743, served in two voyages out and back in the 1740's, was with Admiral Boscawen in the 1750's, and returned to England in the sixties, but could not stand the "British climate." Having considerable money laid by, he had come back to Madras with the idea of supplying the Company with fresh water. In the next year or two he built the Madras water-works which he superintended himself until he sold his plant to the government in 1782 for 30,000 gold pagodas (£12,000). In 1787, he was, as it were, first citizen without portfolio, consulted on every occasion of importance by government as well as by his fellow citizens, whom he continually impressed with the reiteration of his hatred of the British climate and his love for his adopted city. He did not stand at the apex of the non-official social pyramid. That position was occupied by the leading lights of the legal and mercantile fraternity who were not in the Company's service.

As might be expected, the attorneys at Madras were not the best of their profession. Anyone who stood the slightest chance of success at the English, Scottish, or Irish bar would never have set foot in Madras in the 1780's. It was the refuge of the "climber" and the lawyer who had made a bad start at home. India provided many opportunities for such persons. Vast numbers of Indians were being brought within the scope of the Mayor's Court at Madras, which was chiefly concerned with petty debt actions brought by Indians as well as Europeans.[3] Many of these actions were stimulated by attorneys eager for fees. Europeans in India were more disorderly than Europeans at home. Murder was common, duels were frequent, and piracy of all types was prevalent. One Robert Watson, who ran off from Masulipatam with a ship belonging to a Company servant, took her to the Malay archipelago, lost her to two other scoundrels, was captured at Macao by the Company's China supercargoes, was sent to Goa for trial by the Portuguese, was released and made his way back to Bengal by stealing another ship only to be recaptured off Masulipatam by accident, was probably more adventurous and less fortunate than others who engaged in similar activities. Lawyers loved then as now to exercise every artifice of delay. The year 1787 saw the culmination of the case of an Indian named Malem against a Captain Cuthbert Fenwick who had recaptured from Hyder Ali in 1781 a sloop belonging to Malem loaded with elephants and other war material, the value of which had grown with the years to the enormous sum of 35,000 pagodas, interest being compounded at 12 per cent. The attorney for Malem in this case, which ended in an arbitral award giving neither side a victory, was Stephen Popham, the leading attorney of the day, who was building a life anew in Madras on the fees paid by Indians and Europeans in actions for similar debts.[4] He had begun life in England,

[3] India Office: Madras Mayor's Court Records.

[4] The story of the cases of Watson and Fenwick is scattered through the Madras Public Consultations for 1787 at the India Office, see especially: range 240, vol. 66, p. 220; r. 241, v. 2, p. 2401; r. 240, v. 68, pp. 1095, 1592 *et seq.*

but had transferred his hopes to Ireland when the death of an uncle left him a law practice which made it necessary for him to enter the Irish House of Commons. The expenses of borough mongering and of fighting the attempts to reform the borough of Swords in the late 1770's forced him to flee to India as a bankrupt. Within three or four years he had made a considerable fortune, evolved a plan for policing Madras which commanded the government's attention, and bought a site on which a new Indian market was erected. From the correspondence of the year 1787, he would seem to have "climbed" with success and was even able to ward off the displeasure of Lord Cornwallis, who was inclined with his usual candour to consider Mr. Popham a "pest to society." [5] An attorney more to the manner born was Mr. Charles Inglis, one of the few Europeans not in the Company's service who paid his own way out to India. "I came out to this country," he wrote, "on the Asia Indiaman in the year 1785 a passenger and paid in London to Captain Soulker, commander, for my passage one hundred guineas." On the same ship arrived Peter Walker, then a personal assistant to Lord Macartney, but soon to be an attorney at the Mayor's Court. Pullein Spencer, another leading attorney, came out on the Danish frigate *Hussar* in 1784 and at once began to practice.

The private merchants, with Andrew Ross at their head, were, next to the governor and council, the leading citizens of eighteenth-century Madras. Andrew Ross arrived in 1752 with "free merchant's covenants" from the Court of Directors. In thirty-five years, he had built a substantial fortune and had served the city as mayor and alderman. James Amos, another substantial merchant, "came passenger to India on board the ship Earl of Ashburnham in

[5] *Loc. cit.*

the year 1774 without leave of the Company." These two still operated their own businesses in 1787, but most of their competitors had formed partnerships or companies. In Sir Archibald Campbell's day, Balfour and Spalding, Francis Lautour & Co., and Pelling and DeFries were the great mercantile firms of Madras. William Balfour and John Spalding, who had both recently been in the Company's civil service and were related to several leading civil servants, did a great agency business on behalf of the Company's servants who, though debarred from the trade to Europe, were permitted to engage in all forms of "country" trade, and, as is well known, traded to Europe clandestinely under foreign flags. Francis Lautour & Co. conducted a similar, but less extensive business. Francis Lautour, a Swiss, arrived in Rear Admiral Sir Robert Harland's squadron in 1777. After serving many years on board the King's ships, he remained in India "in the prosecution of a considerable line of business that I commenced when acting under Admiral Harland and Admiral Vernon." In 1787, he was "acting as agent for His Majesty's two Hanoverian regiments," and was chiefly employed in making up his affairs with a view to returning with his family to England. Thomas Pelling and John DeFries represented a union for business purposes between the English and the Portuguese community at Madras. Their firm helped to finance the Portuguese and Armenians who engaged in the coastal trade of India. Pelling had come from England with the Company's permission in 1769; DeFries was a Portuguese born in Madras. Other substantial merchants were Sir John Menzies, John Robson, Thomas Davies and Thomas Parkison. Sir John Menzies, who arrived in the *Fortitude* in 1781, considered himself above the necessity of writing a letter giving an account of himself, and was much incensed to find his name on the list of those who had disobeyed the governor's order. John Robson stayed in India to engage in trade after taking over charge of the Company's ship *Hinchinbroke* on her recapture from the enemy by Captain Pasly of H. M. S. *Jupiter*. Thomas Davies had recently transferred his activities from Canton to Madras. He claimed the protection of the Company's supercargoes at Canton on the ground that he traded between Madras and China "without the least injury to the Honourable Company's interest." Thomas Parkison, having been in India under "free merchant's indentures" in the 1760's, had come out again in 1785 to settle down to ship-building and "exchanging the produce of Bengal and the Coast" at Bandamalanka. He had with him two young protégés, Thomas Lloyd and Robert Weir, whose parents had sent them out to India as private soldiers with the intention he should launch them on the road to Indian fame and fortune at a proper moment. They had both resigned from the army by paying substitutes for taking their places, in order to wait until a Company cadetship or an opportunity in the "sea line" presented itself.

Merchants of less note who had had rather unusual careers were William Moore, Frederick Colebit, and Thomas Barter, all three of whom had come to India from America or the West Indies. Moore, an Irishman, had come out to Pondichéry in 1784 as supercargo on the first American ship to arrive in India, the *United States* of Philadelphia. In 1787, he was carrying on a trading business at the Arcot cantonment. Colebit, also an Irishman, and formerly employed in the trade between West Indian and American ports, came out on an American ship in August, 1786 in order to enter the Indian "country" trade. Thomas Barter's West Indian career had been ruined by the failure of David Scott of Antigua during the American

War. Through the kind offices of Mr. Donald Cameron, a banker in London, he was able to come out as a midshipman on the *Earl Talbot* to join his brother as a merchant at Masulipatam.

The affairs of the European merchants were inextricably mingled with those of the Company's civil servants, for the Company itself was a mercantile concern which had taken up governing as a "side-line" only to find that the "side-line" had gradually absorbed almost the whole of its energies. It was Sir Archibald Campbell's duty not only to look into the affairs of the non-official European community, but to find out how the heads of Company departments were actually doing their job. These gentlemen were accordingly asked to explain in detail how they and the sixteen hundred Indian clerks and messengers under them carried on the business of the Company's government in 1787. Their letters together with the proceedings of the governor's council in its various capacities present a fairly complete picture of the Company's affairs on the Coromandel coast in 1787.

In order to understand the economic life of the European community in Madras as a whole, it is necessary to remember the difficulties of doing business on a continent where many kinds of coins passed current and where the lack of actual ready cash was a problem confronting not only the Company, but all other sections of the European community. Business in India was then carried on in almost every conceivable kind of coin which circulated in the various sections of the East, but Europeans were primarily concerned with four coins, the Bombay rupee, the sicca or Bengal rupee, the Arcot or Madras rupee, and the Madras gold pagoda. The business and official community kept their books in terms of a gold pagoda whose exchange value was generally reckoned to be about eight shillings.

There were many kinds of gold pagodas in the southern part of India as there were many kinds of silver rupees all over India, but at Madras all were brought to account in terms of the Madras current or "star" pagoda. Arcot rupees circulated freely, and the bills of exchange drawn on the government or on individuals in which most European business was done were written sometimes in Arcot rupees but more usually in star pagodas.[6] The difficulties of doing business seem to have been not so much those of exchange, for the values of Bombay, Bengal and Madras coins in terms of one another did not fluctuate widely in 1787. The real problems were those of transfer. When, for example, the Bombay government, with no great supply of silver on hand, wished to pay the Rajah of Travancore three lakhs of Bombay rupees for pepper, it required a year's correspondence between the governors of the Company's three Presidencies to accommodate the rajah. Bombay wrote to Bengal; Bengal wrote to Madras; Madras wrote to Indian money-lenders in southern India through the Company's Resident at Tanjore, and the three lakhs were finally arranged for through a government purchase of Porto Novo pagodas. In the course of these negotiations, the Rajah of Travancore refused to accept an earlier offer of Porto Novo pagodas, and the Madras government refused to pay over good Madras pagodas to Danish merchants who were creditors of the Rajah at Tranquebar.[7] A similar problem of transfer arose when, in 1787, the Bengal government could not make payments to the Madras government in silver, but had to ship thousands upon thousands of bags of rice instead.[8]

[6] The exchange value of the Arcot rupee in 1787 was, normally, 375 Arcot rupees to 100 Madras pagodas.

[7] India Office, Madr. Pub. Con. r. 240, v. 67, pp. 697, 805; v. 68, pp. 1200, 1354; r. 241, v. 2, pp. 2663, 2765.

[8] *Ibid.*, r. 240, v. 67, p. 487.

Currency problems such as these caused the Company at Madras to encourage Europeans and Indians to bring every kind of Eastern coin to its mint to be melted down into gold pagodas or Arcot rupees of standard fineness. The mint was in charge of a European assay-master who reported the "touch of gold," but the work was done by an Indian mint-contractor, Chippermall Chitty, who received 6½ pagodas per thousand or 17½ rupees per thousand, and was responsible for all the work of the gold and silversmiths. The Company received ½ of 1 per cent on every amount coined out of a total custom on coinage of about 1 per cent for gold and 2 per cent for silver.[9]

The great activity of the port of Madras was brought about chiefly by the "country" trade of small sloops and "snows" under both Indian and European commanders. The Company kept no exact record of it, but some idea of its size can be gained by occasional references to it. In July of 1787, the government Board of Trade spoke of the "roads" as "alive with shipping from every port of India."[10] In the spring of 1787, fifty-seven ships, only eleven of them under European captains, were solely occupied in carrying to Madras from Bengal the 126,000 bags of rice shipped by a private merchant at Calcutta under contract with the Governor-General.[11] At least 2500 bales of Surat cotton were brought to Madras on "country" ships during the year, often so heavily stowed that cotton bales covered the decks and were slung out over the gunwales.[12] "Country" ships were used and sometimes owned by Company servants for carrying to non-British ports the goods they wished to export illicitly to Europe

[9] Madras Record Office, Public Department; Sundries, XL, Report of the Assay-Master.

[10] India Office, Madr. Pub. Con. r. 240, v. 68, p. 1528.

[11] *Ibid.*, v. 67, p. 618.

[12] *Ibid.*, r. 241, v. 1, p. 1944; r. 240, v. 68, p. 1174.

under foreign flags. On this subject, Andrew Ross wrote the governor on March 28, 1788, that "very large sums of money belonging to British subjects have for many years gone through the hands of foreign nations," and mentioned the presence off the Indian coasts of ships under the following flags: French, Portuguese, Danish, Tuscan, Imperial, Prussian, Swedish, American, and Savoyard.[13] The "country" trade at Madras itself was large enough to occupy the time of five European searchers and fifteen Indian clerks at the Company's custom-house.[14]

Contrasted with the activity of private traders of all kinds the Company's own transactions of a strictly commercial character at Madras in 1787 seem very small. They were in fact so small that, in order to fill up their ships, the Company often allotted the vacant space to private traders. The report of the import warehousekeeper is especially eloquent on the sorry state of the Company's imports from Europe. He informed the governor bluntly: "The Import Warehouse department receives charge of the consignments to this place of woolens, copper, pig lead, Madeira wine, hospital stores and soldiers hats." [15] These then were the only European imports of the Company. Of these, only woollens, copper, and Madeira wine were sold for profit; the other items were brought out for the Company's own use. Since Madeira wine was a luxury article saleable almost entirely to Europeans, woollens and copper were alone sold to Indians. During the year, two attempts were made to sell the Company's woollens at public outcry. Both were utter failures; not a single

[13] *Ibid.*, r. 241, v. 5, p. 933. See also r. 241, v. 2, p. 2774. List of ships calling at St. Helena May 2, 1786 – May 28, 1787 gives names of 76 ships, 45 British, 3 Swedish, 6 Danish, 4 Portuguese, 7 French, 9 Dutch, 2 American.

[14] Madras Record Office, Public Dept., Sundries, XL, Report of the Sea-Customer.

[15] *Ibid.*, Report of the Import Warehousekeeper.

bidder appeared. The Board of Trade sadly attributed this to the results of the war between Tipu, Sultan of Mysore, and the Marathas.[16] They had to take what comfort they could in the proceeds of the copper sales which went off very nicely at profits of 26 per cent and 31 per cent on the invoiced value of the ordinary copper, and 43 per cent on that of the Japan copper. Of this one hundred and ninety-three tons of copper, about one half was bought by Indian dealers, a small quantity by Mr. Amos, and the rest by Messrs. Kindersley and Hughes, two Company servants who intended to resell it at a higher profit.[17] The Company's one hundred and seventy-two pipes of Madeira wine were sold at the high profit of 72 per cent over the invoiced cost at Madras.[18]

The East India Company had therefore ceased to bring to Madras European goods of any appreciable value. All the copper and wine could have been brought upon one ship. More interesting is the record of the export warehousekeeper for 1787. The Company provided only two cargoes for export to Europe from Madras in the winter of 1786–87, and only one and a half in the winter of 1787–88.[19] These cargoes consisted of Indian manufactured cloths known as "piece goods" to the invoiced value of about one lakh of pagodas (£40,000) annually. As far as its commercial business at Madras was concerned, the Company's trade was therefore hardly greater than it had been in the early days of its connection with India. One ship out and two ships back can hardly be said to be of great account. From one point of view, the Company, looked upon as a Madras merchant, was utterly bankrupt. The old system of Anglo-Indian trade was the exchange

16 India Office, Madr. Pub. Con. r. 240, v. 67, p. 934; v. 68, pp. 1528, 1725.
17 *Ibid.*, r. 241, v. 2, p. 2354.
18 *Ibid.*, r. 241, v. 2, p. 2368.
19 *Ibid.*, r. 240, v. 66, p. 128; r. 241, v. 2, p. 2488.

of European hardware and bullion against India "manufactures," chiefly the fine cloths. Since the acquisition of political power by the Company, the surplus of revenue over expenditure was presumed to take the place of bullion brought from Europe. In the Madras of 1787, there was no such surplus, no matter in what light the Company's budget was considered. Madras ran at a huge deficit made up by Bengal, but the Company continued the policy of collecting a small commercial "investment" of cloths there, and, as a matter of fact, the exigencies of other branches of its trade caused it to become considerably involved with the affairs of private merchants.

If the only Company ships which called at Madras had been those used for bringing out and taking home the Company's Madras import and export cargoes, the scope for private connection with its shipping would have been small indeed. It would have been confined to the so-called "privilege" of private trade of fifteen tons per ship granted to the officers of Company ships who usually did business with private merchants at the Company's factories.[20] In this way many of the Europe articles retailed by the ex-soldiers and midshipmen keeping shops and taverns at Madras came to India. At most, such trade would have consisted of this petty "privilege" business plus an occasional venture such as that of Balfour and Spalding who shipped four tons of indigo to England with the government's permission on the *Berrington*, a Company ship carrying home half the Madras "investment" of 1786–87.[21] In fact, most of the Company ships calling at Madras each season at this period belonged to the China fleet. In June and July eight or ten of them, loaded only with chests of

[20] India Office, Madr. Pub. Con. r. 241, v. 1, p. 1967; r. 240, v. 68, p. 1366, and other references to tonnage of ships in these volumes.

[21] *Ibid.*, r. 240, v. 66, p. 212.

silver and lead with occasionally a small invoice of broadcloth, called at Madras on their way to Canton, and nothing was more natural than that Balfour and Spalding, Andrew Ross, Francis Lautour and Co. and others should solicit the government's permission to use the large amount of vacant space on these ships for the purpose of shipping cotton to China, cotton which they had brought around from Bombay on "country" ships. In 1787, this trade was fairly free; the government granted the privilege as applied for under the merchants' promise to buy bills on the Court of Directors in London with the proceeds of their sales at Canton. The government charged no freight, and Andrew Ross and Balfour and Spalding got the lion's share of the business. The ships, with their return cargoes of tea, did not stop at Madras on the voyage home, a circumstance which forced many a Madras army officer and civil servant to go to England via China, there being not enough room available on the few ships sailing from Madras direct to England via the Cape.[22] Late in 1787, the practice of shipping private cotton to China had attracted such attention that the Company's supercargoes at Canton suggested to Sir Archibald Campbell that the Company might as well charge freight. This caused the Madras government to open the Company's expected vacant tonnage on the China ships of the next season to competitive bidding. Balfour and Spalding accordingly offered to take up all the vacant tonnage paying three pagodas a bale freight, and agreeing to pay £10,000 per ship into the Company's treasury at Canton for bills on London, which would mean an approximate total for the season of £100,000. John Beatson of Calcutta offered to freight 3000 tons at three pagodas two fanams a ton making a total cargo worth at

[22] *Ibid.*, r. 240, v. 66, pp. 206, 213; v. 67, p. 727; v. 68, pp. 1172, 1267, 1344, 1362, 1366, 1492; r. 241, v. 1, pp. 1944, 1967, 1983; v. 2, p. 2377; v. 3, p. 3020.

Canton £30,000 to be made up not only of cotton, but of some redwood and opium as well. Andrew Ross offered to ship 2000 bales and pay one and one half pagodas a bale for freight or 3000 bales at a freight of one pagoda a bale, but he objected to the principle of paying freight and agreeing also to pay the proceeds of his shipment into the Company's treasury for bills on London. He promised to pay more freight, if not obliged to deposit his money with the Company at Canton. Naturally, Balfour and Spalding's offer was accepted by the governor and council.[23] In this way, the Company's commercial affairs were blended with those of private merchants and with those of Company servants acting on their own account. Because of the China fleet of ten or a dozen ships, Madras roads saw many ships outward bound but very few homeward bound. The European ships bound for Bengal often did not call at Madras, and those bound home from Bengal only called at Madras to pick up despatches and collect the small Madras "investment." Madras roads saw practically none of the Company's Europe ships during the months from August to December.

The Company's affairs at Madras were even more intermixed with those of private merchants as a result of circumstances having a political rather than a commercial origin. In other words, political power on the Coromandel Coast had gradually involved the Madras government in a financial morass in the midst of which it could not possibly act at all without the facilities provided by its own servants in their private capacities and by the private European merchants. It was a debtor government, dependent in the last analysis for its stability on a market for the bills which it drew on the Governor-General-in-Council

[23] India Office, Madr. Pub. Con., r. 241, v. 3, p. 3088.

at Calcutta. Some idea of the financial resources of the private mercantile firms is gained from the offers they made to take up these bills. In the financial year 1786–87, one crore of Bengal rupees (£1,000,000) were transferred to Madras, partly in the Company's Bengal bonds, partly in rice, and partly in bills of exchange. Since the bonds were issued to the amount of 44 lakhs of rupees, and the amount transferred in rice was comparatively small, about 50 lakhs of rupees were marketed at Madras in bills of exchange bought up by private individuals and merchants.[24] In the winter of 1787–88, the Madras government advertised publicly for tenders for its bills on Bengal. Francis Lautour and Co. offered to take up bills on Bengal to the amount of five lakhs of rupees (£50,000), paying into the Madras treasury 100 pagodas for every 407 rupees. Pelling and DeFries offered to supply pagodas at the rate of 100 for every 410 rupees in bills to a total value of two lakhs of rupees, one half the total to be available in two weeks, the other half in thirty days, or if the governor preferred, they would guarantee pagodas at the same exchange for bills up to five lakhs of rupees to be paid into the treasury, one third in fifteen days, one third in thirty days, and the final third in sixty days.[25]

These tenders provide a clue not only to the resources of private merchants, but to the actual "hand to mouth" manner in which the Madras government was carrying on its business. As he looked over the Company's Madras books, and surveyed the reports of the heads of government departments, Sir Archibald Campbell could easily have imagined himself the president of a concern which was constantly on the verge of ruin. He had about one hundred and seventy-five employees, the Madras civil

[24] *Ibid.*, r. 241, v. 2, p. 2384.
[25] *Ibid.*, r. 241, v. 6, p. 1287.

servants, busily engaged in the double operation of collecting revenue and buying cloth. About one half of these employees were stationed in Madras itself. The rest were scattered in the "subordinate settlements"; in the north, as chiefs and members of council at "factories" of the old type; in the south, as residents in native territories whose rulers had promised to pay for the Company's protection. Each "out-settlement" kept its own books, reporting its financial condition monthly to Madras. Sir Archibald and his council presided not over one cash chest, but over several. When they were in low water at Madras, they paid the most pressing demands on them by drawing bills, for example, on the chief and council of Ganjam. When Ganjam was hard-pressed, the chief looked to Madras for authorization to draw on Madras or on some other "out-settlement."[26] When all were equally hard-pressed, the governor and council had one invariable rule: arrange for the military expenditure, let the rest wait, sell bills on Bengal, or, if authorized from home, advertise to receive cash and give in exchange either bills on London or their own 8 per cent bonds. In times of great stringency, Company servants and army officers were paid in bonds, not in cash. All these transactions in bonds, bills of exchange, and bills on London made business for the private merchant. A Company servant at Madras paid, for example, by a bill on the chief and council at Vizagapatam, or a King's army officer paid by a bill on Bengal took his bill to Balfour and Spalding, who took it up often at a heavy discount.

The year 1787 was not one of great stringency. Laying aside for the moment the question of extinguishing any of the Madras bond debt of 28 lakhs of pagodas, Sir Archibald

[26] Sundry letters to and from the subordinate settlements recorded in India Office, Madras Pub. Con. r. 240, v. 67, 68; r. 241, v. 1, 2, 3, 4.

was able to keep his head tolerably above water. In fact, it was quite a good year at the start. The revenue came in regularly at the "out-settlements," so regularly that he could plan to spend an extra lakh of pagodas in buying cloths for the "investment," and would have done so if corruption and mismanagement at Masulipatam had not thwarted him.[27] Nevertheless, it was not a bad year; he could, with the help of the annual subsidy from Bengal, meet his interest charges and his current military and civil expenditure with a fair degree of success. It was perfectly obvious to him, as to everyone else, that what really kept his government in constant hot water was the heavy load of military expenditure. His company had, in the language of today, to pay too much for "protection." As governor of Madras, he was never able to ask himself how much of a surplus he could save this year, but only to hope against hope that the figures representing the Company's arrears on current account at the end of the financial year in March would not be too high. In March 1788, he thought he was doing fairly well when he was only in arrear 68,000 pagodas with the pay of the civil servants, 164,000 pagodas on the military budget, 251,000 pagodas on the amounts due the creditors of the Nawab of Arcot, 105,000 pagodas on interest due on Company bonds, and 52,000 pagodas on the commissions due to the civil servants collecting revenue, in all a total deficit on current account of about six and a half lakhs of pagodas to carry over into the next financial year.[28]

The Court of Directors at home were not unaware of the rather anomalous condition of Madras finances. It was certainly rather ridiculous that their government at Madras was so hard up for cash that it even refused to receive

[27] *Ibid.*, r. 241, v. 2, p. 2641.
[28] *Ibid.*, r. 241, v. 5, p. 840.

payment of a commercial debt to the Company in the Company's own bonds, but insisted on cash instead.[29] The measures the directors were taking in 1787 to remedy this situation were merely palliative, and involved their affairs still further with those of private merchants. For years they had been complaining that Englishmen in India remitted their property home through foreign channels. One remedy for this evil was of course the granting of further facilities to private traders on the Company's ships. This remedy the directors did not propose to take. In 1787, they were really enforcing the prohibitions against a private trade which infringed their monopoly. An amusing instance of this is the immediate alarm they took when some busybody noticed that their ship *The Royal Admiral* was lying lower in the water than she should have as she left Gravesend on her voyage to China. News of this was sent post-haste to India on a faster ship. On arrival at Madras, *The Royal Admiral* was forbidden all communication with the shore; a military guard was placed on board; she was searched from top to bottom, and, after an unnecessary amount of fuss and bother, it was proved to Sir Archibald Campbell's satisfaction that she carried only the amount of her invoices and lay low in the water because she had taken an unusual amount of water into her hold which her pumps could not get rid of.[30]

Short of allowing greater facilities for private trade, there were two ways in which the directors thought they could divert more of the stream of British remittances from India into British channels. In the first place, they were attempting, as they expressed it, to "bring home"

[29] *Ibid.*, r. 241, v. 1, pp. 1796, 1831, letters concerning the debt of John Beatson.

[30] *Ibid.*, r. 240, v. 67, pp. 986, 1045; v. 68, pp. 1220, 1258.

their bond debt. At Madras, this debt stood at about 28 lakhs of pagodas (£1,120,000) which the Company had borrowed at an average rate of 8 per cent. Quite obviously the directors would make a nice saving of interest charges if the owners of these Madras bonds in pagodas would exchange them for obligations in sterling bearing the lower rate of 5 per cent.[31] Moreover, the debt was variously held; a large block of these Madras bonds were in Indian hands, and Indians in the eighteenth century wanted to keep their money in India. The bonds had been sold to Indians chiefly by European army officers who wanted ready money after the war. The directors' plan was intended to encourage British subjects in India to buy back these bonds from Indians and hence induce them not to remit their money to Europe through the foreign East India companies or foreign traders. According to the records, the scheme was not working very well in 1787. The Indian holders of Company bonds were not eager to sell their bonds. The Europeans were not eager to buy because the directors had made the mistake of not offering an exchange value of the pagoda sufficient to compete with the profit in sterling ultimately realized through foreign channels. After a year of public advertising and governmental persuasion, the directors succeeded in bringing home from Madras in this way only two and one fourth lakhs of pagodas (less than £900,000), hence relieving the Madras government of an interest charge of only 18,000 pagodas.[32]

The other and more common method by which the directors tried to divert the stream of Indian fortunes from foreign hands was to authorize their Indian govern-

[31] *Ibid.*, r. 240, v. 66, p. 10; v. 67, pp. 990, 1083, 1694; India Office, Madr. Abstracts of Despatches to Ct. of Directors, Secret letter of Nov. 10, 1786; Public letter of Feb. 24, 1787, July 17, 1787.

[32] India Office, Madr. Abs. of Despatches to Ct. of Directors, Public letter of July 17, 1787.

ments to sell bills on London to anyone who brought cash to their Indian treasuries. This was a direct method of increasing their annual investment of Indian cloths for export. Like the employment of surplus Indian revenue for that purpose, it took the place of direct export of bullion to India, but it was a method which could only be resorted to when the Company's home finances were in a state to enable them promptly to pay the bills when presented in London. In the spring of 1787, they authorized Sir Archibald Campbell to advertise their readiness to grant bills on London at Madras to the extent of £150,000, all of which was to be allotted to increasing the "investment" in cloths. No money so received into the Madras treasury could be used to pay off current arrears or arrears of debt. The reception given to this announcement by the Madras European community is of considerable interest. Formerly special leave had occasionally been granted to an executor or guardian to transfer an estate to England through bills on the Court of Directors, but there was no great demand for this privilege, and, when the doors were thrown open wide again for the first time since the close of the war in India in 1784–85, the response was not encouraging. Sir Archibald Campbell was not immediately confronted with a host of offers of money. On the first publication of the official advertisement in the *Courier*, only four offers came in: Pelling and DeFries offered 30,000 pagodas at 8s. the pagoda for bills on London at twelve months' sight, or eighteen months' sight bearing 4 per cent interest for the last six months; John Balfour of Balfour and Spalding offered 16,000 pagodas at 7s.6d. the pagoda at twelve months' sight; William Hamilton, a Company servant, offered 3700 pagodas at 7s.6d. the pagoda, and F. H. Drake, one of the council at Vizagapatam, offered 1430 pagodas at 8s. the pagoda. Only two of these offers complied with the directors' terms as to exchange, namely 7s.6d. the pagoda at twelve months, or at eighteen months with 4 per cent interest for the last six months, or 7s.9d. the pagoda at two years' sight or at two and a half years' sight with interest at 4 per cent during the last six months.[33] It is perfectly clear that it was the rate of exchange set by the directors and not a lack of funds in the hands of the European community seeking remittance to England that caused their plans to fail in 1787. In reporting in 1788 that only 35,000 pagodas had thus been offered, Sir Archibald Campbell was quite positive on this point. He advised the directors to raise the exchange rate to 8s. the pagoda and hope to make up the difference by greater profits at their annual sales of Indian "piece goods." [34]

If an examination of the Company's finances at Madras in their broader aspects made it perfectly clear to Sir Archibald that the Company's affairs were either stagnating or being run at a loss in the midst of a European community becoming more prosperous every day, an examination of the Company's affairs in their more particular aspects would have revealed the sources of that increasing prosperity. He did not undertake such an investigation. In a sense, he did not need to. He knew perfectly well that the resources of Balfour and Spalding and the other merchant houses were in large measure supplied by the earnings of Company servants. Company servants would not commit to public record the manner in which many of them acquired their illicit gains, but they did commit to public record many details as to their methods of earning their legitimate salaries, emoluments, or commissions. From these, it is possible to gather some idea of the way in which illicit gains were made.

[33] India Office, Madr. Pub. Con. r. 240, v. 68, p. 1269; r. 241, v. 1, pp. 1803, 1956; v. 2, pp. 2426, 2438, 2677.

[34] *Ibid.*, r. 241, v. 5, p. 840.

The one hundred and seventy-five civil servants were concerned with getting in the revenue and purchasing the cloths for the "investment." In both these functions there were more opportunities for irregularities in procedure outside the area directly controlled by the governor and council at Madras than in it. In the Madras area, methods of revenue collection, even though there was no permanent revenue "settlement" with the Indian landowner small or great, had become standardized by 1787. Petty corruption might be possible, but large "plums" were seldom to be had. The manner of purchasing the "investment" had also become standardized near Madras. In the environs of Madras, the Company owned fifteen weaving villages called "poyakets" for the provision of their coarse cloths. The export warehousekeeper at Madras dealt directly with the weavers through one or two Indians at each village who were employees of the Company and not private "contractors." The Company issued thread and money to the weavers and received cloth in exchange. At Madras, the coarse cloths were washed, bleached and beaten by the Company's own corps of washers and beaters, and taken to the export warehouse to be put in bales for shipment. The fine goods, muslins, chintzes and ginghams, were provided in almost the same way at a more select group of villages except that the weavers bought their own thread, and the Indian servants concerned were "contractors" but not independent "contractors." [35] This was known as the "thread and money" system and gave little scope for gross corruption either by Europeans or Indians.

Outside the Madras area, the revenues were collected

[35] Madras Record Office, Public Department, Sundries, XL, Report of the Export Warehousekeeper. These contractors were not independent merchant middlemen. The Company supervised their dealings with the weavers.

and the cloths provided in a much looser manner. The chiefs and councils at the "subordinacies" were in a close net of financial relationships with the wealthier Indians in their districts both as land-owners and as providers of cloth. Getting in the "kists" of revenue on time was a matter of bargaining between the chief's servants and the "zemindar" land-owners. There was much opportunity here for the acceptance of "douceurs" of all sorts. The "investment" at the "subordinacies" both north and south of Madras was in 1787 being provided not by the "thread and money" system, but by the "contract" system, namely the farming out, in the Roman sense, of the right to collect the Company's cloths to "contractors" who might be either Europeans or Indians.[36] In spite of appeals by loyal and conscientious Company servants to maintain the "thread and money" system in the south, the Board of Trade at Madras insisted that the war had ruined it beyond repair.[37] A perusal of their reports for 1787 leaves a strong suspicion in the mind that they did not wish to revive a system which would cut into the illicit gains of fellow-servants who were friends of theirs.[38]

The extent of illicit gains made by civil servants on the Madras establishment cannot be gauged with any certainty. The records of the year 1787 show that honesty and character were far from being absent in the service, that Pitt's Act and the reforms of Lord Cornwallis were having a salutary effect, and that gross irregularities often

[36] India Office, Madr. Pub. Con. r. 240, v. 67, 68; r. 241, v. 1, 2, 3, 4; letters to and from Masulipatam and other subordinate settlements. See especially reports of the Madr. Bd. of Trade of Feb. 22, July 13, Sept. 21, and Oct. 9, 1787; r. 240, v. 66, p. 362; v. 68, p. 1528; r. 241, v. 2, pp. 2488, 2641.

[37] *Ibid.* r. 240, v. 68, p. 1237.

[38] The Board of Trade also turned a deaf ear to suggestions for extending the Company's markets for European goods in the south and left to individuals the risks of opening up new lines of European trade in Tanjore and in the Nizam's dominions (Hyderabad). See their reports during 1787 cited above.

brought searching investigation. Masulipatam was the black spot of the year,[39] but at Madras itself and at the other stations, the civil servants were not greatly overstepping the bounds of legality. There are occasional indications in the records of 1787 as to the exact way in which illicit gains were won. In September, 1787, Sir Archibald Campbell wrote the directors that the embezzlement of military stores at Madras had been going on for forty years. Some months before, a Captain Thomas Bedford had stabbed himself fatally in the Fort while awaiting trial for this offence.[40] Much of the corruption was effected by that age-old method, the collusive contract. George Westcott at Masulipatam was an adept at this. He had apparently learned the art during the war when he paid Indian bullock-contractors 1600 pagodas less than the Company paid him for the bullocks. At Masulipatam, he bought the grain for the garrison at market prices and charged it to the Company at slightly higher prices, making on one transaction a neat little profit of 4000 pagodas.[41] An ironical indication of the extent to which fees, emoluments, commissions, legal and illegal, were part of the accepted system is the fact that the Company's two chaplains were the only servants paid a fixed stipend.[42]

The number of letters sent to the governor by servants of many years' standing who complain of being barely able to make both ends meet in their family budgets indicates clearly that the opportunities for illicit gain were in the

[39] See especially India Office, Madr. Pub. Con. r. 241, v. 1, pp. 1855, 1875, 2265, and many other letters from Masulipatam.

[40] India Office, Madr. Abs. of Despatches to C. of D., Secret letter of Nov. 10, 1786.

[41] India Office, Madr. Military Con. r. 252, v. 19, p. 783; Madr. Pub. Con. r. 241, v. 2, p. 2548.

[42] India Office, Madr. Pub. Con. r. 240, v. 67, p. 771. List of Civil Servants.

higher ranks of the service. The most informative of these letters is one from Robert Hughes who was continually being passed over when any important post in the service fell vacant. The immediate occasion of his complaint was the appointment of John Mitford as export warehouse-keeper. Hughes had been twenty-one years in the service and was in 1787 making less money than he had twelve years before. He was forced to stand by and see many servants junior to him able to lay by two, three, four, or five hundred pagodas a month. He wanted any one of the following appointments: paymaster, Trichinopoly; garrison-storekeeper, Madras; civil or military paymaster, Madras.[43] These posts were therefore regarded as some of the most lucrative in the government's gift. Assuming for lack of better evidence that each Madras civil servant was able to lay aside out of his gains, either illicit or not, an average of 200 pagodas a month, we arrive at a rough estimate of 420,000 pagodas as the amount civil servants had available for investment in private trade in 1787, either on their own account or with the assistance of private mercantile houses.

The extent of the gains of the military servants on the Coromandel Coast is far more difficult to gauge. The European personnel of the Madras Army consisted of about 850 officers and 6000 rank and file.[44] Of the rank and file, about 2000 were the Company's Europeans universally known to be recruited from the scum of eighteenth-century Europe. The rest made up the four regiments of King's troops and two regiments of Hanoverian troops serving at Madras and paid by the Company. These pri-

[43] *Ibid.*, r. 241, v. 2, p. 2346.

[44] The India Office has a rare printed list of officers serving on the Coast of Coromandel in 1788. Other lists are found in Madr. Army Lists A, vol. 3, and in Madr. Mil. Con. r. 252, v. 20, p. 1579.

vate soldiers made no Indian fortunes of an appreciable extent. They contributed to the wealth of the Madras European community chiefly through the business they gave to the grog-shops and petty retail shops kept by Europeans many of whose Indian careers have already been described. Of the officers, about two hundred were King's officers with the traditions of their class. They were not above making money during their stay in the East, but India was not to most of them either a way of life or a means to retirement at an early age with a competence or a fortune. Their six hundred and fifty Company colleagues were men of a different stamp. The great majority of them were officers in command of sepoy regiments. These were the positions which provided opportunities for gain. There were a host of legitimate subsistence allowances and perquisites, which the unscrupulous officer could supplement by levying tribute on the Company through collusive buying of all kinds of stores and supplies for the sepoys. In spite of these practices, the sepoys in 1787 never complained except when rice of inferior quality was served out to them.[45] It is impossible to judge how much the army officers and the fifty military surgeons had available for investment, but they were unquestionably the backbone of the European community at Madras. Many of them had reserves of cash which they did not hesitate to use for the Company in a time of emergency like the American war.[46] From the records of 1787, it would appear that they accepted a state of affairs which left their pay always in arrear as a matter of course and that their "private concerns" bulked almost as large in their lives as in the lives of civil servants. Applications for leave to come to Madras to attend to these "private

[45] India Office, Madr. Pub. Con. r. 240, v. 67, pp. 717, 864.
[46] *Ibid.*, Madr. Mil. Con. r. 252, v. 18, p. 555, letter of William Fullarton.

concerns" appear frequently in the records. If each officer was able to save even as little as 50 pagodas a month, over 360,000 pagodas a year would have been brought to Madras for speculation in private trade or for remittance to Europe.

The wealth of the Madras Indian community in 1787 cannot be easily compared with that of the European. There were obviously Indian merchants whose credit and resources were as great or greater than those of European merchants. The affairs of the two communities were becoming more and more blended with each other. The records of the Mayor's Court show that in 1787 Indians sued to recover 18,000 pagodas from Europeans, and 23,000 pagodas from their fellow-Indians, while Europeans sued Indians for 17,000 pagodas, and other Europeans for 40,000 pagodas.[47] The prosperity of both communities was growing. The Europeans were busy with various schemes of municipal improvement. They had welcomed the establishment of a newspaper and were about to establish a bank.[48] Peter Massey Cassin was planning the building of an "Exchange" by means of a public lottery. At such an "Exchange," the Europeans of small means like the shop-keepers and Company sea-captains could deal directly with the Indian merchant without the need for the services of "dubashes" and servants eager for exorbitant fees and commissions.[49] The government had already appointed a commission for the regulation of prices of foodstuffs, which were now all brought for sale to one great market, built by Mr. Stephen Popham. The report

47 India Office, Madr. Mayor's Court Records, r. 329, v. 42.

48 *Ibid.*, Madr. Pub. Con. r. 240, v. 67, p. 835; r. 241, v. 1, p. 2138; v. 6, p. 1454. See Love, H. D., *Vestiges of Old Madras* (3 vols., London, 1913), III, 422.

49 *Ibid.*, Madr. Pub. Con. r. 240, v. 68, p. 1567; r. 241, v. 1, p. 2011; r. 241, v. 3, p. 2874. Also Love, *op. cit.*, III, 363.

of this committee shows the ease with which they could establish uniform rates for palanquin boys, coolies and domestic servants. They had more trouble with basic food prices. The only way to prevent the small Indian dealer from being victimized by a powerful monopolist was apparently to regulate monopolies. In veal, for example, one Cawdor Sahib had cornered the market in calves. He was brought before the committee and compelled to sell calves at lower prices. In fish, the fishermen were suffering because of the exactions of three castes of fish retailers. They all testified that they would prefer a regulated monopoly under the Company's eye to the chaotic system which prevailed. After calling before them the head-fishermen of twenty-six villages, the committee gave the farm for fish to Polycondar Chitty, head of the Malabar fishermen, under an elaborate plan of fixed retail prices for fish.[50] With the Madras price level as it was in 1787, a liberal estimate for a European unmarried gentleman's total annual living expenses was 1200 pagodas (£480).[51]

Many of the Europeans in Madras had their wives in India with them and were bringing them out in increasing numbers. One indication of this is the increase from one to four as the number of ladies' hairdressers in Madras during the years 1786–1789.[52] An increasing feminine population meant an increasing interest in religious and charitable affairs. Sir Archibald Campbell's government encouraged the improvement of the Charity School for boys and the establishment of the Orphan Asylum for girls under the patronage of Lady Campbell. Both these institutions were run for the benefit of the unfortunate off-

[50] India Office, Madr. Pub. Con. r. 240, v. 66, p. 161. Love, *op. cit.*, III, 327.

[51] *Ibid.*, r. 241, v. 4, p. 325. Captain Fenwick's monthly estimate of his living expenses while awaiting the trial of the case against him.

[52] India Office, Lists of Europeans: Madras, vol. 4.

spring, both European and Eurasian, of Company officers.[53] In religious matters, the Company, though glad enough of the counsel of Christian Frederick Schwarz, the eminent missionary at Tanjore, still held aloof from all missionary effort among the Indians. Sir Archibald Campbell dealt with ecclesiastical affairs only through his contacts with the Roman Catholic community which comprised, Indians and Europeans together, 100,000 souls in the Madras Presidency, of whom 17,000 lived in Madras itself. Deeply suspicious of the French Capuchin monks who were doing the missionary work, Sir Archibald Campbell determined to bring all Roman Catholics in the Presidency under the jurisdiction of the Portuguese vicar-general at San Thomé. In 1787, he forced the Capuchins to put their funds in the hands of a board of lay trustees and obliged the vicar-general at San Thomé to go to Goa for consecration as a bishop. The new bishop was so arbitrary in carrying out the new regulations that the Capuchins sought the support of Governor Conway at Pondichéry, who accordingly wrote to Sir Archibald Campbell complaining of this Portuguese prelate who "still thinks himself living in the fourteenth century." Sir Archibald was not thus to be swerved from his purpose of bringing the Roman Catholic priests under the close supervision of the Company's government, and held to his original course.[54]

Europeans at Madras also engaged in literary and scientific pursuits. Several Company servants and other Europeans had such hobbies, which were cordially encouraged by the Court of Directors at home. Sir Archibald Campbell himself bought a law library of six hundred volumes so that aspiring attorneys should not lack books.[55]

53 India Office, Madr. Pub. Con. r. 241, v. 1, p. 1763. Love, *op. cit.*, III, 349, 353.
54 *Ibid.*, r. 241, v. 2, p. 2752; r. 241, v. 3, p. 3240. Love, *op. cit.*, III, 390, 394.
55 *Ibid.*, r. 240, v. 68, p. 1404.

William Petrie, a prominent Company servant and former member of council, had a private astronomical observatory which was of assistance to Michael Topping, a surveyor then engaged in laying down an accurate chart of the east coast of India by taking observations for latitude and longitude at all important points between Calcutta and Cape Cormorin.[56] Dr. Anderson of the medical establishment was carrying out experiments with the cochineal insect for the production of better dyes.[57] In the north, two scientists, who later made reputations for themselves, were working under the Company's protection. At Samulcotah, Dr. William Roxburgh was in 1787 carrying out experiments for the cultivation of pepper and coffee in a part of India where neither crop had ever been tried.[58] At Vizagapatam, Dr. Patrick Russell, while visiting his brother, then a member of council, was working on the classification of plants and fishes of the Northern Circars and reporting his results to Sir Joseph Banks in London. He also took the time to compile a treatise on Indian snakes, which was printed by the Company for the prevention and treatment of snake-bite in the army and civil service.[59]

The Madras European community of the year 1787, as revealed in the documents laid before its new governor, was an expanding society, full of life, movement and variegated interest. In many ways, it resembled what Americans have learned to call a "frontier" society. There was the same overshadowing presence of danger, the diversity of opportunity, the chance to scramble for wealth quickly

[56] India Office, Madr. Pub. Con. r. 241, v. 1, pp. 2298, 2343. Love, *op. cit.*, III, 345.

[57] *Ibid.*, r. 240, v. 66, letter of Dr. Anderson, dated Mar. 8, 1787. Love, *op. cit.*, III, 406.

[58] *Ibid.*, r. 241, v. 5, p. 816; r. 240, v. 67, p. 1787. Love, *op. cit.*, III, 408.

[59] *Ibid.*, r. 241, v. 1, p. 2479; v. 2, p. 2811; v. 3, p. 3129. Love, *op. cit.*, III, 333, 410.

acquired, the lack of settled law and order, the possibility of easy shift from one way of life to another, the scope for building a new life in a new land after disgrace in the old, and finally the presence in a community primarily of British stock of elements from other nations of Europe, but there was not, of course, the environment which tended to produce those aspects of political freedom so inseparably characteristic of the life of "frontier" communities of British origin in the New World. A century and a half ago, conditions in the East gave the European scope for economic, but not for political, freedom. In the West he then had opportunities for both, but the "frontier" on which he lived was not constant. It was ever ceasing to be a "frontier" as the wilderness gave way to the settled community. In the East, the "frontier" was constant. Because of her tropical climate, India was always a "frontier" for the European. The new adventurer came out to step into the shoes either of his unfortunate predecessor who lay buried in some palm-shaded cemetery beneath a monster headstone often made by Indian craftsmen, or of his fortunate predecessor, who was sailing home to take his ease in Europe. Whether he landed in Bombay, Calcutta, or Madras, he became a member of a European society on a "frontier" which was ever young, and never stable.

HOLDEN FURBER.

GEORGE III: HISTORIANS AND A ROYAL REPUTATION

THERE can be no doubt that it is as one of the villains of history that the British Monarch of American Revolution times nowadays figures in the mind of the "average man." For all the masters of appeal to that phantom, whether from press, platform, or radio, turn the evil-doing associations of the King's name to account in coupling it with that of their political enemies. "Let the Tories of high finance learn from their prototype, George III," cries, Patrick-Henry-like, our most widely heard ecclesiastic.[1] "Finds new George III in Roosevelt"[2] reads the headline of the press report of the speech of an eminent lawyer, while the publisher of the "World's Greatest Newspaper" attacks the "Monarchic theory so ably upheld by Louis of Bourbon, George of Hanover, and Franklin Roosevelt."[3] Meantime that last-named statesman, not to be outdone in the manipulation of popular prejudice for his own purposes, links by implication the name of that British King with present-day abominations when he speaks of the "reasons that compelled our Revolutionary ancestors to throw off the Fascist yoke."[4]

While this public tossing about of the name of the third Hanoverian King of England has coincided with a revived interest on the part of dry-as-dust historians with his period and his personality, the George III who emerges to smaller audiences from their pages is unrecognizable as

[1] *N. Y. Times*, Mar. 12, 1935, p. 13.

[2] *N. Y. Herald Tribune*, Aug. 29, 1935, p. 19.

[3] *Boston Herald*, Jan. 9, 1936.

[4] Speech at D.A.R. Meeting, April 21, 1938. *Boston Herald*, Apr. 22, 1938, p. 1.

the gentleman of the same name of the headlines and radio speeches. "While thrones were crashing and monarchs were cringing," writes one of these historians," it was no small gain for England to be led by a King of genuine virtue and piety, strong common sense and indomitable courage," and he adds, "no sovereign ever took more seriously his responsibility to his subjects in all parts of his Empire."[5] Nor has Sir John Fortescue been alone in this appraisal, for in general, careful contemporary investigators are finding in the chronicle of that reign the story of an able, businesslike, and even statesmanlike King.

The easy conclusion, however, that this divergence of view is a simple conflict between study and market-place would prove most misleading. For Father Coughlin, Colonel McCormick, President Roosevelt, and all the other present-day popularizers of George III's villainy might call to witness the most distinguished names in historical writing, both English and American, of the last century, who had outdone them all in vivid portrayal of his wickedness. And similarly, dwellers in the ivory tower of our day may look back, if indeed they desire to do so, to a time when journalists and men of affairs could bring their audiences to a flush of enthusiasm by an affectionate mention of the "good old King."

The course of circumstance and the development of doctrine combine to mold and re-mold historical reputations, and write and rewrite history. For the writing of history, even when practised by its most devoted craftsmen, is dependent only partially on the state of development and availability of sources of information and their technical interpretation. The idols of the tribe and of the market-place play their part both in shaping the historian's conclusions, and along with the effectiveness of

[5] Sir J. Fortescue, *Historical and Military Essays* (London, 1928), p. 4.

the historian's presentation, in determining the reception which will be accorded his results. The interweaving of all these factors is well illustrated in a sketch of the course of the reputation of the man whose sixty-year reign over Britain spanned the period from 1760 to 1820.

During those sixty years of great change and controversy, the triple series of momentous events known collectively as the American Revolution, the French Revolution, and the Industrial Revolution, began their transformation of the world. "Bliss was it in that dawn to be alive, and to be young was very Heaven," sang one of the era's poets, but to be King of England in that time no one can claim was easy. It was, indeed, small wonder that in his own day, the period of these great conflicts, George III first appeared to one group as a "wicked tyrant" and came to appear to another as "the good old King."

Most of the controversy has centered upon George III's conduct in the days of the American Revolutionary war. In the decade of the 1760's, several frequently disunited cabinets, mostly Whiggish, followed each other in rapid succession, each adding its bit of legislation in regard to the Colonial problem. In 1770, Lord North, not connected with the Whigs, succeeded in establishing in power a ministry which had to meet the challenge of the American war. They stayed in office until 1782, but lost the war. Whose fault was it? — that of the King, said the Whigs, for he intrigued and caballed to defeat the Whigs and establish in power his friend, the Tory North, whose bungling and threats to English liberties at home and abroad lost England her first colonial Empire. Indeed no, said the Tories, — it was the fault of the Whigs, who bungled the problem from the beginning, with their colonial legislation of the sixties, and whose obstructive tactics in Parliament during the seventies made impossible the vigorous conduct of the war and nullified the struggles of a patriot King and his ministers to save the Empire.

Because the argument over a personality is more tangible and appealing than are most abstract discussions of linked cause and circumstance, the whole question of the interpretation of American Revolutionary history has often centered in contrasting views of the character of George III. The American Declaration of Independence hit upon this vivid means of popular appeal and described him as "a Prince whose character is marked by every act which may define a tyrant." The politically astute phrase-makers in the colonies were matched by sympathizing Whig pamphleteers in England, who pictured George as conspiring against the liberties of his subjects at home and abroad in his determination to "be his own minister," and filled their vigorous pages with tales of his bribery, corruption and backstairs intrigue. The greatest of these was Burke, who himself played the part of a modern party whip for that section of the Whigs who formed, in the decade of the seventies, a determined but hopeless minority opposition to George III. His pamphlet, "Thoughts on the Causes of the Present Discontents," is a straight political and party tract, but its vivid flowing style, its plausible arguments, have so impressed its readers for the century and a half and more since its publication, that its success in influencing later, if not to any large extent, contemporary opinion, has been quite out of proportion to the reasonableness of its thesis.

The bulk of the English people did not, however, believe the Whig journalists. On the events of the American Revolution, about which most of the dispute has centered, most of his subjects in England felt as did George III. Two men, who would have agreed on little else, John

Wesley and Samuel Johnson, were one in their admiration and reverence for the King, and both wrote best-selling pamphlets defending his colonial policy. To more lowly subjects, the stories of his domestic virtues made an appeal as strong as did those of his granddaughter to Englishmen of the next century. Anecdotes which showed his simple friendly manners, his kindliness, and his interest and skill in farming, were common gossip, and these with the picture of the King walking each evening on the terrace at Windsor with the little Princess Amelia clinging to his hand, combined to make most of his subjects believe, in the words of one of them, that "there never lived a more virtuous and patriotic prince; nor any man in any station of life, whose character from youth to age was more consistently pure and dignified."[6] His golden jubilee in 1810 called forth such an outpouring of affection and reverence for himself and his throne as was familiar to us a few years ago at the silver jubilee of his great-great-grandson. For it was not Victoria, but her grandfather, George III, who first linked the Hanoverian dynasty in the hearts of the English people with the universal and enduring sentiments for the virtues of family affection and of home, thereby establishing a tradition, of the strength of which we have recently had dramatic evidence.

If the political struggles of the reign developed opposing characterizations of the King, the fashions in historical writing helped to keep both views alive. For the rationalistic writers of the eighteenth century had seized upon history to point a moral and make clear a lesson. Compilers of the early accounts of the reign, well-named as "chronicles," "annals," and "memoirs," usually wished to illustrate the merit of Whig or of Tory political principle, and dealt with George III accordingly. Most of those volumes

[6] J. W. Croker, *Quarterly Review* (1837), XXXVI, 285.

which appeared during the reign and just after the King's death in 1820, are now forgotten. One partaking a little of their nature, but much superior to the others, is still read, that of John Adolphus, himself the son of a Hanoverian emigrant, who published the first of his volumes in George III's lifetime. He believed the throne filled by a "monarch who sought the love of his subjects through the means of public spirit and private virtue," and he was persuaded "that liberty has been better and more effectually and practically promoted during this period than in any which preceded."[7] For in general the Tory writers at this time took the honors both in numbers and effectiveness. For indeed, it was the great period of Tory ascendancy, and Tory principles established in politics in the 1780's under the premiership of the younger Pitt, with Hume and Blackstone its mentors in historical and legal precept, were controlling English political life, and, except for the small vanguard of the day which was to come, controlling English thought also.

Likewise, with the first considerable historian who wrote of the reign, Tory principles still predominated. Lord Mahon, whose first volume appeared in 1838, had begun to compose his history while the Tory party was still ruling England, and he remembered as a child the Golden Jubilee of "the good old King." His final judgment on George III, from which it is difficult to see how any careful student can dissent, was that "the better he was understood, the more his subjects felt how closely his general views and principles, his tastes and habits were in accordance with their own."[8]

[7] J. Adolphus, *The History of England from the Accession to the Decease of George III* (London ed. 1840), I, vi–vii.

[8] Lord Mahon, *History of England from the Peace of Utrecht to the Peace of Versailles* (ed. 1853), IV, 207.

So to Sir Archibald Alison, the historian of Europe in the French Revolutionary period, whose volumes appeared about the same time as Lord Mahon's, George III seemed to have been a bulwark to his people, for "he possessed in a very high degree . . . native sagacity and discrimination," and far from blaming the King for the loss of the colonies, Alison maintained that "but for the incapacity of the generals in command of his armies, his firmness would have been rewarded with success."[9]

Even as these historians wrote, however, the age of the Tories, both in politics and in history was passing. During the years between the publication of Mahon's earliest volumes, and the appearance of the last in 1852, the nineteenth-century Liberals, who looked upon themselves as inheritors of the traditions of the eighteenth-century Whigs, had become well launched on their conquest of the English mind and the English statute book. Historians linked the triumph of the Whig tradition with the glories and optimism of Mid-Victorian England. As they looked back upon the rise and final triumph of these doctrines, the process looked to them like a conflict between devils and angels, with those who fought on the Whiggish side in the struggles of the late seventeenth and the eighteenth centuries responsible for the glorious outcome. They did not recognize that the opponents of their heroes had made any contribution to the final result. They did not see the development of society as the resultant of a conflict of diverse forces, with the acts of the Tories as well as the words of the Whigs speeding the newer England on its way. To them George III was cast as the villain, as the obstructor of the glories which were to come; his opponents were the champions of light, and the only molders of

[9] Sir A. Alison, *History of Europe from the Commencement of the French Revolution to the Restoration of the Bourbons*, III, 365.

the future. To them Charles James Fox, for long so bitter an opponent of the King during his life-time, played the part of the shining hero, and ever since, to those to whom George III has appeared as the wicked tyrant, Charles James Fox has seemed the defender and preserver of liberty and righteousness and the herald of nineteenth-century liberalism.

An early and a vigorous proponent of this nineteenth century Whig view of George III was Lord Macaulay. In 1845, fresh from a reading of Horace Walpole's journals, then still in manuscript, and familiar with the Whig pamphleteers and journalists of the Revolution period, he published in the *Edinburgh Review* his second essay on Chatham. Treating in detail of the first decade of the reign, which saw the fall of many cabinets, and which ended in the establishment of the Tory, Lord North, as Prime Minister in 1770, Macaulay's clear-cut narrative launched well on its way the story of how George, nurtured in the idea that he must "be a King," determined on a system of personal rule, resolved to overthrow the Whig oligarchy, intrigued and caballed to have his way and to exclude Chatham from the ministry. Thus Macaulay spread the tradition "how imprudence and obstinacy broke the tie which bound the North American colonists to the parent state."[10]

Several factors combined to assure the triumph of these opinions. While in England the nationalistic historical writing of the day had taken the form of glorifying the Whigs, and hence attacking George III, likewise the nationalistic spirit in American historical writing resulted in attacks on him, since it sang the praises of the glorious beginnings of American nationality. During the eighteen-

[10] T. B. Macaulay, quoted in G. O. Trevelyan, *American Revolution* (1899–1907), II, 188.

fifties, the volumes dealing with the Revolution period by Bancroft, America's foremost representative of this school, appeared, and in them the King is described as "singly responsible" for the American Revolution."[11]

But it is not, of course, only the new idols of the tribe or of the market-place which affect historical writing. In this decade another factor played into the hand of the Whigs, namely the nature of new historical material. The journals of Walpole, which Macaulay had used in manuscript, were published, and thus the story of George's subservience to his mother and Bute, of his duplicity, indolence and hypocrisy, vividly told in Walpole's flowing manner, reached a wide audience. At this time, too, families of the great Whig opponents of George III began to ransack their garrets for material to feed their ancestors' fame, so that in this decade of the fifties, several volumes of selected correspondence of the great Whig leaders of the period saw the light, — those of Burke, Bedford, Rockingham, Grenville, and Fox. We do not know how carefully selected they were, since in the case of none of them is the complete collection of manuscript available as yet to inspection. It is certain, however, that the selection was made by apologists and admirers. This, too, played into the hands of those attacking the King. So far had the ideas of the Whig historians triumphed by the year 1861, that Sir Archibald Alison, after publishing a life of Lord Castlereagh, that anathema to the liberals of the "great dawn," laid down his pen, thinking it useless to provoke hostility by his resolute refusal "to worship the Dagon of Liberalism."[12]

At this beginning of the Whig triumph, however, the

[11] G. Bancroft, *History of the United States of America* (Boston, ed. 1875), X, 650.

[12] Quoted *DNB* article on Sir Archibald Alison.

"good old King" view still kept alive. Many English and American schools were still using as texts the "improved edition" of Oliver Goldsmith's *History of England*, with additional chapters edited by Pennock, which quotes the lines on George III:

"And unborn millions from earth's farthest shore,
Shall bless the Christian King till the last sunrise is o'er."

Lady Maria Callcott's *Little Arthur's History of England*, which elderly English gentlemen still recall as the companion of their childhood, was at the height of its popularity. It said of George III, "I think he was one of the best men that ever was a King."[13] Gladstone on the public platform could still refer to the way in which George III "endeared himself to the hearts of his people."[14]

However, just after the end of the decade which saw the establishment among the professionals of the Whig-liberal traditions, signs appear of the beginning of its triumph in the popular mind. For in 1861, the general reader at the appearance of Thackeray's *Four Georges*, seized with delight on the Whig idea of the King made vivid and readable, and revelled in the tales of the gentlemen "who slipped Lord North's bribes so elegantly under their ruffles."[15]

All these inter-workings toward the ascendancy of the Whig portrayal of the King reached a climax in the great work of Lecky on the eighteenth century, the first volume of which appeared in 1878. In his pages the Whig pamphleteers of a century earlier are out-Whigged. For Lecky describes George as "a sovereign of whom it may be said without exaggeration that he inflicted more profound and

[13] Callcott, M. D. G., Lady, *Little Arthur's History of England* (N. Y. ed. 1884), p. 246.

[14] Hansard, CCX, 300.

[15] W. M. Thackeray, *The Four Georges* (London, 1861), p. 117.

enduring injuries upon his country than any other modern English King." And, he continues, "ignorant, narrow-minded, and arbitrary, with an unbounded confidence in his own judgment and an extravagant estimate of his own prerogative, resolved at all hazard to compel his ministers to adopt his views, or to undermine them if they refused, he spent a long life in obstinately resisting measures which are now universally admitted to have been good, and in supporting measures which are as universally admitted to be bad."[16]

In these last phrases, Lecky rather gave the show away, for indeed he was judging the acts of George III solely on the basis of what the Liberals of a century later would have approved. Whatever might have been expected of that monarch, it is unreasonable to have insisted that, born as he was in the year 1737, he should have grown up to be a nineteenth century liberal.

Nevertheless, Lecky's picture of George III was to win almost universal acceptance for a generation to come. In earlier days, as we have seen, the old Whig and the old Tory picture of the King had existed side by side, though the Tory view, in England at least, had the upper hand. Now the Whig view triumphed everywhere, both in England and America, and established its long period of ascendancy which is only just now being broken. Not only the professional historians, but the popular writers and speakers made the Whig view of the King a quite unchallenged one. The manuals, constitutional histories, and historical series, of which there was a great outpouring during that time, adopted it substantially. Sir George Otto Trevelyan, nephew of Lord Macaulay, in the course of several volumes devoted to the praise of Charles James

[16] W. E. H. Lecky, *A History of England in the Eighteenth Century* (ed. 1882) III, 14.

Fox, added his indictment and even censured George for doing his own dirty work, for he says, "he was at home in the darkest corners of the political workshop, and up to the elbows in those processes which a high-minded statesman sternly forbids, and which even a statesman not so high-minded leaves to be done by others."[17]

Even as Lecky and Trevelyan wrote, however, the seeds of disillusion and destruction for nineteenth century Liberalism were sown and sprouting. The Liberals had carried most of their points, it is true, but the results had not been what they had hoped. Salvation was not forthcoming. As all this became clearer, the day of the Whig historians, dependent as they were on the Liberal theory, must likewise pass. New ideas and new methods would produce new histories. Literary fashion, new social theory, new facts turned up through precise methods of historical investigation, and new political practice were to transform the reputation of a King long dead.

By the turn of the century, movements and not men were to the fore in historical writing, and with a decline in emphasis on the force of personality in history, villains, as well as heroes, tended to disappear, as indeed they had done in literature in general. People began to talk about a "revolutionary atmosphere" and a "revolutionary era." Clearly George III had created neither of these. He had been accused of responsibility for the American Revolution, but no one could accuse him of responsibility for the French Revolution. Perhaps the times and not the man were at fault.

A Canadian, eager to justify the cause of the United Empire Loyalists and their steadfastness to the King, was the first to write, in 1907, a popular biography in praise of

[17] Sir G. O. Trevelyan, *The Early History of Charles James Fox* (New York, 1881), p. 114.

"George III: Man, Monarch, and Statesman." "George III of England," he wrote, "was a man — strong, earnest, virile, brave, loyal, kind-hearted, religious. He was a plain liver, a hard worker, and devoted to his duty. If he could not, owing to the feebleness of his generals and the party schism at home, crush the revolt, he at least stemmed the tide of republican success in America."[18] This was the first challenge to the Whigs which had been heard for many a day.

With the issue drawn by a publicist active in Imperial affairs, help from men more purely of the study was soon forthcoming. A few years later a young Cambridge don produced the first of two volumes on the first ten years of the reign, the tale of which, made traditional by Macaulay, had so damaged George's reputation. In this work,[19] the similarity of the constitutional position of George and of Macaulay's idol, Chatham himself, with their common repugnance of strict party organization, was emphasized. At the same time, Americans, examining their own history more closely, were beginning to see how far the colonies had advanced toward feelings of nationalism before 1776, and how all but unbridgeable were the differences and conflicts of interests with England. Could George or anyone else have stemmed the tide?

As far as the course of affairs was concerned, the developments within the Empire vividly illustrated the tendency of colonies to pull away. The dominions had set up tariff barriers against England; soon after the war they were to be represented by ambassadors of their own at foreign courts. All these changes in the intellectual and

[18] Beckles Willson, *George III, as Man, Monarch and Statesman* (London, 1907), p. xi.

[19] D. A. Winstanley, *Personal and Party Government, 1760–1766* (Cambridge, 1910); *Lord Chatham and the Whig Opposition* (Cambridge, 1912).

political scene set the background for a new view of George III already emerging.

It was during the late Edwardian era, the period of "the death of Liberal England," that the Canadian champion of George III had published his book. Soon afterward, historical criticism began to take a hand in revising the accepted chronicle of the epoch of the American Revolution, and therefore inevitably, the reputation of George III. We recall that the journals of Horace Walpole, when still in manuscript, had helped outline Macaulay's Whig picture of the King, and their appearance in print, and subsequent great popular appeal a decade later, had helped to find for the Whigs an even wider audience. In 1911, an American historian, Professor Carl Becker, published in the *American Historical Review*[20] an analysis of these journals as an historical source, in which he demonstrated that large portions of them, rather than having been actually composed at the time at which they are dated, were in fact either entirely written or greatly revised many years later, when not only had Walpole's memories of events become dim, but when his Whiggish opposition to George III had hardened into an unrelenting bitterness. At about the same time as the appearance of Becker's article, Professor Sydney George Fisher in a lively essay on "Legendary and Myth-Making Processes in Histories of the American Revolution" exposed some of the more farcical and obvious distortions of the truth by both English and American historians.[21] These beginnings in biography and in history toward a new view of the King, and the discrediting of an important source for his

[20] C. Becker, "Horace Walpole's Memoirs of the Reign of George the Third," *American Historical Review*, XVI (1911), 255–272, 496–507.

[21] S. G. Fisher, "The Legendary and Myth-Making Processes in Histories of the American Revolution," *Proc. Am. Philosophical Society*, LI, no. 204, Apr.–June, 1912.

detractors, had combined with the changes in the political and intellectual scene to diffuse new light at least among historians. It was not, however, until after the World War that wide results were forthcoming.

Just before the war began, the British Royal family had recovered several ironbound boxes which contained the correspondence of George III, and which had not been in their possession since his death. But it was not until 1927 that the first six volumes of this correspondence covering the first twenty-three years of his reign were published.[22] The editor was the then royal librarian at Windsor, Sir John Fortescue. All the reverence of so many of George III's loyal subjects during his lifetime shows itself again in Fortescue's editorial introductions and in his separately published essays. Of the King's grief and despair at the outcome of the American War, Fortescue says, "He wrote thus bitterly because he knew that it was the faction headed by Fox in Parliament which had brought about the loss of America."[23] The position taken by the nineteenth century Whig historians has been, therefore, reversed. It is no longer George III but the Whigs who caused England the loss of the colonies. However, this new-old Tory view did not score an immediate and easy victory even among historians. Indeed the reviews of these six large volumes of some four thousand documents demonstrated the truth that each man will see in them what his own nature enables him to see. Those who before held to the Macaulay-Lecky-Trevelyan view found this judgment still called "traditional" strengthened by the new evidence, while others hailed these volumes as clear demonstration of the truth of the view of the volume's editor.

[22] Sir J. Fortescue, *The Correspondence of King George the Third from 1760 to December 1783* (6 vols., London, 1927).

[23] Fortescue, *ibid.*, VI, xii.

But this was ten years and more ago, and since then much water has gone under the bridge. For not only new ideas and new documents, but new interpretations and uses of already known documents may rewrite history. Professor Namier,[24] with enormous industry, has learned to know all the members of the House of Commons of the early years of the reign by their first names, has studied their ages, families, businesses, professions, and their voting. Old tales of the bribery of members of Parliament by henchmen of the King prove mythical in the realistic picture of Parliament which unfolds beneath his mass of statistics and tables. The tyrannical King who ruthlessly strove to be "his own minister" metamorphoses into a most industrious, patriotic, and able monarch, who wished, in his own words, "to do his best for England," who sought for his friends those who would get the necessary business done, the floor-management of the House of Commons, and the work of the administrative departments. So, too, the conclusions of the very recent monograph on George and William Pitt by Mr. Donald Barnes of Western Reserve University will doubtless aid the rehabilitation of the reputation of George III,[25] for it pictures him as a more powerful partner in the alliance with Pitt the younger than many historians have supposed.

Nevertheless, the Whig story, superbly narrated as it was first by Burke, then by that nineteenth-century line of masters of English prose and Whig principle, dies hard even among historians. While George Macaulay Trevelyan, son of that Sir George Otto Trevelyan who was, we remember, a nephew to Macaulay, now writes of "the

[24] L. B. Namier, *The Structure of Politics at the Accession of George III* (2 vols., London, 1929); *England in the Age of the American Revolution* (London, 1930).

[25] D. G. Barnes, *George III and William Pitt, 1783–1806* (Stanford University Press, 1939).

fine strength of character" and "great political ability" of George III, he must at once return to the theme of "the obstinacy which wrecks Empires."[26] There can be no doubt, however, that the more favorable view of the King has won or is winning the battle within the guild of historians. Moreover, there are signs that it has begun the process of sifting down to wider audiences.

There have appeared during the last few years two popular biographies of George III.[27] The two authors of these volumes were aware of the new trend in the interpretation of the King's character by the dry-as-dust historians, and paid due homage to it in their introductions and in the obituaries in their final chapters. An examination of the body of their books, however, yields strange results, for there they have repeated almost all of the old saws of the Whigs. Maternal influence, meddling in office-giving, bribery, personal government, obstinacy, all are there. The Whigs did their work well, for they could write, and for that their words have lived long after them. The authors of these books are quite unknowingly still under the Whig spell, although their pronouncements of purpose at the beginning are the straws which show which way the winds of doctrine are at present blowing.

There remains to be recorded a curious chapter in the history of the reputation we have been tracing. George III, so tradition had it, was admonished to "be a King," his model supposed to be the "patriot King" of Bolingbroke. He was supposed to have striven to raise the monarchy again up out of the position of subordination to the Whig oligarchy which it had occupied in the reign of his two predecessors. From those Englishmen, then, who are

[26] G. M. Trevelyan, *British History in the Nineteenth Century, 1782–1901* (London, 1923), p. 36.

[27] C. E. Vulliamy, *Royal George* (London, 1937); J. D. G. Davies, *George the Third: a Record of a King's Reign* (London, 1936).

at present telling us that "the world is hungry for monarchy," we would expect high praise for George III. Such, however, has not been forthcoming. Mr. Belloc, we feel, does not like him, nor does, it is certain, Sir Charles Petrie, Mr. Compton Mackenzie, nor Sir George Young.[28] For the Monarchists have not to this day ceased to lament the White Rose, and they now seek to capture for the Monarchic theory of today all the glamor which still lingers about the exiled Stuarts and their train. Since George III was the first of the Hanoverians to gain for the House of Guelph the love of the English people which had once belonged to the Stuarts, and to establish beyond a shadow of a doubt that Protestant, parliament-given, non-legitimist dynasty, he is not to be forgiven. Perhaps, too, they dimly realize that the old words of Lord Mahon were true, and that "the better he was understood, the more his subjects felt how closely his general views and principles, his tastes and habits, were in accordance with their own." If this is then true, and George III really represented well his age in English history, then we cannot expect modern monarchists to approve of him.

For authoritarians of any hue, whether adherents of Monarchy, Marx, or Mussolini, will never be cordial to the eighteenth century in England. For it was an age of individualism which saw the loosening along all fronts of the reins of control, and it was one which forsook loyalty and fostered liberty. Perhaps, then, if authoritarians of whatever cult finally triumph, the reputation of George III will decline again after a brief glimpse of the light, by a similar chain of circumstance which left it no defenders

[28] Sir Charles Petrie, *The Four Georges; a Revaluation of the Period 1714–1830* (London, 1935), pp. 108–115; Compton Mackenzie, *The Windsor Tapestry; being a Study of the Life, Heritage and Abdication of H. R. H. the Duke of Windsor* (London, 1938), pp. 244–257; Sir George Young, *Poor Fred, the People's Prince* (London, 1937), pp. 170, 171.

when, for different reasons, both English and American nationalist historians turned against him. Or perhaps it will follow the more usual course of a sifting down of the view held of him now by most of those professional historians who concern themselves with his era, so that audiences of the same sort which now, at the mention of his name, shiver at their recollection of a villainous tyrant, will warm to a future familiar picture of a "good old King."

GERDA RICHARDS CROSBY.

MARITIME ADVENTURES OF NEW YORK IN THE NAPOLEONIC ERA

THE neutral trading of New York during the long struggle of England with Revolutionary and Napoleonic France was one of the most exciting episodes in the history of the port. Profits were heavy for a while, as they were at the other American ports, since the war gave shipping and commerce tremendous stimulus. Those gains tended to dwindle, however, as time went on, through the seizure and condemnation of New York vessels by one belligerent or another. Daring, ingenuity, and luck were required in that trading where success often depended upon the eluding of cruisers and blockading squadrons or the outwitting of port officials. An added threat of uncertainty came from the oppressive belligerent commercial measures which grew worse as the war dragged on.

As far as American commerce as a whole was concerned, the story is a familiar one. Its major outlines find their way into every history textbook; its more complicated aspects have been ably analyzed by Miss Clauder and other scholars.[1] Rather than go over that well-plowed ground again, it seems desirable here to give a few intimate pictures of what actually happened to some particular ventures. Considerations of Berlin and Milan Decrees, Orders in Council, Non-Intercourse, and the like may perhaps assume more of a flesh-and-blood aspect when translated into terms of ships, cargoes, and men. Our maritime history, moreover, has on the whole failed to approach the subject from the standpoint of the individual seaports.

[1] A. C. Clauder, *American Commerce as Affected by the Wars of the French Revolution and Napoleon, 1793–1812.*

Here we shall limit ourselves to New York alone, during the very years when it was drawing ahead of Philadelphia toward the secure primacy which lay not far in its future.

That period of neutral trading fell into two natural parts. Starting with the outbreak of war in 1793, it gained momentum until the end of the century. Then there was a brief interval of peace before fighting was resumed more energetically in 1803. That is where we shall pick up the story here, for the next four years saw our commerce flourish even more vigorously until late in 1807, when belligerent decrees and American counter-measures exercised a disrupting effect, ultimately culminating in the War of 1812.

To give a compact picture of the fluctuations of the period, to indicate the relative success of the three leading seaports, and to avoid littering the rest of the article with too many figures, it seems desirable to present here the essential available statistics, boiled down to their simplest form, from 1792, which shows the pre-war commerce, to 1812, when the United States also became a belligerent. One may see graphically, for instance, the crescendo from 1805 to 1807, followed immediately by the deadening effects of the Embargo. Likewise, the statistics indicate how Massachusetts (which then included Maine) led the nation in shipping tonnage, even though its imports and exports lagged behind New York's and also, most of the time, behind Philadelphia's as well.

Aside from the general quantitative gains in imports, exports, and tonnage, the most significant feature of the new commerce was the beginning of the re-export trade, with its profitable, long, transatlantic haul. The lack of such a practice, by which New York and its rivals served as entrepôts between the European belligerents and the Caribbean colonies, had been one of the chief reasons for

COMMERCIAL STATISTICS: LEADING AMERICAN STATES: 1792–1812

(*Figures represent millions of dollars, except tonnage, in thousands of tons*)

	Import Duties			Total Exports			Domestic Exports			Foreign Re-exports			Reg. Tonnage		
	N. Y.	*Pa.*	*Mass.*	*N. Y.*	*Pa.*	*Mass.*	*N. Y.*	*Pa.*	*Mass.*	*N. Y.*	*Pa.*	*Mass.*	*N. Y.*	*Pa.*	*Mass.*
1792	1.2	1.1	.8	2.5	3.8	2.8							50	65	112
1793	1.2	1.9	1.1	2.9	6.9	3.7							45	60	135
1794	2.4	2.0	1.4	5.4	6.6	5.2							71	67	143
1795	2.7	3.0	1.9	10.3	11.5	7.1							93	83	171
1796	3.0	3.6	2.3	12.2	17.5	9.9							103	90	186
1797	2.9	2.9	2.1	13.3	11.4	7.5							110	88	187
1798	2.3	2.0	2.1	14.3	8.9	8.6							111	85	178
1799	3.5	2.2	2.8	18.7	12.4	11.4							120	90	191
1800	3.6	3.1	3.1	14.0	11.9	11.3							97	95	213
1801	4.9	3.7	4.4	19.8	17.4	14.8							106	109	241
1802	3.5	2.7	3.4	13.7	12.6	13.4							79	64	209
1803	4.0	2.2	3.4	10.8	7.5	8.7	7.6	4.0	5.3	3.1	3.5	3.3	89	67	222
1804	5.1	3.5	5.4	16.0	11.0	16.8	7.5	4.1	6.3	8.5	6.8	10.5	105	71	250
1805	6.9	3.6	5.9	23.4	13.7	19.4	8.0	4.3	5.6	15.3	9.3	13.7	121	77	285
1806	7.3	5.1	6.2	21.7	17.5	21.1	8.0	3.7	6.6	13.7	13.8	14.5	141	86	306
1807	7.6	5.1	6.3	26.3	16.8	20.1	9.9	4.8	6.1	16.4	12.0	13.9	149	93	310
1808	3.6	2.5	2.2	5.6	4.0	5.1	2.3	1.0	1.5	3.2	2.9	3.6	146	94	266
1809	3.7	2.3	2.6	12.5	9.0	12.1	8.3	4.2	6.0	4.2	4.8	6.1	169	106	324
1810	5.2	3.3	3.9	17.2	10.9	13.0	10.9	4.7	5.7	6.3	6.2	7.2	188	109	352
1811	2.4	2.3	2.7	12.2	9.5	11.2	8.7	5.6	6.0	3.5	3.8	5.1	161	78	273
1812	3.3	2.4	3.1	8.9	5.9	6.5	6.6	4.6	3.9	2.3	1.3	2.6	162	71	266

Figures for fiscal year ending Sept. 30. N. Y. and Pa. figures represent N. Y. C. and Philadelphia chiefly; Mass. figures include not only Boston but also Salem, Maine ports, etc. Adapted from *Hunt's Merchants Magazine*, I (1840), 186, 187, 273.

the commercial vicissitudes of the American seaports in the trying decade of readjustments following the Revolution. The British had broken up the old colonial sugar triangle by barring American vessels from their West Indian islands and prohibiting the importation of those Caribbean products into England from the United States. The Americans had turned to the adjacent French, Dutch, Danish, and other islands which would admit American vessels. New York could swap its flour for Caribbean products, but the Americans had had to eat most of the sugar and drink most of the rum themselves, since re-exportation to Europe was generally prohibited. With only a moderate overseas demand for its local offerings of flour, flaxseed, ashes, and the like, New York had been hard put to it to find exports enough to pay for the wares it desired from across the Atlantic.

The outbreak of the Anglo-French war in 1793 suddenly changed all that. The belligerents relaxed their rigid peace-time regulations, because neutral American bottoms made a safer mode of trading with the Caribbean. New York immediately began to trans-ship large quantities of colonial goods to Europe and similar amounts of overseas manufactures and wines to the Caribbean. In 1792, the last year of peace, the New York custom house had refunded in re-export drawbacks less than 4 per cent of the import duties collected. Three years later, the drawbacks had risen to more than 25 per cent and by 1798 to more than 33 per cent. During many years of the period, the re-exports amounted to more than the port's domestic exports.

Typical of this lucrative new trade was the voyage in 1805 of the ship *Ambition*, belonging to Isaac Clason, one of New York's wealthiest merchants. Built at Haddam, Connecticut, in 1800, the *Ambition* was a typical full-rigged ship of that day, measuring 332 tons, with a length of 102 feet and a beam of 27. Clason had sent her in May, 1805, to Havana with $34,000 in specie and a cargo valued at $13,000, consisting of flour, butter, wine, and brandy. In exchange at the Cuban capital, she took on 850 boxes of white and 570 boxes of brown sugar (big boxes — sometimes used as coffins afterwards) and 15 tons of Campeachy logwood, which made blue dye cheaper than indigo.

By August 17, she was back at New York. The local regulations prohibited summer Caribbean arrivals from approaching within 300 yards of the city until after several weeks of quarantine; but there was no time to wait for that. The logwood and part of the sugar were left undisturbed in the lower hold, while the sugar boxes stowed between decks were carried ashore in boats and lighters for customs inspection. Two or three days later those identical boxes, with contents untouched, were brought back to the *Ambition* and re-stowed. New officers and crew were shipped; she now had, under 33-year-old Capt. Jeremiah Freeman from Portland, a crew of fifteen men, including four Swedes and a Dutch mate. She sailed for Amsterdam on September 12, bearing letters from Clason to two commission merchants there. They were instructed to sell the sugar and logwood, purchase "100 pipes of the best quality of Geneva," as gin was called, and ship them back on the *Ambition* to New York with all possible speed. The balance of the proceeds was to be remitted "in unexceptionable bills of exchange to Messrs. Mullet & Co., merchants of London." The cargo was now valued at $75,000, a gain of more than 50 per cent over the original cargo shipped to Havana.

The purpose of that farcical unloading and reloading at New York was evasion of the British regulations against trading between enemy ports. Since Spain and Holland were both at war with England, a direct voyage from Havana to Amsterdam would have involved grave risk of condemnation in England. By putting the cargo ashore at New York and reloading it, the Americans could claim that the *Ambition* was making two separate voyages, each involving the neutral port of New York.

For some time, the British admiralty courts had been toying with the idea of recognizing the actual situation and declaring that, despite the stop at New York, this was actually a "continuous voyage" from Havana to Amsterdam. For several years, they had winked at the practice, but early in 1805 a British author, James Stephens, pointed out in his book, entitled *Warfare in Disguise; the Fraud of Neutral Flags*, that such leniency was depriving England of the opportunities afforded by her sea power to cut off the trade between her enemies and their overseas possessions. That helped to harden English hearts against the "continuous voyage," and by the summer of 1805, the admiralty courts began to crack down on the practice.[2]

In that day of slow communications, Clason had no chance to learn of that change and the *Ambition* plowed steadily eastward, unaware of the trouble that lay ahead. She was not to be as lucky as the ship *Ann Alexander* which sailed from New York for Leghorn at about the same time with flour, tobacco, salt fish, apples, and a deckload of lumber. Eighteen days out, she ran into the British fleet off Cape Trafalgar, just after the great battle which had left some of the ships rather battered. That deckload of lumber was just the thing for temporary repairs; a boat from the *Victory* brought over an officer who paid well for

[2] See the protest of the New York merchants against this change of policy in a memorial to Congress, December 28, 1805, in *Am. State Papers, Foreign Relations* (hereafter *A. S. P. Forn.*,) II, 737–739.

it, together with some flour and apples, in good English gold.[3] The *Ambition's* contact with the Royal Navy two weeks later was a different story. His Majesty's gun brig *Haughty* overhauled her "seven leagues south of Falmouth" and sent her into Plymouth with a prize crew. On "continuous voyage" charges, the case was brought before the High Court of Admiralty which released her on July 8, 1806. The captors, however, appealed the case in hope of securing their prize money. Almost four years after she had originally sailed from New York, the Lords Commissioners of Appeal in Prize Causes reversed the original decision and condemned her "because the ship and cargo were engaged in a direct voyage from the Havannah to Amsterdam." The officers and crew of the *Haughty* had to share their spoils with those of the *Ramillies*, 74, which had been in sight at the time of the capture.

The voluminous printed briefs presented in those appeal cases reveal a wealth of detail in scores of similar instances, for they reproduce not only the narrative of the voyage and capture but also, in most cases, the ships' papers, crew lists, manifests, and commercial correspondence. They show that the original release or condemnation by the High Court of Admiralty, or the vice admiralty courts scattered around the Empire from Halifax to Bombay, came within a few months, but that the costly and tedious appeal litigation generally dragged out from three to five years.[4]

Less typical than the *Ambition's* voyage, but interesting as an instance of Yankee swapping and re-swapping of wares, was one of the last of the regular slaving ventures;

[3] L. B. Ellis, *History of New Bedford*, pp. 153–154.

[4] N. Y. P. L. Lords Commissioners of Appeal in Prize Causes, Briefs: New York Ships (hereafter L. C. A.). For description of these printed briefs, see author's notes in *Am. Hist. Review*, XXXIII, 593–595. The papers, now in the Reference Division, are listed under "Great Britain, Courts, Prize Causes."

the case of the *Cotton Planter*. Smaller than the *Ambition*, she was a full-rigged ship of 267 tons, built at Stonington, Connecticut. She was five years old when Matthias Nicoll of New York purchased her for $9500. He gave the command to Capt. Benjamin Gardner of Newport, but went along on the voyage himself as owner-supercargo. On July 27, 1806, she sailed out past Sandy Hook with a crew of twelve in addition to Nicoll and Gardner. Below decks were 27,000 oak staves and headings, for the making of wine casks, carried as freight for two New York houses, in addition to Nicoll's own venture. The latter consisted of some 45,000 staves and headings, 450 barrels of flour, 33 barrels of rum, some 30 pipes of brandy, 4 hogsheads of tobacco, 4 crates of crockery, 2 bales of broadcloths, and a few bales of gingham and "britannias."

His first objective was Madeira, long familiar to the New Yorkers who were particularly fond of its wine. There he delivered the staves, carried as freight, and sold 318 barrels of flour for $3176 to the firm of Sheffield & Young, who made partial payment with a sterling bill of exchange for £405. Moving on to Teneriffe, he sold $966 worth of staves to one James Barry. Then the *Cotton Planter* set out for the slave stations of Africa. At Senegal, late in October, Nicoll dealt with one J. P. Derime, who took two bales of blue cloth for $800 and 15 barrels of rum, at 75 cents a gallon, for $356.25. In exchange, Nicoll bought ten Negroes at $130 a head. Similar negotiations followed at the Isle of Goree, where one "Monsieur Pepin" took the four hogsheads of tobacco, at ten cents a pound, for $370 and sold Nicoll fourteen Negroes at $130 a head, while a "Doctor Hughs" sold ten apparently better Negroes at $180 each. Nicoll paid for part of the balance with the sterling bill of exchange received at Madeira for flour. Heading westward, the slave ship stopped at the Isle of

May in the Cape Verdes, where Nicoll bought 2040 bushels of salt from one Emmanuel Toquin at twenty cents a bushel.

South America, which was just being opened to Anglo-American trade, next attracted Nicoll. Steering for the Rio Plata, he encountered Admiral Popham's British fleet, which was attacking Buenos Aires. It was necessary to wait at Maldonaldo for several weeks until hostilities ceased. To pay for ship's stores during that interval, Nicoll sold at retail part of his cloth for $1522 and a crate of earthenware for $57. An extra unexpected profit of $3867 for salvage came from assisting the partly wrecked ship, *Bengal*; part of her cargo was rescued and she was towed up to Buenos Aires after the British finally occupied that port. At Buenos Aires Nicoll sold the slaves and the salt, each at a profit of about $1200. In fact, the salt proved the better venture of the two for it sold at 81 cents a bushel, a gross profit of more than 300 per cent over the price paid in the Cape Verdes, whereas the slaves, a much more perishable and risky commodity, yielded only $6188, a gain of 25 per cent over their cost in Africa. Through "Don Louis Godfrey," who received a commission of 3½ per cent for his services, Nicoll purchased 5400 quintals of jerked beef at $2.00 and 600 quintals more at $2.50, hoping to sell them at Havana for $10.00 a quintal.

Since Havana was an enemy port in British eyes, Nicoll cleared for the neutral port of Charleston. On July 31, 1807, almost a year after first sailing from New York, the *Cotton Planter* was overhauled by H.M.S. *Latona* fourteen leagues west of Antigua. With confidence, Nicoll and Gardner produced the ships' papers, with the innocent destination, to the British captain. To their consternation, he confronted them with several intercepted letters which Nicoll had written from Buenos Aires to New York.

In one he had said "I feel fully persuaded that the sooner my beef arrives in Havana, the greater price it will bring." Just before leaving, he had written:

> "The Ship Cotton Planter is now cleared out and ready for sea; Tomorrow morning, wind permitting, I hope to leave this; we have yet to undergo an examination from the Admiral's ship, about four miles below this; as soon as I take my departure from there I will sing Te Deum; and now that it may please the Supreme Dispenser of all Things to send the Ship *Cotton Planter* to her destined port in safety, and there incline the hearts of his faithful Spaniards to give me ten dollars per quintail for my beef is the most cordial and sincere wish of M. Nicoll."

Those damning words transferred the profits of the voyage from Nicoll to the *Latona's* captain and his subordinates. Three days later, ship and cargo were condemned in the vice admiralty court at Antigua. Nicoll appealed but on June 3, 1809, the Lords Commissioners of Appeals upheld the original decision.

Many other New York vessels during those years engaged in "tramp" voyages, wandering from port to port wherever there seemed to be prospects of profit. The brig *Industry*, for instance, took a cargo of sugar, cotton, and logwood from New York to Nantes; herrings from there to St. Petersburg; hemp, iron, and duck back to New York; and was carrying flour and pipe staves from New York to Barcelona when she was stopped off Malaga in 1807. She was condemned at Gibraltar for breach of the Orders in Council.[5] The ship *Comet*, on the other hand, confined herself to a shuttle trade between New York and Nantes, carrying sugar, ashes, logwood, and mahogany

[5] L. C. A. *Industry*.

eastward and bringing back wines in return. She had made six such voyages when a British privateer caught her off the Loire.[6]

Even in the distant Eastern seas, the New Yorkers ran foul of the far-flung Royal Navy. With Holland included among England's enemies, Dutch ships could not be safely employed in bringing coffee from Java; and the obliging Yankees made the most of their neutral services in that profitable long haul. Minturn & Champlin, a prominent firm of transplanted Rhode Islanders, were among the leaders in this trade, and lost more than one vessel. In the summer of 1807, their little 175-ton brig *Cora*, built up the Hudson and with her officers from there also, unloaded a cargo of provisions at Samarang and took on a load of Java coffee and sapan wood. She was armed with four guns and carried small arms as protection against the Sunda pirates, but did not try to put up a fight when, three days out from Samarang, she was overhauled near Batavia by the British sloop-of-war *Fox* and sent into Bombay for condemnation.[7] Three years earlier, H.M.S. *Tremendous* had captured in the Indian Ocean the New York ship *Penman*, which was engaged in a voyage from Batavia to Muscat and back, after being chartered by a New York firm to sail from New York to the Java capital by way of Antwerp. The vice admiralty court at Colombo, Ceylon, condemned her for trading between enemy ports.[8]

The bulk of the captures, however, occurred on lesser voyages to or from the West Indies. Now and then interesting features appeared in such cases. In the summer of 1806, the ship *Franklin* was captured by his Majesty's sloop, *Ferret*, for violating the blockade of Martinique. A British prize crew of six men and a prize master were

[6] L. C. A. *Comet.*
[7] L. C. A. *Cora.*
[8] *A. S. P. Forn.* II, 765.

put aboard her and she was ordered to Bermuda for condemnation. A week or so later, at dusk, the *Franklin's* captain, James Forsyth of New London, snatched the prize master's dirk — the signal for his men to throw overboard the cutlasses of the prize crew. He informed the latter that if they chose to work and do their duty as men, he would give them water and victuals; otherwise, they would get neither. He altered the course for an American port, but his good luck did not last. Two more British warships appeared, and this time the *Franklin* was condemned at Gibraltar.[9] Lengthy disputes occurred in the case of the *Buhlah Maria* and several other New York vessels, as to whether or not the British navy was maintaining an adequate blockade of the island of Curacao.[10] In most cases, however, there is a general sameness to those records of British captures in Caribbean waters — "three leagues west of Dominica," "off Old Cape Francois," "four or five leagues leeward of Guadeloupe," — where the ubiquitous British warships and privateers seem to have been everlastingly on the watch. The aftermath was likewise a fairly uniform story — condemnation in the vice admiralty courts of Jamaica or Antigua on charges of carrying enemy property, or of trading between enemy ports.

While the French and Spaniards appreciated the services of neutral Yankee shipping in those Caribbean waters, on occasion they did a little capturing and condemning on their own account. These seizures by no means approached the wholesale arbitrary condemnations of the previous decade, which gave rise to so many of the French Spoliation claims, but the French were incensed at the manner in which the New Yorkers and others were fur-

[9] L. C. A. *Franklin.*

[10] *A. S. P. Forn.* II, 760; L. C. A. *Buhlah Maria.*

nishing supplies and perhaps munitions to those parts of Haiti under anti-French Negro control. Perhaps we should discount a certain amount of disappointment and bombast in the threat of the French Admiral Willaumez, whose squadron had failed in its objective of intercepting the big British Caribbean convoy in the summer of 1806. From Havana, he reported to the French minister of Marine that on July 28th:

> "A schooner — which I boarded at midnight afterwards informed me that it was part of a convoy of Americans, consisting of eight sail, under the escort of two small frigates, bound to New York, laden with coffee, &c. &c., by the revolted negroes of St. Domingo. The news not being disclosed to me by the master of the schooner till some days after the convoy had time to escape to the northward, indignant at the conduct of the Americans, I immediately put the master of the schooner in irons, and all his people, and made sail in search of said convoy, determined to hang at the yard-arm the captains and supercargoes, in the face of their countrymen, at New York; but being nearly off Cape Hatteras, the weather changed, and the gathering storm left me no hope of arriving off New York in time to intercept the pirates."

After riding out a gale off Hatteras and approaching "within ten leagues of Long Island," he spoke a vessel which reported that the Americans had safely put into the Chesapeake and Delaware.[11] New York was thus spared an international incident of the first magnitude — if the admiral was not bluffing.

The Spaniards had a particular source of grievance

[11] Adm. Willaumez to Minister of Marine, Sept. 30, 1806, quoted in translation in N. Y. *Evening Post*, Jan. 24, 1807.

against New York in those years; from the port had come one of the first revolutionary attacks against the Spanish Main. Early in 1806, the ship *Leander*, belonging to Samuel G. Ogden and employed in the trade with Santo Domingo, was fitting out in New York harbor. Several dozen young New Yorkers were lured aboard her with the prospect of going to New Orleans as mail guards or artisans. She put to sea on February 3; a few days later, the dupes realized that the expedition was not as advertised. Francisco Miranda, the Venezuelan revolutionary leader, who was aboard with several Latin American subordinates, took charge of the men as military officers. At Jacmel in Haiti, two schooners were acquired and the little squadron set out for the Spanish Main. Running afoul of the Spaniards, the two schooners were captured. The unfortunate New York dupes were tried for piracy at Caracas; ten were hanged and beheaded; and the rest, some three dozen, were sentenced to ten years of slavery at hard labor on the public works.[12] Yet, despite that provocation, the Spaniards seem to have captured and condemned fewer New York vessels than did the British or French. One unlucky vessel was taken by a Cuban privateer and its crew forced to run the gauntlet, in which they were brutally beaten; — a foretaste of the West Indian piracy of twenty years later. By and large, however, the Spaniards caused relatively little trouble to New York vessels.

One unfortunate brig, the *Hope*, was captured by both the French and British on a single voyage. In 1804, a New York merchant named George Barnwell loaded her with staves, pine boards, fish, and flour for the Jamaican market. A French privateer caught her, put the captain and crew ashore on Turks Island, and sent her into

[12] *A. S. P. Forn.* III, 257–258; Sherman, *A General Account of the Miranda Expedition* (N. Y., 1808), pp. 96–98.

Samana Bay in Santo Domingo. There she was libelled in the Court of Admiralty but later restored. In the meantime, however, the privateer's crew had "totally plundered, stolen, or destroyed" her cargo and a considerable part of her rigging. Finally, one William Walton, a Baltimore merchant who was serving as United States commercial agent, tried to salvage something for the owner, and, incidentally, win a commission for himself. Securing a Maryland captain whose vessel had been condemned as unseaworthy, Walton refitted the *Hope* on Barnwell's account and loaded for him a cargo of mahogany and lignum vitae. Some shipwrecked sailors from the French navy agreed to work their way to New York as crew, while two French naval officers came along as passengers. Some twenty miles from Sandy Hook, with her destination almost in sight, she was overhauled by a British frigate on June 6, 1806. She was sent to Halifax with a prize crew and condemned on the ground that, since the title to vessel and cargo were not clear, they were presumably enemy property. On appeal to London she was eventually released in April, 1809, five years after she had set out upon that unlucky voyage.[13]

New York vessels did not have to travel to the East Indies, to the English Channel or even to the West Indies to meet the far-flung naval forces with which England was exercising the crushing effects of sea power, because for two years a British squadron haunted the waters around Sandy Hook. By coincidence, the two vessels which made the greatest maritime stir at New York in 1806 were both named *Leander*. One was the ship which took Miranda's raiders to the Caribbean; the other was the British frigate, which captured the *Hope* and in other ways made herself the most obnoxious of that squadron. From the summer

[13] L. C. A. *Hope II.*

of 1804 until the summer of 1806, the frigates *Leander* and *Cambrian*, accompanied by the sloop-of-war *Driver*, steadily patrolled the sea approaches to New York and even frequently operated in the Lower Bay inside Sandy Hook. According to one story, the vessels had originally come at New York's request. The president of one of the marine insurance companies, it was said, had asked the British consul to provide local protection against French privateers.[14] A more likely reason for their first appearance in June, 1804, however, was the presence of two French frigates, which were waiting in New York to convey Jerome Bonaparte and his Baltimore bride to France.[15]

Whether invited or not, the *Leander* and her consorts soon made their presence extremely distasteful to the New Yorkers. A midshipman on the *Leander* later described the squadron's practices in his memoirs:

> "Every morning at daybreak, we set about arresting the progress of all vessels we saw, firing off guns to the right and left to make every ship that was running in heave to, or wait until we had leisure to send a boat on board "to see," in our lingo, "what she was made of." I have frequently known a dozen, and sometimes a couple of dozen, ships lying a league or two off the port, losing their fair wind, their tide, and worse than all their market, for many hours, sometimes the whole day, before our search was completed." [16]

Scarcely had the squadron arrived at their station when De Witt Clinton, then mayor of New York, began sending protests to Washington, protesting the violation of terri-

[14] J. B. McMaster, *History of the People of the U. S.*, III, 239, 246.

[15] I. N. P. Stokes, *Iconography of Manhattan Island*, V, 1423–1426, quoting original sources.

[16] Basil Hall, R.N., *Fragments of Voyages and Travels* (1832 ed. 1st series), vol. I, p. 289.

torial waters. He urged that the blockaded French frigates be given a twenty-four hour start; he protested against the impressment of twenty seamen from the incoming British ship *Pitt* and of later impressment of American seamen; and he complained of the operations carried on so close inshore.[17] The *Hope* was by no means the only New York vessel stopped off the Hook and sent with a prize crew to Halifax. Three weeks later, another brig *Hope*, four days out from New York for Bordeaux, was captured by the *Driver* and sent to Halifax. A mile and a half off Sandy Hook Light, the *Leander* caught the ship *Aurora*, inward bound from Havana with sugar and logwood, and sent her in the same direction. The ship *Enterprize* and the brig *Eugenia*, inward bound from Bordeaux, met a similar fate, their wine cargoes being condemned as enemy property.[18] Nor were they the only victims.

Aboard that squadron which cruised back and forth almost in sight of the New York waterfront were dozens of reluctant seamen whose claims of American citizenship had not saved them from impressment. In the lengthy list submitted by Madison to Congress of those applying to the State Department for release from impressment were more than thirty specified individuals aboard the three warships, most of them having been impressed during the early months on the station. On a single day, August 4, 1804, the *Leander* had bagged Samuel Howard, Andrew Richee, William Right, Jack Bowier, Samuel Gain, and Thomas Auld; during the ensuing month she added Thomas Williams, William Smith, Noah Becks, and William Gray, while Robert Blaway, Nathaniel Moore and Samuel Moore were also taken, at dates unspecified. Even more were aboard the *Cambrian*, six impressed before

[17] *De Witt Clinton Letter Book*, quoted in *Stokes*, *loc. cit.*
[18] L. C. A. *Hope I*, *Aurora*, *Enterprize*, *Eugenia*.

she arrived at Sandy Hook and twelve more, including Patrick Cunningham, first mate of the ship *Juno*. The little *Driver* also acquired three. Most of these men had certificates of protection as American citizens and this list does not include the considerable number of seamen impressed from British merchantmen.[19]

New York cursed the whole squadron for its seizures and impressments but the *Leander* roused the port's rage to white heat with the "Pierce murder" on April 24, 1806. The little sloop *Richard*, coming up the Jersey coast from Brandywine on the Delaware, was about a quarter mile off shore from Sandy Hook, when the *Leander* spotted her and started firing. One shot landed forty feet ahead; another flew directly over the sloop. She started to heave to when a third shot struck the quarter-rail. A splinter carried off the head of the helmsman, John Pierce, brother of the master. His body was carried to the city and viewed by angry crowds along the waterfront before being laid in state at the City Hall. Several boat loads of stores, ordered by the purser of the *Leander*, were intercepted at the docks or pursued down the Bay, while a pilot boat was sent out to intercept two of the *Leander's* latest prizes en route to Halifax. A great mass meeting at the Tontine Coffee House passed vigorous resolutions against the "repeated outrages committed by foreign ships of war at the mouths of our harbours" and recommended that no further assistance in the form of supplies or pilotage be accorded to them. The whole city turned out for the public funeral procession of Pierce, with bells tolling and the flags at half mast on all the harbor shipping. Within ten days, President Jefferson issued a proclamation calling for the arrest of Capt. Henry Whitby of the *Leander*; commanding the three warships to leave the ports of the

[19] *A. S. P. Forn.* II, 790–797.

United States; forbidding the three captains ever again to enter United States waters; and prohibiting any shore assistance in the form of food, pilotage or repairs.[20]

The squadron did not leave immediately — the two *Hopes* were captured in June of that year. A year later, following the *Chesapeake-Leopard* affair off the Virginia Capes, the President made a more sweeping proclamation on July 2, 1807 but, in defiance of it, the Royal Navy made its appearance at Sandy Hook again early in September in the form of the frigate *Jason* and brig *Columbine*. An armed boat pursued a pilot who refused his services; the *Columbine* fired on a gunboat and forced it to send a midshipman aboard; and when the custom house barge was sent down to warn them off, it was boarded and searched in insolent fashion. The greatest excitement came when the *Jason* sent its barge up to the city with a message for the British consul. As soon as the boat touched the shore, six of the sailors made a dash for liberty. The British lieutenant drew his pistols and threatened to fire if they did not return; a mob assembled, sheltered the men and had begun to handle the officer roughly when the commandant of the Navy Yard intervened and managed to save him.[21]

Yet, despite British frigates, port activities were thriving at New York as never before, in that summer of 1807. The exports for the year ending September 30 reached a peak which would be equalled only once again (in 1825) before 1835, while imports were in an equally flourishing condition. Despite occasional seizures, the vessels which escaped capture and condemnation were making extraordinarily profitable voyages. The municipal common

[20] N. Y. *Commercial Advertiser*, April 26, 1806 *et seq.*; N. Y. *Spectator*, May 6, 1806; Stokes, *op. cit.*, V, 1445–1446; McMaster, *op. cit.*, III, 237–239.

[21] N. Y. *American Citizen*, Sept. 5 *et seq.*; Stokes, *op. cit.*, V, 1472.

council was voting to build new piers to accommodate the increasing shipping and there seemed every evidence that neutral profits were outweighing the occasional attendant irritations. In July, while New York was planning new fortifications for the harbor, Robert Fulton after several trials blew up a 200-ton brig between Governors and Ellis Islands with the new torpedo he had invented. Just a month later, on August 17, he started the steamboat *Clermont* on her epochal trip up the Hudson to Albany, two weeks before the *Jason* made her appearance. Altogether, that summer of 1807 was the high water mark in the history of the old port of New York before its great boom after 1815.

Before the year was out, the Embargo had shut down with deadening effect upon that rushing business. Alarmed at the possible consequences of the new foreign decrees, Jefferson on Tuesday, December 22, 1807, signed the Embargo Bill which he had pushed through Congress. On Thursday forenoon, the twenty-fourth, one vessel cleared for Dublin and six for the West Indies — the last regular clearances for more than a year. That afternoon, the *Evening Post* published a letter written at Havre de Grace in Maryland, stating that when the writer left Washington Monday night, the Embargo legislation seemed likely. "Do not be surprised," he wrote, "if, by the next mail orders should be received at New-York preventing all vessels from going to sea. I say this in hope it may prove of service to some of your mercantile friends." [22] Meanwhile, a hard-riding courier was speeding northward with the news of the accomplished fact. The next day turned out to be the most exciting Christmas in the history of the port. McMaster has vividly described the effect of the news at New York:

[22] N. Y. *Evening Post*, Dec. 24, 1807.

"So well did the messengers perform their task that at five o'clock on Friday morning one of them crossed the ferry from Paulus Hook and roused the collector of the port of New York from his slumbers. The nearest Republican printer was sought, and by seven o'clock copies of the law in the form of handbills were distributed about the streets. Then followed a scene which to men not engaged in commerce was comical. On a sudden the streets were full of merchants, ship-owners, ship-captains, supercargoes, and sailors hurrying toward the water-front. Astonished at this unusual commotion, men of all sorts followed and by eight o'clock the wharves were crowded with spectators, cheering the little fleet of half-laden ships which, with all sail spread, was beating down the harbor. None of them had clearances. Many were half-manned. Few had more than part of a cargo. One which had just come in, rather than be embargoed, went off without breaking bulk. At the sight of the headings of the handbills, the captains made crews of the first seamen they met, and, with a few hurried instructions from the owners, pushed into the stream. That the Collector was slack is not unlikely, for it was ten o'clock before his boats were in pursuit." [23]

The following day, the *Evening Post* announced several arrivals and then remarked "No Clearances in the Future." Hundreds of vessels were still left in port — 537 by one estimate and 666 by another.

The deadening effect of the Embargo upon the business of the port was graphically described by John Lambert, an English traveler, who contrasted the situation in November 1807 and April 1808:

[23] McMaster, *op. cit.*, III, 279.

"When I arrived at New York in November, the port was filled with shipping and the wharves were crowded with commodities of every description. Bales of cotton, wool, and merchandize; barrels of pot-ash, rice, flour, and salt provisions; hogsheads of sugar, chests of tea, puncheons of rum, and pipes of wine; boxes, cases, packs and packages of all sizes and denominations, were strewed upon the wharves and landing places, or upon the decks of the shipping. All was noise and bustle. The carters were driving in every direction; and the sailors and labourers upon the wharves, and on board the vessels, were moving their ponderous burthens from place to place. The merchants and their clerks were busily engaged in their counting-houses, or upon the piers. The Tontine coffee-house was filled with underwriters, brokers, merchants, traders, and politicians; selling, purchasing, trafficking, or insuring; some reading, others inquiring the news. . . . The coffee-house slip, and the corners of Wall and Pearl-streets, were jammed up with carts, drays, and wheel-barrows; horses and men were huddled promiscuously together, leaving little or no room for passengers to pass. Such was the appearance of this part of the town when I arrived. Every thing was in motion; all was life, bustle and activity. . . .

"But on my return to New York the following April, what a contrast was presented to my view! and how shall I describe the melancholy dejection that was painted upon the countenances of the people, who seemed to have taken leave of all their former gaiety and cheerfulness? The coffee-house slip, the wharves and quays along South-street, presented no longer the bustle and activity that had prevailed there five months before. The port, indeed, was full of shipping; but they were dismantled and laid up. Their decks were cleared, their hatches fastened down, and scarcely a sailor was to be found on board. Not a box, bale, cask, barrel, or package, was to be seen upon the wharves. Many of the counting houses were shut up, or advertised to be let; and the few solitary merchants, clerks, porters, and labourers, that were to be seen, were walking about with their hands in their pockets. Instead of sixty or a hundred carts that used to stand in the street for hire, scarcely a dozen appeared, and they were unemployed; a few coasting sloops, and schooners, which were clearing out for some of the ports in the United States, were all that remained of that immense business which was carried on a few months before. The coffee-house was almost empty. . . . In fact, every thing presented a melancholy appearance. The streets near the waterside were almost deserted, grass had begun to grow upon the wharves, and the minds of the people were tortured by the vague and idle rumours that were set afloat upon the arrival of every letter from England or from the seat of government." [24]

The remark "No Clearances" appeared day after day with monotonous regularity throughout 1808 and into 1809 as ships and seamen lay idle in port, with now and then exceptions. The most conspicuous evasion came with the sailing of John Jacob Astor's *Beaver* for Canton on August 17, 1808. The astute Astor had the blessing of President Jefferson himself for this voyage, which had as its excuse the desire of a Chinese "mandarin," Punqua Wingchong, to return to his native land. Other merchants in New York and in Philadelphia attacked the permission;

[24] John Lambert, *Travels through Canada and the United States in the Years 1806, 1807 & 1808* (London, 1810), II, 155–158.

some said that he was "a Chinaman picked up in the Park" or "a common Chinese dock loafer"; a group of Philadelphians pointed out that the high-class Chinese never left their country. When the *Beaver* finally returned to New York on June 1, 1809, "with a full cargo of teas, silks and nankeens" it was said that she bore "two hundred thousand dollars more than she left with." [25]

Another clearance, in April 1808, involved an amazing piece of international connivance between England, France, Spain and, to a lesser degree, the United States. Readers of the novel *Anthony Adverse* will recall how the author served up this episode, based upon the memoirs of the international financial adventurer, Vincent Nolte. It was no less than an understanding between the chief belligerents, through the medium of their leading financiers, whereby the silver of Mexico, bottled up by British sea power, might be made available in Europe. Small, fast vessels plying between Vera Cruz and various ports of the United States conducted one stage of this business. Among the American merchants involved was Archibald Gracie of New York. There is an interesting supplement to Nolte's account in the *Voyages* of George Coggeshall, a Connecticut mariner operating from New York, who served as mate on five such Vera Cruz voyages in Gracie schooners; two from New Orleans in the *Centurion* in 1807 and three from New York in the fast pilot-boat *Hamilton* in 1807–08. The last of these trips came during the Embargo period, under the dispensation which allowed merchants "to send out vessels in ballast, to collect and bring home whatever they could gather together, either in money or other available property." The *Hamilton* sailed in ballast and two months later was at Philadelphia with a large quantity of silver aboard. Taking full advantage

[25] K. W. Porter, *John Jacob Astor, Business Man*, I, 144–150.

of the situation, Coggeshall netted a profit of 150 per cent on a $600 venture in the Vera Cruz market. He pointed out that "in consequence of the Embargo, seamen's wages were extremely low; our crew consisted of twenty picked men before the mast, and their wages were but six dollars per month."[26]

The wits of the merchants were sharpened during the period of the Embargo and subsequent interruptions of trade. Clever evasions of American as well as of foreign regulations might well bring in huge profits. Stephen Whitney, one of that numerous swarm of Connecticut Yankees operating at New York, is said to have become one of the city's first millionaires through sending cotton abroad by way of Amelia Island, just below the Georgia border. The letterbook of Stephen Jumel, a Frenchman who was a leading wine merchant at New York, shows that he was constantly on the *qui vive* to make the most of any opportunity. Late in 1808, when it became apparent that the pending repeal of the Embargo would radically increase the price of exportable products in American ports, he sent the brig *Stephen* to New Orleans, instructing Captain Berry to leave the vessel in the lower Mississippi and go ahead by boat to New Orleans alone, without letter bag or passengers, delivering instructions to Jumel's correspondent so that he could buy up a return cargo before the town learned the latest news.[27]

When, at last, Congress substituted Non-Intercourse for Embargo in 1809, New York shared in the general boom, for trade was permitted with regions outside the British and French domains. Jumel wanted to replenish his stock of wines from Bordeaux; since direct trade with

[26] George Coggeshall, *Voyages*, etc., Second Series, pp. 39–57; Vincent Nolte, *Fifty Years in Both Hemispheres*, pp. 77–153.

[27] N. Y. P. L. *Jumel & Desobry Letter Book*, Dec. 6, 1808.

France was prohibited, he planned to have Joseph Perry at Bordeaux send the wine overland to Pedro Quehille at the Spanish port of St. Sebastian. Jumel pointed out the necessity of removing all the French labels from the bottles, substituting Spanish ones instead, and doing likewise with the corks. He instructed Capt. Decasse of his schooner *Collector* to say nothing to the crew about the source of the wine; otherwise there might be trouble with the American customs officers. He likewise informed Quehille at St. Sebastian that another vessel of his would be coming over in five or six weeks and that as soon as her Jumel & Desobry house flag was seen, he was to hoist a white flag on shore if the coast were clear; otherwise a red and white flag to warn her captain to try another, safer port.[28]

In the face of such American tricks, the naval officers and port officials of both England and France became keenly suspicious. We have already seen the condemnation of the *Cotton Planter* because the British had intercepted incriminating letters from other vessels. A British privateer was overhauling the brig *John*, bound from Guadeloupe to New York, when they saw a heavy object thrown overboard; inquiries brought out the fact that several damaging letters had been tied to a brick.[29] The ship *Dispatch* of New York, bound from Cadiz to Tonningen, was captured by another British privateer off the Bill of Portland and sent into Weymouth. The customs "tide surveyor" there became suspicious of the absence of a register and ordered the stern to be scraped. Successive layers of paint eventually revealed that she had been a French ship, bearing the names *Bonaparte* and *Le Vainqueur* in turn.[30]

[28] *Ibid.*, instructions to Capt. Decasse, Oct. 4, 1809; instructions to Pedro Quehille, Oct. 7, 1809.

[29] L. C. A. *John.*

[30] *Ibid.*; *Dispatch*; incidentally, the Danish name painted by the German

During 1808 and early 1809, several New York vessels, trading from port to port overseas rather than returning home to be interned by the Embargo, were condemned by the French Imperial Council of Prizes. Under the Milan Decree, it will be recalled, any vessel which had touched at a British port or had been visited by a British warship was liable to seizure. Consequently the Yankee shipmasters tried to prove that they came from innocent neutral ports. The ship *Minerva*, for instance, lay at Charente, chartered to carry a cargo of brandies to Bremen. According to Capt. Jenkins, she had left New York on Oct. 9, 1807; arrived at Rotterdam, Jan. 4, 1808; remained there until June 21, when she sailed for Bergen, Norway; and left there in ballast for Charente on July 8. During the first week of 1809, when 450 pipes of brandy were aboard and she was all ready to sail for Bremen, the customs officers discovered that her health clearance for Bergen was printed in different type from the others issued at that port. They re-examined Capt. Jenkins and his crew, who stuck to their story although, on the strength of that suspicious document, they were thrown into prison and fined 11,000 francs for perjury. The same fate befell the officers and crew of the *Wareham*, whose captain swore that he had come to Charente directly from Teneriffe and had not visited a British port; only to have witnesses appear from Rochelle to testify that they had seen his ship undergoing repairs at Plymouth, England.[31]

The brunt of these captures fell upon the marine insurance underwriters, who in most cases were shipowners and merchants themselves, seeking to spread out the risks involved in the capture of individual ships. The insurance

prize crew on the American *City of Flint* in 1939 failed to deceive Norwegian port officials.

[31] *A. S. P. Forn.* III, 334-336.

policies of the day protected the owner against a wide range of contingencies, the usual printed form reading:

> "Touching the adventures and perils which we, the assurers are contented to bear and take upon us in this voyage, they are of seas, men of war, fires, enemies, pirates, rovers, thieves, jettisons, letters of mart or countermart, surprizals, takings at sea, arrests, restraints, detainment of all Kings, Princes or Peoples of what nation condition or quality soever, barratry of the master of mariners, and all other perils, losses and misfortunes, that have or shall come to the hurt, detriment or damage of said vessel, or any part thereof."[32]

Marine insurance rates might be called a barometer of sea power, but in those days of slow communication they were a much less sensitive gauge than they are today. The normal peacetime sea risks, which were about 2 per cent for a one-way trip to England or the West Indies, were increased to meet the extra risks as far as they were known in New York at the time the policy was signed. In 1810, for instance, the rate to Liverpool or Belfast was only 2½ per cent, little more than normal, but to St. Petersburg, involving the risky Baltic passage, had jumped to 20 per cent.[33] Naturally, these were simply guesses in the dark, based on information weeks or months old. The insurance companies suffered their heaviest losses when some new belligerent decree shut down upon a trade in which they had already made heavy commitments. "Premiums dip deep in profit," wrote Nicoll, after the seizure of the *Cotton Planter*, "but are frequently repaid with heavy interest." [34]

[32] Policy of Commercial Insurance Co., of N. Y., quoted in L. C. A. *Hope II*; similar in original policies of other companies.

[33] N. Y. Hist. Soc. *Howland & Grinnell Account Book, passim.*

[34] L. C. A. *Cotton Planter.*

Between losses to their own shipping and underwriting for others, numerous New York merchants suffered terrific reverses during these years. Scoville, the chronicler of the group, declares that Daniel Ludlow had lost nearly a half million by underwriting ships captured by the French before 1800, and that Archibald Gracie, perhaps the foremost New York trader of the day, never recovered from losing a million dollars through captures in the Napoleonic period. The house of Minturn & Champlin, with its activity in the East Indian trade, was another distinguished victim of the times.

Yet, with all that, profits were to be made when flour was selling, as it was in 1811, for $8 or $9 a barrel at New York, and at the same time, for $18 at Lisbon and $20 at Gibraltar. With England in need of cotton, with Wellington's army to be fed in the Peninsula, and with many other parts of the world ready to pay handsomely for goods which could be brought to them, plenty of New York houses were willing to take chances with their vessels and cargoes ventured in their holds. Some of these firms, such as Leroy, Bayard & McEvers, managed to weather the trying times with good profits.

Captures and condemnations continued during the interval between the Embargo and the War of 1812, with Denmark joining England and France in the practice. Here it has been possible, however, to touch only upon a small fraction of New York's high adventure afloat but the circumstances were in general similar to those already cited. No other voyage, nevertheless, can compare in dramatic interest with that of Astor's *Tonquin*, which sailed on Sept. 8, 1810, for the Northwest Coast. The following May, her company laid the foundation of Astoria on the Columbia River and then sailed away to a tragic fate; early in June she was blown up after the Indians had massacred her crew.[35] That, however, lay far remote from the sphere of British and French commercial decrees. For a first-hand picture of conditions on the Atlantic, one may dip into Capt. George Coggeshall's delightfully explicit account of five voyages to Europe between 1809 and 1812; two to Tonningen, two to Lisbon, and one deep into the Baltic as far as Riga.[36] Other ventures might be cited by the score, if space permitted.

By the spring of 1812, it was evident that these belligerent interferences with American shipping were leading the nation toward war. Early in April, Congress laid a ninety-day embargo on American shipping and the events of Christmas Day of 1807 were re-enacted. As soon as the news arrived, dozens of vessels slipped away to sea — "had the city been enveloped in flames," said one newspaper, "property could not have been moved off with greater expedition."[37] Interest thereafter shifted from merchantmen eluding the British, to warships which were preparing to fight them. On April 14, two frigates from the Navy Yard fired seven shots at the newly completed nine-foot masonry walls of Castle Williams on Governors Island, "for the purpose of trying her strength," and found that the walls stood the shock even better than anticipated.[38] News of the declaration of war reached New York on June 20; the following day, Commodore Rodgers stood out to sea with a squadron — the *President*, *United States*, *Congress*, *Argus*, and *Hornet* — which would be, before long, writing one of the most thrilling chapters in American naval history.

35 Porter, *op. cit.* I, 185–192; Washington Irving, *Astoria*.
36 Coggeshall, *Voyages*, 2nd series, pp. 61–120.
37 Guernsey, *N. Y. City and Vicinity during the War of 1812–15*, I, 16.
38 N. Y. *Evening Post*, April 15, 1812.

ROBERT GREENHALGH ALBION.

ENGLISH GAME LAW REFORM

The eighteenth century in England was the country gentleman's century. Despite all the busy commerce, the rising industrialists, and the mushroom factories, he dominated society and ruled the kingdom much as he pleased. The nineteenth century was likewise in many respects his century, but then he governed only on sufferance and as long as he recognized his masters in the middle class capitalists, who found him a convenient instrument for their policies. The change from domination to sufferance constitutes a well defined class struggle, which has its well established landmarks in the Reform Bill of 1832 and the repeal of the corn laws, but one of its most instructive illustrations is to be found in the intimate skirmish which resulted in the Game Act of 1831.

The French game laws, which played an important part in causing the savage extremes of the great French Revolution, have received their merited attention from historians. Perhaps it was because no such striking upheaval graced the annals of England that their English counterparts waited until recently for an appreciation of their high social significance. For England also had a well developed, ancient, and elaborate institution of sporting privilege and game preservation; and this game system, too, insofar as it incorporated the principles of the old régime, aristocratic, blood-given, legally established right, perished under the advancing Juggernaut of new ideas and conditions. But it was an industrial revolution and the appearance of a powerful mill-owning non-landed middle class, rather than a surge of democratic and peasant individualism, that brought about the reform in England.

The English game laws had a history reaching back to the forest laws of the middle ages.[1] As the barons had filched from the king his ancient prerogatives they had bit by bit secured an extension of the royal sporting privileges to themselves, at first individually by personal grant and then generally by statutes. The tangle of game legislation, spread over centuries, culminated in 1671 in a law which remained as the principal foundation of the game system for a hundred and sixty years. This sporting charter disqualified almost all except the landed classes from indulgence in the amusement of pursuing game. For its purposes the privileged were classified as persons possessing special personal rights of forest or the franchises of chase, park, or free warren (which in fact were already decaying); persons owning lands or tenements producing an income of at least one hundred pounds a year; persons having leaseholds of ninety-nine years or more worth half again as much; and the eldest sons of men who ranked as esquires or higher.[2] No doubt these provisions opened the gates to floods of litigation but their general intent is apparent. In order to render it even more unmistakable the legislature, under cover of a concern lest the lower classes waste their time in vain amusements, stipulated baldly a few years later that "inferiour tradesmen, apprentices, and other dissolute persons" should not "presume to hunt, hawke, fish, or fowle." [3]

These laws may be regarded as the kernel of the game system. As the revolution of 1689 signalized the fact that the landed aristocracy had arrived in the political world,

[1] Chester and Ethyn Kirby, "The Stuart Game Prerogative," *English Historical Review*, XLVI (April 1931), 239–254; and Chester Kirby, "The English Game Law System," *American Historical Review*, XXXVIII (Jan. 1933), 240–262, and the references there given.

[2] 22–23 Car. II, c. 25.

[3] 4 Wm. and M., c. 23.

so they crowned the process by which the country gentlemen secured themselves an exclusive position in the sporting world. It had been a long process, just as the political climb had been, and the history of the early game laws is a maze which the unwary may well avoid; but in its essence the sporting right was a part of the reward or booty which came with the responsibilities of government. It was the enviable perquisite associated with the duties of an unpaid magistracy and legislature.

As such it required constant attention and there grew up accordingly an elaborate game code, remarkable for its complexity, encumbered with a host of obsolete but unrepealed statutes, eloquent of the immensely difficult and never successful attempts to protect the most precarious of possessions. For game presented peculiar difficulties. It had little or no value for sport unless it was wild and free to come and go as it pleased. But its wildness made it impossible to identify as ordinary property was identified, since it passed constantly from estate to estate. The property rights in a hare, a pheasant, or a partridge changed from moment to moment; in fact, strictly speaking, they did not exist.

To make the most of these tenuous rights the ruling classes exerted themselves without stint. Every conceivable restriction was laid upon those sporting practices which were supposed to be characteristic of the poacher. Killing game at night, or on Sunday or Christmas day, or during closed seasons, selling game, or, if one were disqualified, even having it, were all made illegal. The possession of nets, lurchers, harepipes, and such other instruments as were commonly used only by poachers, was prohibited. The heaviest penalties were imposed upon poaching, death under the Black Act of 1723 for deer stealing while disguised, seven years' transportation for deer stealing under the act of 1802, six months' imprisonment and a whipping for gang poaching under the act of 1800, and so down to a fine of a few unpayable shillings and a few days in gaol.[4]

The enforcement of these measures rested in the hands of the country gentlemen and their agents. The act of 1671, by authorizing every lord of a manor to appoint a gamekeeper with the power of confiscating paraphernalia of sport found in the possession of unqualified persons, provided the landed classes with a kind of private game police, who prowled about the copses and fields on the alert for any laborer so misguided as to indulge his sporting instincts or his love of a full stomach. When he had apprehended his culprit the gamekeeeper brought him before the Justice of the Peace, almost invariably a member of the landed classes, and there, unless the offense had been of a sort to require heavy punishment, such as transportation, the offender received his summary trial and sentence. Not satisfied with the mere machinery which the law provided, the gentlemen organized private associations to assist in the protection of their exclusive rights, and there came into existence about the middle of the eighteenth century various regional organizations which provided by subscription the funds necessary to bring to justice poachers and especially the tradesmen who marketed the illegally procured game. For a time at least, there was a "Society of Noblemen and Gentlemen for the Preservation of the Game" which looked upon the whole country as its sphere of activity.[5]

And finally, as if all these measures were not enough, the legislature introduced a new qualification by the im-

[4] See, for example, 9 Geo. I, c. 22; 39–40 Geo. III, c. 50; 6 Anne, c. 16; 28 Geo. II, c. 12; 42 Geo. III, c. 107.

[5] See *ante*, note 1.

position of taxes on sport. William Pitt, in his youthful enthusiasm for balancing the budget by the imposition of excise taxes, required every sportsman to procure a two-guinea game certificate and every gamekeeper to be deputed with his authority only on paper stamped at the rate of half a guinea. So satisfactory did this arrangement of 1784, with some necessary tinkering in 1785, prove, that both the government, which desired the revenue, and the sportsmen, who welcomed the additional exclusiveness and protection which it afforded, gladly saw it extended until in 1812 sportsmen were taxed at three and a half guineas and gamekeepers at one pound five shillings.[6] A tax on sporting dogs was introduced in 1796, and in 1812 it also had reached substantial rates, greyhounds being assessed at twenty shillings and other sporting dogs at fourteen.[7]

These measures, beginning with the acts of 1784 and 1785, which established the game tax as a permanent institution, rested upon a principle not altogether identical with that of the old game system. For they concerned themselves, not with the land or birth of the sportsman, but merely with the payment of a small sum for the privilege of the chase. As long as the old game qualifications remained in force the new laws served as a reënforcement of the old system of privilege; but they demonstrated that the ownership of land by no means constituted the only possible test for the sporting restrictions which in some form were inevitable in such a densely populated country as England.

The sportsmen did not then trouble their minds about such fundamental questions. Instead they were enjoying

[6] 24 Geo. III, c. 43; 25 Geo. III, c. 50; 31 Geo. III, c. 21; 52 Geo. III, c. 93.

[7] 36 Geo. III, c. 124; 52 Geo. III, c. 93, schedule G. Dogs not of the sporting kind were charged for at fourteen shillings also where more than one was kept, otherwise only one shilling; a blanket duty was levied upon packs of hounds.

their privileges to the utmost and in the process transforming into abuses what had doubtless at one time been, in a measure, rational and acceptable amusements. In the seventeenth century, English field sports had followed rather simple lines. In the eighteenth, the growth of wealth and luxury led to many refinements in the direction of efficiency and artificiality. The breeding of fleeter horses and hounds, the rise of the subscription pack, the progress of the enclosure movement contributed to transform hunting at force from an almost leisurely to a highly elaborate pursuit. Hounds and red-coated gentlemen multiplied beyond all reason and the fox hunt became a craze.

But the fox, although closely associated with the game system, was not technically game. It was the change in the sport of shooting which most vitally affected the game laws. Improvements in the fowling piece had already in the last decades of the seventeenth century brought the introduction of the practice of shooting game on the wing, and continued increases in efficiency made shooting flying game universal by 1750 and rapidly augmented the demand for game to be shot by the marvelous new weapons. Thus the shot gun had become an instrument of precision, convenience, and almost unlimited execution long before the introduction of the percussion principle, which made possible the copper cap gun in the early years of the nineteenth century and led to the decline of the flint lock.

In fact, the new guns of the eighteenth century proved almost too successful. The sporting world shot to a constant refrain of laments in which old and new sportsmen alike grieved at the dearth of game, for the natural increase was no match for the terrific destruction. The sportsmen, therefore, resorted to artificial preservation. The gamekeepers devoted their attention, not merely to poachers, but to the blood-sucking stoats and weazels, to the egg-eating rats, to the marauding cats and dogs; and not merely to the protection of the game, but to fostering it, hatching the pheasant eggs in the barnyard and stacking buckwheat, peas, and beans in the coppices during severe weather. Such nursing brought the accumulation of game in favorable circumstances to vast numbers and made possible the development of the battue, which seems to have been introduced from the Continent about the beginning of the nineteenth century, or possibly a few years earlier. In this sport human beings beat for the game and drove it in immense numbers to the waiting shooters, who, without being obliged to exert themselves beyond taking aim and pulling the trigger, mowed it down. The bags mounted into the hundreds. The battue, although subsequently refined, was in the beginning an orgy of slaughter, a fashionable pastime for grandees like the Duke of Wellington and the Duke of York.[8] Such were the mighty hunters of the land of William Rufus and Richard the Lion Hearted.

Even aside from this abuse, and indeed before it appeared, the game system caused much discontent. An institution of class privilege, bolstered up by class legislation, must inevitably generate some dissatisfaction, for no one likes inferiority and few can see any justice in it when applied to themselves. The poacher, encouraged by old principles of the common law and by the philosophy of the day, rationalized his law-breaking into a virtue and declared that he had a natural God-given right to whatever

[8] William B. Daniel, *Rural Sports* (London, 1801–1802), II, 406–407; William B. Daniel, *Supplement to the Rural Sports* (London, 1813), 399–406; *Sporting Magazine*, XIX (Jan. 1802), 231; XXI (Nov. 1802 and Jan. 1803), 99, 225; XXIX (Feb. 1807), 247; XXXIII (Jan. 1809), 202; LXIII (Jan. 1824), 227; *Annals of Sporting*, V (Feb. 1824), 141–142; VII, 120, 182; IX, 51; X, 364; XI, 109; XIII, 109–110.

wild animals he could secure. If the game preservers increased the breed, so much the better for him. The townsman who bought the poached hares, partridges, and pheasants was inclined to agree.

It was the farmer who had most cause to feel dissatisfied in the eighteenth century. He lived in the midst of the game system and was in some, though a moderate, degree a capitalist; but rarely did he possess, when a freeholder, the amount of land sufficient to give him a qualification under the game laws. And the tenants, whose numbers were rapidly increasing in consequence of the enclosure movement, were excluded from sport by their landlords, who generally reserved the game to themselves. This exclusion was irksome enough to a person in the farmer's position, but it was not the principal of his grievances. Hares, it appeared, loved nothing so much as a diet of luscious growing crops, and not only the wheat but the forage crops, the turnips and grasses which played such an important part in the new agriculture. As the preservation of game increased, the devastation increased. William Marshall, the agriculturist, gave it as his considered opinion that "To a person who has not been an eye-witness to the destruction which accompanies an inordinate quantity of game, the quantity of damage is in a manner inconceivable."[9] And there were other marauding pests. A host of poachers, shooters, and fox, stag, and hare hunters stalked and galloped about the meadows and fields, trampling grass and crops, breaking hedges, and generally doing a vast deal of damage, while the farmer stood helplessly by and reflected on the wantonness of human beings where other people's property is concerned.

Still in the eighteenth century this discontent did not go very far. The landed gentlemen continued to be the

[9] *Rural Economy of Norfolk* (London, 1787), I, 171–178.

genuinely dominant class. The farmers were not only impotent but they were divided, because a few were actually qualified in their own right, a few sported on sufferance, and still others indulged in fox hunting, that branch of field sports which required no qualification. The urban middle class had not yet become aroused. But the discontent was present and growing. Perhaps its first great impulse came in 1752 when the Society of Noblemen and Gentlemen for the Preservation of the Game attempted to revive the enforcement of the game laws, previously not much attended to in the metropolis of London. A loud outcry greeted this venture. The society was described as a menace to liberty.[10] The game laws were denounced — a little mysteriously — as depriving the farmers of rights which belonged to them by "the laws of nature and of nations."[11] During the Seven Years' War, Englishmen asked themselves why they should fight for British freedom when it did not permit them the liberty of killing game.[12]

Such sentiments gained a slow but increasing momentum as the years wore on. As early as 1772, a bill was introduced into the House of Commons for the purpose of lowering the property qualifications almost to the vanishing point.[13] Ten years later, during the debate on a bill of

[10] *Remarks on the Laws Relating to the Game, and the Association Set on Foot for the Preservation of It* (London, 1753), pp. 15–17.

[11] [Clubbe, John], *The Farmers Queries and Resolutions Concerning the Game* (Ipswich, [1770]).

[12] *Public Advertiser*, 29 July and 13 Aug. 1756; *London Chronicle*, 5–7 May, 1757. See also *An Alarm to the People of England; Shewing Their Rights, Liberties, and Properties to Be in the Utmost Danger from the Present Destructive, and Unconstitutional Association, for the Preservation of the Game All over England, Which is Proved to Be Illegal* (London, 1757).

[13] *Journals of the House of Commons*, XXXIII, 956–957; *A Letter to Richard Whitworth, Esq.; Member of Parliament for the Town of Stafford; on His Publishing a Bill, Proposed to Be Brought into Parliament, for Amending the Laws Relating to the Game, and Pretended to Be for the Ease and Liberty of the People* (London, 1772). The bill does not appear to have been debated.

Thomas Coke's to increase the stringency of the poaching laws, the House of Commons for the first time (as far as can be ascertained) listened to a general attack on the game system. Charles Turner described the game laws in no uncertain terms as

> "cruel and oppressive on the poor: he said it was a shame that the House should always be enacting laws for the safety of gentlemen; he wished they would make a few for the good of the poor; if gentlemen were not safe in their houses, it was because the poor were oppressed. . . . He had been down in Dorsetshire, and he was shocked to see game there more numerous than the human species. For his own part, he was convinced, that if he had been a common man, he would have been a poacher, in spite of all the laws; and he was equally sure, that the too great severity of the laws was the cause that the number of poachers had increased so much. He earnestly wished to see the game laws revised, and stripped of more than half of their severity; this wish was not an interested one, for every shilling of his estate was in lands only, and he was a sportsman as well as other men." [14]

But Turner's was a voice in the wilderness. And if Richard Sheridan at the time of the enactment of the game tax declared "that it was utterly impossible to frame a rational system of game laws," he did so rather from faction than from conviction, and without any serious intention to secure a reform.[15]

The fact is that, after all, this discontent did not penetrate very deeply. Shortly after the French Revolution had swept away the exclusive sporting rights of the privi-

[14] *Parliamentary Register*, VI (1782), 283; VI, 210.
[15] *Parl. Reg.*, XVI (1784), 404.

leged classes in France,[16] there took place in the House of Commons a debate on the English game laws which reveals clearly how far England fell short of such extreme measures. Charles Fox's friend, John Christian Curwen, a man of "levelling principles," was convinced that the game laws were both unnecessary and in principle "cruel, oppressive, and contrary to the spirit of the constitution."[17] He moved, therefore, on March 4, 1796, that the old qualifications be totally abolished and only the game tax and the laws on closed seasons, reënforced by new restrictions on trespass, be retained.[18] His case he rested simply on justice and reason. The qualifications were not rational, and they could not be enforced. Reform would leave the gentlemen with their game and their sport, much as before, but would remove the injustice.[19]

The House of Commons took the matter, at first, very much as an exercise in dialectics. The conservatives looked askance at the matter, misinterpreted it, and obscured it with suggestions of their own. They especially feared unforeseen consequences. William Windham declared that he did not especially object to game law reform in itself, but English society, in contrast to French, depended upon the residence of the upper classes on their country estates and without the game laws the incentive for doing so would be lacking.

> "And this single circumstance [he observed] might instruct gentlemen, who are fond of changing laws, in how many unforeseen collateral points society might be af-

[16] Ernest Demay, *Recueil des lois sur la Chasse en Europe et dans les Principaux Pays d'Amérique, d'Afrique, et d'Asie* (Paris, 1894), pp. 16–17.

[17] *London Times*, 17 Feb. 1796.

[18] *Parl. Reg.*, XLIV (1796), 239.

[19] *Ibid.*, XLIV, 232; *Parliamentary History of England, from the Earliest Period to the Year 1803* (London, 1806–1820), XXXII, 831–832.

fected by a change, in its direct view, simple and salutary."[20]

Charles Fox, penetrating a little more deeply into the question, pointed out that the game laws, entirely aside from natural rights, on which out of respect for the sensibilities of his hearers he forbore to touch, hardly harmonized even with the principle of property. For some of the most opulent persons, because their wealth did not consist in land, were excluded from sport. He did not hesitate to score the game laws roundly as arbitrary and tyrannous in principle and pernicious in practice because of the animosity which they fostered in their beneficiaries.[21]

The conservative forces were not endangered by these remarks, nor by William Wilberforce's "utmost abhorrence" of the game laws. Windham's smugness, Dudley Ryder's indignation at disrespectful, inconsiderate, and hasty tampering with ancient institutions, Robert Banks Jenkinson's deprecation of any change at such an inappropriate moment — indeed, he made no secret of his desire that "game should not only be preserved, but be preserved expressly for gentlemen" — these were the sentiments of the landed classes. And if the House decided to discuss the question further, there were nevertheless only seventy-seven members present to enter the division lobbies.[22]

Curwen's bill to give effect to his ideas, duly introduced, came up for discussion on April 29th. It had now attracted the attention of the prime minister, probably not so much because it was considered an important question

[20] *Parl. Reg.*, XLIV (1796), 242.

[21] *Parl. Hist.*, XXXII, 842–844.

[22] *Ibid.*, XXXII, 846; *Parl. Reg.*, XLIV (1796), 246–247; *Journals*, LI, 475. Jenkinson's motion for adjournment was rejected by 27 to 50; discussion was resumed on the 11th. See *Gentleman's Magazine*, LXVI, pt. 2 (Oct. 1796), 839; *Sporting Magazine*, VII (March 1796), 290.

in itself, but from fear lest the reforming elements fasten upon it for a serious agitation. William Pitt, therefore, thought the bill should be disposed of as soon as possible, rather than left to "be afloat to agitate men's minds."[23] Once the conservatives mobilized their forces it was, indeed, a simple matter. Curwen, anticipating a mere discussion and germination until the next session, was caught off his guard, had to admit that the bill contained inaccuracies, and was forced back to a defense merely of its principles.[24]

So Fox's twitting the sportsmen with their own frequent violations of the game laws made no impression and the opponents of the bill could describe it as mischievous and nonsensical. "In these times of democratical doctrines," Sir Richard Sutton "did not hesitate to utter the aristocratical opinion that the game laws of this country were founded on good principles, and secured to the landed proprietors that superiority of privilege and of enjoyment which they could best exercise without injuring themselves or interfering with any other pursuits." But it was from Pitt himself that there came the classic defense of privilege which finally and effectively settled the game question for those days. To him, although he would not oppose all modifications, the restrictive principles of the game laws were perfectly sound.

> "In viewing the degree of right to kill game [he said] as enjoyed by different orders of men in society, it was not from partiality, but from reason and reflection, that he would indulge that privilege in a superior degree to the highest orders of the state. From their situation and habits of life, it was an amusement better suited to

23 *Parl. Reg.*, XLIV (1796), 332–333; *Sporting Mag.*, VII (March 1796), 291.
24 *Parl. Reg.*, XLIV (1796), 560.

them than to others, and their gratification claimed, he thought, the first attention. The second class, to whom a participation of this right might properly be given, were the occupiers of land, but in a more limited degree, and only on their own grounds; lest by too liberal an indulgence in this amusement, they might be diverted from more serious and useful occupations. They ought to enjoy this privilege, however, merely as an amusement and by no means on the notion of property; for property was a creature of the law. . . ."[25]

Out of doors this rather academic discussion attracted some attention, but it did not create any great excitement. For the most part the public interest seemed to be chiefly on the side of the sportsmen, who were able to follow the debate in the columns of the *Sporting Magazine*. Lord Verulam expressed in private correspondence his fear of the "introduction of French anarchy"[26] if reform were made; and a savage pamphleteer in *Some Considerations on the Game Laws, suggested by the late motion of Mr. Curwen* rang the changes on the subjects of leveling principles, the rights of property, and the destruction of the constitution. Curwen, it seemed, would place arms in the hands of the whole population, render sedition easy, and undermine laws which required no further justification than that they had been enacted by the ancestors of the gentlemen of England.

On the other side there were only occasional and not very violent expressions of dissatisfaction. At Sheffield an "Association for Preserving the Liberty of the Subject" urged the farmers to destroy game and foxes,[27] and the

[25] *Parl. Hist.*, XXXII, 851.

[26] T. Estcourt to Lord Verulam, 18 and 20 [?] March 1796, Historical Manuscripts Commission, *Report on the Earl of Verulam MSS*, pp. 164–165.

[27] *Sporting Mag.*, VII (March 1796), 330–331.

Committee of Secrecy in 1799 discovered a pronouncement of the London Corresponding Society which attacked the game laws as class legislation:

> ". . . even the farmer, on whose property the game is fed, is robbed of every constitutional right of a Briton, and subjected to the brutality of a bashaw in the form of a Country Justice, from whom there is no appeal." [28]

All this sounds very unreal, as unreal as the whole still-born revolutionary movement of Hardy and Horne Tooke. A pamphleteer in 1797 made some very unpoetical *Poetical Remarks on the Game Laws* and the *Sporting Magazine* published protests against the injustices in the sporting system — almost every one admitted some defects and expressed a willingness to see some not too drastic reforms made — but when Lord Mountmorres in 1789 told Fanny Burney that the revolution would cross the Channel to England with the game laws as a chief stimulus, he was speculating on the basis of an analogy rather than an understanding of the situation. On the contrary, the Parliament showed its views by more severe poaching laws in 1800 and 1802.[29]

The fact is that the time of the Napoleonic wars was a time when the national crisis turned attention outward. In such circumstances men will endure many abuses. After 1815, when peace presented the opportunity and economic depression gave the occasion for a careful examination of the social structure, the game laws, in company with other institutions, became a great grievance. All the discontent

[28] *Parliamentary Papers, 1797–1799, Report of the Committee of Secrecy* (1799), pp. 53–54.

[29] *Sporting Mag.*, XXI (Dec. 1802), 113–114; XXIV (June 1804), 141; cf. Daniel, *Supplement to the Rural Sports*, p. 69; Elie Halévy, *Histoire du Peuple Anglais au XIXe Siècle* (Paris, 1912–1923), I, 224; 39–40 Geo. III, c. 50; 42 Geo. III, c. 107.

and lawlessness which had always accompanied the game system were now increased an hundredfold and the theoretical humanitarian and personal convictions of the iniquity of the game laws, convictions widely but not very earnestly held, became suddenly real and personal. The system, in short, collapsed and reform became imperative.

But it was not the farmer, evidently the chief sufferer during the eighteenth century, who contributed most to bring about this change; nor was it any other rural class. The rapid development of the towns, growing out of the rise of manufactures, with their consequent impulse to commercial activities, on which they depended in a much greater degree than the earlier industries, meant an immense and rapid increase in the urban middle classes. These people were merchants, mill owners, fundholders, bankers, officials; they were wealthy but they were not to any great degree sportsmen and most of them had no intention of leaving their countinghouses, warehouses, and exchanges, for the purpose of shooting the game for dinner. It was not that they had no taste for game. On the contrary, they loved it as much as their country cousins and refused to be without it. Indeed, it was not proper to be without game. No fashionable hostess could think for a moment of serving her dinner in the season without a game course; and no corporation banquet was complete unless it was similarly adorned. Accordingly the urban game eaters went into the market, as they said, with their "silver guns" and came home as well supplied as the squires, if not better. Silver bullets served their purposes much better than lead. "I send my guinea to market," declared one urban buyer, "and that's as sure as a gun."[30]

[30] William Cobbett, *Rural Rides* (Everyman's Library, London, n. d.), I, 174; Daniel, *Supplement*, pp. 403–404.

This practice placed the rapidly growing middle class in direct opposition to the country gentlemen, for in order to prevent poaching, the sale of game had been prohibited since the beginning of the seventeenth century.[31] Unqualified persons had subsequently been forbidden to possess game at all, and special penalties had been laid on poulterers, fishmongers, and public carriers.[32] As a result there grew up a vast illegal traffic; the townsmen would have their game; the ruling class in the interests of sport forbade them. The traffic had been a thriving business in the eighteenth century, often carried on almost openly, and it would appear that it, more than anything else, had occasioned the activity of the Society for the Preservation of the Game.[33] Now, after 1815, it was discovered to be a vast and rapidly growing business.

London was the great center of the traffic. At Leadenhall and Newgate markets the wholesalers exposed the game almost as openly as poultry, taking a double commission of five per cent from the retail poulterers, who with slight competition from fishmongers and hawkers disposed of the contraband commodity to the consumers. The inns, serving game to travelers with their meals, were also great centers of distribution.[34] It was, of course, a seasonal trade, although some game was on the market the year round, and at Lord Mayor's day and Christmas time such quantities came into London that special pro-

[31] 1–2 Jac. I, c. 27, s. 3; cf. the temporary provisions in 32 Hen. VIII, c. 8.

[32] 6 Anne, c. 16; 28 Geo. II, c. 12, s. 1.

[33] See *ante*, pp. 348, 353.

[34] *Parliamentary Papers, 1823, Reports of Committees*, I, *Report from the Select Committee on the Laws Relating to Game* (hereafter referred to as *Rep. Sel. Comm.*, 1823), 6, 7, 16, 18, 33, 34; *Parliamentary Papers, 1828*, VIII, *Report from the Select Committee of the House of Lords, Appointed to Take into Consideration the Laws Relating to Game* (hereafter referred to as *Rep. Sel. Comm.* 1828), 9, 20; *Three Letters on the Game Laws, Pamphleteer*, XI (1818), 447–450 (erroneously paged, should be 347–350).

vision had to be made by the coach companies to carry it. Often the deluge glutted the market and the surplus, in those days of inefficient refrigeration, had to be thrown into the Thames. A wholesaler at Leadenhall testified to selling over 19,000 head of game in a year.[35]

The poulterers understood very well that they were violating the law, and despite the luxury prices which they received they wished to avoid the trade. But when the London Association of Poulterers in 1818 adopted resolutions looking to the enforcement of the law, they discovered that it had fastened too strong a hold upon them. A "parcel of Jews and porters" came into the business, dissension arose among the poulterers, who hesitated to prosecute their fellows, and customers took offense. "Good God, what is the use of your running your head against the wall!" exclaimed one nobleman's servant to the secretary of the poulterer's committee.[36] The tradesmen therefore relapsed, sold more game than ever, and contented themselves with advocating that the game traffic be legalized under a licensing system.

This was only natural. Public opinion simply disregarded the law. Actions brought to enforce the statutes were regarded with abhorrence, and the public informer, surrounded with general hostility, had little opportunity to secure convictions. There was a tacit and universal conspiracy to abide by the old adage, "*Non est inquirendum unde venit venison.*" The law permitted persons qualified to sport to have game in their possession; so it was impossible to enforce it against others. Until 1818, by a curious lapse, the country gentlemen had omitted to lay any

35 *Rep. Sel. Comm.*, 1823, 8, 13, 20, 21, 26; *Rep. Sel. Comm.*, 1828, 26–27, 42–43, 97.

36 *Sporting Mag.*, LII (Sept. 1818), 260; *Rep. Sel. Comm.*, 1823, 11, 18; *Rep. Sel. Comm.*, 1828, 20–21.

penalty on the actual purchase of game, but when this error of logic was corrected it made no difference, for the tradesmen "never sold a bird less."[37] The only results of the new law putting a penalty on purchasers were the unsuccessful attempt of the tradesmen to abandon the game traffic and the immunity which they could in an extremity secure by informing on their customers.

Now, this whole game traffic was built up on a foundation of the most widespread, vicious, and demoralizing thievery in the rural districts. It was the custom of the country gentlemen, as a means of flattering their own vanity, to flatter their friends with presents of game, but this could account for only a small quantity of the thousands of hares and pheasants which poured into London during the game season; and indeed the social distinction which attached to it only rendered it the more necessary for those who had no such resources to make their purchases in the shops. So the town was a market; the squires' preserves were a source of supply. And as the available supply was particularly abundant, poaching became an extremely serious problem.

There had always been poaching, but the nature of the game system at the opening of the nineteenth century aggravated this chronic nuisance into a crying evil. Intensive game preservation, necessary for the battue, increased immensely the game available for poachers, and by concentrating it in small areas facilitated their work. They imitated the policy of their betters and in organized gangs attacked the swarming birds on a large scale. Gang poaching, of course, was not a new phenomenon in 1815, just as intensive preservation was not new, but now the conjunction of that economic distress which caused an outbreak of rick burning and rioting, the sullen discontent

[37] 58 Geo. III, c. 75; *Rep. Sel. Comm.*, 1823, 18.

of many farmers with the game system, the remarkable opportunities for disposing of stolen game in the towns, and the exaggerated ease with which coverts could be raided, all combined to produce an epidemic of poaching and poaching affrays which shocked the country into an acute consciousness of the game evil.

On the night of January 18, 1816, the first of the great game battles took place. Some thirty game watchers of Colonel W. Fitzhardinge Berkeley, Lord Ducie, and Miss Langley, patroling the lands near Berkeley Castle, encountered a band, variously estimated at from fifteen to thirty in number, of poachers. The enemy drew themselves up in military array, advanced to battle, killed a gamekeeper, injured several others, and marched off in true martial spirit, crying "glory! glory!" It was afterwards discovered that the band had assembled at the home of their leader, a supposedly respectable farmer and rate collector, who furnished them with powder and flints for their guns, blacked their faces, and obliged them to take an oath "not to peach on each other." Though the "Bible" which the swearers kissed turned out to have been only a ready reckoner, the affray gave evidence of such discipline and organization that all the forces of law and order were brought to bear on it. Bow Street was called in, and a dozen of the culprits were captured. Two paid for their enterprise with their lives and eight more went off to penal colonies to enjoy a living death.[38]

This affair placed strikingly before the country the problem of game violence which was evident from the opening of the game season in 1815. Near Loughborough

[38] *Sporting Mag.*, XLVIII (April 1816), 25–31; *Rep. Sel. Comm.*, 1823, 38; Berkeley to Lord Sidmouth, 24 Jan., 1816; Berkeley to Home Secretary, 29 Jan., 1816, Home Office Papers (Public Record Office), H. O. 42/148; *Annual Register*, LVIII (1816), 10.

in October 1815 a gang brutally beat a gamekeeper; in Berkshire a gamekeeper shot in cold blood a poacher who refused to halt; in December a gang of seven poachers from Biggleswade murdered a keeper; a battle of keepers and poachers took place in January, 1816, near Ferrybridge in Yorkshire; the vicinity of Downham in Norfolk was terrorized with impunity until a police officer from London broke up the gang there.

Nor was this a temporary disturbance. It continued year after year. Every season witnessed the renewal of the poaching war, the affrays, the inhuman brutality of the poachers, who, knowing that capture meant at least transportation, resisted the keepers with all the ferocity of their kind. And the malefactors were not by any means mere starving laborers, who, indeed, all too often had not the spirit for this hazardous occupation. Of the men tried in the Berkeley Castle case nine were sons of respectable farmers.[39] A gang of forty, who in 1818 all but beat to death a Bedfordshire keeper, was led by a farmer named Field and had the encouragement of several local gentlemen and farmers, enemies of the game system.[40] In the vicinity of large towns the increasing numbers of the factory operatives made it impossible to keep a large head of game.[41]

Despite the violence which he committed, the lives which he took, and the public attention which he forced, the gang poacher probably had less success than the solitary and confirmed transgressor. With his silent lurcher and his nets the individual could slip out at night and bag a few hares or, with the assistance of a friend or two, net a covey of partridges without much danger of detection. A

[39] *Sporting Mag.*, XLVIII (April, 1816), 25.
[40] *Annual Reg.*, LX (1818), 153; *Sporting Mag.*, LIII (Dec. 1818), 136–137.
[41] *Rep. Sel. Comm.*, 1828, 38–39, 82; *Annals of Sporting*, V (March 1824), 164.

snare set in the hedge meant more risk, perhaps, but then the penalty was small. Pheasants perched on the naked branches at night could be dropped easily enough with a gun, though, to be sure, if a "cracking" gun were used instead of an air gun it would be heard by the keeper, and the poacher would have to remove himself quickly from the vicinity.

With the poachers, no doubt, there were many motives. The opportunity for profit, either by using the game directly as food or by disposing of it to the poulterers, must have predominated, but many of the gangsters regarded poaching also as an amusement. It was universally maintained among them that there was nothing wrong in it, no moral transgression. Orator Hunt, in gaol for his ideas, discovered that the poachers and their gaolers alike felt that the game takers had been convicted under unjust laws when in fact they were only doing the farmer a service by relieving him of a nuisance.[42] The fact was that game was an exceedingly precarious form of property and no amount of legislation could give it adequate protection.

What legislation could not do the preservers were determined to do by their own individual efforts. They proposed to defend their legal rights with all their might. Having imbibed with their mothers' milk the doctrines of rural paternalism and the sacredness of property, stocked their manors with expensive pheasants, and hired gamekeepers to watch over the game with fostering care in order that it might be slaughtered wholesale on the battue days, the country gentlemen found themselves totally unable to discover any truth in the absurd theory that man has a natural right to wild animals, or, if he has, to believe that the theory applied to their coverts. The

[42] *Rep. Sel. Comm.*, 1828, 50; but cf. *Rep. Sel. Comm.*, 1823, 43.

higher the preservation, the greater the hatred directed toward the poacher. Sir Walter Scott, in his poem "The Poacher," depicted a loathsome, prowling, lawless creature, who lived by plundering, if not the preserves, then the farmer's barns. He was "the most proper blackguard commonly in his native village," "the very scum of the territory upon which he crawls." Nothing could exceed the squire's indignation when he heard the villagers or saw the newspapers extolling the prowess, uprightness, and enterprise of the hero-poacher.[43]

Game, therefore, was preserved by armed force, and the keepers and watchers stood guard night and day over the coverts. Robert Peel, who declared that he preserved his game in the mildest manner, kept five or six keepers on regular duty and a reserve force of twenty or thirty more who could be called out in an emergency to do battle.[44] Another member of the House of Commons boasted that he had at his disposal a little army recruited from his tenants and laborers.[45] Thus were assembled the forces which struggled for the mastery of the fields and copses, and there ensued the dreadful affrays which disgraced the annals of the day.

"'Seized you the poachers?' said my lord — They fled
And we pursued not — one of them was dead,
And one of us; they hurried through the wood,
Two lives were gone, and we no more pursued.
Two lives of men, of valiant brothers lost!
Enough, my lord, do hares and pheasants cost!"[46]

43 Walter Scott, *Poetical Works* (Edinburgh, 1833), VI, 377–378; see also II, 352, and George Crabbe, *Poetical Works* (London, 1834), VII, 274, note; *Sporting Mag.*, LXXI (Dec. 1827), 93–94.

44 *Parliamentary Debates* (Hansard), ser. 2, XII, 954.

45 *Rep. Sel. Comm.*, 1828, 77–78, 80.

46 "Smugglers and Poachers," *Poems of George Crabbe* (Cambridge, 1905–7), III, 176.

Still, if the sportsmen (in a day when an efficient rural police was unknown) had maintained their forces merely to repel or capture the marauders who were carrying off their expensively raised game they could perhaps not have been greatly blamed. But this was not enough for them. To them the only good poacher was a dead poacher. The keepers all too frequently carried guns on their rounds and showed little compunction in shooting at their enemies, with the result that feuds arose and revenge and counter-revenge embittered the struggle. Dog spears set in the hare runs impaled the pursuing lurchers. Steel mantraps with wide-gaping, ferociously spiked jaws struck terror into the surrounding peasantry and sometimes embraced their offending legs in a terrible grasp.

Spring guns, set to be discharged at poachers who might touch a wire strung along the ground, mangled and killed innocent and guilty alike who wandered into the forbidden coverts. Learned lawyers were to be found who considered it just as murderous in law to kill with a spring gun as to shoot a man in cold blood,[47] but the courts, before legislation upon this subject in 1827, could not be induced to take such a view. A man was fined five pounds for setting a spring gun in his garden to protect it against the depredations of hares, but his offense consisted in the want of a qualification. It remained uncertain whether the killing of men, which, it seemed, required no qualification, was equally illegal.[48]

No one could say, therefore, that the game preservers

[47] Edward Christian, *A Treatise on the Game Laws* (London, 1817; another edition, 1821), pp. 278–279, 281; Edward, Lord Suffield, *Considerations on the Game Laws* (London, 1825), p. 81.

[48] *Annals of Sporting*, V (April 1824), 294; *Sporting Mag.*, L (April 1817), 6 (case of "Jay v. Whitfield"; cf. "Osborne v. Gough" in Christian, *Treatise*, 283); LV (Jan. 1820), 189–194; "Ilott v. Wilkes," Barnewall and Alderson, *Reports*, III, 304–307.

wanted energy in the application of the laws. The poachers swarmed in the parlors of the Justices of the Peace, the Quarter Sessions, the Assizes, where fines, imprisonment, and sentences of transportation were dealt out with a liberal hand. Commitments to gaols under the game laws, if we may believe the very incomplete statistics gathered by the House of Commons, numbered 868 in 1816; 1147 in 1817; 1467 in 1820; convictions under the game laws by Justices of the Peace in years 1827 to 1830 numbered about two thousand a year.[49] It was an age of disorder, no doubt, but all the evidence goes to show that the game system had collapsed. The game, at best a precarious form of property, had been the first objective of hungry and restive men, who found that the towns offered them an unlimited and rapidly growing market. Not jealousy of the farmers on the subject of the privileged system, nor yet desire of the townsmen for participation in sport, had caused the breakdown of the game laws, but the silver bullets of the urban game eaters, who had, thoughtlessly and selfishly, no doubt, but none the less effectively, riddled an old institution until it seemed ready to crumble and collapse forever. For the sporting privileges of the landed classes necessitated that the sale of game be prohibited; and the prohibition had become a mockery of the facts.

In 1815, the anomalies of the game system first aroused serious general attention, and there commenced a steady movement for its radical modification, a movement which

[49] *Parl. Papers*, 1822, XXII, No. 420, "An Account of all commitments . . . under the game laws . . . from the year 1815 . . ."; *Parl. Papers*, 1830–1831, XII, No. 144. For 1827 the convictions before the Justices of the Peace were 2033; for 1828, 1943; for 1829 they were 2123; for 1830 they were 1874; in addition there were convictions in the assize courts of 52, 65, 106, 92 in the respective years. These figures are in some cases very incomplete, as, for example, some Justices of the Peace did not turn in their summary convictions at all.

runs through the reform agitations of the day like a colored thread, always present, highly significant, and hitherto strangely ignored. The outbreak of peace, which produced fewer immediate blessings than a war weary world had anticipated, saw the rehabilitation of the national life while at the same time horror of revolutionary anarchy still remained fresh in the minds of the governing classes. The game law agitation took its place in this pattern of forces.

A *Letter on the Game Laws*, which came from the press in 1815, assailed the system with promising spirit. Claiming to be a member of the privileged gentry, the anonymous author described the game laws as demoralizing the habits of the whole population, and suggested as remedies the legalizing of the sale of game, which would destroy poaching by permitting a legitimate supply of the market, and throwing open the game privilege to tenants on their holdings subject to the permission of their landlords.[50] The next year Joseph Chitty, the prominent scholar of law, who had published a valuable lawyers' manual on the game laws, expressed his general endorsement of these views in his *Observations on the Game Laws*. And Sir William Elford in 1817 fulminated vigorously in *A Few Cursory Remarks on the Obnoxious Parts of the Game Laws*, assailing them as "scandalous and disgraceful," unjust and inexpedient, impossible to enforce or obey.[51]

It was Colonel Wood, member for Brecknockshire, who on May 20, 1816, opened the subject in the House of Commons by moving for a select committee to inquire into

[50] This pamphlet was also reprinted in 1818 with two other letters under the title "Three Letters on the Game Laws," in *The Pamphleteer*, XI.

[51] Joseph Chitty, *Observations on the Game Laws, with Proposed Alterations for the Protection and Increase of Game, and the Decrease of Crimes* (London, 1816; in *The Pamphleteer*, IX, 1817). Sir William Elford, *A Few Cursory Remarks on the Obnoxious Parts of the Game Laws* (in *The Pamphleteer*, X, 19–31).

the propriety of legalizing the sale of game. In the existing situation, with the bloody Berkeley Castle affray to point his case, he had no difficulty in securing what he desired. But the psychology of 1816 was not one of concessions and the committee, admitting the undeniable poaching evil, could only recommend that the farmer be given some interest in the enforcement of the law by making game "the property of the person upon whose lands such game should be found." Even upon this proposal, totally meaningless as it was, they deprecated any action in the near future.

> "The commercial prosperity of the country [ran the report of the committee], the immense accumulation of personal property, and the consequent habits of luxury and indulgence, operate as a constant excitement to their [the game laws'] infraction, which no legislative interference that Your Committee can recommend appears likely to counteract."

In short, they confessed in the same breath full knowledge and complete incompetence.[52]

It suited the genius of the country gentlemen rather to enact a new law imposing the penalty of seven years' exile for the first offense of night poaching.[53] Colonel Wood in 1817 proposed a bill for legalizing the sale of game but he only afforded the game preservers an opportunity for a parade of their ideas. George Bankes, sponsor of the poaching act of the previous year, explained that the game law system "was three hundred years old, and therefore was supported by the wisdom and experience of their ancestors. . . ." "This was not the time," Lord Deerhurst warned, "to disgust resident gentlemen." "Was it . . .

[52] *Parl. Papers*, 1816, IV, no. 504, 1–3.

[53] 56 Geo. III, c. 130. Romilly protested but secured no material alteration in a new measure of 1817, 57 Geo. III, c. 90.

a time," asked Curwen, "to disgust the country?"[54] The "resident gentlemen," however, were not so much interested at this moment in the country as in logical consistency and they decided that since the law punished — or at least prohibited — the sale of game, it ought to do likewise for its purchase. Bankes' measure of 1818, duly enacted, imposed accordingly a penalty of five pounds for each head of game bought, whether the purchaser were qualified to kill game or not. This was logic, but it was not statesmanship; the law was unenforceable and the game traffic went on uninterrupted.[55] There was one flaw in this prohibitory legislation; it omitted to abolish the Englishman's appetite for game.

At last in 1819, despite the unrelieved discouragement which they had received, the unbroken front of the conservatives, both Whig and Tory, and the uncertain passions of the Peterloo year, the reformers brought forward a full and thorough measure for discussion. Introduced by Thomas Brand,[56] it proposed to abolish all qualifications and all restrictions on the game traffic, declared game the property of those on whose land it should be found, and retained those parts of the old game system, the poaching laws, the game taxes, the closed seasons, which were not vitiated by the principle of exclusion. Brand made out a complete and unanswerable case for his bill. He spoke of the injustice of the qualifications, the failure to enlist the interest of the farmers, without which the game laws could never be enforced, and the consequent terrible poaching evil, and concluded that the system was "the best and shortest way to demoralize a whole people."[57]

[54] *Parl. Deb.*, ser. 1, XXXV, 878, 921–925; *Sporting Mag.*, L (June 1817), 111.

[55] See *ante*, p. 363. The act is 58 Geo. III, c. 75.

[56] Later Lord Dacre.

[57] *Parl. Deb.*, ser. 1, XXXIX, 937–943.

That the case was unanswerable did not prevent the conservatives from answering it — after their fashion. They protested against untried theories, predicted that poaching would be unrestrained, and dreaded lest the yeomen should become sportsmen and lose their "respectful submission and manly dependence on the laws." George Bankes fell back on the resident gentlemen theory and prophesied that "if any disgust were excited by the abolition of laudable country amusements, the most dreadful results might ensue. The country," he urged, "would be impoverished, and that indeed would end in the total demoralization of the inhabitants of the provinces." In the face of such an attitude the reformers could accomplish but little. It did no good for Colonel Wood to point out that gentlemen resided in those parts of the country where game was not preserved, as well as where it was; nor to suggest that they turn to fox hunting, not subject to qualification laws, as a single fox could amuse hundreds of gentlemen while hundreds of pheasants were required for a single shooter. The bill was finally thrown out by a large majority.[58]

Exhausted by their efforts and discouraged by ill success, the advocates of a change lost hope and the question receded from the public attention. In 1821, when Lord Cranborne moved for a game law committee it was apparent that interest was lacking.[59] But the question did not solve itself and after the reconstruction of the Cabinet in 1822 it came to the fore once again, Cranborne's motion for a committee in 1823 being received with a new respect. Robert Peel, who had succeeded Lord Sidmouth as Home Secretary, offered a carefully qualified and cautious en-

[58] On the report stage, the vote being 119–59; the second reading had passed by 110–83. *Ibid.*, XXXVIII, 541; XXXIX, 945, 1078–1090; XL, 374–383.

[59] *Ibid.*, ser. 2, V, 38–42.

dorsement, accepting the need for inquiry but upholding the principle of exclusion. He did not welcome a committee, but neither did he reject it; the government had never before taken such a view.[60]

The committee, confining its investigation chiefly to the commerce in game, exposed the whole traffic to the view of the public, which, now that a deluge of evidence from police officers, porters of inns, and poultry tradesmen poured forth from the committee, no longer had the slightest excuse for refusing to recognize that the silver gun had mortally wounded the old game system. Nevertheless the committee blindly insisted that the only reform necessary was to legalize the sale of game under careful restrictions without in the least touching the qualifications.[61] Cranborne's bill to give effect to these views had Peel's support. But its excessive moderation insured it a double attack; that unblushing Tory, Sir John Shelley, declared it would lead to the destruction of field sports, while Lord Brougham denounced it as entrenching the worst parts of the game system. The cross fire was fatal and the bill was ultimately rejected.[62]

So the weary struggle dragged on through the twenties, the reformers urging their measures year after year with relentless emphasis on the demoralization which arose out of poaching, the complete ineffectiveness of the restrictions on the commerce in game, and the injustice, as well as impolicy, of excluding many of the most powerful and wealthy subjects of the King from the right to kill game. For a time the leadership of James Stuart Wortley, a large landholder of Yorkshire, a game preserver, and a

60 *Ibid.*, ser. 2, VIII, 542–543.

61 *Rep. Sel. Comm.*, 1823, 4–5.

62 *Parl. Deb.*, ser. 2, IX, 646–647; *Journals of the House of Commons*, LXXVIII, 439.

member of Lord Cranborne's committee of 1823,[63] seemed about to lead the cause to success. Robert Peel, the Home Secretary, already busy at the acquisition of his ultimate enviable reputation for inconsistency, became converted and gave expression to one of the strongest arguments for reform.

> "If laws stand upon our statute-book [he declared] which are practically evaded and violated every day, this is of itself a sufficient reason for their repeal. I will ask, whether these laws are not perfectly inoperative — whether they are not constantly, notoriously, and openly violated in every great town — and whether it is possible in the present state of society, that it should be otherwise? . . . If the law really prevented the sale of game there would be a ground for objecting to an alteration of it; but as it is notorious that it is wholly inoperative, this is one of the strongest grounds for its repeal."

And if the erratic Home Secretary dashed all hopes by starting sudden doubts in his own mind in 1824,[64] his hearty support in the following year carried Stuart Wortley's bill through the Commons and up to the Lords, where it encountered a determined and fatal opposition.[65] Stuart Wortley then entered the House of Lords as Baron Wharncliffe and carried on the struggle there. A success of no mean proportions was secured in 1827, although without Wharncliffe's support, when the murderous spring guns were prohibited as a means of preserving game.[66]

[63] His full name was James Archibald Stuart Wortley Mackensie. *Dictionary of National Biography*, XIX, 110.

[64] *Parl. Deb.*, ser. 2, X, 912–919, 1420; XI, 956–959; cf. X, 225, 267; XI, 1097, 1199–1201.

[65] *Ibid.*, XII, 953–956; XIII, 300–307, 450–453.

[66] 7–8 Geo. IV, c. 18.

The next year another select committee convinced the Lords of the necessity of reform, as that of 1823 had converted the Commons,[67] and Lord Suffield could congratulate the noble gentlemen on their generosity in giving up voluntarily their exclusive game privileges, while Lord Wharncliffe a bit incongruously imparted to them the secret that they were not giving up anything substantial, as there would under the new arrangements be more game and more sport than ever. But it was now the House of Commons which proved remiss, allowing the session to come to an end without action, perhaps because of the more engrossing religious controversies of the day.[68] Consequently the only advance which could be achieved for the time being was a new poaching act which modified the barbarous harshness of the act of 1817 and deferred the penalty of transportation for night poaching to the third offense.[69]

Only the violence of the political quarrels of the day prevented some reform action in 1829.[70] Public opinion had, indeed, now come round to a genuine demand, not for a mere legitimation of the commerce in game, but for a thorough revision of the whole game system. Support by Lord Wharncliffe, an influential and telling pamphlet by Lord Suffield, devastating articles in the *Edinburgh Review* by Sydney Smith, the acquiescence of Peel, rendered reform respectable and imperative.[71] The *Sporting*

67 *Rep. Sel. Comm.*, 1828, 3–5, 57–59, 62–65.

68 *Parl. Deb.*, ser. 2, XIX, 280–282, 287.

69 9 Geo. IV, c. 69; see *ante*, note 53.

70 *Parl. Deb.*, ser. 2, XX, 369–370; XXI, 1247–1249, 1252.

71 Suffield, *Considerations on the Game Laws* (London, 1825). The *Edinburgh Review* articles, all of which would seem to be by Sydney Smith, are as follows: "The Game Laws," in vol. XXXI (March 1819), 294–309; "Spring Guns and Man Traps," vol. XXXV (March 1821), 123–134; "Man Traps and Spring Guns," vol. XXXV (July 1821), 410–421; "Game Laws," vol. XXXIX (Oct. 1823), 43–55; "Lord Suffield on the Game Laws," vol. XLIII (Nov. 1825), 248–262; "The Game Laws," vol. LXIX (March 1829), 55–102.

Magazine, organ of the sportsmen themselves, discussed reforms receptively. Chief Justice Best at the Northampton Assizes in 1829 informed a jury of his sincere wish for a speedy change in a code which had produced so much crime.[72]

Many of the advocates of reform were themselves sportsmen, who had the wit to see that no great harm could come to any reasonable amount of sport. Suffield was one of the greatest preservers of Norfolk. But others clung to privilege for its own sake and cried out at the dangers to be feared from its abolition. Charles James Apperley, the famous "Nimrod," painted the game system in glowing colors and warned against the friction among landholders, the increase of poaching, and the general demoralization to be expected. In particular he could not bear the thought of landless men having game and gentlemen selling it;

> "in God's name [he exclaimed] don't oblige an English gentleman to turn poulterer, and make a tradesman-like bartering of what he has been so long accustomed to look upon as merely objects of his amusement; and induce him to sell what he had before so much pleasure in giving!"[73]

Blackwood's Magazine, as usual, sounded the tocsin of "the sacred, indestructible rights of property." The movement for game law reform, it declared in 1827, not altogether without justification, was part of a general attack on the aristocracy, "the object of which is to degrade it from its place in society, and to accom-

[72] *Sporting Mag.*, LXXI (April 1828), 418–425; LXXII (May, June 1828), 54–67, 81–110; LXXIV (May 1829), 60. See also *Observations on the Game Laws* (by Philanthropos, London, 1827).

[73] *Sporting Mag.*, LXVI (Aug. 1825), 300–301; see also numbers for Nov. and Dec. 1825 and March 1827.

plish its virtual annihilation as a separate estate of the realm. . . ."[74]

But such ranting could not stave off action. Even the press of business, although crowding out a game bill in 1830, could not prevent the Whig ministry in the next year from proceeding with determination. The Tories attempted to save what they could from the general wreck and on November 19, 1830, three days after the resignation of the Duke of Wellington's fatal ministry, the Marquess of Chandos brought in a bill which, for all its radical revision of the game system, still retained low game qualifications and therefore the principle of exclusion. It would have suited well enough, perhaps, if it could have been enacted in 1816, when the country gentlemen were not prepared for any concessions at all, but it did not satisfy the reforming temper of 1831. For the government now was prepared to make a game reform of its own. Lord Althorp, leading in the House of Commons, assured the House that "the government would readily support any measures that could improve the present system." Lord John Russell insisted on the necessity of doing something "to clear out this blot on the country, and something to reconcile the people of England to the landed aristocracy. . . ."[75]

In these circumstances, unable to reach any agreement with the Marquess of Chandos, the Whig government introduced a radical game bill on February 15, 1831. It ran a long, dreary, and sometimes perilous course through the greater part of the year, passing safely by the shoals of Peel's warning — after fifteen years of public attention — against undue haste, and the rocks of the Duke of Wellington's naïve assurance that gentlemen would cease

74 "The Game Laws," *Blackwood's Mag.*, XXII (Dec. 1827), 644, 649–650.

75 *Parl. Deb.*, ser. 3, I, 811–812.

to spend money or employ gamekeepers in the country unless they retained their exclusive rights, until at last it reached its harbor in September and became law.

By the Game Act of 1831,[76] exclusive sporting privileges were sunk almost without a trace. The remains of the old special franchises, already nearly extinct, were left untouched, and lords of manors retained their rights of appointing gamekeepers, but the qualifications for killing game were abolished completely. Game, defined as hares, pheasants, partridges, grouse, heath or moor game, black game, and bustards, might be killed by any one supplied with a properly stamped license, subject only to the necessary police restrictions regarding trespass, poaching, and closed seasons. All the massed confusion of the old game acts was removed at a single stroke, only the laws of 1827 and 1828 regarding spring guns and night poaching and the game certificate legislation were retained, and the rest of the game system was consolidated into a single and comparatively simple statute.

The sale of game became legal, sportsmen supplied with the proper game certificates being authorized to sell it to dealers licensed by the Justices of the Peace. Thus the silver gun proved triumphant and the game traffic restrictions, without which privilege in sport could not exist, were swept away. This, then, was the heart of the reform, from which, despite the surface appearances to the contrary, the abolition of the qualifications followed as a necessary consequence. The Game Act of 1831, like the Parliamentary reform of 1832, was essentially a victory of the urban middle class in a struggle with the old ruling landed classes.

Nothing demonstrates this fact more clearly than the fate of the farmer. For while he was given the theoretical

[76] 1–2 Wm. IV, c. 32.

right to kill game, supposing he could afford to purchase the rather expensive game certificate, he received very little besides. Whatever the urban middle class might think about aristocratic pretensions they had the greatest respect for the rights of property, and the Game Act very carefully guaranteed to the owners of land the power to reserve to themselves the right of killing game on their own land.[77] The tenants, who composed most of the farmers of England, therefore discovered that as far as concerned their crops and the actual land in their occupation, the new law was a very empty thing. The battues, the excessive preservation of game, and the devastation of crops continued unabated, and indeed increased. Phoenix-like the sporting system arose again out of its ruins. To please the middle classes privilege had been abolished, but for the farmer it continued as lusty as ever.[78]

[77] Section 8; but cf. section 7.

[78] On this phase of the subject see an article by the present writer: "The Attack on the English Game Laws in the Forties," *Journal of Modern History*, IV (March 1932), 18–37.

CHESTER KIRBY.

FROM HUSKISSON TO PEEL: A STUDY IN MERCANTILISM

In 1828, after several years of vigorous effort in renovating the commercial and colonial aspects of English policy, William Huskisson left the Board of Trade. During the remaining two years of Tory rule other issues held the stage. For eleven years thereafter, the period of the Whig administrations of Grey and Melbourne, the mercantile structure, unaffected by any changes of major importance, remained substantially as Huskisson had left it. It has been the custom for historians to pass over this period with the casual remark that the Whigs were interested not in finance but in other and more pressing subjects of reform. This explanation seems unsatisfactory and merits examination.

Mercantilism for the first empire, which nature had made almost self-sufficient, was perhaps not too illogical, but the efforts made after 1783 to set up a new self-contained British world were foredoomed to failure. After the American Revolution, the nice adjustment of food-producing units to units of tropical products, and of both to the industrial fabric of the mother country, was broken, and the remaining North American colonies were either too poor in raw material or too unfavorably situated to take the place of those that had gone. It was the historic function of the years 1783–1820 to prove, first of all to the "intelligentsia" of Great Britain, secondly to some of her statesmen and "practical business men" and finally to none of her North American colonists, that the task of reconstituting the profitable and almost self-contained world of the eighteenth century was an impossible one.

Nevertheless, it required the full length of this term of thirty-seven years for the arguments of the intellectuals and the logic of circumstances to make any breach of consequence in the walls of the old fortress. In other words, rules and regulations, bounties, prohibitions, preferences and the vast structure of the Navigation Acts, save for incidental changes here and there, stood in 1820 much as they had done in the years previous to the Revolution. If, beyond the letter, there had been any change in the spirit of mercantilism, it had been in the direction of a more rigid enforcement of acts and regulations.

Finally a time favorable for change arrived. Under the pressure of commercial depression, the economist Thomas Tooke in 1820 had succeeded in having the merchants of London sponsor the well-known petitions which he drew up pressing for inquiry into the state of trade. Consequently, these petitions were then presented to Parliament by Alexander Baring,[1] of the famous City firm of that name. In response, both Lords and Commons set up committees whose reports may be regarded as the point of departure for the ensuing period of reform. By 1828, the structure of mercantilism had undergone major alterations.[2]

Yet after Huskisson's enactments, much of the original mercantile edifice was still visible. The basic principle of the old colonial system remained untouched. In all the reforms there had not been the slightest suggestion that the colonies should be left to themselves to work out the regulation of their own trade. Indeed, the very essence of the reforms lay in their constituting a sort of Imperial trading code, enlightened, it is true, but resting as firmly as ever upon the central authority. The audacious suggestion

[1] Later, first Lord Ashburton.

[2] For description of these, see A. Brady, *William Huskisson and Liberal Reform* (Oxford, 1928), ch. IV.

that the regulation of the empire's trade could and possibly should be conducted from points other than London was yet to be made.

In detail, the infinite complexities of the customs administration, with its plethora of forms, fees and officials, still remained, all carefully controlled, as before, from London. The East India Company still monopolized the tea trade and colonial vessels were not allowed to trade to ports within its preserves. The baffling mysteries of regulation governing the trade between the British North American provinces, the British West Indies and the United States were almost as impenetrable as ever. More especially, save for the slight reduction of the timber preference in 1821, the old preferential duties on timber and sugar, the most conspicuous parts of the mercantile structure, remained untouched. Other preferences, such as that on Cape of Good Hope wines, were growing up. The Corn Laws, the third member of the great trinity of prohibitions, continued, and their effects were almost as hard on the colonies as on foreign countries or the English poor. Colonial tariffs made at Westminster invariably gave exports from Great Britain preference in the colonies over those from other countries.[3] Not until Sir Robert Peel's great ministry of 1841–1846 were further advances made.

It was not from want of trying that the Whigs failed to carry further the task of simplifying the Empire's fiscal structure and of approaching what to a considerable section of the party was a great ideal, free trade. During their period of office the subject was under frequent discussion and various attempts at additional reforms were made. Except for the abolition of the East India Company's monopoly none of them succeeded.

[3] In some cases, a substantial preference was given, in the majority only a moderate one. The range was from 7 per cent to 30 per cent.

These attempts chiefly took the form of attacks on the differential duties on foreign timber. The differential duties on sugar went untouched and the corn laws were not interfered with. The day-to-day administrative regulation of colonial trade, even in very minute particulars, carried on by the Colonial Office, was never even a subject for discussion in Parliamentary circles.[4] The general principle of centralized control of all Imperial trade was seldom put in question.[5] But the differential duties on timber were constantly under fire. Consequently the remainder of this essay will be confined to a discussion of the timber duties, as illustrating practically all of the points at issue in the fiscal controversies of the period and as much the most striking examples of post-revolutionary mercantilism. These duties in their extreme form had come into existence during the Napoleonic wars, when Napoleon's control of the continent had threatened to interfere with Britain's supply of ship-timber. In order to encourage colonial production, heavy duties had been imposed on wood of all sorts coming from foreign countries. "Foreign countries" meant in practice the countries about the Baltic Sea, Russia, Prussia, Sweden and Norway. After the war, the vested interests concerned in the importation of colonial timber were powerful enough to prevent much interference with the duties. Save for a

[4] For examples of this and the endless negotiation and bickering between colonial and home authorities, reference may be made to the running controversy that went on between the Legislature of Nova Scotia and the Colonial Office on such matters as rates of Imperial duties on particular commodities, payment of customs officials, the opening or shutting of "out-ports," the question of free ports, etc. See *Journals* of Assembly, Nova Scotia, March 10, 29, 1834, Jan. 2, 6, 1835, App. 1 to *Journals* of 1835 (Mr. Stewart's report of his interview with the Imperial authorities on the subject of free ports), Feb. 12, 1836, also Geo. R. Young, *Letters on the Treaties with France and America as regards their "Rights of Fishery," with a General View of Colonial Policy* (Halifax, 1834).

[5] Those who challenged this never put forward the alternative of decentralization and local control but that of the dissolution of the Empire.

slight reduction in 1821 they continued to stand unaltered, affording timber from the colonies protection in the British market to a rate of some 275 per cent.

The Whigs began their attack shortly after assuming office on November 19, 1830. In December of that year the word went round that the timber duties were in danger. Sir Howard Douglas, who had just ended a term as Governor of New Brunswick, immediately wrote in protest to Under-Secretary Hay, predicting the ruin of the North American colonies and their eventual loss to the Empire, should the protection on their great staple be withdrawn.[6] Word seems to have crossed the ocean at about the same time, for in January, 1831, petitions from the colonial legislatures began to be drafted. The two houses of Nova Scotia maintained that without the timber trade, which they took for granted would end with the repeal of the acts imposing the duties, the colonies would not be able to buy British manufactures. The fisheries would also be ruined, for the fishermen were dependent on the cheap salt that the timber ships brought out at low freights. They were not slow to evoke their rights as "children" and the terms *justice*, *parental regard*, etc., were prominent in the document.[7]

A joint petition from both houses of the legislature of Upper Canada[8] used much the same kind of argument. There were vested interests which would lose their capital if the trade were destroyed. The trade would cease because freights from Canada to England were so much higher than from the Baltic countries and wages of British seamen were higher than those of Baltic sailors. Emigration would stop because the timber ships would no longer

6 Canadian Archives, "Q" series, vol. 195–A, Howard Douglas to Hay, Dec. 24, 1830 (hereafter cited as Q, with volume number appended).

7 Nova Scotia, *Journals of Assembly*, Jan. 5, 1831.

8 Q356, p. 69, Feb. 17, 1831.

afford cheap passages. Similar petitions came in from various localities in the colonies, most of them centres of the timber industry.[9] The colonial newspapers joined in the outcry, the Montreal *Gazette* and the Quebec *Mercury* being particularly active in their protests.[10]

Meanwhile in England, Grey's ministry was proving so weak that Greville freely predicted a short life for it.[11] The Chancellor of the Exchequer, Lord Althorp, though popular, was no speaker and was not a man of business. He appears to have relied very fully on his young familiar, Charles Poulett Thomson, whose family had been engaged in the Baltic timber business for generations and who might therefore reasonably have been expected to have decided views on the unwisdom of the preference to British North America. Thomson was also the associate of Jeremy Bentham, Charles Villiers, Nassau Senior, and other intellectuals.[12] While not a Philosophical Radical himself, he was closely associated with that group and his ideas were hardly distinguishable from theirs. Greville speaks jeeringly of the consequences "if Althorp and Thomson are to goven England,"[13] and declares that Thomson furnished Althorp's ideas.[14]

Greville declares that not a soul knew of the new ministry's budget proposals before Althorp introduced them.[15] He cannot then have been aware that, for nearly two months before they were introduced, one of the chief

[9] Q356, p. 156.

[10] See Quebec *Mercury*, Jan. 15, 1831; Montreal *Gazette*, Jan. 20, Feb. 17, March 17, April 14, etc., 1831.

[11] C. C. F. Greville, *Journal of the Reigns of George IV and William IV*, (New York, 1875), I, 455–456.

[12] Greville, *op. cit.*, p. 442. See Adam Shortt, *Lord Sydenham* in *Makers of Canada* series (Toronto, 1908), p. 12; G. B. Scrope, *Memoirs of Charles, Lord Sydenham* (London, 1843), *passim.*

[13] Greville, *op. cit.*, p. 454.

[14] *Ibid.*

[15] *Ibid.*, p. 453.

among them had been the subject of attack on both sides of the ocean. Two weeks before the budget was brought down, a correspondent of the Montreal *Gazette*, writing from London, predicted a decrease in the Canadian preference of twenty shillings, which was within five shillings of the actual proposal.[16] In England, Douglas followed up his letter to the Colonial Office with a pamphlet in the best mercantilistic tradition.[17] It was frankly non-economic in tenor. If Britain wished to continue to be a great power, she must have colonies and she could not long retain her colonies without the commercial tie, which would be snapped by wiping out the timber trade. The colonies would then become either independent or of no importance. The great "nursery for seamen" which the timber shipping provided would be lost. Letters to the same effect began to appear in the English press. It was maintained that a reduction in the preference would inflict on holders of stocks of timber in Quebec, owners of the fixed capital in the trade and the owners of timber ships, especially those of the poorer sort, heavy and unjust losses.[18]

Althorp brought down his budget on February 11.[19] Two hundred and sixty-three articles were to be freed from taxation and the loss made up by new duties. Among these, those on timber were the most prominent. He proposed to take five shillings off the duty on European timber, bringing it down to fifty shillings a load and to increase that on colonial timber from ten shillings to twenty shillings. Thus there would still be a differential

[16] Montreal *Gazette*, March 17, 1831, London letter of Jan. 27.

[17] *Considerations on the Value and Importance of the British North American Provinces*, 1831.

[18] See two letters to the *Mercantile Journal*, Feb. 26 and March 5, 1831, reprinted as a pamphlet.

[19] In this essay all accounts of Parliamentary proceedings, extracts from speeches, etc., are based on Hansard. It has not been thought necessary to give references in each case.

of thirty shillings a load,[20] which was equal to half as much again as the purchase price at Quebec.

The proposal was vigorously opposed by members for the city of London and other commercial districts.[21] Althorp was accused by a member representing the West Indian interest[22] of taking a "new view of the policy of this country as regards its colonies . . . the first step to a radical change of policy." Alderman Thompson stood up for the shipping interest.[23] Mr. Spring-Rice and Mr. Poulett Thomson made the principal speeches in defence of the plan. Spring-Rice denied that the whole budget was anti-colonial. He agreed that it was the duty of government to view the colonies as wholly dependent upon the motherland and since they were not represented, to extend to them "a larger sympathy." But this must be tempered with discretion and he felt that the change would not injure Canada, since it had often been declared that the timber trade was too precarious to be of any real benefit to her. Poulett Thomson at this juncture confined himself to practical arguments minimizing the probable injury to shipping and it was not until later in the debate that he put the case in academic terms that must have delighted the orthodox *laissez-faire* economists of the day. In his speech of March 18, he was to say that "if the country took the ships engaged in the colonial timber trade, paid the owners their freight and kept them sailing about the Atlantic doing nothing, the country would be a gainer." This sort of talk was to be remembered against him when,

[20] A load was fifty cubic feet. The average price in Quebec was about 20 shillings. Freight was about 30 shillings. The selling price in England was about 100 shillings, so that all the duty was added to the cost.

[21] Aldermen Waithman and Thompson, Mr. G. Robinson and others.

[22] Mr. K. Douglas.

[23] He also objected to another of the budget proposals, the equalization of the duty on wines from the Cape of Good Hope with that on wines from France.

eight years later, he was appointed Governor-General of British North America.

The budget debate was adjourned until March 15. In the interval, opposition appears to have been organized. Henry Warbuton, M.P., member of an old Baltic timber firm, one of Althorp's confidants, a friend of Ricardo's, and a *laissez-faire* doctrinaire of the most uncompromising type, had already been singled out as perhaps the most dangerous enemy of the colonial preference. "His speeches go directly to annihilate" the Canadian trade.[24] But he was only one individual. It was in organized opinion that trust was to be placed. "They seem to think that the shipowners' voice will be most attended to."[25]

As might have been expected, on the resumption of the debate, petitions were presented from the "Merchants of the City and shipowners connected with the port of London," from a similar body in Glasgow and another in Dublin.[26] Speeches in the debate went over familiar ground. Those supporting the budget resolutions either libelled Canadian timber by asserting its worthless quality, proved to their own satisfaction that the trade was morally defenceless because of the anti-social nature of the lumberjack's calling, refuted the idea that it was useful for carrying out emigrants cheaply, denied that the shipping engaged would suffer, or stated a clear economic case, which, as the quotation from Thomson given above shows, it was easy enough to do. Those defending the trade affirmed the opposite side of all these points, asked if Britain were once more to make herself dependent on foreign supplies, stressed the value of the timber trade in maintaining

[24] Quebec *Official Gazette*, quoted in Montreal *Gazette*, Jan. 1, 1831.

[25] Liverpool letter, Feb. 16, to Montreal *Gazette*, April 14, 1831.

[26] Before the committee of 1835, Henry Bliss, provincial agent, stated that he had received in 1831, too late for presentation, a whole boxful of petitions from the colonies, all protesting against any reduction in duties.

large numbers of seamen under rigorous conditions, or waved the flag in a style familiar enough to anyone who has ever argued the question of free trade versus protection.

Three days later, March 18, Althorp gave ground. He had decided that there was no need for immediate additional revenue, so that he was free to leave the Canadian duty unraised and to lower the Baltic duty. This he proposed to do in three successive years, beginning on January 1, 1832, the total reduction to be fifteen shillings. Poulett Thomson followed his patron and this time suggested it would be cheaper for England to buy the colonial timber ships and burn them and their cargoes on the shore rather than to go on buying colonial timber at the excessive rates imposed by the differential duties.

Althorp's change of front seems to have tripped him up. Two opposition front-benchers, Peel and Herries, intervened to counsel delay, and Peel added that Althorp seemed to have been so well satisfied with the budget he had made for 1831 that he proceeded to make one for 1832 too. Peel is credited by Thomas Tooke [27] with having defeated the proposal. Whether that be so or not — and Peel's part in the debate was small — defeated it was by 236 to 190. It is more probable that other factors were responsible. Among these were the savage attacks of the representatives of the ship-owners, the hasty and amateurish nature of the budget, which had alienated the City,[28] and, more particularly, the general political situation. Then too, the ministry had cut a poor figure in debate, having no one who could speak very effectively on such subjects.[29] When the actual defeat came, the vote was taken not so much on the concrete proposal of reduction in

[27] See his *History of Prices*, II, 343.

[28] Greville, *op. cit.*, p. 453.

[29] Thomson, an effective though by no means a brilliant speaker, was a junior.

the differential duties as on the greater issues of the day. The Reform bill was the measure that displaced all others in interest and any blow that the opposition could give to the ministry would make its chances so much poorer. Hence the defeat of the timber duties proposal, which extended a ridiculous and costly tariff arrangement for another eleven years, was an incident and can hardly be taken seriously as an expression of considered opinion on the subject.[30]

The remainder of 1831 and virtually the whole of 1832 were taken up with Reform. In 1833 the first reformed Parliament met and its attention was concentrated on the emancipation of the slaves, poor law reform and the other important measures of the day. But this period from the meeting of the first reformed Parliament in February, 1833, to the resignations of Grey and Althorp in July, 1834, represented the summit of Whig constructive statesmanship and it would have been surprising if fiscal reform had not been thought about again.

While the Chancellor announced that no change would be made at the time, though he refused to pledge himself for the future,[31] there was a persistent rumour during the winter of 1833–34 to the effect that a new attack on the duties, again led by Poulett Thomson, was in contemplation.[32] This brought on another outburst of petitioning from various colonial bodies with reiterations of the con-

[30] See Greville, *op. cit.*, pp. 456, 457, 467. It is amusing to find the Colonial Secretary assuring colonial governors in the very midst of the debate that there was no intention of altering the timber duties to the detriment of the colonies, and then shortly afterward, but before the defeat of the proposals, sending out a circular letter to them defending the "late" decrease of duty on Baltic timber! See Goderich to Maitland, March 7, 1831, and Goderich's circular letter of April 1, 1831.

[31] Feb. 21, 1834.

[32] Montreal *Gazette*, April 1, 1834, quoting the Newcastle (England) *Journal* of some weeks before.

ventional arguments against reducing the duties.[33] But the danger passed and then towards the end of the Parliamentary session came the resignation of Grey and Althorp.[34] The reconstruction of the ministry under Melbourne and its dismissal by William IV quickly followed.[35]

Peel's first ministry[36] never had a majority. Consequently, its achievements consisted in marking time. When Melbourne came back, he promoted Poulett Thomson to the position of President of the Board of Trade, Mr. Spring-Rice becoming Chancellor of the Exchequer. Almost at once Thomson began another attack on the anachronism of the trade system.

This attack took the form of a committee to inquire into the whole question of the timber trade. Thomson had apparently made a "window-dressing" motion for a committee even while Peel was still in office,[37] and now, almost immediately after assuming office he made a declaration that he would try to have the timber duties equalized.[38] He followed this up with his proposal for a committee, which, presented by him as President of the Board of Trade, was of course accepted by the House.[39]

This committee sat from June 6 until August 14, 1835, when it reported. It heard thirty witnesses (some of them at great length) representing every aspect of the timber trade of Great Britain and most sects of economists.

33 See Quebec Committee of Trade, Memorial of Jan. 27, 1834, in Q215, p. 72; Petition of the Merchants of Montreal to the House of Commons, in Montreal *Gazette*, March 4; Joint Address of the Council and the Assembly of Nova Scotia to the King, March 8, in *Journals* of Assembly, Nova Scotia, etc.

34 July 7.

35 Dismissed, Nov. 15, 1834.

36 Nov. 15, 1834–April 8, 1835.

37 March 15, as reported in the Montreal *Gazette*, May 2, 1835.

38 Reported in the Quebec *Gazette*, June 20, 1835.

39 The committee was ordered June 1 and named June 6.

Its proceedings are embalmed in a stout volume of the Parliamentary papers for 1835.[40] They constitute a mine of information on one of the great staple trades of the time.

The membership of the committee reflected its origins. Thomson "has named such a committee as will surely swamp your colonial protection. It is a committee of the philosophers. . . ."[41] There were thirty-two members. Of these two were ministers, the Chancellor of the Exchequer and Thomson, the latter being chairman, two were Conservative leaders (Peel and Herries), one was a former Whig in process of becoming a Conservative (Sir James Graham), one was the highest of the high Tories (Sir R. Vyvyan), and at least eight, not including Thomson, were either Philosophical Radicals or persons of doctrinaire free trading views.[42] The rest belonged to no well-defined group. Mr. Bingham Baring (afterwards second baron Ashburton), the representative of the great City house of that name, was a moderate Whig. G. R. Robinson, chairman at Lloyd's was connected with a colonial firm and "a gentleman who has earned the distinction of being Colonial Member in the House of Commons."[43] William Smith O'Brien was an Irish Nationalist, Viscount Lowther, a respectable aristocrat of the minor ministerial type, Alderman Thompson, the representative of the City of London. The others were obscure private members. The report of such a body (as indeed the reports of all Parliamentary committees named by the government of the day and weighted with a party majority) was a foregone conclusion. Its interest therefore lies, not in the report, but in the evidence and the manner of taking it.

[40] *Parl. Papers*, 1835, XIX, 519.

[41] London Letter, June 6, in Montreal *Gazette*, July 23, 1835.

[42] William Ewart, Benjamin Hawes, William Hutt, Edward Strutt, Charles A. Tulk, Henry Warburton and the better known Radicals Roebuck and Grote.

[43] *The Nova Scotian*, Apr. 13, 1837.

It is impossible here to give more than a very general idea of this evidence. The nature of the majority of questions asked, makes it apparent that there was a strong effort made to put the colonial timber trade in as unfavorable a light as possible, an effort only partially countered by questions from members favourably disposed towards it. The "philosophers" naturally did not conceal their extreme doctrinaire bias. Again, while the list of witnesses appeared to display a wide catholicity, it was in reality heavily weighted against the colonies. James Deacon Hume, well known in his day as a free trader and a founder of the Political Economy Club,[44] was the first witness. Aided by his friends on the committee, he made out a very black case against the colonial trade. Its non-economic and monopolistic nature was revealed in the clearest light. Far from being a benefit to the colonists, it appeared to be a curse and far from being an object of colonial anxiety, it was simply the affair of certain vested interests at home.

Certain other doctrinaires with colonial experience were also examined. John McGregor was in his day fairly well-known as a statistician and economist.[45] Samuel Revans was a self-educated man who had attempted to establish a newspaper in Montreal devoted to free trade and anti-colonial opinions.[46] His journal, needless to say, had not met with much success. Neither's evidence was very reliable. Thus McGregor's attempt to discredit the character of colonial lumbermen was itself discredited by one of the timber importers, Allan Gilmour.[47]

44 Hume was the official who under Huskisson reduced the Customs laws of England from the accumulated complexities of centuries to three or four simple statutes.

45 "A Utilitarian of the most extreme type, identifying civilization with material prosperity" — *Dictionary of National Biography*.

46 *The Daily Advertiser*.

47 MacGregor had stated that all lumbermen were dishonest, and in illustration had asserted that one of them had secured advances of some £25,000 from

Also, a wide range of persons engaged in trade with the north of Europe appeared. Their testimony was all to the same effect — that it was impossible to do the business of the good old days, because of the enormously increased prices necessitated by the heavy duties. It was capped by that of a member of the committee, Henry Warburton, the Radical M.P. and ex-Baltic timber merchant,[48] whose firm had been in business since about 1757. Warburton supplied most exhaustive accounting details of timber transactions, from that period to the date of his retirement in 1831, his object apparently being to show the exact incidence of the preference on these factors. But the results, as in all inquiries into the incidence of the tariff, were not conclusive.[49]

On behalf of the colonial timber trade the men who were engaged in it testified first. While some of these men had visited the colonies and one or two had even lived there for some years, there was not one of them who was permanently domiciled there or who could have been called a colonial. They were for the most part merchants engaged in importing colonial timber, or shipowners, or both. Then there were two witnesses who might be styled "protectionist" as contrasted with "free-trade" doctrinaires, in that they were not business men, had no individual axe to grind and gave to their evidence an intellectual aspect by casting it in general terms: these were John Neilson, proprietor of the Quebec *Gazette*, who had been in Canada for over forty years, had become a colonial statesman of

the firm of Pollock, Gilmour and Co., and had then decamped. Allan Gilmour of this firm in his evidence stated that no such thing had occurred.

48 It is significant that at least three of this school were both extreme free-traders and connected with the Baltic timber trade: Poulett Thomson, Warburton and Thomas Tooke, the economist. A significant number of the others were products of Trinity College, Cambridge.

49 It seems virtually impossible to establish conclusive results, no matter how complete the data, for there are always factors which elude investigation.

repute and had indicated his distrust of the centralizing, paternalistic school of imperial thought by espousing the cause of the French-Canadians, and Henry Bliss, who had lived for many years in Nova Scotia and was at the time agent for the legislature of New Brunswick and for the Committees of trade of Montreal and Quebec.

Neilson testified that the trade was a matter of very great importance for the population of Lower Canada (previous testimony had tried to show that it was not) and that the calling of lumber-jack was no more demoralizing than was that, say, of the sailor. He particularly dissociated the French-Canadian political agitation of the period from the timber trade, though if the trade were lost he predicted an increase of political trouble because of economic discontent.

Bliss was a colonial mercantilist of the old school. He claimed for all colonial goods an "adequate" protection. When it was pointed out to him that the timber differential represented a protection of about 225 per cent as compared with 30 per cent, the highest differential between British and foreign goods entering the colonies, he would have none of this arithmetical measurement. Are the colonies part of the motherland? Are they "our own children"? Is protection to British capital and labor part of British policy? If so, then you must protect your colonial industries, no matter what the figure is. Otherwise, you in effect cast them off and it were better if they were given free trade and the empire broken up. These were the sort of rhetorical questions he posed, those of the thoroughgoing colonial sentimentalist, the type for whom the Empire was the grandest of concepts but who could grasp that concept only in terms of trade.

The case carrying the greatest weight in popular opinion, though intellectually a weak one, was probably that of the shipowners trading to British North America. While the sentimental note was not unduly conspicuous,[50] the difficulty of competing in the Baltic was abundantly stressed and the necessity for retaining a great British mercantile fleet upon the ocean no doubt constituted the undertone of all this type of evidence. In the Baltic trade, Swedish ships drove out British ships and Norwegian ships drove out both. Even in the Prussian trade, it was difficult for British ships to compete, because, it was said, of the superior excellence of Prussian ships, the infinitely greater sobriety and industry of the Prussian sailor and his low rate of wages. Only in the voyages from the Russian ports was British shipping still predominant. Thus, cut off the colonial trade and you destroy a large volume of British shipping.[51] Here was an argument that the public could understand and with which it would sympathize.

It is significant that no one was heard who could be said to represent the public, and that several witnesses contended that the consumer was not interested in the question. It was, thus fairly evidently, a battle between two sets of vested interests, one of which was aided by and partially identified with an academic group fighting mainly for the sake of a principle.

When the committee reported, its recommendation was found to be the fifteen shilling reduction in the Baltic duty which Thomson, speaking with the voice of Althorp, had attempted to effect in 1831 — that and some minor points.[52] The mountain thus seems to have labored and

[50] "Where will Britain find a 'nursery for seamen' equal to the North Atlantic trade?" "What would Britain do for ships and timber in time of war if this great trade were destroyed?" etc.

[51] About a thousand timber ships came to Quebec alone every year.

[52] The chief of which were that the deal duties should be levied on cubical contents and not by prescribed sizes and that the changes recommended, in

brought forth the proverbial mouse. Moreover, the mouse was still-born, for after the report was presented to Parliament hardly another word was heard of it.

Instead of acting on the report in the next session, the government, indeed, seemed to devote itself to denying that it had any intention of interfering with the duties. Thus Lord Lansdowne, Lord President of the Council, stated[53] that Government had no intention of bringing in a timber bill but if it did so decide, ample notice would be given. About the same time, Thomson said about the same thing in the Commons. He had reason to believe that a bill embodying the recommendations of the report would be brought in later in the session but in any case no change would be made in the duties until after the session of 1837. He was probably whistling to keep up his courage. A little later Lord Glenelg, the Colonial Secretary, also denied that any change was contemplated. So the free traders had ended by denying their principle thrice.

That was virtually the end of the battle. The next elections eliminated many of the doctrinaire Radicals from Parliament. Left to itself and without strong conviction on the subject, the government of the easy-going Melbourne preferred to let sleeping dogs lie. Not until 1840–41, when a government sinking in the bog of financial embarrassment attempted to rescue itself by a series of desperate manoeuvres, were the timber duties even seriously discussed again. When they were, it was to provide once more the occasion for a report which has become a classic in English economic literature.[54] This document, insofar as a mere intellectual exposition is ever responsible for anything, may be regarded as fundamental in the tariff

---

order not to disturb commitments already embarked upon, should not apply to the shipments of the year 1836.

[53] Feb. 22, 1836.

[54] *Parl. Papers*, 1840 (601), 99.

revolution of 1840–46. It re-enforced the evidence against the differential duties submitted to the committee of 1835, provoking on that account the same set of colonial reactions as had been stimulated in the previous year, exposed the absurdities and illogicalities of the English tariff system and gave free traders and the Anti-Corn Law League an enormous amount of ammunition for their fight. Perhaps few were surprised more than the free traders themselves when, in 1841, the government, after having for several years displayed little sympathy with tariff reform and after having disregarded this report in very much the same way as the previous one, suddenly underwent a conversion and brought in a budget that attacked the three classical monopolies, sugar, corn and timber. Unfortunately no one was convinced by what appeared to be a death-bed repentance and the proposals were defeated on the floor of the House. "I cannot conceive," said Sir Robert Peel, in moving the vote of want of confidence, which completed their downfall, "a more lamentable position than that of the Chancellor of the Exchequer, seated on an empty chest, by the side of bottomless deficiencies, fishing for a budget."[55]

The general surprise at the sudden conversion of the Whigs was only equalled by the shock administered to vested interests and Tories by Peel's almost immediate appropriation of their programme. In the next year, 1842, came the first of his reforming budgets, which swept away much of the apparatus of trade monopoly he himself had previously been so zealous in defending. In his revolutionary changes the timber duties occupied a prominent place. They were greatly reduced and within four years became only moderate preferences, no longer large enough to be the occasion for pitched battles involving the fate

[55] Quoted in John Morley, *Cobden*, I, 183.

of governments. With them went the whole structure of mercantilism and another chapter in Imperial history opened.

Meanwhile the stormy petrel in this whole matter, the scorpion to successive easy-going Whig ministries, Poulett Thomson, had disappeared from the immediate scene of action. After doing his best for several years to antagonize not only colonial traders but the colonists themselves, he had in 1839 taken the rather surprising step of accepting the post of Governor-General to those very colonies. It is hard to understand why he should have done it except on the assumption made in his brother's biographical memoir,[56] that he saw that the Whigs were falling on evil days and that there was little to be expected in the immediate future by the ambitious young politician — that, and a certain self-distrust and timidity which made him think that his place was in administrative work rather than in the hurly-burly of politics. But his was a queer selection and it is no wonder that the word of his appointment astonished and dismayed the colonists. However, there are other things in life besides economics and Thomson was to prove not only capable of conciliating the business interests of the colonies by appearing to moderate his free-trading zeal but also consummately successful in helping to solve one of the most difficult political situations with which they had ever been faced — that resulting from the rebellions of 1837.

When the experience of these eleven years is summed up, certain conclusions stand out. In the first place, the general public never at any time seems to have evinced much interest in the fiscal battle, one way or another. Secondly, all the efforts of the intellectuals, able as they were, logical as was their case, went for very little before the strength

[56] G. B. Scrope, *op. cit.*, p. 102.

of vested interests. Still, the presence of a numerous body of these men in Parliament, their learning and ability, the disinterestedness of the majority of them and above all their devotion to abstract principle constitutes an interesting social and political phenomenon in English public life and provides a comment on the Englishman's frequent assertion that he is entirely a practical man, who will have nothing to do with theory. Thirdly, colonial opinion was almost unanimous in desiring the continuance of the preference and in repudiating any suggestion for the relaxation of Imperial control. The only dissenting voices seem to have been William Lyon Mackenzie, Papineau and a little later, William Hamilton Merritt. Mackenzie was merely a Philosophical Radical in Canada, though even as such he opposed Imperial regulation of colonial trade on the practical grounds of want of knowledge by Imperial officials.[57] Papineau and other French politicians did not like the timber trade because it brought in English immigrants, but they were not very much interested in economic matters. Merritt, a very sagacious practical man, was opposed to Imperial trade control because of its inefficiency. He rightly thought that the people most directly concerned would best know their own interests and appears to have been ready to sacrifice British preferences for this object.[58] It appears probable from Thomson's despatch to Russell of May 26, 1840,[59] that Merritt's numerous letters made an impression on Thomson. In that despatch Thomson described the inconvenience of detailed regulation from London and recommended that within the general principle of Imperial control, the colo-

57 Mackenzie to Neilson, Dec. 28, 1835, Canadian Archives, Neilson Papers, Vol. 8.

58 Merritt to Thomson, Feb. 13, 1839, Canadian Archives, "Sundries, Upper Canada."

59 Q272, p. 193.

nies be allowed to formulate the details of their own trade policies.

But these exceptions were not of much practical importance. All the official and semi-official bodies within the colonies did their best to have the preference continued. The representations of these bodies appear to have constituted only minor determinants of policy, likely to be easily crowded out of ministerial attention by the more immediate pressure of groups closer to hand. In other words, government through "pressure groups," as the current phrase is, is no new thing, but an inevitable part of the political life of any state.

Among these groups, the timber merchants trading with northern Europe were the oldest and the weakest. Many of their firms had been established for over a century and they numbered among them men of wealth and prestige. Yet not even the strategic possession of the presidency of the Board of Trade by one of their number sufficed to gain anything for them. Only the accidental coincidence of hard times, bad Whig finance and a Conservative Prime Minister who spent his life in being converted to his opponents' views at last destroyed the abuses they fought.

They were doubly unfortunate in that the interests of their opponents exactly coincided. The merchants engaged in the colonial timber trade were powerful and well-organized, and they found themselves in natural alliance with a large body of shipowners, who could draw on all the prestige, sentiment and patriotism that surrounded the sailor's calling. Some details will illustrate the nice way in which all these factors worked in together. William Price went out to Quebec in 1810. He soon established a timber business of large proportions and became an influential personage in the province. He appears from the first to have had some connection with James Dowie, who was a partner in the London firm of Gould, Dowie and Co., merchants in the Canada trade.[60] Their business was the export of British manufactures and the import of all colonial produce, ashes, furs, wheat, flour and timber. They had a branch in Canada. Gould, the senior partner, had been the chairman of "The North American Colonial Association," which seems to have been a society of merchants in the Canada trade. It kept in close touch with similar bodies in the colonies, such as the Montreal Board of Trade and the Quebec Committee of Trade,[61] arranging for publication of correspondence and other propagandist material.[62] There were also various colonial journals published in London in which such bodies were interested.[63] When in 1837 the Bank of British North America was organized in London, James Dowie became one of the directors, George Richard Robinson, M.P., the "colonial member" mentioned above, of the firm of Robinson, Brooking, Garland and Co., of London and St. John, Newfoundland, being another. Robinson was a member of the timber committee of 1835, Dowie was a witness, as was also John Miller, another merchant in the Canada trade, a shipowner and chairman of the North American Colonial Association for 1835. Behind this close little knot of vested interest stood the General Association of Ship-Owners,[64] and various local ship-owners' associations,

60 Report of the Timber Committee of 1835, evidence of James Dowie.

61 See the long letter of George Auldjo, well-known Montreal merchant, and Chairman of Montreal Committee of Trade, to Gould as Chairman of the North American Colonial Association, Nov. 25, 1831, published in the Montreal *Gazette*, Feb. 12, 1835.

62 It seems to have been organized in the late 1820's and was still in existence in 1864. About 1840 there was added to it "The North American Colonial Association of Ireland." Names prominent in the Canada timber trade appear as Chairmen, members of committees, etc.

63 One of these had the name, the *Colonial Journal.*

64 This body lasted until 1915, by which year it had become "The Ship-Owners' Society."

whose power in Parliament seems to have been quite as great in its own sphere as that of the "landed interest." More remotely connected were certain great banking houses, especially that of Baring Brothers, which through its members seems to have had its feet in both political camps.[65] The house of Baring, with its vast interests in the affairs of the North American continent, could not have stood idly by while a great trade like the timber trade was destroyed.

Thus a period usually dismissed as somewhat empty in so far as fiscal reform goes, turns out to be one during which hard battles were waged. If little was accomplished by the fighting, that was not for lack of definition of the issues but because they were dwarfed by others and because the government of the day was not powerful enough to make head against the various interests which opposed it. For the fiscal policy of that government one man above all others stands out as responsible, Poulett Thomson, with whom conviction was superimposed upon family interest. Into such a heterogeneity of elements does the unsystematic "mercantile system" upon analysis break down.

[65] Alexander Baring, 1st Lord Ashburton, was President of the Board of Trade in Peel's ministry of 1834–35.

A. R. M. Lower.